EXPERT EVIDENCE AND CRIMINAL JUSTICE

Expert Evidence and Criminal Justice

MIKE REDMAYNE

OXFORD

UNIVERSITY PRESS

OXFORD
UNIVERSITY PRESS

Great Clarendon Street, Oxford OX2 6DP

Oxford University Press is a department of the University of Oxford.
It furthers the University's objective of excellence in research, scholarship,
and education by publishing worldwide in

Oxford New York

Athens Auckland Bangkok Bogotá Buenos Aires Calcutta
Cape Town Chennai Dar es Salaam Delhi Florence Hong Kong Istanbul
Karachi Kuala Lumpur Madrid Melbourne Mexico City Mumbai
Nairobi Paris São Paulo Shanghai Singapore Taipei Tokyo Toronto Warsaw
and associated companies in Berlin Ibadan

Oxford is a registered trade mark of Oxford University Press
in the UK and certain other countries

Published in the United States
by Oxford University Press Inc., New York

© Mike Redmayne 2001

First published 2001

British Library Cataloguing in Publication Data

Data available

Library of Congress Cataloging in Publication Data

Data available

ISBN 0-19-826780-0

1 3 5 7 9 10 8 6 4 2

Typeset by Graphicraft Limited, Hong Kong
Printed in Great Britain
on acid-free paper by
T.J. International Ltd,
Padstow, Cornwall

For Louise

General Editor's Preface

This monograph examines the ways in which the evidence of experts is constructed, presented, interpreted and incorporated into decision-making in criminal justice. It brings depth and sophistication to an area of the law that may be said to have been relatively neglected in academic circles despite its considerable significance in many high-profile criminal cases. Granted the fallibility of much of the oral evidence given in courts, can expert evidence claim a greater degree of objectivity and reliability? Much depends on probabilities, in theory and in their practical application; much also depends on the foundations of the expert 'knowledge', whether in the spheres of DNA, psychiatry or psychology. In this study, Mike Redmayne subjects these and other issues to careful scrutiny; he demonstrates the problems of interpretation in forensic science; and he links these difficulties to the practical rules of evidence, both in this country and in other jurisdictions, and to the expectations and working assumptions of decision-makers in criminal justice. The result is a fine, scholarly book which is of importance to criminal lawyers, the wider criminal justice community and policy-makers.

Andrew Ashworth

Acknowledgements

I have been interested in expert evidence for a decade. Back in 1990, looking for a research topic in the criminal justice field, my interest was drawn by prominent miscarriage of justice cases that had involved expert evidence. There is very little in this book about those cases. Over the years my interest in experts has paralleled a growing interest in evidence, and in ways of thinking about this rich subject that draw on work in a number of disciplines. This book reflects that. It also reflects the aid and encouragement I have received from a number of people. When I started out as a research student at Birmingham University, Roger Leng, David Feldman, and Mike McConville helped out. From my time at Brunel University, I am grateful to my then Head of Department, Ian Loveland, for helping to give me the time to concentrate on writing. I am also grateful for participants in a staff seminar in the Law Department of the University of Leicester for hearing out some of the ideas in Chapter 6, and for their comments on them. Andrew Ashworth, the general editor of the Oxford Monographs on Criminal Justice, gave advice and encouragement as this work progressed. At Oxford University Press, John Louth, Mick Belson, and the copy-editor, Vicky Harris, have seen the project through with enthusiasm and efficiency. I am particularly indebted to those who read and commented on drafts of various chapters. They are: Colin Aitken, Craig Callen, Andrew Choo, Sean Doran, Neil Duxbury, and Robert Reiner.

LSE
December 2000

Contents

Table of Cases

UNITED KINGDOM

Table of Statutory Material

UNITED STATES

1

Introduction

Apart from the obvious—its being about the use of expert evidence in the criminal process—there is no single theme that runs through this book; no one argument that develops to reach a conclusion at the end. The individual chapters are relatively free-standing, each developing a single topic in a fairly hermetic manner. This structure does not seem to me to need much justification: the topics chosen are all important in their own right. Nevertheless, I do approach expert evidence from a particular standpoint, and certain themes run beneath the surface of this study. These matters deserve some development in this brief introductory chapter, a process that will also allow me to sketch what lies ahead.

Expert evidence presents a number of challenges to the legal system. What links them, perhaps, is the need to defer to, yet exert a degree of control over, the experts employed in it. Each chapter of this book examines a particular difficulty that the criminal justice system faces when dealing with experts. Chapter 2 looks at how actors in the system decide to use expert evidence and how forensic science services are regulated. In highlighting the increasing use of forensic science and the strengths and weaknesses of scientific evidence, this chapter serves as an introduction to issues focused on later, because it establishes the need to scrutinize expert evidence with care. Chapters 3 and 4 explore the difficulties caused by the use of statistics in forensic science. This subject may seem esoteric, but the problem is pressing. In a recent article aimed at a legal audience, a group of forensic scientists have expressed their frustration at what they perceive to be the reluctance to take it seriously.[1] I have considerable sympathy with this view—although the conclusions I draw about the best way to tackle the problem are rather different from theirs. Chapter 3 introduces and explains the issues; Chapter 4 focuses on the core of the problem: presenting statistics to juries. Some may find the discussion of probability theory and the use of notation in these chapters off-putting. That is understandable. For the many lawyers who—like me—gave up any subject involving maths at the earliest opportunity, getting to grips with even basic equations is scary. But it is not something that can reasonably be avoided. Nozick has observed that, even outside the sciences, a degree of technical knowledge is now required of those

---

[1] Ian W. Evett, Lindsey A. Foreman, Graham Jackson, and James A. Lambert, 'DNA Profiling: A Discussion of Issues Relating to the Reporting of Very Small Match Probabilities' [2000] *Crim. LR* 341; see esp. 354.

who want fully to understand some of the intellectual debates of our time.[2] Evidence law, it seems to me, is of this nature. For those unfamiliar with probability theory, I have attempted to present the key ideas as simply as possible. Chapter 3 introduces them at a relatively slow pace, using concrete examples. It also includes a short appendix explaining some of the concepts that are not developed in the main text.

Chapters 5 and 6 move on to more traditional evidence law territory: admissibility rules. The first of these chapters contains a detailed analysis of a subject that is only just beginning to receive attention from evidence scholars on this side of the Atlantic: exclusionary rules for unreliable scientific evidence. Drawing on American law and scholarship, I argue the pros and cons of such rules—with the emphasis on the pros. The second examines a rule—the *Turner* rule—that has generated a fairly large case law in England and Wales. Although the *Turner* cases are often criticized, the jurisprudence has received no satisfying synthesis. By picking apart the principles underlying the cases, I show that the *Turner* jurisprudence is both more and less coherent than it is usually taken to be. With these two topics the challenges for the courts are partly doctrinal—rationalizing the principles underlying the admissibility rules. In part, they are wider than this, for they involve the need to scrutinize and control the evidence offered by experts. In relation to these two chapters, the point about the difficulty of avoiding technical discussion in evidence scholarship needs reiteration. Small parts of the analysis rely on an understanding of likelihood ratios— a concept introduced in Chapter 3.

The final chapter deals with the tension between expert evidence and the adversarial system. This is such a perennial topic in discussions of expert evidence that it needs no introduction.

This leads to a second standpoint which informs the analysis in this book. '[T]he rules of evidence', Twining suggests, 'are only one small part of the subject of evidence and proof. The rounded study of evidence, as part of the study of law, would include logical, philosophical, psychological, processual, and other dimensions.'[3] That is quite a tall order, but it is one I try to make good on. Evidence is a complex, multi-dimensional subject. In order to give a thorough picture of the use of expert evidence in the criminal process I have drawn on work in a number of disciplines, and this has pulled the discussion into topics lying beyond expert evidence. In certain respects, as this study has developed, expert evidence has become a lens through which to view wider issues in evidence and criminal justice. In Chapter 2 there is an analysis of the epistemological issues raised by the concept of case

[2] Robert Nozick, *The Nature of Rationality* (Princeton: Princeton University Press, 1993), xv–xvi.
[3] William Twining, 'Identification and Misidentification in Legal Processes: Redefining the Problem' in *Rethinking Evidence: Exploratory Essays* (Evanston: Northwestern University Press, 1994) (essay orig. 1983), 155.

construction; Chapters 3 and 4 are relevant to debates about the uses and limits of Bayesianism in evidence scholarship; Chapter 5 contains a detailed examination of justifications for reliability-based exclusionary rules, while Chapter 7 touches on the relative merits of adversarial and inquisitorial systems.

There is much in this book—it will be no surprise—about expert evidence. I say rather less about the topic that forms the second half of my title: criminal justice. At least, I say little about it directly: the arguments I develop, however, would play out differently were this book about scientific evidence in the civil justice system. In a system that does not use lay fact-finders, less emphasis needs to be put on exclusionary rules. The nature of the forensic sciences and the resource advantages possessed by the state also play a role in my diagnosis of the problems and their solutions. That expert evidence in criminal cases frequently addresses questions of identity drives much of the discussion in Chapters 3 and 4, as well as some of the arguments in Chapter 5. Still, readers may feel that too little is said about process values: the need to protect defendants, to give them their say, and to ensure that criminal verdicts are legitimate.[4] My response has two prongs: first, that these values do not play a particularly important role in the rules governing expert evidence, and, secondly, that to the extent that they do, they largely coincide with a more basic evidentiary concern: the need to produce accurate verdicts. This needs some explanation. The starting point is to ask the question 'why do we use expert evidence in the criminal justice system?' The answer seems obvious: to improve decision-making. But this just leads one to ask 'what constitutes good criminal justice decision-making?' It is not too much of an exaggeration to say that the whole of the literature in criminal law, criminology, and criminal evidence is an attempt to answer this question. Both the size of this literature and the level of disagreement within it indicate its intractable nature. Nevertheless, when it comes to expert evidence, good criminal justice decision-making involves, primarily, making accurate decisions: distinguishing between the innocent and the guilty and between degrees of culpability. There are caveats to this: some applications of forensic science might operate successfully only at the price of substantial invasions of privacy. That is an appropriate concern, but it is not a subject I explore in this book because it is irrelevant to the topics I choose to treat.[5] There are also good arguments for excluding expert

---

[4] The notion that the decisions of criminal courts should be 'legitimate' in some sense is embraced by a number of evidence scholars. See, e.g., I. H. Dennis, *The Law of Evidence* (London: Sweet & Maxwell, 1999), 36–43. In the following passages I use the term 'legitimate' to refer to any perspective that incorporates some value other than accuracy in its theory of adjudicative fact-finding, i.e. including those who prefer to emphasize rights rather than the somewhat vague notion of legitimacy (see, e.g., Katharine Grevling, 'Fairness and the Exclusion of Evidence Under Section 78(1) of the Police and Criminal Evidence Act' (1997) 113 *LQR* 667).

[5] For discussion of this issue in the context of DNA evidence, see Mike Redmayne, 'The DNA Database: Civil Liberty and Evidentiary Issues' [1998] *Crim. LR* 437, 437–46.

evidence from the courts if it has been obtained illegally, thus sacrificing accurate for legitimate decision-making. This is a controversial issue, but, beyond some forms of scientific evidence being so powerful that they render the dilemma especially vivid,[6] the issues are identical to those arising when other forms of evidence are obtained illegally. This is not a topic, therefore, requiring discussion in a book devoted to expert evidence.

Nevertheless, the question of balancing accuracy and legitimacy does impinge on parts of the discussion in this book. It plays a small role in the discussion of unreliable expert evidence in Chapter 5. It arises most vividly in Chapter 6, where I discuss the merits of admitting expert evidence on the subject of witness credibility. There, the argument favours verdict accuracy over process values. Some reasons are offered in support of this choice, but they may not convince everyone. It would be nice to offer a better defence for the conclusion reached—perhaps a theory of the role of process values in adjudication—but I am not sure that it would be very much help. In this particular context I suspect that the arguments boil down to little more than intuition and assertion.

The emphasis on accurate decision-making has certain parallels in recent work by Goldman, in which he assesses the extent to which 'veritism'—the pursuit of truth—is achieved by various social institutions.[7] Mostly, this theme lies in the background of the study. The only serious engagement with Goldman's work comes in Chapter 5, where I make use of, and attempt to supplement, his analysis of exclusionary rules. Nevertheless, this book might be read as an attempt to assess the extent to which the criminal process, in its use of expert evidence, achieves veritistic ends. Needless to say, no very clear answer to this question emerges. Various criticisms of the rules and procedures governing expert evidence are put forward, but there is no bottom-line calculation of how well the criminal justice system performs on the veritism scale. One conclusion, though, does come out of this aspect of the study, and it serves as a counterpoint to Goldman's own analysis. Even when accuracy is not being traded off against legitimacy, we have to accept that there are limits on our ability to achieve it. Perfect solutions are difficult to find because lay decision-makers (here including judges) have cognitive limitations, and different experts have different cognitive needs. When it comes to expert evidence, verdict accuracy is an appropriate goal; but we must accept that in aiming for it we will frequently be disappointed.

---

[6] See *R. v. Nathaniel* [1995] 2 Cr. App. R. 565; *R. v. B. (A.G.'s Ref. No. 3 of 1999)*; *R. v. Weir, The Times* 16 June 2000; Michael Zander, 'All the Evidence Suggests that we Should Change Our Minds Over DNA', *The Times*, 30 May 2000. The powerful nature of evidence based on DNA profiling has also played a role in recent proposals to relax the rules on double jeopardy: see Law Commission, *Double Jeopardy*, Law Com. Con. Paper 156 (London: Stationery Office, 1999), 36.

[7] Alvin I. Goldman, *Knowledge in a Social World* (Oxford: Oxford University Press, 1999); see esp. ch. 9.

2

Constructing Cases with Science

In Chapter 1 it was stated that, in the criminal process, the *raison d'être* of expert evidence can broadly be thought of as the promotion of accurate decision-making. This chapter examines the potential of forensic science to contribute to that end. I look in some detail at how forensic science is used in police investigations; what emerges from this is a picture of the potential strengths and weaknesses of scientific evidence. The opening section introduces this theme with some relatively theoretical considerations. It explores what it might mean to say that scientific knowledge and police cases are constructed. This serves as an introduction to the rest of the chapter. But the discussion also serves a broader purpose; in later parts of the book I talk about good and bad science, and the need for courts to exclude the latter. Some find this distinction naïve.[1] The somewhat theoretical observations developed here—together with brief discussions in other parts of the book —are intended to address concerns of this sort.

Forensic science—the subject of this chapter—has been described as being 'not a scientific discipline as such, but rather the application of the whole range of sciences and some skills which are not commonly thought of as sciences'[2] to the investigation of crime. In order to keep the enquiry within limits, I shall concentrate on the use of trace evidence: physical material and marks found at the crime scene, used for purposes of identification and reconstruction. I shall, however, offer a few observations on other uses of forensic science in the criminal process.

1. POLICE INVESTIGATIONS AND CASE CONSTRUCTION

There is broad consensus on the principal features of police investigations. A quotation from Steer sums this up: 'the great majority of crime detections involve little of what the public would perceive as real detective ability. Information, forensic evidence even, contribute directly to very few detections.'[3] Suspects are generally identified through being caught in the act, or

---

[1] See, e.g., Gary Edmond and David Mercer, 'Trashing "Junk Science" ' [1998] *Stan. Tech. L. Rev.* 3 <http://stlr.stanford.edu/STRL/Articles/998_STLR_3> (visited 27 November 1999).

[2] House of Lords Select Committee on Science and Technology, *Forensic Science: Report*, HL 24, 1992–3 (London: HMSO, 1993), 10.

[3] David Steer, *Uncovering Crime: The Police Role*, Royal Commission on Criminal Procedure Research Study No. 7 (London: HMSO, 1980), 71.

by members of the public.[4] Rarely are they caught through trace evidence. The investigatory process does not end, however, with the identification of a suspect. The police and Crown Prosecution Service are interested in the successful prosecution of crime; to this end they must present convincing cases to the courts. The typical police investigation, then, begins with a suspect, and continues by building up a convincing case against him. The questioning of suspects, in order to elicit incriminating remarks, is a key part of this process.

A way of describing these characteristics of police investigations that has had considerable mileage in the literature is that the police are involved in a process of 'case construction'.[5] It is worth examining this notion and its implications for the use of science in the criminal process. What is interesting about the case construction metaphor is that, as Jones notes, it appears to parallel a constructionist literature in science studies.[6] This is significant because, if scientific knowledge is constructed in just the same way that police cases are, then perhaps it has little potential to contribute to accurate decision-making.

On one reading, the idea that the police are constructing cases against suspects is not one that says anything particularly surprising about police investigations. It is fairly obvious that police investigations are goal oriented, the goal usually being the presentation of a strong case against the believed perpetrator. Cases are not pre-given: they must be put together from the evidence generated during the enquiry. In contrast, it is startling to read that quarks are constructed.[7] One would have thought that quarks are natural kinds. It is evident that a case will only exist because of police work, but how can this idea be applied to an elementary particle? And whereas the instrumental character of police investigations is apparent upon reflection, it is not immediately obvious that the work of scientists is goal oriented in any parallel sense.

To gain a better understanding of the constructionist literature, its theoretical claims require closer scrutiny. There is one relatively straightforward way in which construction is happening in both science and the

[4] See John Burrows and Roger Tarling, 'The Investigation of Crime in England and Wales' (1987) 27 *Brit. J. Criminol.* 229; Michael McConville and John Baldwin, 'The Role of Interrogation in Crime Discovery and Conviction' (1982) 22 *Brit. J. Criminol.* 165.

[5] See Andrew Sanders, 'Constructing the Case for the Prosecution' (1987) 14 *J. Law & Soc.* 229; Mike McConville, Andrew Sanders, and Roger Leng, *The Case for the Prosecution: Police Suspects and the Construction of Criminality* (London: Routledge, 1991). For a review of some of the literature, see David Dixon, *Law in Policing: Legal Regulation and Police Practices* (Oxford: Clarendon Press, 1997), esp. 34–6, 40–8. The case construction model is thoughtfully applied to police use of forensic science in Paul Roberts, 'Science in the Criminal Process' (1994) 14 *Ox. J. Leg. Stud.* 469.

[6] Carol A. G. Jones, *Expert Witnesses: Science, Medicine and the Practice of Law* (Oxford: Clarendon Press, 1994), 1.

[7] Andrew Pickering, *Constructing Quarks: A Sociological History of Particle Physics* (Edinburgh: Edinburgh University Press, 1984).

criminal process. In order to draw distinctions, I term this 'building'. As
I have stated, cases do not come pre-formed: they have to be built out of
evidence. This will involve a degree of discretion, because the police will
have to decide what lines of enquiry to pursue, what evidence to include in
the file, and how to describe certain pieces of evidence. As McBarnet puts
it: '[e]vidence, the facts of the case, strong and weak cases are not simply
self-evident absolutes; they are the end product of a process which organises
and selects the available "facts" and constructs cases for and in the courtroom.'[8] Sociological studies of laboratory science suggest that a similar
process occurs. In Knorr-Cetina's account of research on food proteins,
scientists continually make 'selections';[9] in Latour and Woolgar's study of
the analysis of thyrotropin releasing hormone, they are confronted by a
'seething mass of alternative interpretations' from which a single one is
chosen.[10] In both science and the criminal process, the outcome does not
result from some algorithmic process, but is contingent and negotiated.
Thus far no epistemological claim has emerged: the process of building is
unremarkable. Looking further, though, one finds that writers in the science
studies field make theoretical claims about the nature of scientific knowledge.
By way of contrast, the theoretical aspects of case construction are not well
developed in the criminal justice literature.[11] There are some suggestive
comments, though. Walker refers to 'the constructed nature of both "truth"
as well as "guilt"',[12] and McBarnet writes that 'the incident under investigation or in dispute cannot be conceived of as some absolute—"truth" or
"reality"—nor as a simple objective thing'.[13] It might be said that these stronger
constructionist claims involve 'fabrication' rather than simple building. The
science studies literature provides a better insight on the epistemological issues
lurking here. Latour and Woolgar's study is strongly anti-realist: scientific
knowledge neither describes, nor, perhaps, is it caused by, reality. For them,
reality is created by the process of fabrication that occurs in the laboratory.[14]
Such strong claims rarely appear in the criminal justice literature. Indeed,

[8] Doreen J. McBarnet, *Conviction: Law, the State and the Construction of Justice* (London: Macmillan, 1981), 3.
[9] Karin D. Knorr-Cetina, *The Manufacture of Knowledge: An Essay on the Constructivist and Contextual Nature of Science* (Oxford: Pergamon Press, 1981).
[10] Bruno Latour and Steve Woolgar, *Laboratory Life: The Construction of Scientific Facts* 2nd edn (Princeton: Princeton University Press, 1986), 36.
[11] See David Dixon, 'New Left Pessimism' in Lesley Noaks, Mike Maguire, and Michael Levi (eds), *Contemporary Issues in Criminology* (Cardiff: University of Wales Press, 1995), 222.
[12] Clive Walker, 'Miscarriages of Justice in Principle and in Practice' in Clive Walker and Keir Starmer (eds), *Miscarriages of Justice: A Review of Justice in Error* (London: Blackstone Press, 1999), 43.
[13] *Supra* n. 8, 11. See also Donald Nicolson, 'Truth, Reason and Justice: Epistemology and Politics in Evidence Discourse' (1994) 57 *Modern L. Rev.* 726, esp. 737; Anita Kalunta-Crompton, *Race and Drug Trials: The Social Construction of Guilt and Innocence* (Aldershot: Ashgate, 1999), 55–67.
[14] For an exploration of Latour and Woolgar's brand of anti-realism, see Ian Hacking, 'The Participant Irrealist at Large in the Laboratory' (1988) 39 *Brit. J. Phil. Sci.* 277.

one influential group of case-constructionists has distanced itself from a parallel anti-realism about facts.[15]

These epistemological issues raise many questions, but this is not the place to pursue them.[16] Instead, I want to explore some of the ways in which it might make sense to talk about a stronger sort of construction than the simple sense of building taking place in the criminal process. Hacking has drawn a distinction between 'interactive' and 'natural' kinds.[17] With natural kinds one has to be careful about identifying precisely what is constructed when a constructionist claim is made. If quarks exist, for instance, they are a natural kind. We cannot construct them: they simply exist or do not. But our ideas about quarks, and even the concept 'quark', have been constructed by physicists. Interactive kinds differ, because here the entity interacts with our knowledge of it. Some forms of mental illness are a good example of this: because people are aware of how they are classified, they interact with medical categories.[18] Social categories, such as gender, or bodies of knowledge, such as finance theory, provide other illustrations.[19]

Turning back to the criminal process, the interactive dimension adds a twist to the simple concept of case building. Confessions are usually elicited through a process of police questioning in which legal categories, such as 'recklessness', 'theft', or 'offensive weapon', may be suggested to, and adopted by, suspects.[20] These evaluative categories may then provide suspects with a way of understanding their actions. The questioning of witnesses can involve a similar interactive process. But it seems that physical evidence, because it is not interactive, is less subject to the process of case construction.[21] It is possible, though, to imagine various ways in which

[15] See Mike McConville, Andrew Sanders, and Roger Leng, 'Descriptive or Critical Sociology: The Choice is Yours' (1997) 37 *Brit. J. Criminol.* 347, 349–50. The authors resist the anti-realist interpretation of their work made in David J. Smith, 'Case Construction and the Goals of the Criminal Process' (1997) 37 *Brit. J. Criminol.* 319.

[16] For evaluation of constructionist claims in the science studies literature, see Arthur Fine, 'Science Made Up: Constructivist Sociology of Scientific Knowledge' in Peter Galison and David J. Stump (eds), *The Disunity of Science: Boundaries, Contexts and Power* (Stanford: Stanford University Press, 1996); Ronald N. Giere, *Explaining Science: A Cognitive Approach* (Chicago: University of Chicago Press, 1988), 50–61, 111–40.

[17] Ian Hacking, *The Social Construction of What?* (Cambridge, MA: Harvard University Press, 1999), 103–17.

[18] For a detailed study, see Ian Hacking, *Mad Travellers: Reflections on the Reality of Transient Mental Illnesses* (Charlottesville: University Press of Virginia, 1998).

[19] On the latter, see Donald MacKenzie, 'Fear in the Markets', *London Review of Books*, 13 April 2000, 31.

[20] For illustrations, see Martin Wasik, Thomas Gibbons, and Mike Redmayne, *Criminal Justice: Text and Materials* (London: Longman, 1999), 296–8.

[21] On this point, see Andrew Sanders, 'Some Dangers of Policy Oriented Research: The Case of Prosecutions' in Ian Dennis (ed.), *Criminal Law and Justice* (London: Sweet and Maxwell, 1987), 206. Sanders suggests that the degree to which cases are subject to construction 'depends on the extent to which [they] are determined by objective concrete evidence (for example, blood samples, photographs, fingerprints) as compared to evidence which is not just susceptible to manipulation, but which relies for its existence on questioning or prompting by others (for example, eyewitness identification, incriminating statement, failure to explain suspicious actions)'.

other types of expert evidence might be interactive.[22] The most obvious examples involve psychological and psychiatric expertise. Battered woman syndrome (BWS) provides psychiatrists and battered women with a way of conceptualizing a woman's actions during a violent relationship.[23] One aspect of BWS—the concept of learned helplessness—affords victims of domestic violence a way of understanding their difficulties in leaving a relationship. Usually, this happens retrospectively, as when a woman is the subject of psychiatric evaluation after having killed her violent partner, but, as the concept of learned helplessness gains popular currency, it may give women a means of interpreting their actions during a relationship, in the process, perhaps, changing the way they act. In this scenario, there would be the sort of 'looping effect' of which Hacking writes.[24] Another syndrome, rape trauma syndrome (RTS), may have similar repercussions.[25] RTS, a type of post-traumatic stress disorder, describes the psychological sequelae of rape. Some suggest that it might be used in the courts to corroborate complainants' claims that they did not consent to intercourse. Should this happen, we might see a shift in the concept of rape—and in complainants' understandings of their experiences—from sexual intercourse without consent to sexual intercourse followed by trauma. Given the difficulty in defining consent, it is understandable that such a shift might appear attractive. Finally, consider an example involving a confession: the case of Andrew Evans.[26] In 1972 Evans came to believe that he had killed a 14-year-old girl

---

[22] Instead of being interactive, forensic science may play a role in the process of interaction. An illustration of this is provided by Mullin's account of how expert evidence was used to justify using coercive tactics in order to elicit confessions from the Birmingham Six. See Chris Mullin, *Error of Judgement: The Truth About the Birmingham Bombings*, revd edn (Swords: Poolbeg, 1990), esp. 48. Later in the saga of this case, the confessions and the scientific evidence played a mutually supporting role in upholding the convictions, each covering for the defects of the other.

[23] BWS is discussed in more detail in Ch. 6 § 9.

[24] *Supra* n. 17, 34, 105–8. Some writers have suggested that interactions will happen in larger ways: they worry that allowing more claims of excuse in the criminal law—what are often referred to as 'abuse excuses', some of which may depend on expert evidence—will lead to general shifts in our notions of responsibility, and hence in our behaviour. For an analysis of this claim, see Michael Stocker, 'Responsibility and the Abuse Excuse' in Ellen Frankel Paul, Fred D. Miller, and Jeffrey Paul (eds), *Responsibility* (Cambridge: Cambridge University Press, 1999), 180–7. Thinking about the interactive effects of syndrome evidence sheds light on other claims, too. Some feminists criticize BWS on the grounds that learned helplessness constitutes an unflattering portrayal of victims of domestic violence. See, e.g., Fiona E. Raitt and Suzanne Zeedyk, *The Implicit Relation of Psychology and Law: Women and Syndrome Evidence* (London: Routledge, 2000), ch. 4. I have always been somewhat puzzled by this claim—if learned helplessness exists among battered women, why deny it? Looking through the lens of interaction, however, I have more sympathy for this criticism.

[25] See, generally, Patricia A. Frazier and Eugene Borgida, 'The Scientific Status of Research on Rape Trauma Syndrome' in David L. Faigman, David H. Kaye, Michael J. Saks, and Joseph Sanders (eds), *Modern Scientific Evidence: The Law and Science of Expert Testimony*, Vol. 1 (St Paul: West Publishing, 1997). For a constructionist account of RTS, see Shirley A. Dobbin and Sophia A. Gatowski, 'The Social Production of Rape Trauma Syndrome as Science and as Evidence' in Michael Freeman and Helen Reece (eds), *Science in Court* (Aldershot: Ashgate, 1998).

[26] *R. v. Evans*, No. 97/1544/Z3 (CA, 3 December 1997).

whose murder had been reported in the papers. The principal evidence against him was his own confession, but, as he was unable to recall events on the afternoon of the murder, he had no good way of knowing whether his confession was true. His belief in his own guilt appears to have been bolstered by medical diagnoses that his amnesia was triggered by an emotional shock—by implication, the shock of killing the girl. When he finally appealed his conviction in 1997, medical opinion had shifted: four experts agreed that the earlier diagnoses were unsound. When one's self-definition as a murderer depends on expert evidence, which itself depends upon a consensus among psychiatrists which is apt to change over time, the idea of the construction of guilt carries far more weight than the simple image of building with which this discussion started.

It may also be possible to move construction beyond the basic building conception without using the notion of interaction. MacKenzie's account of nuclear missile guidance systems starts out with the fact that such systems are tremendously accurate.[27] A missile could be fired at me from the United States and land within a block of where I am sitting. But on enquiring into the matter, this hard fact begins to soften: none of the tests of nuclear missiles are quite close enough to the actual conditions of firing a missile in anger to establish accuracy in such a way as to dispose of all doubts. The facts generated by testing exist 'only within a wider web of assumptions and procedures',[28] many of which can be questioned. I shall refer to this sort of construction as 'reification'. The gist of this idea is that what we take to be facts have become so because the assumptions on which they rest are largely hidden; these facts might, though, be pulled apart by a determined enquirer who uncovers and questions those assumptions. This idea of reification can be seen in Latour and Woolgar's account of the analysis of thyrotropin releasing hormone (TRH).[29] The chemical structure of TRH became a fact in 1969 after analysis in two American laboratories. Because TRH only occurs naturally in tiny amounts, the reification of this fact would be particularly difficult to undo. One of the laboratories needed 500 tons of pig brains to extract just 1 mg of TRH. Scientists are unlikely to repeat that sort of work, just as the ultimate test of missile accuracy—firing one armed with a nuclear warhead across the globe—is—we may hope—not going to be undertaken.

The case construction literature parallels this idea of reification. The cases constructed by the police may be difficult to challenge for a variety of reasons: because the discretionary decisions used in their construction are well hidden, because the process of interaction has led witnesses to believe the police interpretation of events, or because defendants lack the resources to mount an effective challenge. But one should be cautious about drawing

---

[27] Donald A. MacKenzie, *Inventing Accuracy: A Historical Sociology of Nuclear Missile Guidance* (Cambridge, MA: MIT Press, 1990).
[28] Ibid. 341.   [29] *Supra* n. 10.

too strong a parallel with the scientific literature. In Latour and Woolgar's account, those 500 tons of pig brains lend credence to their anti-realism, to the shift from building to stronger forms of constructionism.[30] Unless ideas about interaction and memory distortion can be made to bear an awful lot of weight, it makes rather less sense to say that there is no fact of the matter against which to measure the authenticity of police case constructions.[31] The past is not completely inaccessible: it is always possible that new evidence will throw doubt on the case constructed by the police. Might the similarities be stronger when it comes to the technologies used by forensic scientists? One can certainly imagine an account of the development, testing, and use of DNA profiling along the lines of MacKenzie's work on nuclear missile guidance systems.[32] DNA match probabilities are certainly based on a web of assumptions and procedures, involving topics ranging from the genetic structure of human populations to the effectiveness of laboratory protocols for avoiding contamination. However, many of these assumptions have been tested and it is now difficult, I think, to be tremendously sceptical about them. (Things were different in the early 1990s, when there really was a sense of unpacking the 'black box' of DNA technology to reveal the frailty of the assumptions on which it was based.) There are counters to this sort of argument: Latour and Woolgar remark of the reproducibility of phenomena accompanying successful testing that, 'considering that the same set of operations produces the same answers there is little to marvel at'.[33] This addresses the ontological status of entities such as TRH: ontological

---

[30] See Hacking, *supra* n. 14.

[31] McBarnet's comments, quoted above, suggest otherwise. Elaborating them (*supra* n. 8, 11–12), she makes the point that for a witness 'what happened' is 'what *struck* him as happening; how he made sense of what he saw'. There is a useful insight here, but I am cautious about putting too much weight on it. It is valuable to note that when we describe actions, we often use evaluative terms—they become actions under a description, as the philosophers say. We say X hit Y, not that X's hand moved through the air until it met Y's body. Often these descriptions are not problematic. But if they are, we do have available to us those more narrowly visual terms. For examples of how these can be used to dilute controversy, see Philip Kitcher, *The Advancement of Science: Science Without Legend, Objectivity Without Illusions* (New York: Oxford University Press, 1993), 226–7; Dudley Shapere, 'The Concept of Observation in Science and Philosophy' (1982) 49 *Phil. Sci.* 485, 519. There may, however, be more troubling examples, such as when new descriptions become available to us, allowing us to redescribe past events. What, twenty years ago, was touching or fondling may become redescribed as child abuse. For an analysis, see Ian Hacking, *Rewriting the Soul: Multiple Personality and the Sciences of Memory* (Princeton: Princeton University Press, 1995), ch. 17. Hacking suggests that, to a limited extent, the past is indeterminate, a conclusion that lends some support to McBarnet's claims. A slightly different reading of McBarnet is that she is arguing that agent-relative descriptions of facts are constitutive of those facts, thus that there are different facts for different people (for this claim, see also Nicolson, *supra* n. 13, 737). But while it is true that we always describe the world from a point of view, it is false that this has ontological significance: see John Searle, *Mind, Language and Society: Doing Philosophy in the Real World* (London: Weidenfeld and Nicolson, 1999), 20–3.

[32] For an account of this sort, see Mike Redmayne, 'Expert Evidence and Scientific Disagreement' (1997) 30 *UC Davis L. Rev.* 1027, 1047–62.

[33] *Supra* n. 10, 183.

questions, however, are not a central issue with a technology such as DNA profiling. Whatever DNA is, the tests of the technique of DNA profiling suggest that it provides reliable answers to the questions we ask of it, questions about the identification of people by their body materials.[34] More pertinent is MacKenzie's observation: 'testing inevitably involves "the construction of a background against which to measure success"'.[35] Tests of DNA profiling technology do involve background assumptions, but these do not seem radically to destabilize the results.[36] While it is possible that the genetic structure of human populations does not resemble those produced by laboratory tests, it is doubtful that the differences are great. At some point, scepticism about this sort of technology begins to resemble the scepticism of flat-earthers.[37] So while it is possible to talk of the technology of DNA profiling being constructed, or reified, these labels would not, I think, signify anything very interesting about the technology. There might, however, be other areas of forensic science where talk of construction would lead to the sort of profitable debunking of assumptions that it does in other areas.[38]

There is another direction in which the idea of construction in forensic science can be developed. The case construction literature emphasizes that the way in which cases get built depends upon police goals, which lead the

[34] This attempt to separate the ontological from the instrumental is open to objections. Assumptions about the structure of DNA, for example, doubtless are crucial to the process of extracting DNA from body materials and amplifying it. But the level of manipulation involved here supports a strong argument for realism about entities such as DNA: see Ian Hacking, *Representing and Intervening: Introductory Topics in the Philosophy of Natural Science* (Cambridge: Cambridge University Press, 1983), esp. ch. 16.

[35] *Supra* n. 27, 373–7, quoting John Law, 'Technology and Heterogeneous Engineering: The Case of Portuguese Expansion', in Wiebe E. Bijker, Thomas P. Hughes, and Trevor Pinch (eds), *The Social Construction of Technological Systems: New Directions in the Sociology and History of Technology* (Cambridge, MA: MIT Press, 1987), 126.

[36] See, generally, National Research Council, Committee on DNA Forensic Science: An Update, *The Evaluation of Forensic DNA Evidence* (Washington DC, National Academy Press, 1996), chs 4, 5; Lindsey A. Foreman, Adrian F. M. Smith, and Ian W. Evett, 'Bayesian Analysis of DNA Profiling Data in Forensic Identification Applications' (1997) 160 *J.R. Stat. Soc. (Series A)* 429.

[37] There is a more general point here, which is that the constructionist literature in science studies generally lacks an account of the warrant for, or justification of, scientists' beliefs. While scientists in the laboratories described in the literature do have a large degree of choice in conducting their work, I suspect that the choices they make among competing interpretations are usually rationally justified. On this theme, see Larry Laudan, 'The Pseudo-Science of Science?' in *Beyond Positivism and Relativism: Theory, Method and Evidence* (Boulder: Westview Press, 1996) (essay orig. 1982); Susan Haack, 'Science as Social?—Yes and No' in *Manifesto of a Passionate Moderate: Unfashionable Essays* (Chicago: University of Chicago Press, 1998).

[38] Fingerprinting may provide an example. See Simon Cole, 'What Counts for Identity? The Historical Origins of the Methodology of Latent Fingerprint Identification' (1999) 12 *Science in Context* 139. Once again, though, I think that our ability to test the claims of fingerprint experts (to see how many false positives they generate) tends to undercut some of the arguments emerging in this area. That relatively simple tests can be undertaken distinguishes the forensic sciences from the sort of field described by MacKenzie: the limitations on testing nuclear missiles in realistic settings opens up many more questions about what counts as a successful test.

police to interpret events in particular ways, to neglect certain lines of enquiry, and to suppress specific items of information.[39] The building is done with a purpose, and this leads to the reification of the police interpretation of the case. One might, naïvely, expect the forensic scientist to approach her investigation with an extreme objectivity that would rule out these practices. To debunk this view, there is no need to turn to the sociological literature; the Court of Appeal's judgment in *R. v. Ward* will do:

> For lawyers, jurors and judges a forensic scientist conjures up the image of a man in a white coat working in a laboratory, approaching his task with cold neutrality, and dedicated only to the pursuit of scientific truth. It is a sombre thought that the reality is sometimes different. Forensic scientists may become partisan. The very fact that the police seek their assistance may create a relationship between the police and the forensic scientists. And the adversarial character of the proceedings tends to promote this process. Forensic scientists employed by the government may come to see their function as helping the police. They may lose their objectivity. That is what must have happened in this case. It is illustrated by the catalogue of non-disclosures which we have set out.[40]

There are plenty of illustrations of this process—which can be referred to as 'biased building'—in the literature on forensic science. The official inquiry into the Chamberlain case in Australia found that scientists were over-eager to interpret results of tests in ways consistent with the Chamberlains' guilt.[41] To take just one example, one scientist explained away experimental results that undermined her belief that an anti-serum she was using to test for foetal blood would not react with non-foetal blood. 'For inadequate reasons', the inquiry concluded, 'Mrs Kuhl accepted as correct results which tended to confirm the specificity of the anti-serum and rejected those results which cast doubt upon it.'[42] Similarly, scientists involved in the prosecution of the Maguire family went beyond agreed parameters when declaring positive results, and did not disclose results that undermined their conclusions.[43] And in the United States, scientists in the FBI laboratory have also, it seems, distorted the results of their analyses in order better to fit prosecution cases.[44] Bias appears to be a universal tendency in forensic science.

---

[39] For a take on case construction that emphasizes the psychological biases of police investigations, see A. A. S. Zuckerman, 'Miscarriages of Justice—A Root Treatment' [1992] *Crim. LR* 323. For a study of police officers, which found evidence of over-confidence in investigative hypotheses, see Roger Mullin, 'Good Judgment?' (1995) 11 *Policing* 272.

[40] [1993] 1 WLR 619, 674.

[41] T. R. Morling, *Report of the Royal Commission of Inquiry Into the Chamberlain Convictions* (Darwin: Government Printer, 1987).

[42] Ibid. 81.

[43] See Sir John May, *Return to an Address of the Honourable the House of Commons dated 12 July 1990 for the inquiry into the circumstances surrounding the convictions arising out of the bomb attacks in Guildford and Woolwich in 1974*, HC 556, 1989–90 (London: HMSO, 1990), esp. §§ 11–12.

[44] See John H. Kelly and Phillip K. Wearne, *Tainting Evidence: Behind the Scenes at the FBI Crime Lab* (New York: Free Press, 1998). Cf. US Department of Justice, Office of the

What implications do these accounts of biased building have for forensic science? One might take issue with the whole notion of bias here, because it carries the implication that it is possible to carry out scientific enquiry without bias.[45] A common theme in the science studies literature is that scientific investigations are frequently shaped by scientists' goals, interests, and political allegiances.[46] It is certainly true that it is difficult to give any clear definition of bias in scientific practice.[47] It cannot be presumed that every scientific disagreement, or every departure from the mean opinion, involves bias. In much of science, there exists no simple, algorithmic methodology that would produce answers against which we could compare the views of scientists accused of bias. Nevertheless, some practices can fairly uncontroversially be labelled biased. The psychological literature distinguishes motivational and cognitive bias. The former is close to the popular notion of bias (the referee is biased because he wants one side to win). In *Ward*, the Court of Appeal suggests that prosecution scientists were biased in this way because they came to see their role as helping the police, which led them deliberately to keep relevant information from the defence. One might try to combat such forms of bias by clarifying the forensic scientist's role and obligations. But motivational biases can also be more subtle: most academics think that they are better at their job than their average colleague, but we cannot all be right.[48] The Maguire scientists may have interpreted the results of tests in ways that supported their belief in the defendants' guilt, without even being aware of the bias involved. However, there are limits to motivation-based belief: '[p]eople will come to believe what they want to believe only to the extent that reason permits.'[49] Further, people may be motivated by a desire to be accurate, and this can reduce bias.[50]

Cognitive biases are potentially more problematic, for these result from unconscious reasoning strategies that can lead us to unwarranted conclusions.

Inspector General, *Special Report: The FBI Laboratory: An Investigation into Laboratory Practices and Alleged Misconduct in Explosives-Related and Other Cases* (Washington DC: US Department of Justice, 1997).

[45] For an analysis that comes close to this stance, see Gary Edmond, 'Judicial Representations of Scientific Evidence' (2000) 63 *Modern L. Rev.* 216, 220–6, 244.

[46] See, e.g., Barry Barnes, David Bloor, and John Henry, *Scientific Knowledge: A Sociological Analysis* (Chicago: University of Chicago Press, 1996), ch. 5. Accepting that all scientific enquiry is moulded by value judgements need not lead one to take a very sceptical view of science, nor to abandon objectivity. As Schrader-Frechette puts it, '[v]alues threaten objectivity only if they alone determine the facts. . . . Conceptual and logical reasons also ground theory choice and hence objectivity.' K. S. Schrader-Frechette, *Risk and Rationality: Philosophical Foundations for Populist Reforms* (Berkeley: University of California Press, 1991), 44.

[47] See Nancy E. Shaffer, 'Understanding Bias in Scientific Practice' (1996) 63 *Phil. Sci. (Proceedings)* S89.

[48] Thomas Gilovich, *How We Know What Isn't So: The Fallibility of Human Reason in Everyday Life* (New York: The Free Press, 1991), 77.

[49] Ziva Kunda, 'The Case for Motivated Reasoning' (1990) 108 *Psychological Bulletin* 480, 483.

[50] See ibid. 481–2.

A group of such biases may lead us to overestimate the amount of support for a hypothesis we favour. We tend to look for confirming, rather than disconfirming, evidence;[51] we may judge evidence of better quality if it agrees with our theory, of worse quality if it does not;[52] and our beliefs can persevere even after being discredited.[53] It also appears that extraneous information supporting a hypothesis will affect our judgement of that hypothesis, and of the evidence for it, even when we know we should not take the extraneous information into account.[54] Biases such as these may well have played a role in the Chamberlain and Maguire cases. How deep do these cognitive biases go? Some people think that they can affect perception. When developing his account of scientific revolutions, Kuhn drew on Gestalt psychology to argue that scientists can see different things when confronted with the same visual stimulus.[55] Influenced by this work, Nordby, writing about disagreement in forensic science, claims that '[w]hen expectations conflict, experts do not see the same thing, so they are not presented with the same evidence.'[56] There are examples in the history of science which appear to bear out this sort of talk. Blondlot famously claimed to have discovered N-rays, evidenced by small variations in the brightness of a screen; he persisted in this claim even when other scientists could not see the effect.[57] This sort of episode is sometimes taken—via the 'theory laden' nature of observation—to provide support for constructionist accounts of science. But there are grounds for caution here: the plasticity of observation should not be exaggerated.[58] Cases like that of Blondlot are probably rare, confined to phenomena which are barely (if at all) visible: Blondlot himself argued that the ability to see the variations was a carefully acquired

[51] See Gilovich, *supra* n. 48, 30–7.

[52] See ibid. 52–60; Jonathan J. Koehler, 'The Influence of Prior Beliefs on Scientific Judgments of Evidence Quality' (1993) 56 *Organizational Behavior & Human Decision Processes* 28. For evidence of confirmation bias in forensic science examinations, see Larry S. Miller, 'Procedural Bias in Forensic Science Examinations of Human Hair' (1987) 2 *Law & Hum. Behav.* 157; cf. Jean C. Beckham, Lawrence V. Annis, and David J. Gustafson, 'Decision Making and Examiner Bias in Forensic Expert Recommendations for Not Guilty by Reason of Insanity' (1989) 13 *Law & Hum. Behav.* 79.

[53] See Craig A. Anderson, Mark R. Lepper, and Lee Ross, 'Perseverance of Social Theories: The Role of Explanation in the Persistence of Discredited Information' (1980) 39 *J. Personality & Soc. Psychol.* 1037.

[54] See, e.g., Jonathan D. Casper, Kennette Benedict, and Jo L. Perry, 'Juror Decision Making, Attitudes, and the Hindsight Bias' (1989) 13 *Law & Hum. Behav.* 291.

[55] Thomas S. Kuhn, *The Structure of Scientific Revolutions*, 2nd edn (Chicago: University of Chicago Press, 1970), 111–22.

[56] Jon J. Nordby, 'Can We Believe What We See if We See What We Believe?—Expert Disagreement' (1992) 37 *J. Forensic Sciences* 1115, 1121.

[57] See Alan Chalmers, *Science and its Fabrication* (Milton Keynes: Open University Press, 1990), 49.

[58] See Jerry Fodor, 'Observation Reconsidered' (1984) 51 *Phil. Sci.* 23. Cf. Paul M. Churchland, 'Perceptual Plasticity and Theoretical Neutrality: A Reply to Jerry Fodor' (1988) 55 *Phil. Sci.* 167; Jerry A. Fodor, 'A Reply to Churchland's "Perceptual Plasticity and Theoretical Neutrality"' (1988) 55 *Phil. Sci.* 188. For a brief review of this debate, see Alvin I. Goldman, *Philosophical Applications of Cognitive Science* (Boulder: Westview, 1993), 33–9.

skill. When talking about the impact of theory on science, it seems best to concentrate on its impact on interpretation, not on observation.

This account of biases suggests some of the limitations of forensic science: forensic science examinations may be a continuation of, rather than a constraint upon, police case construction practices. But there are problems in regarding motivational and cognitive biases as an all-pervading and ineliminable feature of enquiry. To the extent that we are aware of our vulnerability to bias, we may be able to control it.[59] In fact, a feature of good scientific practice is the institution of processes—such as blind testing, the use of precise measurements, standardized procedures, statistical analysis—that control for bias.[60] Thus Blondlot's N-rays lost credibility when he continued to see them after the prism that was supposed to produce them had been removed by a sceptic. More will be said about bias in forensic science later, as well as in Chapter 7. All that need be noted now is that although bias may affect enquiry, this does not necessarily lead to strong constructionist conclusions.

I have spent quite a lot of time here looking at the idea of case construction and at how it might apply to scientific evidence. There are two reasons for this. First, case construction has become a widely used metaphor in the criminal process literature, yet there has been relatively little attention paid to the different ways in which cases can be said to be constructed and, in particular, to the epistemological and ontological claims associated with constructionism. While this book is a study of expert evidence, one of its purposes is to use this subject to explore wider issues in criminal evidence and procedure, and the science studies literature surveyed here has served this end. The second reason is connected to the first: it is tempting to pick up on some of the claims in the science studies literature and to draw rather strong conclusions about the use of forensic science in the legal system. In Jones's work on expert evidence, scientific facts are viewed as 'negotiated constructs'; the police's position as the main customer of the Forensic Science Service (FSS) 'more or less guarantees that the facts will be structured after a particular fashion'; and if defence experts 'use the State's resources [i.e. FSS laboratories] they will always come to the same answer as the State'.[61] On this account, the construction of cases in the criminal process seems rather directly to reflect the social interests of actors. Facts and evidence appear to play little constraining role. My view is that the constructionist literature does not generally support such conclusions. Construction in the legal system should generally be understood in the minimal sense of 'building'. Although bias, reification, and interaction also enter the picture, these should

---

[59] See, generally, Timothy D. Wilson and Nancy Brekke, 'Mental Contamination and Mental Correction: Unwanted Influences on Judgments and Evaluations' (1994) 116 *Psychological Bulletin* 117.

[60] See Gilovich, *supra* n. 48, 56–60.

[61] Jones, *supra* n. 6, 273, 218, 220.

not lead one to abandon naive assumptions (there are facts, and the careful analysis of evidence can help us to discover what they are). Forensic science, moreover, to the extent that it is performed well, will utilize procedures that minimize the extent to which scientific input to criminal cases is built in a biased fashion. At least, that is the potential of forensic science. Whether this potential is fulfilled in practice is the question to which I now turn.

2. POLICE USE OF FORENSIC SCIENCE

As the analysis moves from potential to practice, a preliminary question concerns the availability of trace evidence. There is relatively little information on this, but brief reflection suggests that some form of physical evidence can be found at the majority of crime scenes. Locard's principle—that 'every contact leaves a trace'—is one of the founding presumptions of forensic science.[62] A wide range of forensic science techniques is available: analysis of fibres, hair, body fluids, soil, handwriting, shoe-marks, tool-marks, finger-, ear- and foot-prints, and, with advances in DNA technology, the analysis of single skin cells. Of course, even if traces are ubiquitous, that does not mean that they will be practically usable. The perpetrator might be identified through a single skin cell left at the crime scene,[63] but finding such minute traces and establishing their relevance to an investigation would be no mean feat. Nevertheless, more obvious traces will often be readily located. Even with the range of forensic science techniques available some thirty years ago, Parker and Peterson found that physical evidence was present at 88 per cent of US crime scenes.[64] The potential contribution of forensic science to the criminal process seems almost unlimited.

Yet in practice, it seems, forensic science is only used in 1.7 per cent of notifiable offences.[65] One should not be too quick to interpret this as dramatic under-utilization. Even before taking resources into account, there may be good reasons for not using forensic science evidence in the majority of cases. As I observed earlier, successful investigations usually start with a clear suspect. The majority of suspects confess, and nearly all of these cases

[62] See Brian H. Kaye, *Science and the Detective: Selected Reading in Forensic Science* (Weinheim: VCH, 1995), 71.

[63] See I. Findlay, A. Taylor, P. Quirke, R. Frazier, and A. Urquhart, 'DNA Fingerprinting from Single Cells' (1997) 389 *Nature* 555.

[64] Cited in Joseph L. Peterson, Steven Mihajlovic, and Michael Gilliand, *Forensic Evidence and the Police: The Effects of Scientific Evidence on Criminal Investigations* (Washington DC: Government Printing Office, 1984), 24. These figures presumably do not apply to crimes carried out in public spaces, or to white-collar crime. For a more conservative estimate (physical evidence available at 40 per cent of burglary scenes), see Forensic Science Service, *Annual Report and Accounts 1997/98*, HC 878, 1997–8 (London: Stationery Office, 1998), 14.

[65] See National Audit Office, *Report by the Comptroller and Auditor General: The Forensic Science Service*, HC 689, 1997–8 (London: Stationery Office, 1998), 23.

can be expected to generate straightforward guilty pleas.[66] Even if use of forensic science imposed no cost on the police, it would be understandable that it would not occur in such cases. Indeed, forensic science is used far more often in contested cases: 30–40 per cent of trials in the Crown Court involve expert evidence.[67] In a good proportion of the remaining 60–70 per cent of cases, it seems likely that forensic science could add little. Many cases will be contested on grounds of *mens rea* rather than *actus reus*, and here the potential contribution of trace evidence is minimal.

At this stage, the available figures have told all that they can: more qualitative sources must now be consulted to judge how effectively forensic science is used in the criminal process. It will be helpful, first of all, to know something about the organization of forensic science services in England and Wales. Forensic science laboratories have existed since the 1930s. In the early days, local laboratories were set up by the police; it was not until 1966 that these came under the control of the Home Office, which amalgamated them into a smaller number of laboratories, each of which served several different police forces. This restructuring was perceived as giving forensic scientists a certain amount of independence from the police. During the next twenty-five years, considerable thought was given to balancing the workload of the FSS against increasing police demand. Implementation of the recommendations of the Rayner Scrutiny Programme[68] led to a policy whereby FSS resources were only increased in relation to increases in police personnel. To stop the FSS being overwhelmed by referrals, a policy of 'selectivity' was also introduced. This meant that exhibits from minor crimes, or cases in which a guilty plea was expected, were not to be referred. Despite this, the FSS workload continued to increase. Forensic science services were reviewed in the 1980s by management consultants from Touche Ross, as well as by the Home Affairs Committee.[69] The outcome of this was a major change in the management of the FSS, which in 1991 became an executive agency of the Home Office.[70] As an executive agency, the FSS is expected

[66] See Mike McConville, *Corroboration and Confessions: The Impact of a Rule Requiring that no Conviction Can be Sustained on the Basis of Confession Evidence Alone*, Royal Commission on Criminal Justice Research Study No. 13 (London: HMSO, 1993), 32–3.

[67] See Michael Zander and Paul Henderson, *Crown Court Study*, Royal Commission on Criminal Justice Research Study No. 19 (London: HMSO, 1993), 83–5. Not all of this expert evidence is what I term trace evidence, but much of it is.

[68] For a general account of the Rayner programme, see Committee of Public Accounts, *The Rayner Scrutiny Programme, 1979 to 1983*, HC 365, 1985–6 (London: HMSO, 1986).

[69] Home Affairs Committee, *The Forensic Science Service: Report*, HC 26-I, 1988–9 (London: HMSO, 1989).

[70] The FSS agency is still subject to Home Office control, although this will generally be exercised only as a last resort. The FSS has a large degree of financial and operational independence from government, and operates more like a business than it did previously. On the general characteristics of executive agencies, and the political background against which they were created, see Gavin Drewry, 'Revolution in Whitehall: The Next Steps and Beyond' in Jeffrey Jowell and Dawn Oliver (eds), *The Changing Constitution*, 3rd edn (Oxford: Clarendon Press, 1994). In 1999 the FSS gained trading fund status. This allows more financial autonomy: it

to recover its operational costs by charging the police for each referral they make. 'Direct charging' is obviously now a significant element in police decisions to use forensic science. Its introduction was controversial, and in the following sections of this chapter I shall try to discern the impact that it has had.

One of the principal factors structuring police use of forensic science is crime seriousness.[71] In homicide cases, forensic science is used almost automatically,[72] and its use is frequent in other serious cases. This generalization, however, obscures huge variation between forces. McCulloch found that referrals were made, on average, in 36.2 per cent of murder/suspicious death cases, with one force sending items for testing in 6 per cent and another in 80 per cent of these cases.[73] And while most forces submitted items in more assault than burglary cases, this trend was occasionally reversed: one force made submissions in 1.4 per cent of burglary, but only 0.7 per cent of assault cases.[74] In fact, this latter profile may more accurately reflect the potential contribution of forensic science. There seems to have been a tendency for the police to regard forensic science as being of little use in the investigation of 'volume crime'—burglary, car theft, and the like. Steer found that in this sort of case investigations quickly came to a halt when there was no suspect,[75] yet it seems that physical evidence can provide an important tool for linking together crimes as the work of a single perpetrator.[76] Volume crime is an area that the FSS has recently been targeting for increased submissions, achieving an 85 per cent growth in volume crime submissions in the years 1996–9, the largest increase in any crime category.[77] The FSS view is that strategies of this sort can double or treble police detection rates.[78]

can now borrow from banks and accumulate profits for the purposes of long-term investment. This move was perceived as enabling greater efficiency and allowing the FSS to compete in the developing forensic science market. See *Home Office Consultation Paper on Forensic Science Service Agency Move to Trading Fund Status* (London: Home Office, 1998).

[71] See Paul Roberts and Chris Willmore, *The Role of Forensic Science Evidence in Criminal Proceedings*, Royal Commission on Criminal Justice Research Study No. 11 (London: HMSO, 1993), 16–17; Malcolm Ramsay, *The Effectiveness of the Forensic Science Service*, Home Office Research Study No. 92 (London: HMSO, 1987), 12.

[72] Ramsay, ibid. at 4, found that there were referrals in 92 per cent of recorded homicide cases in 1984.

[73] Helen McCulloch, *Police Use of Forensic Science*, Police Research Series Paper 19 (London: Home Office Police Research Group, 1996), 9.

[74] Variations in submission rates are ongoing: see National Audit Office, *supra* n. 65, 24.

[75] Steer, *supra* n. 3, 71–8. For the view of one police officer that forensic science plays no role in volume crime, see D. C. Blakey, 'Does Forensic Science Give Value for Money?' (1995) 35 *Science & Justice* 1, 3.

[76] See O. Ribaux and P. Margot, 'Inference Structures for Crime Analysis and Intelligence: The Example of Burglary Using Forensic Science Data' (1999) 100 *Forensic Sci. Int'l* 193.

[77] Forensic Science Service, *Annual Report and Accounts 1998/99*, HC 679, 1998–9 (London: Stationery Office, 1999), 5–7.

[78] Committee of Public Accounts, *The Forensic Science Service*, HC 321, 1998–9 (London: Stationery Office, 1999), 11.

As well as case seriousness, the availability of other evidence against a suspect also influences police referral decisions. Like Roberts and Willmore,[79] Ramsay found that submissions usually occurred in cases where there were suspects, sometimes as a last resort when other avenues of enquiry had foundered. 'The FSS was not asked to reveal "who dunnit", but to corroborate suspicions already well-formed.'[80] Temkin reports that in rape cases, although vaginal swabs were taken from complainants as a matter of course, samples were not always sent for analysis, the police instead waiting to see if a prosecution was probable.[81] Sometimes, though, the fact that there is a clear suspect counts against making a referral: Saulsbury *et al.* found that two of the commonest reasons given for not submitting evidence to the FSS were 'suspect arrested' and 'availability of other evidence'.[82] So it seems that trace evidence is used as a corroborating tool: if there is no case to speak of, or a case that stands on its own, it will not be sent for analysis.[83] This practice is open to criticism on two counts. Forensic science gets used, not to investigate crime, but to construct cases. This doubtless satisfies the short-term priorities of the police, but longer-term goals might be met by using trace evidence more proactively, to link different crimes to a single perpetrator and to build up databases. If the FSS is right that proactive use of forensic science can increase detection rates, the case construction model may well indicate a degree of short-sightedness on the part of the police. Another problem reflects a more traditional criticism of police case construction practices: the case may get constructed around the wrong person, especially if it is built with the bias that ignores contrary evidence. 'Given that eyewitnesses can make mistakes, and that police officers can sometimes be misled,' Ramsay observes, 'the FSS clearly has an intermittent but vital role to play in protecting the innocent, as well as in strengthening the case against those who commit offences.'[84] The factors structuring police use of forensic science suggest that this role is not fully exploited.[85]

[79] *Supra* n. 71, 17.
[80] Ramsay, *supra* n. 71, 17. Ramsay found that in nearly 80 per cent of cases referred to the FSS the police already had a suspect.
[81] Jennifer Temkin, 'Medical Evidence in Rape Cases: A Continuing Problem for Criminal Justice' (1998) 61 *Modern L. Rev.* 821, 835. In all likelihood, the creation of the DNA database has changed this practice, because a DNA match may lead the police to the suspect in the first place. Nevertheless, the police do not take or submit samples in all cases, including sexual cases: see David Blakey, *Under the Microscope: Thematic Inspection Report on Scientific and Technical Support* (London: Her Majesty's Inspectorate of Constabulary, 2000), 14, 20. Nor, when samples are submitted, do they always follow up leads generated by the database: ibid. 33–4.
[82] William Saulsbury, Malcolm Hibberd, and Barrie L. Irving, *Using Physical Evidence: An Examination of Police Decision Making* (London: The Police Foundation, 1994), 32.
[83] Studies from other jurisdictions confirm this picture: see Frank Horvath and Robert Meesig, 'The Criminal Investigation Process and the Role of Forensic Science Evidence: A Review of Empirical Findings' (1996) 41 *J. Forensic Sciences* 963. Again, the increasing availability of databases may be changing this picture. But the police still appear reluctant to make full use of these new means of detection, as if they are foreign to the dominant culture. See n. 81, *supra*.
[84] *Supra* n. 71, 20.   [85] See further Roberts and Willmore, *supra* n. 71, 25–8.

A third factor affecting referral decisions is cost. The police have a financial incentive not to use forensic science, and Saulsbury *et al.* found that 'financial considerations' was the most common reason given for not submitting evidence to a laboratory.[86] When direct charging was introduced, there was much concern about the detrimental effect that it might have on police decisions to use trace evidence.[87] West Midlands Police immediately announced that they would send fewer items to the FSS,[88] while FSS scientists feared that the new regime would affect both police clear-up rates and their own morale.[89] The year immediately following agency status did see a fall in police case submissions to the FSS.[90] Now, after nine years of the new system, it is possible to make some reasonably well-informed judgements about the impact it has had on referral decisions. Looking at direct charging in the most general terms (its impact on the number of cases submitted to the FSS), it must be said that charging has, if anything, increased referrals. Since agency status, there has been an increase of some 55 per cent in the number of cases the police refer to the FSS.[91] Of course, it is not easy to interpret these figures. There had been a downturn in submissions during the 1980s, when selectivity was introduced, and one might wish to draw comparisons with the pre-selectivity position.[92] The available figures, however, do not allow such comparisons to be made. The figures in the 1990s also need to be seen against a background of changes in crime rates, and there have also been advances in technology, which will have increased the potential use of forensic science.[93] In the period 1991–9, however, crime rates have decreased.[94] As for changes in technology, these are unlikely to

[86] *Supra* n. 82, 32.

[87] See Mike Redmayne, 'The Royal Commission and the Forensic Science Market' in Mike McConville and Lee Bridges (eds), *Criminal Justice in Crisis* (Aldershot: Edward Elgar, 1994); Paul Roberts, 'What Price a Free Market in Forensic Science Services? The Organization and Regulation of Science in the Criminal Process' (1996) 36 *Brit. J. Criminol.* 37; W. J. Rodger, 'A Police Laboratory Point of View' (1994) 34 *J. Forensic Sci. Soc.* 118; A. M. C. Gallop, 'Market Forensics' (1994) 34 *J. Forensic Sci. Soc.* 121.

[88] 'Detectives Protest at Fee for Forensic Testing', *The Times*, 25 April 1991.

[89] 'Forensic Charges Defended', *The Times*, 26 April 1991.

[90] House of Lords Select Committee on Science and Technology, *Forensic Science: Evidence Received After 31 July 1992*, HL 24-II, 1992–3 (London: HMSO, 1992), 23–5.

[91] Figures are given in Committee of Public Accounts, *supra* n. 78, v, updated in Forensic Science Service, *supra* n. 77, 9. The figures exclude DNA suspect samples, but include DNA crime-scene samples. See also Her Majesty's Inspectorate of Constabulary, *What Price Policing? A Study of Efficiency and Value for Money in the Police Service* (London: HMIC, 1998), 73–4.

[92] See House of Lords Select Committee on Science and Technology, *supra* n. 2, 81.

[93] See Clive Walker and Russell Stockdale, 'Forensic Evidence' in Walker and Starmer, *supra* n. 12, 131.

[94] David Povey and Judith Cotton, *Recorded Crime Statistics—England and Wales, October 1998 to September 1999*, Home Office Statistical Bulletin 1/00 (London: Home Office, 2000), 2. These figures, too, need careful interpretation: forensic science is used most often in serious crime, and the rate of violent crime has not decreased during the period in question (although there are individual years in this period where it has decreased while the overall increase in submissions to the FSS has continued). At the same time, one must bear in mind that serious crime only accounts for around one third of FSS casework.

account for the whole increase, especially as some new techniques (e.g. DNA analysis) will have replaced old ones (e.g. blood grouping). Although it might initially be surprising that the direct charging regime has led to an increase in police submissions, there is actually a good explanation for this. Now that the FSS operates something like a business—it must recover its costs each year, although it cannot make a profit[95]—it has an interest in encouraging the police to make submissions to it (previously there was no financial incentive to maximize submissions). The FSS has successfully pursued this strategy in relation to volume crime by educating the police about the benefits of forensic science in routine cases.[96] This is not to say that similar increases in the use of forensic science would not have occurred outside agency status—there is no way of proving causation here—but it might have been more difficult to achieve them without market mechanisms.

The picture painted by case submissions, though, is a little simplistic. In the first years of agency status, the FSS imposed a relatively crude uniform charge for each item submitted for analysis. This meant that, by increasing the number of cases referred, but decreasing the number of individual items submitted from each case by a greater amount, a police force could still cut its forensic science costs. Item-based charging certainly appears to have had an impact: between 1991 and 1995 the average number of items submitted per case decreased from 4.7 to 4.1.[97] More recent figures do not appear in the literature, perhaps because they are no longer critical. In 1995 the FSS switched from item-based charging to a system more closely based on the amount of work actually performed, a system further fine-tuned in 1996.[98] In crude terms, then, the drop in the number of items submitted does not appear to offset the increased use of forensic science that has accompanied direct charging. Nevertheless, one should not paint too rosy a picture of the impact of agency status on submission policies. First, there is some evidence that cost has caused police forces to be over-selective,[99] and here financial pressure may feed into case construction tendencies, because the police will be particularly disinclined to send for analysis material that is likely to weaken their case.[100] Secondly, many police forces set budgets for the use of forensic

---

[95] Since 1999 the FSS may, as a trading fund, carry surplus earnings over from one year to the next, but these must be reinvested.

[96] See further Committee of Public Accounts, *supra* n. 78, xii.

[97] Forensic Science Service, *Annual Report and Accounts 1994/95*, HC 623, 1994–5 (London: HMSO, 1995), 11. Slightly different figures, which show a similar trend, are given in R. J. Weddell, 'The Way Forward—Raising Educational Standards for Scientific Support Personnel in the UK' (1997) 37 *Science & Justice* 9, 12.

[98] Forensic Science Service, *Annual Report and Accounts 1995/96*, HC 551, 1995–6 (London: HMSO, 1996), 8.

[99] See *Using Forensic Science Effectively: A Joint Project by the Association of Chief Police Officers and the Forensic Science Service* (Birmingham: Forensic Science Service, 1996), 55–6; Blakey, *supra* n. 81, 4, 11, 35; *Report of Her Majesty's Chief Inspector of Constabulary for the Year 1993*, HC 446, 1993–4 (London: HMSO, 1994), 36.

[100] See Roberts and Willmore, *supra* n. 71, 27–8.

science, and it can happen that the budget is overspent, with drastic consequences.[101] Finally, some police officers have tried to gauge whether forensic science delivers value for money, a question there probably is no good answer to,[102] and which may lead to some rather crude calculations. Here is one approach:

I have to be sure that forensic science is a better use . . . of my . . . budget than spending it on informants, computers, more police officers, horses, dogs or helicopters. . . . Now, £1.3 million per annum would buy me a very big helicopter every year, or 70 extra police constables for the beat, and that is what the public demands. I have never yet had a politician or a member of the public say to me, 'Chief, what we need is a bigger forensic science budget'.[103]

It is easy to overlook a further set of factors that govern police decisions to use forensic science, yet these are perhaps the most fundamental of all. Trace evidence cannot be used unless the police are aware of its existence and usefulness, and know how to collect and preserve it. The police have specialist Scene of Crime Officers (SOCOs) to do some of this work. In recent years SOCOs have become increasingly well trained; the post has also been largely civilianized.[104] Yet there are still problems with the current system. SOCOs do not attend crime scenes automatically: the Audit Commission found that SOCOs were overstretched, and managed only to visit a third of relevant crime scenes.[105] And there is no guarantee that SOCOs are targeted on the most useful crime scenes: the decision whether to call a SOCO is frequently left to the first officer attending the scene, whose knowledge of the potential of trace evidence is frequently poor.[106] SOCOs often are not called out because of the apparent lack of evidence at the scene, even though much trace evidence is barely visible.[107] Tilley and Ford comment:

---

[101] Tilley and Ford found one force where 'the usage of forensic science is erratic because of . . . budgetary and decision-making arrangements—discretionary spending is simply stopped for periods of time.' Nick Tilley and Andy Ford, *Forensic Science and Crime Investigation*, Crime Detection and Prevention Series Paper 73 (London: Home Office Police Research Group, 1996), 20–1. See also *Using Forensic Science Effectively, supra* n. 99, 108 (one force imposed 'a virtual moratorium on submissions for a 3-month period'); Blakey, *supra* n. 81, 15 ('[e]vidence was found of one force where DNA submissions reduced dramatically as the financial year-end approached').

[102] Tilley and Ford, *supra* n. 101, 38–40.

[103] Blakey, *supra* n. 75, 2. Blakey was then Chief Constable of the West Mercia Constabulary.

[104] See House of Lords Select Committee on Science and Technology, *supra* n. 2, 28.

[105] Audit Commission, *Helping With Enquiries: Tackling Crime Effectively* (London: HMSO, 1993), 34–5.

[106] See Saulsbury *et al.*, *supra* n. 82, 24; Blakey, *supra* n. 81, 8, 19, 29, 30.

[107] Ibid. 29. See also Peter R. De Forest, 'Proactive Forensic Science' (1998) 38 *Science & Justice* 1. Note, too, that a careful scene search that uncovers no trace evidence linking the defendant to the scene can be exculpatory evidence. See J. W. Thorpe and M. D. Cole, 'An Armed Robbery—Hypothesis Testing and Preservation of Evidence' (1994) *J. Forensic Sci. Soc.* 151.

There are serious weaknesses in systems which depend heavily on the judgements of the first officer attending. Tests of their understanding of the potential discriminating powers of varying physical evidence types revealed widespread gaps in understanding, so much so that most would have done better by simply randomising their responses.[108]

Even when SOCOs are involved, their work may leave much to be desired. They do not have the level of expertise of forensic scientists and may overlook or destroy important evidence. One study found SOCOs to give a significant proportion of wrong answers in a forensic science awareness survey, scoring little better than other police personnel.[109] Given the ease with which trace evidence can be destroyed or contaminated, this is a significant problem: Saulsbury *et al.* found that 12 per cent of respondents reported that 'procedural or other errors' had been a reason for not submitting evidence in a case they had worked on in the last year.[110] Obviously, it would be preferable if forensic scientists attended crime scenes, as they are the people best placed to find trace evidence and to make decisions about the items that should be submitted to the laboratory. But forensic scientist scene attendance is rare: they are called out only in the most serious or complex cases. The cost imposed on the police for a scene visit by the FSS is a significant factor here. Scene attendance has declined by 25 per cent since agency status.[111]

3. QUALITY SCIENCE?

Poor quality science contributed to the miscarriage of justice cases of the 1970s. Techniques such as Greiss and Gas Chromatography/Mass Spectrometry (GCMS) were insufficiently specific to identify the substances that they were used to test for, and the results of their application were interpreted poorly. More recently, Kevin Callan has been convicted of shaking his child to death on the basis of flawed expert evidence,[112] and equipment at the Fort Halstead Laboratory was found to be contaminated with traces of explosives.[113] What procedures exist to prevent the prosecution from constructing cases on the basis of poor quality science?

[108] *Supra* n. 14. See also *Using Forensic Science Effectively*, *supra* n. 99, 17–18, 23; Blakey, *supra* n. 81, 45, 49, 76.
[109] *Using Forensic Science Effectively*, *supra* n. 99, 95.
[110] *Supra* n. 82, 32. For stories of the disastrous techniques sometimes used by SOCOs, see R. Stockdale, 'Exploding Myths' (1997) 37 *Science & Justice* 139.
[111] See Weddell, *supra* n. 97, 10. See also Tilley and Ford, *supra* n. 101, 16.
[112] See Kevin Callan, *Kevin Callan's Story* (London: Little, Brown, 1997), 59–94, 100–1, 118–29. On the poor quality of evidence given by another pathologist, see 'Lawyers in Dispute Over Expert Witness', *The Times*, 17 July 2000.
[113] See Brian Caddy, *Assessment and Implications of Centrifuge Contamination in the Trace Explosive Section of the Forensic Explosives Laboratory at Fort Halstead*, Cm 3491 (London: Stationery Office, 1996).

Starting with the procedures employed by the FSS, things are much improved since the 1970s. Fairly elaborate quality assurance procedures have been set up. These involve external accreditation by the United Kingdom Accreditation Service and the British Standards Institute. These auditing systems examine the calibration of equipment, staff training and internal quality assurance mechanisms. They have their limitations: they are not well suited to auditing the more subjective parts of the forensic science process, nor to setting standards that the FSS should attain. They do not cover the input to the process, i.e. procedures for the collection of evidence at crime scenes.[114] Internally, casework is reviewed by a second scientist, and the FSS runs its own casework quality assurance trials, some of which involve blind submission of dummy cases. In 1996–7, 1.5 per cent of these tests resulted in an 'unsatisfactory result', but only one of these (from among 1,000 tests) was a false positive.[115] One gets the sense, though, that this sort of quality audit is not the FSS's highest priority: in that same year only 66 per cent of scheduled audits were undertaken.[116] There are sometimes other gaps: Caddy found that quality assurance at the Forensic Explosives Laboratory did not extend to testing the centrifuge at the centre of the contamination scare.[117] As for the scientific techniques themselves, these are validated before they are used in casework. The validation involves an external element: the FSS must demonstrate that 'the method has been reviewed by scientific experts, published (if sufficiently novel) and generally accepted by the relevant scientific community'.[118] Those last words were not casually chosen. They invoke the *Frye* test for novel scientific techniques, which until recently was the dominant admissibility standard for scientific evidence in courts in the United States.[119] Unfortunately, when it comes to forensic science, the *Frye* standard is not awfully helpful. What is the relevant scientific community that must generally accept, say, mitochondrial DNA profiling? Details of this new technique might be published, but this will be in a limited range of journals—*Science and Justice, Journal of the Forensic Sciences, Forensic Science International*—that probably does not get read much outside the forensic science community. Publication here obviously counts for something, but it is usually only when a technique becomes controversial that the wider scientific community—including, sometimes, those best placed to judge its validity—will take an interest in it.[120] The *Frye* test tends to collapse in on itself, becoming, in practice, general acceptance by those forensic scientists likely to use the technique in question. To note this is not to criticize the

---

[114] For a discussion of these quality assurance systems and their limitations, see House of Lords Select Committee on Science and Technology, *supra* n. 2, 26–33. See also National Audit Office, *supra* n. 65, 49–62.

[115] National Audit Office, *supra* n. 65, 56.   [116] Ibid. 55.

[117] *Supra* n. 113, 11.   [118] Ibid. 52.

[119] *Frye* v. *United States* 293 F. 1013 (1923). *Frye*, and its demise, are discussed in detail in Ch. 5 §§ 3–4.

[120] See Redmayne, *supra* n. 32.

FSS, which may be trying as hard as it can to get external validation of its techniques. But these characteristics of forensic science should not be ignored. I return to them below.

The FSS, though, is not the only source of forensic science evidence. Some forensic science disciplines, such as pathology, fingerprinting and hand-writing analysis, exist largely outside the FSS. Beyond these areas the police would, prior to the switch to agency status, sometimes use other sources of expertise when the FSS could not help them. But agency status and direct charging have changed the forensic science landscape. These changes were instituted partly in order to spark the development of a forensic science market which, by providing competition for the FSS, would prevent abuse of its monopoly. The police are now able to shop around for forensic science services. In the early 1990s, there was already concern about the unregu-lated nature of forensic science and the existence of 'cowboy' experts.[121] These, though, were used largely by the defence; now they may be used by the pro-secution too. The prospect of poorly trained scientists trying to make a quick buck by undercutting FSS prices was a second reason—beyond fears about the impact on police submissions—why many greeted the move to agency status with apprehension. There are plenty of anecdotes about the grim consequences when the police have been prepared to sacrifice quality for cost.[122] Other evidence comes from a National Audit Office survey of police forces that asked respondents to rank their reasons for using non-FSS sup-pliers: out of six factors, cost was ranked first and scientific quality last.[123] While this is sobering, it is hardly surprising. Forensic science evidence is rarely challenged by the defence, so it need not be of particularly high quality to meet police needs.[124] But even if the police did value scientific quality highly, they would not be well placed to judge which services offer it.

As the switch to agency status is relatively recent, it is unlikely that police use of non-FSS suppliers has yet reached its peak. In 1994 the FSS was still supplying 95 per cent of police forensic science requirements, with the remain-ing 5 per cent falling mainly in niche markets such as analysis of drugs and documents.[125] In 1996 some forces were using non-FSS suppliers in 9 per cent of cases,[126] and by 1997 the market was growing fast. The FSS estimated that during that year other providers had increased their market share

---

[121] See Sean Webster, 'Rounding up the Cowboys', *Solicitor's Journal Expert Witnesses Supplement*, 4 June 1993. For a spectacular example, see 'Fresh Blow to the Image of "Hired Guns"' and 'Fake Doctor Wrecked Lives and Marriages', *The Times*, 9 September 1998. See also 'Lawyers in Dispute Over Expert Witness', *The Times*, 17 July 2000.

[122] See, e.g., House of Lords Select Committee on Science and Technology, *Forensic Science: Evidence Received up to 31st July 1992*, HL 24-I, 1992–3 (London: HMSO, 1992), 146; Stockdale, *supra* n. 110.

[123] *Supra* n. 65, 25.

[124] Cf. Royal Commission on Criminal Justice, *Report*, Cm. 2263 (London: HMSO, 1993), 148. The Commission suggests that it is the duty of the police to ensure the quality of service they are receiving, an aspiration which seems rather naive.

[125] McCulloch, *supra* n. 73, 20–1.   [126] National Audit Office, *supra* n. 65, 24.

threefold, to an income of about £3 million,[127] and a new supplier emerged, offering a complete service for the investigation of serious crime.[128] The FSS predicts that, in the medium term, 20 per cent of the market will go to non-FSS sources.[129] As well as growth in external suppliers, we can expect to see the police attempting to keep more forensic science analysis in-house. The police have always done some of their own forensic science work, for example, basic drugs testing[130] and car engine number reconstruction. Back in 1993, the House of Lords Select Committee on Science and Technology (HLSC) noted reports that in-house work was increasing,[131] and there have recently been suggestions that the expertise of SOCOs be expanded, so that they might act as expert witnesses in more cases.[132]

The growth of an unregulated forensic science market is cause for considerable concern. This point was made by the HLSC as well as by the Royal Commission on Criminal Justice (RCCJ), even before the rapid growth in the non-FSS market. Both bodies suggested that some regulatory mechanism was needed to control the market.[133] For the HLSC, the solution was the registration of individual forensic scientists by a Government-accredited board,[134] while the RCCJ proposed a more ambitious regulatory mechanism: a Forensic Science Advisory Council that would have, as part of its remit, the review of 'the performance and standards of . . . laboratories'.[135] The Government was cautious about the RCCJ's scheme,[136] and in 1997 various forensic science organizations established a working group to consider how to take the question of regulation further. Its recommendations are now being implemented, although it is likely to be some time before they come fully into effect.[137] The working group's report recommends a scheme of registration close to that envisaged by the HLSC—though its proposals are more

[127] Committee of Public Accounts, *supra* n. 78, 2.
[128] Ibid. 13. This is probably the company Forensic Alliance: see R. Stockdale, 'Joined-Up Science' (2000) 40 *Science & Justice* 131.
[129] Committee of Public Accounts, *supra* n. 78, 13.
[130] The circumstances in which the police may perform drug tests are detailed in Home Office Circular 40/1998.
[131] *Supra* n. 2, 39–40. See also Royal Commission on Criminal Justice, *supra* n. 124, 147. There is little quality assurance of in-house work: see *Using Forensic Science Effectively*, *supra* n. 99, 73. See also 'Half of Breath Tests "Flawed"', *The Times*, 24 July 2000.
[132] Weddell, *supra* n. 97.
[133] In contrast, the earlier Home Affairs Committee report concluded that regulation was not necessary. *Supra* n. 69, xxiv.
[134] *Supra* n. 2, 33–6.   [135] *Supra* n. 124, 151.
[136] See *Royal Commission on Criminal Justice: Final Government Response* (London: Home Office, 1996), 55. This document noted that the Government wanted to delay consideration of the question of regulation until the publication of a report on contamination at the Forensic Explosives Laboratory. When published, the report recommended setting up an Inspectorate of Forensic Sciences to monitor laboratory performance. See Caddy, *supra* n. 113, 23 and Appendix 4.
[137] See E. A. V. Ebsworth, 'The Council for the Registration of Forensic Practitioners' (2000) 40 *Science & Justice* 134.

detailed.[138] The goal is to set up a registration council for all forensic practitioners. The council will draw on the knowledge of existing bodies—
such as the Royal Society of Chemistry and the Policy Advisory Board for
Forensic Pathology—to develop standards for admission to the register and
to assess and verify working practices. The council will have disciplinary
powers.

These latest developments are important and welcome. They cannot, of
course, ensure that bad science is never used in the criminal process. They
will, however, provide for a degree of oversight of the forensic science
market, and give its customers (police, defendants, and the courts) a means
of assessing the scientific quality of the work on offer. It is to be hoped that,
once registration is in place, the police will not use unregistered practitioners
(save in exceptional cases that call for unusual expertise). Ultimately, it may
be appropriate for the courts to enforce this aspiration by excluding evidence
from unregistered practitioners. The remaining question is whether registration and scrutiny of working practices is enough to ensure the integrity
of forensic science in the United Kingdom. The impact of agency status on
research and development by the FSS provides a place to start examining
this question. Forensic science should never be stagnant: existing scientific
techniques can be improved upon, and new ones developed. Forensic science resources, such as databases of paint, glass, and fibres, need continual
updating. Yet the forensic science market itself may not ensure that such
developments occur. It has been seen that the principal customer, the police,
does not rate scientific quality highly as a purchasing criterion for forensic
science services. To a certain extent, the FSS has an interest in carrying
out research. By developing new techniques it may extend the amount of
services it can sell to the police, increasing its financial health. The development of the DNA suspect database is a good example of this sort of process.
New developments can also be sold outside the jurisdiction: expertise in
DNA databases has, for example, been sold to New Zealand.[139] Yet if
research simply aims at increasing the accuracy or reliability of an existing
technique, the market alone may not be sufficient to ensure investment—
especially if the cost of the technique is likely to rise.[140] The HLSC heard
evidence that FSS research was being run down[141]—DNA technology being
an exception to this—and even a member of the FSS management team has
recently hinted that the obsession with DNA has had a detrimental effect

[138] *Report of the Forensic Science Working Group* (London: Royal Society of Chemistry,
1997).

[139] See Forensic Science Service, *supra* n. 77, 18; see also Forensic Science Service, *Annual
Report and Accounts 1999–2000*, HC 655, 1999–2000 (London: Stationery Office, 2000), 34.

[140] It is telling that the FSS has cast its own research efforts in terms of market efficiency:
'over the past three years our scientists have continued to develop more cost-effective forensic
techniques.' Forensic Science Service, *Annual Report and Accounts 1993/94*, HC 517, 1993–4
(London: HMSO, 1994), 15.

[141] *Supra* n. 2, 40, 97.

on other areas of forensic science.[142] There are figures, too. In 1991 the FSS spent 16 per cent of its resources on research and development,[143] but in 1998 the proportion was 6 per cent.[144] This comparison may be misleading: if FSS resources have increased since 1991, a diminution in the *proportion* spent on research might not mean that research has been run down. But in real terms, the amount of money spent on research seems to have decreased: the FSS and MPFSL[145] spent about £2.5 million on research in 1991,[146] compared with around £3 million in 1998—and this after a 24 per cent increase in research spending that year.[147] Nevertheless, there are plans to increase research and development investment to around £5 million per annum in the next few years.[148] It may be that a cut in spending on research was a relatively short-term consequence of agency status and that now, with the increased flexibility offered by being a trading fund,[149] research investment will grow. One should be aware, however, that research on the forensic sciences is the sort of public good that may not be delivered by the market.[150] Looking at the field of pathology, for example, it was realized in the late 1980s that research and expertise was in decline.[151] The Home Office has now funded senior posts in pathology in some universities in order to halt this trend:[152] it may be that a similar initiative would pay dividends in other areas of forensic science.

The last point is worth developing. In the brief discussion of general acceptance, above, I noted that there may be little interest in the forensic sciences outside the forensic science community itself. Is this as it should be? There are two problems with the relatively narrow nature of the forensic science community. The first is that it means that some of the mechanisms that give us reason to believe that science is a peculiarly reliable source of knowledge are not engaged in the forensic sciences. Science operates well as a means of finding, testing, and evaluating significant truths about the world partly because of its communal nature.[153] Some of the factors in play in the wider

---

[142] See Rebecca Pepler, 'Meeting Report: Blood and Iron' (1999) 39 *Science & Justice* 269, 271 (summarizing paper given by David Werett). See also 'To Research or Capitulate?' (Editorial) (1996) 36 *Science & Justice* 1.

[143] House of Lords Select Committee on Science and Technology, *supra* n. 2, 23.

[144] See National Audit Office, *supra* n. 65, 16.

[145] The Metropolitan Police Forensic Science Laboratory which, in 1996, was amalgamated with the FSS.

[146] House of Lords Select Committee on Science and Technology, *supra* n. 2, 24.

[147] Forensic Science Service, *supra* n. 77, 6, 14.   [148] Ibid. 14.

[149] See n. 70, *supra*.   [150] See Roberts, *supra* n. 87, 43–5.

[151] See G. J. Wasserman (chair), *Report of the Working Party on Forensic Pathology* (London: HMSO, 1989), esp. 7–12.

[152] See Trevor J. Rothwell, 'The Role of the Policy Advisory Board for Forensic Pathology' in Stephen Leadbeatter (ed.), *Limitations of Expert Evidence* (London: Royal College of Physicians, 1996), 82.

[153] See Philip Kitcher, 'The Division of Cognitive Labour' (1990) 87 *J. Phil.* 5; Haack, *supra* n. 37, 107–8; Alvin I. Goldman, *Knowledge in a Social World* (Oxford: Clarendon Press, 1999), 248–63.

scientific community—intense competition, dissemination of ideas, mechanisms of peer review—do not necessarily operate in the forensic sciences.[154] Thus some forensic science techniques have been applied and relied upon for years without close scrutiny of their validity.[155] Given that the consumers of forensic science (the police, defence lawyers, and the courts) are not well placed to assess its knowledge claims, this is problematic. A second reason for being uneasy about the narrow interest in the forensic sciences is that it has meant that forensic science has lacked an academic base. This may have led to a lack of theoretical development in the discipline. Nearly forty years ago, Kirk lamented that progress in forensic science 'has been technical rather than fundamental, practical rather than theoretical, transient rather than permanent'.[156] These criticisms are repeated today,[157] and fundamental concepts, such as individualization, remain theoretically underdeveloped.[158] This is a deep-seated problem, and has certainly not been caused by agency status. But these aspects of forensic science do suggest a need for caution when it comes to the claims made for forensic science techniques.

4. Interpretation and Bias in Forensic Science

So far, I have reviewed several of the factors that influence the use of forensic science in the criminal process. I now consider another: the *interpretation* of trace evidence. This brings issues of case construction back to centre stage, as well as the question of bias.

Much writing on forensic science evidence stresses the role of interpretation in the process of drawing conclusions from the examination of physical evidence. Analysis of a crime scene will involve the formation of hypotheses about what might have happened, which will then structure the search undertaken, the choice of the exhibits, and the ways in which they are to be tested. But even in the laboratory, when relatively straightforward technical processes are applied, their results need to be interpreted, and this may allow a certain amount of discretion. Examining the work of the Forensic Explosives Laboratory (FEL) at Fort Halstead, Caddy found that:

[154] For the impact that this has had on one area, see William C. Thompson, 'A Sociological Perspective on the Science of Forensic DNA Testing' (1997) 30 *UC Davis L. Rev.* 1113.

[155] Fingerprinting and handwriting identification are good examples. See, generally, Michael J. Saks, 'Merlin and Solomon: Lessons From the Law's Formative Encounters with Forensic Identification Science' (1998) 49 *Hastings LJ* 1069.

[156] Paul L. Kirk, 'The Ontogeny of Criminalistics' (1963) *J. Crim. L., Criminol., & Pol. Sci.* 235, 235.

[157] See G. F. Sensabaugh, 'On the Advancement of Forensic Science and the Role of the University' (1998) 38 *Science & Justice* 211; P. R. De Forest, 'Recapturing the Essence of Criminalistics' (1999) 39 *Science & Justice* 196. The Royal Commission on Criminal Justice suggested that one role of its proposed forensic science advisory council would be to encourage interest in forensic science in the universities: *supra* n. 124, 151.

[158] See John I. Thornton, 'The General Assumptions and Rationale of Forensic Identification' in Faigman *et al.*, *supra* n. 25, Vol. 2.

It is common practice within the FEL not to report to the courts the levels of explosives found in the test kits because of the difficulties which occur in interpreting levels. . . . [T]here does seem to be some disparity in the interpretation by different casework officers of the significance of low levels of explosive. . . . The decision seems to be left to the individual case officers and their interpretation within the context of the case.[159]

This context might, presumably, include whether or not a plausible explanation for innocent contamination has been put forward by the police or defence. Similarly, in cases involving glass evidence, much will depend on the exact formulation of prosecution and defence hypotheses.[160] An important consequence of this is that the police have considerable opportunity to influence the way in which trace evidence is interpreted. It is they, after all, who in the majority of cases select the items to be submitted to the FSS, and supply information about the crime. In this manner, police case construction has a substantial impact on the forensic science process. The forensic science market may feed into this. The extent to which alternative hypotheses are considered 'depends upon the range of other possibilities presented to the scientist. But this in turn now has direct cost implications for the police who, faced with tight financial budgets, may increasingly wish to draw the line sooner than later.'[161] The National Audit Office, as well as Tilley and Ford, noted that the police were reluctant to supply full details of all relevant items found at the crime scene.[162] One reason for this, the latter noted, may be that the police fear that the FSS will then demand to carry out unnecessary analyses of items just to inflate its income.

Might there be good reasons for not giving to the forensic scientist all of the information about a crime and the items found at the crime scene? At one point Home Office policy was to limit the amount of information given to FSS scientists, the reason for this being that it would ensure the integrity of the scientific examination. Blinding the scientist to extraneous information would combat some biases of the kind considered above. It is now generally recognized that this policy was counter-productive; it was 'like asking an architect to design a building but not telling him anything about its proposed purpose and location. Science without context . . . is meaningless at best and dangerous at worst.'[163] But how dangerous is the threat of biased

---

[159] *Supra* n. 113, 10.

[160] See, e.g., I. W. Evett, J. A. Lambert, and J. S. Buckleton, 'Further Observations on Glass Evidence Interpretation' (1995) 35 *Science & Justice* 283.

[161] Angela Gallop and Russell Stockdale, 'Trace and Contact Evidence' in Peter White (ed.), *Crime Scene to Court: The Essentials of Forensic Science* (Cambridge: Royal Society of Chemistry, 1998), 70.

[162] National Audit Office, *supra* n. 65, 46; Tilley and Ford, *supra* n. 101, 21–2.

[163] Gallop and Stockdale, *supra* n. 161, 69. On current policy, and the continued reluctance to give full information to forensic scientists, see *Using Forensic Science Effectively*, *supra* n. 99, 62–3. Even if one accepts that forensic scientists need a considerable amount of potentially biasing case information in order to do their job, there must surely be limits to the sort of information that is appropriate. Thompson relates that he 'heard one forensic

case construction that the provision of background information to the scientist entails? I noted above that one of the features of good science is that it implements mechanisms that control cognitive biases. Some of these can be implemented in the forensic sciences. For example, examinations by scientists working for the FSS are always checked by a second scientist.[164] There are also methods of interpreting data in forensic science that seem likely to check bias. Thus the FSS has been developing Bayesian methods of interpretation which, by drawing attention to such issues as the disconfirming effect of inconsistent or unexpected evidence, will tend to curb bias in scientific judgement.[165] Where subjective interpretation is called for, standardized procedures can be implemented. Thus Caddy was critical of the practices of FEL scientists, noted above. He argued that they had available to them data on background levels of explosives traces in the environment which could have provided a more secure framework for subjective judgements about the significance of finding very small amounts of explosives.[166] A process such as fingerprint comparison is quite subjective. Research has shown that fingerprint examiners give extremely varied estimates of the number of matching points on a pair of prints, and there is, no doubt, plenty of room for confirmation bias here.[167] In the past this may have been controlled adequately by the convention of using a match criterion—sixteen points of identity—that is probably extremely conservative.[168] Other techniques leave less room for bias: in the United Kingdom, DNA profiling is largely automated, and the blurry autoradiographs that were once open to subjective interpretation are now a thing of the past.

Thus far I have concentrated on cognitive biases. One would obviously want to control these wherever possible. But it could be argued that forensic scientists working for the prosecution should be encouraged to have a certain amount of motivational bias. We do not expect the police to approach

analyst defend the scoring of an ambiguous [DNA] band (a judgment that incriminated a defendant in a rape case) by saying "I must be right, they found the victim's purse in [the defendant's] apartment."' Thompson, *supra* n. 154, 1129–30. Information that does not relate directly to the physical evidence being examined should surely be kept from the scientist. For a general discussion of the use of blind procedures in forensic science, see 'The Need for "Blind" Procedures in Forensic Science: An Internet Discussion', *Scientific Testimony: An Online Journal*, <http://www.scientific.org/open-forum/articles/blind.html> (visited 5 April 2000).

[164] National Audit Office, *supra* n. 65, 54–5. Fingerprint identifications are confirmed by a second and third officer: see Blakey, *supra* n. 81, 26.

[165] See, e.g., I. W. Evett, G. J. Jackson, and J. A. Lambert, 'More on the Hierarchy of Propositions: Exploring the Distinction Between Explanations and Propositions' (2000) 40 *Science & Justice* 3. Such methods of interpretation are considered in more detail in Ch. 3.

[166] *Supra* n. 113, 10.

[167] See I. W. Evett and R. L. Williams, 'A Review of the Sixteen Points Fingerprint Standard in England and Wales' [1995] *Fingerprint Whorld* 125.

[168] The sixteen-point standard may soon be abandoned. See R. Knowles, 'The New (Non-Numeric) Fingerprint Evidence Standard—It is Pointless?' [*sic*] (2000) 40 *Science & Justice* 120, and, on the general background to this change, ACPO Crime Committee, *Report of the Quality of Fingerprint Evidence Review* (Thames Valley Police, 1996).

the investigation of crime with extreme neutrality. Given their limited cognitive and financial resources, we expect them to fasten on a suspect and then to build up a strong case against him, rather than exhaustively tracing every possible lead. The fact that the defendant has an opportunity to counter the police case by proposing his own alternative explanations lends a degree of justification to this practice. Unless the police are disastrously bad at judging who the perpetrator of a crime is, a non-neutral strategy will tend to be an effective means of convicting perpetrators. And the motivation of wanting to convict the suspect may lead to evidence being discovered that would be overlooked in a more neutral investigation.[169] Perhaps we should expect something similar of the forensic scientist. Stockdale, an ex-FSS scientist who now works for the defence, employs the metaphor of a fox hunt. The prosecution forensic scientist 'is and should be one of the hunters', and cannot be expected to give evidence that will satisfy both prosecution and defence.[170] One can recognize that there is much merit in this argument, though, without seeing the issue in black and white terms. Even defence barristers, whom we expect vigorously to defend their clients' interests, are held to respect certain broader ethical obligations. And when it comes to the police, the argument from limited resources and adversarial balance only has limited force. We do not expect the police to neglect obvious lines of investigation that point away from their main suspect.[171] As for forensic scientists, it seems to be appropriate that they should strive to be neutral, and be motivated by a desire to be accurate, even though we realize that their dependence on information provided by the police, as well as the ubiquity of cognitive bias, means that these ideals will not always be met. The ideal of neutrality is especially important because crime scenes cannot be preserved forever, testing can destroy exhibits, and defence experts are often not employed to review prosecution work.[172] Nevertheless, these considerations doubtless point to a source of ambiguity in the forensic scientist's role which needs to be addressed. The FSS Code of Practice does just this.[173] But given that the examples reviewed earlier suggest that bias has been a

[169] On the incentives provided by adversarial evidence searches, see Richard A. Posner, 'An Economic Approach to the Law of Evidence' (1999) 51 *Stanford L. Rev.* 1477, 1488–93.

[170] Russell E. Stockdale, 'Running with the Hounds' (1991) 141 *New LJ* 772, 772.

[171] See the Code of Practice under section 23(1) of the Criminal Procedure and Investigations Act 1996, para. 3.4: 'in conducting an investigation, the investigator should pursue all reasonable lines of inquiry, whether these point towards or away from the suspect. What is reasonable in each case will depend on the particular circumstances.'

[172] See, generally, Joseph L. Peterson, 'Ethical Issues in the Collection, Examination, and Use of Physical Evidence' in Geoffrey Davies (ed.), *Forensic Science*, 2nd edn (Washington DC: American Chemical Society, 1986).

[173] Staff should aim to be impartial by: 'objectively considering the items of evidence for examination and ensuring the conclusions based on these examinations are soundly based. Ensuring that opinions are placed into the context of the case as presented giving reasonable possible alternatives where appropriate, dependent on the information supplied.' Forensic Science Service Code of Practice, in Forensic Science Service, *Annual Report and Accounts 1996/97*, HC 129, 1997–8 (London: Stationery Office, 1997), inside front cover.

pervasive influence on forensic science institutions in several jurisdictions, continual vigilance is required. Unfortunately, it seems that there is still a somewhat complacent attitude to bias in forensic science. A document prepared jointly by the Association of Chief Police Officers and the FSS states that '[t]he forensic scientist should be treated as a member of the investigative team. His/her professionalism ensures that the independence and integrity of findings are in no way compromised by actual involvement in the process.'[174] The lessons of three decades of research in cognitive psychology, and of cases such as *Chamberlain* and *Maguire*, do not seem to have been learnt.

5. CONCLUSION

'[T]he hope that science may provide an antidote to the police construction of criminality', Walker and Stockdale write, 'seems forlorn.'[175] Though the picture sketched in this chapter is complex, my conclusion would not be as pessimistic as theirs. But, rather than trying to make this clear by summing up what I have said already, I shall end by introducing a slightly different perspective on the themes of this chapter.

As I have shown, the FSS employs sophisticated instruments, its processes are validated to ISO 9000 and UKAS accredited, and it attempts to give a speedy and efficient service to the police. This is all to the good. But Tilley and Ford found a tendency to treat scientists 'as technicians contracted to answer questions at the lowest possible price, rather than as partners in an integrated investigative process'.[176] There is another vision of the forensic scientist's role in the early stages of the criminal process, one that talks of the scientific investigation of crime. De Forest, one of the proponents of 'proactive' forensic science, laments that:

We appear to have relegated the framing of questions to non-scientifically educated detectives leaving criminalists with technician functions and fancy hardware, operating in a reactive mode, doing only what is asked of them. . . . In what other scientific field are scientific problems circumscribed and defined solely by others?[177]

This problem is not unique to England and Wales. De Forest writes about the United States as well. He suggests that there the fact that early forensic science laboratories were fashioned on the model of clinical laboratories has contributed to the reactive role of the scientist. Even the definition of

[174] *Using Forensic Science Effectively, supra* n. 99, 42. The possibility of bias offers a strong justification for funding defence forensic scientists.
[175] *Supra* n. 93, 148.
[176] *Supra* n. 101, 22. See also Stuart Kind, *The Scientific Investigation of Crime* (Harrogate: Forensic Science Services Ltd, 1987), 1–20.
[177] *Supra* n. 157, 199–200.

forensic science with which I started ('. . . not a scientific discipline as such
. . .') is questionable. It may be that the lack of academic base for forensic
science—which has contributed to the lack of sustained reflection on theoretical concepts, such as individualization—has led us to see diversity
where there should be unity. Much of the next chapter concerns this more
theoretical level. It explores scientific ways of thinking about evidence,
involving the careful selection, delimitation, and investigation of hypotheses.
But these only come into the picture at the laboratory stage, and even here
the market casts its shadow. The new Case Assessment and Interpretation
model, we are told, helps FSS staff 'to take a more consistent approach to
defining customer needs to give best value for money'.[178] I have written at
length here, as have others, on how forensic science plays a role in the construction of cases. But perhaps we should also give some thought to the
way in which forensic science, and the role of its practitioners, have been
constructed, and to what the implications of that construction are.

[178] Forensic Science Service, *supra* n. 77, 12.

3

Probability Models in Forensic Science

One point to come out of the previous chapter is that interpretation plays an important role in forensic science. This chapter takes up that theme and examines it in more detail. One reason for stressing interpretation should already be apparent: the significance of trace evidence often depends on the information available to the forensic scientist and on the assumptions she brings to her work. A second reason is more closely connected to the traditional concerns of evidence scholarship, which focus on the way evidence is used in court. Fact-finders need to analyse expert evidence and combine it with the other evidence that is presented to them; for their part, experts need to present their evidence in a manner that facilitates this task. These points are obvious, even banal. What is interesting is that their implementation is challenging, and even controversial.

1. INTERPRETING FORENSIC SCIENCE EVIDENCE

Suppose that a forensic scientist analyses glass found on a suspect's coat and finds that it is similar to a sample from a window broken during a burglary. What conclusions can be drawn from this? How should those conclusions be communicated to other decision-makers? Forensic scientists recognize that 'expression of the results [of examinations] must receive attention equal to that afforded to the examinations themselves',[1] and there is considerable interest in developing a uniform framework for the reporting of results. It is at just this point, however, that different theoretical commitments in the forensic science community have led to disagreement about the most appropriate way to proceed. Consider two papers on the topic. Brown and Cropp suggest a way of translating probability ranges into verbal expressions. Using this scheme, an expert witness would communicate conclusions in the following form: '[t]his indicates that the (fibres, paint etc) (possibly/probably/very probably/almost certainly) (came/did not come) from the same source as the Known Sample. . . .'[2] In a more detailed review of means of communicating

---

[1] M. E. Lawton, J. S. Buckleton, and K. A. J. Walsh, 'An International Survey of the Reporting of Hypothetical Cases' (1988) 28 *J. Forensic Sci. Soc.* 243, 252.

[2] G. A. Brown and P. L. Cropp, 'Standardised Nomenclature in Forensic Science' (1987) 27 *J. Forensic Sci. Soc.* 393, 396.

forensic science evidence, Rudram suggests that results might be communicated in a form such as: '[i]n my opinion A probably came from
B. Expressed on a scale of 1 (little evidence) to 10 (certain) I would put this
at 7.'[3] Conclusions similar to these are commonly expressed by experts, both
in their written reports and in court. To most lawyers, no doubt, they appear
unexceptional. Yet they are controversial. 'Probability statements such as
those discussed by Brown and Cropp', Aitken suggests, 'are superficially helpful but only serve, on deeper analysis, to confuse the evaluation of evidence
further.'[4] Writing with Taroni, Aitken responded to Rudram's proposals by
claiming that opinions such as the one quoted not only lack theoretical insight,
but also usurp the role of the court.[5] There is more at stake here than the
theory of forensic science; the issues underpinning these disagreements
affect the information that will be presented to other actors in the legal
system. They also impinge upon the decision-making role of the jury. In order
fully to understand what is at stake, it will be helpful to take a step back,
in order to examine more generally the implications of probability theory
for forensic science.

The Bayesian Turn in Forensic Science

In the previous chapter, I drew attention to Kirk's comments on the theoretical under-development of forensic science.[6] While the theory of forensic
science does remain in an impoverished state, there has been, in the last twenty
years, an attempt to develop a coherent theoretical framework for identification techniques. These developments rely on Bayesianism.[7] The *fons et
origio* is a paper by Lindley on the interpretation of glass evidence that adopted
a Bayesian approach to the problem rather than one based on classical
statistics.[8] The paper is technical, but it is worth pausing to try to gain an
understanding of its significance.

   When deciding whether glass found on a suspect is similar to glass
broken at the crime-scene, the forensic scientist measures the refractive
index of each glass sample.[9] However, owing to natural variations in the
measurements, no one measurement can be expected to give the true value

[3] D. A. Rudram, 'Interpretation of Scientific Evidence' (1996) 36 *Science & Justice* 133, 138.
[4] C. G. G. Aitken, 'Statements of Probability' (1988) 28 *J. Forensic Sci. Soc.* 329, 330.
[5] Franco Taroni and Colin Aitken, 'Interpretation of Scientific Evidence' (1996) 36 *Science
& Justice* 290.
[6] Paul L. Kirk, 'The Ontogeny of Criminalistics' (1963) 54 *J. Crim. L., Criminol., & Pol.
Sci.* 235, 235.
[7] The development of the Bayesian approach is described in I. W. Evett, 'Interpretation: A
Personal Odyssey' in C. G. G. Aitken and D. A. Stoney (eds), *The Use of Statistics in Forensic
Science* (Chichester: Ellis Horwood, 1991). For an overview of applications, see C. G. G. Aitken,
Statistics and the Evaluation of Evidence for Forensic Scientists (Chichester: John Wiley, 1995).
[8] D. V. Lindley, 'A Problem in Forensic Science' (1977) 64 *Biometrika* 207.
[9] See, generally, Brian H. Kaye, *Science and the Detective: Selected Reading in Forensic Science*
(VCH: Weinheim, 1995), 78–82.

for the glass examined. Consequently, the measured refractive index of the glass taken from the suspect cannot be expected to match exactly that from the window, even if it *is* from the window. Using classical statistics, the solution to the problem would be to conceptualize the measured values as forming a normal distribution around the true value, and to declare a match if the measurements from the two sources are sufficiently close (say, if the mean measurement from the suspect sample is within 2.6 standard deviations of the mean of the crime sample).[10] Once a match has been declared, the scientist would then consult a database to see how common glass of that refractive index is. One of the odd things about this process is what has been called the 'fall-off-the-cliff effect':[11] the two samples will be treated as though they match perfectly if the means fall within 2.6 standard deviations of each other, but not if they are just a whisker further apart—2.7 standard deviations, say. The criterion appears arbitrary, and ignores the evidentiary value of a match that is close but not quite close enough. The effect is stranger still if the near match involves a crime-scene sample with a refractive index very distinct from that of most glass that is manufactured. The improbability of finding glass with a refractive index just a little bit different from that of the crime-scene glass should, logically, lead the examiner to tolerate a larger 'window' in which to declare a match.

Lindley's innovation was to analyse the glass problem using a Bayesian approach that would not involve a sharp cut-off, and therefore the evidence loss associated with the classical analysis. Nor does the Bayesian approach involve assuming that a 'close enough' match is perfect, a process that tends to inflate the value of the evidence. Instead, it takes into account both the similarities and differences between the two samples, as well as a number of other factors. At the heart of the Bayesian approach is the likelihood ratio, which measures the probative force of a piece of evidence relative to two hypotheses. In the criminal context, the likelihood ratio can be depicted in the following terms:[12]

$$\frac{P(E \mid H_P)}{P(E \mid H_D)}$$

In words, the probability of the evidence (here, the glass evidence) given the prosecution hypothesis, divided by the probability of the evidence given the defence hypothesis. Crudely, it can be assumed that H_P is that the defendant smashed the window, and that H_D is that the defendant did not smash

[10] For a simple explanation of the glass problem, see Bernard Robertson and G. A. Vignaux, *Interpreting Evidence: Evaluating Forensic Science in the Courtroom* (Chichester: John Wiley, 1995), 114–20.

[11] Evett, *supra* n. 7, 12.

[12] Readers who find the technical aspects of the discussion in the following pages confusing may wish to consult the appendix to this chapter, where some of the concepts are introduced in a more basic manner.

the window. Now in the glass example, if the measured refractive indices of the two samples are very close, that evidence will be very probable given H_P but improbable given H_D. The likelihood ratio will be large: the glass evidence will provide strong support for H_P. If, however, the glass found on the suspect has a very different refractive index from the crime-scene glass, $P(E|H_D)$ will be larger than $P(E|H_P)$, and the evidence will support H_D. That is intuitively reasonable because, if the defendant did smash the window, one would expect to find glass on his clothes with a measured refractive index close to that of the crime-scene glass—the absence of such glass points towards his non-involvement (I am making certain assumptions here, the significance of which I explain below). Yet although it is easy enough to understand why the absence of matching glass is evidence that the suspect did not smash the window, that is a conclusion that does not flow naturally from the classical approach to the examination. There, the rejection of the null hypothesis (that the two samples are from the same source) leaves the scientist with no obvious means of analysing the significance of the non-match for H_D. Straight away one of the significant features of the Bayesian approach can be appreciated: it can produce important evidence that might otherwise be overlooked. Finally, note that there will be a point where the dissimilarities between the crime and suspect samples of glass will be such that $P(E|H_P) = P(E|H_D)$. In that case, the evidence will support neither hypothesis. In legal terms, the glass evidence will be irrelevant.

There is more to the Bayesian approach, however, than added precision.[13] The scientist who approaches the glass problem from a Bayesian perspective will ask different questions about the evidence and will need different information about the crime. There are significant ways in which her role will change, as will the nature of the evidence she gives. To explain this, I need to unpack some of the simplifying assumptions made in the previous paragraph. A start can be made by adding another element to the likelihood ratio given above:

$$\frac{P(E|H_P, I)}{P(E|H_D, I)}$$

where I represents the background information available to the scientist. Adding it to the conditioning for E emphasizes that the conditional probability assigned to E is affected by the assumptions made by the scientist. Note also that H_P and H_D may be rather more specific than the crude 'the defendant smashed/did not smash the window' assumed before—in part because they are affected by I. Above, I assumed that if the defendant did smash the

[13] The discussion that follows draws on Ian W. Evett and John Buckleton, 'The Interpretation of Glass Evidence: A Practical Approach' (1990) 30 *J. Forensic. Sci. Soc.* 215; I. W. Evett, J. A. Lambert, and J. S. Buckleton, 'Further Observations on Glass Evidence Interpretation' (1995) 35 *Science & Justice* 283.

window, then it would be surprising not to find matching glass on his clothes. But that depends on the exact content of H_p and I. If there is information— say, an eyewitness report—that the burglar smashed the window with a brick held in his hand, then there would, at least initially, be a high expectation of finding matching glass on his clothes were H_p true. That would not be the expectation, though, if the information was that the burglar threw a brick from across the street. There would only initially be a high expectation of finding matching glass in the first scenario because other elements of I may affect $P(E|H_p, I)$. The expectation would be affected by knowing that the suspect was arrested several days after the offence, because then one would expect much of the glass transferred from the crime-scene to have fallen from his clothes (though here information about the retentive properties of his clothes would be useful: one expects to find more glass on a woollen jumper than on a silk shirt).

Turning to the denominator of the likelihood ratio, the strength of the glass evidence will also be affected by the specifics of H_D and I. If the defendant admits being present when the window was smashed, but denies participating in the burglary, then, even if closely matching glass is found, the likelihood ratio may be sapped of much of its force as support for H_p— though not necessarily all of its force. If the defendant's story is that he was standing some distance from the window when it was smashed, then the discovery of large amounts of glass on his clothes may still support H_p. $P(E|H_D, I)$ will also depend on information about the suspect's lifestyle. Someone who works as a glazier, or who admits smashing windows to commit other burglaries, would be expected to have glass fragments on his clothes; it would be less surprising, therefore, to find glass on his clothes that matched the crime-scene glass, and incriminating glass evidence would provide less support for H_p than it might otherwise do.

A number of points emerge from this description of the Bayesian analysis of glass evidence. The outcome of an approach based on classical statistics would be a statement such as 'the glass recovered from the suspect's clothes matches the glass from the broken window; approximately 2 per cent of glass manufactured in this country has the same refractive index as the glass from the broken window'.[14] Although the other variables—such as the probabilities of transfer and persistence—could be brought to the fact-finder's attention, it is not easy to combine them with the statistical evidence, nor to gauge how far they support or undermine H_p. By combining all of the variables in a single result, the Bayesian approach simplifies the fact-finder's task by reducing her 'aggregation burden'.[15] It does not, however, simplify the scientist's task: the number of variables that must be considered leads to a far more complex calculation. It imposes a considerable

[14] See, e.g., *R. v. Abadom* [1983] 1 All ER 364.
[15] See Joseph P. Kadane and David A. Schum, *A Probabilistic Analysis of the Sacco and Vanzetti Evidence* (Chichester: John Wiley, 1996), 246.

'judgemental burden'[16] on the scientist, who must answer questions such as 'if the culprit was standing three feet away from the window when he broke it, how much glass would I expect to be transferred to his clothing?'; and 'given that the suspect was wearing a woollen jumper, and was arrested two hours after the crime, how much glass would I expect to find on his jumper if the suspect was the culprit?' Rather obviously, these are difficult questions to answer. They have, though, highlighted the need to collect data that can be used to suggest some answers to them.

It should be apparent that the Bayesian approach leads to an expansion of the expert's role. I do not mean to suggest that there is anything sinister about this, but it does merit reflection. The Bayesian expert ideally takes into account all of the information about the crime that is available, including eyewitness reports such as 'the burglar was standing three feet away from the window when he smashed it'. Plainly, such reports cannot be taken at face value: the witness may be mistaken or lying, and the defence might put forward an alternative hypothesis—possibly several of them. The expert has to specify the information on which her evidence is based, but there may still be difficulties to face. If the information changes, or is disputed at trial, the expert will have to give alternative likelihood ratios. In some situations, though, I will contain no relevant information about the crime and H_P and H_D will only be crudely specified. The process involved here, Cook *et al.* suggest, can be conceptualized as involving a choice between different levels in a hierarchy of propositions.[17] At the lowest level, Level I, are source propositions, such as 'the glass came from window X/it came from some other source'. But there are also propositions at a higher level, Level II, of the sort I have been considering, for instance 'Mr A is the man who smashed window X/Mr A was not present when window X was smashed'. To address Level II propositions, the scientist needs to have available some information about the crime to enable her to address transfer and persistence probabilities; without such information, she must restrict herself to Level I. The Bayesian approach allows the expert to jump from Level I to Level II; in doing so, she gives more helpful information to the court. At Level I, however, more questions are left for the court to address.

On occasion, it will not be obvious whether the court or the expert is best placed to answer some of the questions that need to be asked in order to address Level II. Suppose a burglary has been committed and shoe-prints similar to those that would be left by a pair of shoes owned by the suspect are found in the burgled premises. On a Bayesian analysis, the likelihood ratio involves assessing r, the probability that the footwear mark found at the crime-scene was left by the offender, and w, the probability that the

---

[16] See ibid.

[17] R. Cook, I. W. Evett, G. Jackson, P. J. Jones, and J. A. Lambert, 'A Hierarchy of Propositions: Deciding Which Level to Address in Casework' (1998) 38 *Science & Justice* 231.

suspect was wearing the matching shoe given that he was the offender and that he left the print at the crime-scene.[18] Although the expert might be in a good position to assess r if only one set of shoe-prints of unknown origin was found at the crime-scene, often r will be problematic. Suppose several prints that could not be accounted for were found, but the ones matching the suspect's shoes were found near the point of entry (a broken window): is the scientist in a better position to assess r than the jury? With w, too, there may be easy cases: if the suspect was arrested an hour after the burglary and was wearing the shoes found to match, it is surely appropriate for the expert to presume that $w = 1$. But what if the suspect was arrested several weeks after the burglary, especially if he was not wearing the shoes at the time of arrest, their being found, instead, in his wardrobe? It is difficult to argue that the expert's knowledge of shoe-wearing habits puts her in a better position to assess w than the jury. Left to its own devices, though, it is unlikely that the jury will appreciate the significance of either w or r.[19] It might therefore be appropriate for the expert to draw these matters to the jury's attention, and to explain how they would affect the value of the shoe-print evidence; even then, however, one might be sceptical of the jury's ability to incorporate r and w into the evidence,[20] especially as the significance of w, in particular, is likely to seem obscure. Perhaps, then, it is better for the expert to make reasonable, conservative estimates of r and w.[21] I certainly incline towards that view, but I hope to have made it clear that the Bayesian turn involves questions about the role we wish forensic scientists to play in the courts—about what we wish to consider them experts of—that should not be ignored. Moreover, I am less sure about the appropriate division of expert/jury judgement where other evidence types are concerned. In an assault case, where bloodstains are found on a suspect's clothes, they will be analysed to see whether they match the victim's blood. Here, the Bayesian approach highlights the significance of considering the probability that the suspect would have bloodstains on his clothes, whether or not he committed the assault.[22] My concern here is not

---

[18] See I. W. Evett, J. A. Lambert, and J. S. Buckleton, 'A Bayesian Approach to Interpreting Footwear Marks in Forensic Casework' (1998) 38 *Science & Justice* 241.

[19] For some empirical evidence, see F. Taroni and C. G. G. Aitken, 'Probabilistic Reasoning in the Law. Part 2: Assessment of Probabilities and Explanation of the Value of Trace Evidence other than DNA' (1998) 38 *Science & Justice* 179.

[20] The empirical evidence on mock jurors' ability to incorporate error rates into DNA match probabilities suggests that this sort of probabilistic discounting is not easily accomplished. See Jonathan J. Koehler, Audrey Chia, and Samuel Lindsay, 'The Random Match Probability in DNA Evidence: Irrelevant and Prejudicial?' (1995) 35 *Jurimetrics J.* 201. This research, however, raises difficult problems of interpretation: see Jason Schklar, 'DNA Evidence in the Courtroom: A Social Psychological Perspective' in Michael Freeman and Helen Reece (eds), *Science in Court* (Dartmouth: Ashgate, 1998).

[21] For example, Evett *et al.*, *supra* n. 18, suggest that it will often be appropriate to assume that w has a value of 0.5.

[22] See Ian W. Evett and John S. Buckleton, 'Some Aspects of the Bayesian Approach to Evidence Evaluation' (1989) 29 *J. Forensic Sci. Soc.* 317.

so much that forensic scientists are not well placed to address this question —they have in fact collected data that bear on it[23]—but that the jury may intuitively consider that the presence of bloodstains on the suspect's clothes is evidence against him.[24] The danger here is that this particular piece of evidence may end up being double-counted. It is obviously important for the expert to make explicit all of the assumptions she is making in assessing the evidence.[25] Even so, I am not sure that this rules out the possibility that the jury will, consciously or not, take the bloodstains to be incriminating evidence apart from the assessment of the strength of the blood evidence provided by the expert.

There are other concerns about the change in the expert's role that accompanies the Bayesian turn; these are similar—but not identical—to those surrounding the jury's role, which I have just discussed. Responding to a proposal to extend the Bayesian approach into areas beyond the analysis of blood, Davis *et al.* express the concern that

there is a paucity of relevant frequency data. . . . [C]onclusions like '*the left shoe from Colin Donovan was responsible for the partial shoe-marks lifted as BOY/2*' are a reasonable way **at present** of expressing the outcome of our work in terms that courts will understand. Unfortunately, we live in an imperfect world where the data on which to base likelihood ratios in handwriting, toolmarks, shoemarks and so on is simply not available.[26]

Recall the probabilities that must be assessed within the Bayesian framework, such as r and w in shoe-print cases and the probabilities of transfer and persistence in glass cases. One can appreciate that some experts may feel cautious about addressing these issues unless the appropriate data have been collected—even when there are data, there may be doubts about their relevance to the case in hand.[27] The point is that the Bayesian approach relies on some very subjective probabilities, which scientists may feel reluctant about expressing, or about using as the basis for evidence to be presented in court.

The word 'subjective' in that last sentence may be misleading. Especially when used to describe the opinion of a scientist, 'subjective' has a pejorative

---

[23] T. J. Briggs, 'The Probative Value of Bloodstains on Clothing' (1978) 18 *Med. Sci. & L.* 323; G. Gettinby, 'An Empirical Approach to Estimating the Probability of Innocently Acquiring Bloodstains of Different ABO Groups on Clothing' (1984) 24 *J. Forensic Sci. Soc.* 221.

[24] That is partly because the jury may think that the bloodstains were what drew police attention to the defendant in the first place; in other words, that they are what single him out from the rest of the suspect population.

[25] See G. Jackson, 'The Scientist and the Scales of Justice' (2000) 40 *Science & Justice* 81, 83.

[26] Roger Davis, Owen Facey, Pam Hamer, and David Rudram, 'Interpretation of Scientific Evidence' (1997) 37 *Science & Justice* 64, 64 (original emphasis). See also Stuart Kind, *The Sceptical Witness* (Harrogate: Forensic Science Society/Hodology, 1999), 258–9.

[27] Davis *et al.*, loc. cit., note that '[l]ocal surveys have shown different frequency distributions' for the probability of finding glass on a person's clothing, 'pointing to the need for surveys in the specific locality of a crime or an arrest' (citing Evett *et al.*, *supra* n. 13).

ring to it. There is a school of thought, however, in which it is an article of faith that all probabilities are subjective. Probabilities reflect degrees of belief that are personal; they are always relative to the information we have. When I see a coin tossed I am confident that the probability of it landing heads is 0.5, and that probability sounds impressively objective. But if I think about it, I should realize that my belief that 0.5 is the right answer rests on a number of subjective beliefs that I might be prepared to rethink: perhaps the coin is biased; perhaps the person tossing it has given it a phoney flip that guarantees its landing tails; perhaps the pattern on the heads face makes that side slightly heavier, making the coin slightly more likely to land heads down. And so on. One can carry out a similar process with any seemingly objective probability. The forensic scientist who claims that 'approximately 2 per cent of glass manufactured in this country has the same refractive index as the glass from the broken window' is making assumptions about the proficiency with which she carried out her analysis, about the quality of the survey which provided the 2 per cent figure, and about its continuing validity—perhaps manufacturers have recently changed the amount of lead they put in window glass, making glass of the relevant refractive index more or less common than it was previously.[28] The Bayesian approach accepts, in fact emphasizes, the subjective nature of all of the probabilities involved in the forensic scientist's work. Where data are absent or sparse, such as for the probabilities of transfer and persistence in a glass case, the importance of the scientist's professional judgement is stressed.[29]

One can, however, accept that all probability judgements are ultimately subjective, but still consider that there is an important distinction to be drawn between a large-scale study of the refractive indices of various pieces of glass and a scientist's judgement about how many fragments of glass would be transferred to the cotton shirt of a person standing six feet away from a breaking window. It seems reasonable to claim that some probabilities are more subjective than others, and that probabilities at the objective end of the spectrum have a significantly different quality to those at the subjective end. One can even use terms such as 'resilience' or 'weight' to shore up the distinction,[30] or point to the conceptual difficulties in assigning probabilities to unique events.[31] In fact, those who express concerns about the Bayesian

---

[28] For other reasons why classical statistical methods contain subjective elements, see James O. Berger and Donald A. Berry, 'Statistical Analysis and the Illusion of Objectivity' (1988) 76 *Am. Scientist* 159.

[29] See I. W. Evett, 'Expert Evidence and Forensic Misconceptions of the Nature of Exact Science' (1996) 36 *Science & Justice* 118; Colin Aitken and Franco Taroni, 'Interpretation of Scientific Evidence (Part II)' (1997) 37 *Science & Justice* 64. For a description of the process by which transfer probabilities in a glass case might be elicited, see I. W. Evett, 'Criminalistics: The Future of Expertise' (1993) 33 *J. Forensic Sci. Soc.* 173, 175–7.

[30] See Mike Redmayne, 'Bayesianism and Proof' in Freeman and Reece, *supra* n. 20, 63–7.

[31] See L. Jonathan Cohen, 'Can Human Irrationality be Experimentally Demonstrated?' (1981) 4 *Behavioral & Brain Sciences* 317, 329–30.

approach are echoing some long-running philosophical disputes about the nature of probability. Hacking observes that Bernoulli, writing at the end of the seventeenth century, drew distinctions between types of probability that he regarded as qualitatively different, believing that they could not be combined in a straightforward manner.[32] Writing about the problem of defining r in cases involving trace evidence, Stoney observes that it is open to 'considerable philosophical debate' whether a subjective probability relating to r can be combined with population frequencies.[33] I have a little —though not much—more to say about these debates below. But now I want to leave the topic, in order to examine a further important aspect of the Bayesian approach to forensic science.

2. BAYESIANISM, PRIOR ODDS, AND THE EXPERT'S ROLE

I have suggested that the Bayesian framework raises some tricky questions about the expert's legitimate role in evaluating variables such as r and w. According to its proponents, however, one of the principal merits of the Bayesian approach to forensic science is that it clarifies the expert's role in court. I noted earlier that Taroni and Aitken criticized Rudram for endorsing reporting conventions that would lead to the expert usurping the role of the court.[34] An understanding of this criticism involves returning to the likelihood ratio that is central to the Bayesian framework:

$$\frac{P(E|H_P, I)}{P(E|H_D, I)}$$

Thinking in terms of the likelihood ratio, the Bayesian expert's conclusions will be in terms of how much more (or less) likely E is to occur if H_P is true than if H_D is true. The expert addresses the probability of the evidence given particular hypotheses. But, ultimately, the fact-finder wants to know something else: she wants to know the relative probabilities of H_P and H_D, given all the evidence she has heard. The process of transforming statements about the probability of the evidence into statements about the probability of the hypotheses can be conceptualized as an application of Bayes' theorem which, in its odds form, provides that:

---

[32] Ian Hacking, *The Emergence of Probability: A Philosophical Study of Early Ideas About Probability, Induction and Statistical Inference* (Cambridge: Cambridge University Press, 1975), 151–3.

[33] D. A. Stoney, 'Relaxation of the Assumption of Relevance and an Application to One-Trace and Two-Trace Problems' (1994) 34 *J. Forensic Sci. Soc.* 17, 20.

[34] *Supra* n. 5.

$$\frac{P(E|H_P, I)}{P(E|H_D, I)} \times \frac{P(H_P|I)}{P(H_D|I)} = \frac{P(H_P|E, I)}{P(H_D|E, I)}$$

Likelihood Ratio   Prior Odds   Posterior Odds

The first term—the likelihood ratio assessed by the scientist—will be familiar. The third term, the posterior odds, is what the court ultimately wants to know. To relate the likelihood ratio to the posterior odds, the former must be multiplied by the prior odds. The prior odds represent the relative probabilities of H_P and H_D prior to hearing the expert's evidence. They will be assessed on the basis of any other evidence the fact-finder has heard (here represented by I). Although it is conventional to use the term 'prior odds', the information on which those odds are based need not have been heard prior to hearing the expert evidence; they can be conceptualized as an assessment of the strength of support for H_P and H_D on consideration of all of the evidence heard by the fact-finder at any stage during the trial, apart from the expert evidence.

The significance of the Bayesian conceptualization of the fact-finding process is as follows. The only way to get from the likelihood ratio to the posterior odds is to combine it with the prior odds. The expert, however, has no role in assessing the prior odds: these are for the fact-finder, based on the non-expert evidence she has heard. Nor has the expert any business in testifying in terms of the posterior odds; these, too, are for the fact-finder, and because they can only be arrived at by assessing the prior odds, the expert cannot legitimately make statements about them. To put it less abstractly, the expert should not testify in terms such as 'in my opinion the glass came from the broken window', or 'the blood probably came from the defendant', because one can only reach conclusions of this sort by making assumptions about the strength of other evidence against the defendant. In practice, this point can be very significant. Suppose that, during the trial, it has emerged that the defendant has a very strong alibi; suppose also that one of the witnesses to the burglary testified that the culprit was white, but the defendant is black. Then, even if there is strong glass evidence against the defendant (say, a match with glass found in only 2 per cent of windows), one would have very good reasons for concluding that the glass found on the defendant very probably did not come from the window. Where evidence is presented in probabilistic terms, the distinction can be stated more clearly still: the fact that only 1 per cent of people would match the blood found at the crime-scene does not mean that there is a 1 per cent chance that the defendant is guilty.

The distinction between $P(E|H)$ and $P(H|E)$ that is insisted on under the Bayesian approach is important. But I want to be clear about it. It is not a result of Bayes' theorem—it is not axiomatic in the way the theorem is. It is just that Bayes' theorem happens to map neatly onto a distinction that we might otherwise think it sensible to draw. Note, though, that the distinction between $P(E|H)$ and $P(H|E)$ maps onto the evidence given by any witness. When an eyewitness says, 'the person I saw at the bus-stop on Saturday night was the defendant', it could be claimed that she is making an assumption about the prior odds (she had better rethink her conclusion if she finds out that ten independent witnesses place the defendant on a flight to Paris on Saturday). Yet we do not insist that eyewitnesses say things such as 'the observation I made on Saturday night is ten times more probable given the hypothesis that the defendant was at the bus-stop than given the hypothesis that he wasn't'.[35] No one claims that normal witness testimony usurps the role of the trier of fact, because it is presumed that the fact-finder will not take the witness's claim to be certain at face value. Perhaps things are different with expert witnesses, but one should not just assume that they are, that it is always wrong for an expert to testify in terms of $P(H|E)$.

There are two immediate reasons for wishing to impose the $P(E|H)$, $P(H|E)$ distinction on experts when we do not do so in respect of lay witnesses. First, it is possible that expert opinions are treated with a particular degree of deference by witnesses. When an expert witness says, 'in my opinion the glass came from the window' or 'the shoe-print was made by the defendant's trainer', fact-finders may take it that that is the last word on the issue—that no matter what other evidence conflicts with these conclusions, the glass must be from the window, the shoe-print must be the defendant's. There is little empirical evidence on this issue,[36] and, while I suspect that fact-finders will not always take expert claims at face value, it might be thought sensible to play on the safe side, by enforcing the distinction, especially as it is more feasible to do so with experts than with lay witnesses. Secondly, experts sometimes give evidence that involves statistics or probability statements, and here confusing $P(E|H)$ and $P(H|E)$ may significantly distort the value of the evidence. It simply is not the case that if only 1 per cent of people would match the blood found at the crime-scene there is a 1 per cent chance that the defendant is guilty; yet the fact-finder might be misled into thinking otherwise. This confusion is sometimes called the prosecutor's fallacy.[37] When it is committed with numbers rather than words, it may have more impact on the fact-finder; it is also more obviously wrong.[38] There are two more subtle reasons for wanting to make much of the $P(E|H)$,

---

[35] For the suggestion that courts actually should enforce this distinction, see D. V. Lindley, 'Probability and the Law' (1977) 26 *The Statistician* 203, 208–9.

[36] The empirical evidence on juror attitudes to expert witnesses is reviewed in Ch. 5; none of it really answers the question posed here. See, e.g., Schklar, *supra* n. 20.

[37] William C. Thompson and Edward L. Schumann, 'Interpretation of Statistical Evidence in Criminal Trials: The Prosecutor's Fallacy and the Defense Attorney's Fallacy' (1987) 11 *Law & Hum. Behav.* 167. See also David J. Balding and Peter Donnelly, 'The Prosecutor's Fallacy and DNA Evidence' [1994] *Crim. LR* 711.

[38] Equating $P(E|H)$ with $P(H|E)$ is only ever correct when the prior odds are evens (i.e. when H_P and H_D are equiprobable). This will rarely be the case.

P($H|E$) distinction. The first is that it may help the expert to think more clearly about her evidence, for example, about how its value will be affected by changes in H_P and H_D. A second reason is that the likelihood ratio is thought by some to have what might be termed important 'combinatorial properties'. 'If the objective assessment of quantifiable evidence is to make an impact on the courts', Aitken claims, 'then it has to be done with the likelihood ratio, not with simple statements of probability.'[39] Because the likelihood ratio forms a multiplier for the prior odds, the fact-finder may be able to use it to form a precise assessment of the posterior odds; this may not be so easy to achieve when a frequency (e.g. '2 per cent of windows have glass of this refractive index') is presented. It is far more difficult when evidence is given in the form P($H|E$), because there is no obvious way of working out what the value of the evidence would have been had the expert not already—effectively—made an assessment of the prior odds. There is much more to say about this combinatorial claim, and I shall examine it in detail in Chapter 4. Now, though, I want to switch the focus to another model of interpretation in forensic science, which might be termed the 'certainty model'.

3. FINGERPRINT EVIDENCE: ABSOLUTE IDENTIFICATIONS

The technical debates that I have just reviewed stand in marked contrast to the way in which fingerprints are dealt with. Here, there is little concern with either classical or Bayesian statistics. Consider this summary of a fingerprint expert's testimony:

[The expert's] evidence is that he found 12 matching characteristics as between the fingerprint on the cash point receipt, and the print of the defendant's small finger on his left hand. His conclusion is that those fingerprints are identical.

He was asked if the mark on the receipt could have come from somebody other than the defendant and his reply you will recall was 'Absolutely not'.

It was his evidence also that he had never known the ridge characteristics of one person's fingerprint to match those of another person, and that no other fingerprint expert to his knowledge had ever done so either.[40]

Like some of the expert opinions quoted above, there is nothing exceptional about the evidence summarized here. Such absolute opinions are given

---

[39] Aitken, *supra* n. 4, 330. See also Geoffrey K. Chambers, Stephen J. Cordiner, John S. Buckleton, Bernard Robertson, and G. A. Vignaux, 'Forensic DNA Profiling: The Importance of Giving Accurate Answers to the Right Questions' (1997) 8 *Criminal Law Forum* 445, 456 ('the likelihood ratio is superior to expressed probabilities of contact . . . in that it can be combined in a logical way with other evidence in the case'); B. S. Weir, 'Presenting DNA Statistics in Court' in *The Proceedings of the Sixth International Symposium on Human Identification* (Madison, WI: Promega Corp., 1995).

[40] The quotation from the summing up is from a transcript of the Court of Appeal's judgment in *R. v. Charles* CA 9800104Z2 (17 December 1998) (Casetrack transcript).

by fingerprint experts all the time. Indeed, as Stoney observes, fingerprints 'have become synonymous with the concept of absolute identification' and are 'idealized as *the standard* for conclusions of absolute identity'.[41] It is worth considering the inferential process behind these absolute opinions.

When two fingerprints are compared, an examiner will look for similarities between the ridge characteristics of the prints. Specific characteristics, or points, and their relative positions on the two prints are used as the basis for comparison. If a sufficient number of matching characteristics are observed, the examiner will conclude that the prints were made by the same person. The subjective nature of this process has been emphasized by Stoney. When a conclusion of identity is made, what happens, he suggests:

is analogous to a leap of faith. It is a jump, or extrapolation, based on the observation of highly variable traits among a few characteristics, and then considering the case of many characteristics. Duplication is inconceivable to the rational mind and we conclude that there is absolute identity. This leap, or extrapolation, occurs (in fingerprinting) without any statistical foundation, even for the initial process where the first few ridge details are compared. Although founded on scientific observations, the process of comparison and the conclusion of absolute identity is explicitly a subjective process. The conclusions are accepted and supported as subjective—very convincing, undoubtedly valid, but subjective.[42]

Stoney contrasts this with the explicitly probabilistic process involved in DNA profiling, where the probability of finding each allele reduces the probability of finding the set of alleles; as the overall probability diminishes, however, DNA experts tend not to make the leap of faith to identity.[43] Instead, they report a very small probability of a random match.

As before, the label 'subjective' that is applied to fingerprint identification should not necessarily be taken pejoratively. But it is important to understand how the peculiar nature of fingerprint comparison affects fingerprint evidence. If one asks 'how many points of identity between two fingerprints should there be before one can declare a match?', there is no agreed answer. That is largely because of the subjective nature of the process. There have been attempts to develop statistical models for fingerprint comparison—

[41] David A. Stoney, 'Fingerprint Identification: Scientific Status' in David L. Faigman, David H. Kaye, Michael J. Saks, and Joseph Sanders (eds), *Modern Scientific Evidence: The Law and Science of Expert Testimony* (St Paul: West Publishing, 1997), Vol. 2, 70 (original emphasis).
[42] David A. Stoney, 'Reporting of Highly Individual Genetic Typing Results: A Practical Approach' (1992) 37 *J. Forensic Sci.* 373, 375. The use of the phrase 'leap of faith' should not make one view the process with too much suspicion. The decision that, owing to the number of similarities, two prints are from the same source is rather like the rejection of the null hypothesis in hypothesis testing, and fits the inductive process described in William A. Dembski, *The Design Inference: Eliminating Chance Through Small Probabilities* (Cambridge: Cambridge University Press, 1998) (see esp. 22–4). What is subjective about the 'leap of faith' is that the probability of a chance correlation between the two prints cannot be conceptualized in anything but the vaguest manner.
[43] Ibid. 375–6; see further David A. Stoney, 'What Made Us Ever Think We Could Individualize Using Statistics?' (1991) 31 *J. Forensic Sci. Soc.* 197.

which would put it on a par with DNA profiling—but none of these 'even approaches theoretical adequacy, and none has been subjected to empirical validation'.[44] To make up for the lack of statistical base for fingerprint identification, fingerprint examiners have tended to adopt thresholds for identification. For example, many countries have a twelve-point standard, such that a fingerprint examiner will only declare identity if twelve matching features are found between two prints. In England and Wales, however, sixteen points was chosen as the appropriate standard.[45] Whatever the standard chosen, it is obvious that there is something rather odd with having a match threshold—there is the same fall-off-the-cliff effect seen in the classical statistical approach to glass analysis.[46] It makes little sense for an expert to declare that the two prints come from the same source when twelve similarities are found, but to venture no opinion if only eleven are identified. Yet fingerprint examiners are loath to abandon such numerical thresholds and declare only that two prints are 'probably' from the same person.[47] Given the lack of an objective framework for fingerprint comparison, this is not surprising; but it does result in considerable information loss for the courts.[48]

The fact that there is no objective justification for a numerical match threshold also means that there will be considerable pressure to ignore any threshold chosen. In *Charles*[49] a twelve-point match was accepted in an English case, while in *R. v. Buckley*[50] a nine-point match withstood challenge in the Court of Appeal. The sixteen-point standard will soon be abandoned in England and Wales;[51] the situation then will presumably be that it will be up to each fingerprint examiner to decide when identity has been established. In anticipation of this, in *Buckley* the Court of Appeal laid down guidelines on admissibility:

[44] Stoney, *supra* n. 41, 72. For a detailed review, see David A. Stoney and John I. Thornton, 'A Critical Analysis of Quantitative Fingerprint Individuality Models' (1986) 31 *J. Forensic Sci.* 1187.

[45] For the history of the sixteen-point standard, see I. W. Evett and R. L. Williams, 'A Review of the Sixteen Points Fingerprint Standard in England and Wales' [1995] *Fingerprint Whorld* 125, 126–8. The authors note that a practice has developed of giving 'non-provable' identifications, where there are between eight and fifteen matching points. In these instances, an expert will declare a certain match to police officers, but will not testify to it in court. In cases of 'particular importance', however, it is accepted that an experienced expert can give evidence of a certain match on less than sixteen points.

[46] See, generally, Bernard Robertson, 'Fingerprints, Relevance and Admissibility' (1989) 1 *NZ Recent Law Rev.* 252.

[47] See Stoney, *supra* n. 41, 73; Evett and Williams, *supra* n. 45, 137.

[48] The absolute threshold rule will often be conservative: it will protect innocent defendants from being found to match. On occasion, however, being conservative towards one defendant will involve failing to eliminate a co-defendant, e.g. where two defendants are tried together and a close match with one is found on an incriminating object. See Stoney, *supra* n. 41, 73.

[49] *Supra* n. 40.   [50] *The Times*, 12 May 1999.

[51] See ACPO Crime Committee, *Report of the Quality of Fingerprint Evidence Review* (Thames Valley Police, 1996); R. Knowles, 'The New (Non-Numeric) Fingerprint Evidence Standard— It is Pointless?' [*sic*] (2000) 40 *Science & Justice* 120.

If there are fewer than eight similar ridge characteristics, it is highly unlikely that a judge will exercise his discretion to admit such evidence and, save in wholly exceptional circumstances, the prosecution should not seek to adduce such evidence. If there are eight or more similar ridge characteristics, a judge may or may not exercise his or her discretion in favour of admitting the evidence. How the discretion is exercised will depend on all the circumstances of the case, including in particular:

(i)   the experience and expertise of the witness;
(ii) the number of similar ridge characteristics;
(iii) whether there are dissimilar characteristics;
(iv) the size of the print relied on . . . ;
(v)   the quality and clarity of the print. . . .

In every case where fingerprint evidence is admitted, it will generally be necessary, as in relation to all expert evidence, for the judge to warn the jury that it is evidence of opinion only, that the expert's opinion is not conclusive and that it is for the jury to determine whether guilt is proved in the light of all the evidence.[52]

Fingerprint evidence provides an interesting contrast to the Bayesian approach. Some would argue that, in giving an absolute judgement, the fingerprint examiner is usurping the role of the court by confusing $P(E|H)$ and $P(H|E)$. That argument has more bite once the sixteen-point standard—which is thought to be extremely conservative[53]—is relaxed. It is possible that in the future fingerprint evidence will be presented in court in the form of likelihood ratios. But to assess the arguments for and against that move would be to jump well ahead. In the next chapter I consider the issues surrounding the presentation of trace evidence in court. For now, it is enough to know that there is a model of absolute identification that has been around for a long time and works relatively well.

4. CONCLUSION

One of the leading proponents of the Bayesian perspective in the sciences has referred to Bayesianism as 'Bayesianity'.[54] That captures something important: Bayesianism provides a world-view, and its adherents are sometimes inclined to push its solutions to problems with an almost religious fervour, finding no merit in other ways of proceeding. It is important,

---

[52] *Buckley*, LEXIS transcript.

[53] See Stoney, *supra* n. 41, 66. Whether the standard is conservative in practice is not an easy question to answer. The precision afforded by the number 16, Evett and Williams suggest, 'is illusory because the determination of the individual points is subjective' and research shows 'that experts vary widely in their judgments of individual points'. Further, comparison with countries employing a twelve-point rule suggests that experts in such countries can be 'more cautious than their UK colleagues', because they employ more conservative practices of point characterization (*supra* n. 45, 136).

[54] E. T. Jaynes, 'Bayesian Methods: General Background—An Introductory Tutorial' in J. H. Justice (ed.), *Maximum Entropy and Bayesian Methods in Applied Statistics* (Cambridge: Cambridge University Press, 1986).

however, to be able to see problems from outside the Bayesian *Weltans-chauung* as well as from within it. That is why I have evaluated the Bayesian approach to forensic science critically. Evaluating critically, of course, is not the same thing as being a critic. So, as I try to summarize some of the ground that has been covered so far, let me make quite clear that I think that the Bayesian approach to forensic science problems is, in general, a good thing.

The Bayesian approach may lead to decision-makers receiving more information, and information which is more relevant, than they would otherwise. In the broken window example I showed that, in some situations, a failure to find glass on the suspect's clothes can be interpreted as evidence that he did not commit the crime; the Bayesian framework allows the expert to specify when this will be the case, and how significant it is. Because all of the relevant information about the crime can be factored into the Bayesian framework, the expert's results can be more carefully focused on the hypotheses the fact-finder is thought to be addressing.

Bayesian evaluation of forensic science evidence offers insights that classical statistics do not, and appears to offer decision-makers more accurate information about the value of scientific evidence. For example, uncertainty about whether a shoe-print found at the crime-scene was left by the offender, or whether the suspect would have been wearing the matching shoes if he had indeed burgled the house, can be incorporated in the likelihood ratio. When a car seat is examined for fibres matching the suspect's clothes, the overall number of foreign fibres on the seat must be taken into account, rather than just those that match—the more foreign fibres there are, the weaker the evidence.[55] When blood or semen left at a crime-scene is examined, the value of the evidence depends on the number of contributors to the evidence there are believed to be, hence on the specific terms of the hypotheses put to the expert.[56] Importantly, when the number of suggested contributors does not chime with the results of the expert's analysis—for instance, if an analysis of the stain suggests to the scientist that there were two contributors but the defence puts forward the theory that there were three—the evidence is weakened, because the numerator of the likelihood ratio will be less than one. These points are particularly significant, because it seems that if the evidence is communicated in terms of frequencies (the percentage of shoes, fibres or DNA profiles in the population that would match the evidence found at the crime-scene) these variables cannot easily be incorporated in the scientist's evidence. Presentation in terms of frequencies would

[55] See Michael C. Grieve and James Dunlop, 'A Practical Aspect of the Bayesian Interpretation of Fibre Evidence' (1992) 32 *J. Forensic Sci. Soc.* 169; C. Roux and P. Margot, 'An Attempt to Assess the Relevance of Textile Fibres Recovered From Car Seats' (1997) 37 *Science & Justice* 225.

[56] See J. S. Buckleton, I. W. Evett, and B. S. Weir, 'Setting Bounds for the Likelihood Ratio When Multiple Hypotheses are Postulated' (1998) 38 *Science & Justice* 23.

therefore seem to over-weight the scientific evidence. This, then, provides a good reason for insisting on the Bayesian interpretation of forensic science evidence.

I have suggested, however, that there are some concerns about the Bayesian approach, in particular about its occasional use of probabilities that lie towards the subjective end of the subjective/objective spectrum. It seems to me that, judged on its own terms, the Bayesian approach is perfectly coherent. But the criticisms do raise an important issue. The issue is not so much about whether one can assign probabilities without data, or combine different types of probabilities: one certainly can, if one wants to. The real issue is whether that is what the courts want expert witnesses to do. It is perfectly possible that the courts do not want expert evidence that incorporates probabilities which lack the resilience of probabilities that lie towards the more objective end of the spectrum. Connected to this is the question of the division of judgemental labour between expert and fact-finder—who gets to assess which probabilities.

A final criticism: there are situations in which the Bayesian approach can get very complicated if the expert tries to follow it through in court. If the defence or prosecution get into the position of putting forward multiple H_ps and H_Ds, a likelihood ratio should be given for each possible pairing of hypotheses. Even if multiple hypotheses are not put forward, there is an argument that more than one likelihood ratio should be given to reflect plausible alternative hypotheses that the fact-finder might construct for herself.[57] There is much to be said for simplicity. If problems of complexity arise, that will sometimes be because the fact-finder has decided to aim for Level II propositions rather than Level I propositions.[58] Sticking to Level I will also avoid most of the issues surrounding subjective probabilities and judgemental competence. It may be that expert witnesses are sometimes better off being less ambitious, giving evidence in more general terms that are further removed from the issues of interest to the court. I have no very strong opinions about these issues; I certainly do not want to give the impression that they are knock-down objections to the Bayesian approach in forensic science. But they are points that require some thought: it should not just be assumed that the Bayesian approach is better than other ways of doing things. The forensic scientist's choice of evaluative framework is not straightforward; it is wrapped up in questions about how evidence is best presented in court.

---

[57] I made such an argument in 'Science, Evidence and Logic' (1996) 59 *Modern. L Rev.* 747, though I now think that I overstated the case that this was a serious criticism of the Bayesian approach. See further Peter Donnelly, in Ronald J. Allen *et al.*, 'Probability and Proof in *State v. Skipper*: An Internet Exchange' (1995) 35 *Jurimetrics J.* 277, 290–1, 301–4.

[58] Complexity will not always be reasonably avoidable, however, even at Level I. See the discussion of relatedness and DNA match probabilities in Ch. 4 § 7.

The presentation of expert evidence in court, especially expert evidence based on probabilities, raises issues beyond those touched on so far. Because the arguments surrounding the 'presentation problem' are complex, I have devoted the whole of the next chapter to them. The present chapter will, I hope, serve as a primer for the discussion there. But it also stands in its own right, highlighting some subtle issues about the way forensic scientists approach their work. What I hope to have shown is that these are not just technical matters: they raise broader concerns about the most appropriate way of making decisions about guilt and innocence in the criminal process.

APPENDIX: PROBABILITY AND ODDS

This short appendix supplements the discussion of probability and odds that appears in the main text. Readers who are unfamiliar with discussions of probability may wish to read it before starting the chapter.

Subjective Probability

The discussion in the chapter relies on a concept of probability that is subjective. Subjective probability describes how confident a person is about a proposition. Put another way, it describes degrees of belief. The basic idea here should be neither unfamiliar nor controversial. We frequently talk about events in terms of probabilities: 'it will probably rain this afternoon'; 'United have no chance of winning the match'. What is more puzzling is how we can get from these vague expressions to numerical values for degrees of belief. Here is one way of conceptualizing this move. Suppose I make you the following offer: I will pay you £1 if it rains this afternoon, nothing if it does not. How much would you be prepared to pay to accept this offer? That obviously depends on how probable you think rain is this afternoon. To get you to specify that probability as precisely as possible, I could impose the following condition: you set a price, but I get to decide whether you pay me for the offer or whether I pay you the same price for it. Then you will want to set a price that you regard as fair, one that will not allow me to take advantage of you. If you set the price at 32p, then it looks as though your degree of belief in rain is 0.32. If you regarded the probability of rain as 0.35 but set the price at 32p, then you would be worried about my buying the offer from you, which would leave me (in your opinion) with a 0.35 probability of winning £1—so you stand to lose 3p.

It is not difficult to come up with objections to the foregoing. Various aspects of subjective probability are controversial; some of these concerns play a role in the arguments in the main text. Nevertheless, the notion of subjective probability captures, if only crudely, something important about our doxastic attitudes: the existence of degrees of belief. Even if the idea of attaching figures to these degrees is a simplistic way of conceptualizing them, this simplicity at least buys a rigorous way of thinking through various problems.

Conditional Probability

Subjective probabilities are conditional. Our degrees of belief are always relative to the information we have. Your degree of belief in the proposition 'it will rain this afternoon' depends on whether you have heard the forecast, seen the clouds approaching, etc. Your degree of belief in 'United will lose' depends on what you know about their team, about the other team they will play, whether the match is fixed, etc. This means that your degree of belief in a proposition may change when your evidence changes. If I ask you for your probability that I will roll a six with the dice I am holding, and you believe that the dice is fair, you may well answer '0.17'. It could be said that for you, P(*six, given fair dice*) = 0.17. This could be further abbreviated to $P(S|F) = 0.17$. Here, the symbol '|' means 'given' or 'conditional upon'. This idea of conditional probability is being used when probabilities are said to be conditioned on certain evidence, or information; the evidence is sometimes said to be the conditioning for the probability. Note that, to be precise, it should be said that your $P(S)$ is conditioned on more than just the knowledge that the dice is fair; it also depends upon your general background information about dice and the likelihood of throwing a six with one. Writing '*I*' for 'background information', the relevant expression can be written as $P(S|F, I)$.

Your $P(S|F)$ may change when you receive new information. Suppose I roll the dice and tell you that it is an even number (E). Your $P(S|F, E)$ may now be 0.3. This can be seen intuitively, but another way of showing what is happening here is to use Bayes' theorem. 'A six will be thrown' is your hypothesis (H), and 'even number' is evidence (E) relating to the hypothesis. Bayes' theorem describes how your initial $P(H)$ should change when you hear E:

$$P(H|E) = \frac{P(E|H)\,P(H)}{P(E)}$$

The calculation is: $(1 \times 0.17)/0.5 = 0.3$.

Once one decides to conceptualize degrees of belief as numerical probabilities, the probabilities will obviously need frequent updating via Bayes' theorem whenever the evidence available to the subject changes. This is why the term 'Bayesian' is often used to describe a theory of belief updating that relies on subjective probability.

Probability and Odds

Especially when applying probability theory to legal problems, it is often easier to talk in terms of odds than probabilities. The two are not fundamentally different: they are both means of conveying the degree of belief in a proposition. Odds, however, can be a little confusing for those who are not used to using them. Odds are expressions such as 'two to one'. They are apt to confuse because it is not always made clear whether the value of the odds supports or undermines the proposition in question. I might say 'the chances of my ever climbing Everest are a million to one'. The convention is for the figure in the first part of an odds ratio to express the support for the proposition, relative to the figure in the second part. So those who are unaware of my mountaineering abilities might just interpret my statement in the conventional way, as odds of a million to one on. What I really should say is 'the odds are one to a million', or, more elegantly, 'a million to one against'.

This leaves the relationship between probability and odds. It is not too difficult to see that a probability of 0.7 for a proposition implies that there is a probability of 0.3 against it. The odds on it, therefore, are 7:3. Converting the other way is a little less intuitive. To convert odds of x:y into a probability for a proposition, calculate $x/(x + y)$.

Bayes' theorem can be expressed in odds form. Writing '$\bar{H}$' for 'the negation of H', this is:

$$\frac{P(H|E)}{P(\bar{H}|E)} = \frac{P(E|H)}{P(E|\bar{H})} \times \frac{P(H)}{P(\bar{H})}$$

The central term in this equation, the likelihood ratio (or odds ratio), provides a means of conceptualizing the relative support a piece of evidence gives to two hypotheses (here, the hypotheses H and $\bar{H}$). If the odds on the evidence occurring given the hypothesis are 2:1, the ratio is 2/1 and the evidence provides twice as much support for H as for $\bar{H}$.

4

Presenting Probabilities in Court

The urge to make adjudicative fact-finding as rational and accurate as possible has, on occasion, produced some rather cranky proposals. Unhappy that justice was content to require 'less precision than chemistry',[1] Bentham suggested that witnesses might testify more precisely by expressing their degree of belief in a particular fact in terms of a twenty-point scale.[2] But, while the fact-finder would be expected to take the numerical expressions into account, Bentham did not consider that it was possible to devise precise rules for the combination of pieces of evidence. 'To take the business out of the hands of instinct,' he wrote, 'to subject it to rules, is a task which, if it lies within the reach of human faculties, must at any rate be reserved, I think, for the improved powers of some maturer age.'[3]

Others have not been so cautious. In a paper read to the Royal Statistical Society in 1977, Lindley, like Bentham, suggested that evidence might be quantified. This done, there would be no role for the jury. It would be left to a statistician to combine the probabilities according to the rules of probability, in order to compute the probability of the defendant's guilt.[4] A better-known example of the urge to quantify is the prosecution's strategy in *People* v. *Collins*,[5] which involved an expert witness assigning probabilities to various events and then combining them in order to convince the jury that there was only a tiny probability that the defendants were innocent.

The three proposals that I have just described are all deeply flawed, though each for different reasons.[6] That should not lead one, though, to dismiss all proposals of this ilk. After all, the rules of probability theory do appear to impose some constraints on reasoning, and a knowledge of those rules might well improve fact-finding. Moreover, expert evidence is sometimes described in terms of probabilities, and the Bayesian turn in forensic science may mean

---

[1] M. Dumont (ed.), *A Treatise on Judicial Evidence* (Littleton: Rothman, 1981) (orig. 1825), 43.

[2] Ibid., 40–3. The proposed 'decigrade' scale ran from 10 to −10.

[3] John Bowring (ed.), *The Works of Jeremy Bentham* (Bristol: Thoemmes, 1995) (orig. 1827), Vol. 6, 216.

[4] D. V. Lindley, 'Probability and the Law' (1977) 26 *The Statistician* 203, 211.

[5] 68 Cal. 2d 319 (1968).

[6] Those reasons are hardly worth dwelling on here. For reaction to Bentham's scheme, see William Twining, *Theories of Evidence: Bentham and Wigmore* (London: Weidenfeld & Nicolson, 1985), 58–60. The mathematical objections to *Collins* are explored in William B. Fairley and Frederick Mosteller, 'A Conversation About *Collins*' (1974) 41 *U. Chicago L. Rev.* 243. Lindley claims to have made his proposal in all seriousness (*supra* n. 4, 220), but it would obviously face problems of legitimacy and computational complexity.

that this happens more and more often. Familiarizing jurors with probability theory may no longer be the dream of eccentrics; perhaps it is now a necessity. In the following pages, I examine this possibility.

1. The Presentation Problem

To understand why quantification is back on the courts' agenda, it will be helpful to begin with *R. v. Deen*.[7] At Deen's trial for rape, DNA evidence was presented which had a match probability of one in three million—meaning that the probability that a person picked at random from the relevant population would have that profile was one in three million. During the presentation of the DNA evidence, however, the following exchange occurred:

Counsel: So the likelihood of this being any other man but Andrew Deen is one in 3 million?
Expert: In 3 million, yes.

Although this is slightly ambiguous, the natural interpretation of it is that the probability of anyone else having been the source of the crime-scene profile is one in three million. What the expert has done is confuse $P(E|H)$ with $P(H|E)$. During Deen's appeal, it took some time to convince the court of the significance of this distinction. Once it had been grasped, however, the Lord Chief Justice, Lord Taylor, made a telling comment: '[i]t makes it very difficult, even if the scientist gets it right, and the judge gets it right—if this is what is right—what on earth does an ordinary jury make of it?'[8] It is relatively easy for experts to avoid the prosecutor's fallacy, but even if they do, it is not obvious that jurors will not fall into error of their own accord. Nor is it obvious that the jury will understand the meaning of evidence expressed in terms of $P(E|H)$.

To appreciate the problem, consider the facts of *R. v. Adams*,[9] said to be the first case in which the prosecution relied solely on DNA evidence. Adams was charged with rape, the DNA evidence connecting him to the crime having, the prosecution claimed, a match probability of 1 in 200 million. Apart from this, the evidence favoured Adams: Adams was considerably older than the description of the assailant given to the police by the victim.[10]

---

[7] *The Times*, 10 January 1994. For examples of similar testimony, see *R. v. Doheny, R. v. Adams* [1997] 1 Cr. App. R. 369; *R. v. Dalby* CA 94/2819/W2 (1995); *R. v. Hassett* CA 90/3304514/X3 (1999). Although the reports do not contain direct quotations, similar errors are suggested by 'DNA Expert Admits Mistake in Link with Alleged Killer', *The Guardian*, 25 January 1997; *R. v. Docherty* [1999] 1 Cr. App. R. 274, 276.

[8] Transcript of proceedings in the Court of Appeal, 7 December 1993 (transcript by John Larking), 46.

[9] *R. v. Adams* [1996] 2 Cr. App. R. 467; *R. v. Adams (No. 2)* [1998] 1 Cr. App. R. 377.

[10] The victim described her attacker as being between 20 and 25 years old; Adams was 37 and the victim put his age at 40 to 42.

Moreover, the victim did not pick Adams out at an identity parade, and at committal proceedings said that he did not look like her attacker. To boot, Adams had an alibi, which was supported by his girlfriend. In a case such as this, the $P(E|H)$, $P(H|E)$ distinction is crucial. If each piece of evidence favouring Adams is given even moderate weight, the probability that he is innocent, given all the evidence, will be very far from 1 in 200 million. Even if one dismisses *in toto* the evidence favouring Adams, one should be cautious about assuming that the posterior odds against innocence are 200 million to one. That will only be the case where the prior odds on innocence are evens, and, it would seem, that is not a sound assumption in a criminal case when no evidence incriminating the defendant has been heard.[11]

Adams is a hard case—factually hard, rather than hard in the familiar sense of involving conflicting legal principles—because it is difficult to see how to combine the DNA evidence with the exculpatory evidence in terms that enable one to decide whether a conviction is justified. Although cases like it should, by rights, be rare (because the co-occurrence of powerful DNA evidence and credible exculpatory evidence is improbable), the creation of the national DNA database, which allows the police to identify and prosecute suspects on the basis of DNA evidence alone, makes it possible that there will be similar cases in the future. That should be borne in mind as I turn to discuss the presentation of statistical evidence in court.

2. EVALUATING PROBABILITIES: EMPIRICAL RESEARCH

Much has been written about the ability of lay people in general, and jurors more specifically, to evaluate statistical evidence. Looking briefly at the general research, it is fair to say that lay people have not performed well on the various experiments they have been subjected to. Sometimes we are conservative: faced with two urns, one containing 70 per cent blue balls and 30 per cent red, and the other with the proportions reversed, we are too slow to increase our probability that an urn is the predominantly red one when we see more red than blue balls in blind draws from it.[12] At other times we are not conservative, a classic illustration being reactions to the medical diagnosis problem:

The probability of breast cancer is 1% for a woman at age forty who participates in routine screening. If a woman has breast cancer, the probability is 80% that she will get a positive mammography. If a woman does not have breast cancer, the probability is 9.6% that she will get a positive mammography. A woman in this age group

[11] See Richard D. Friedman, 'A Presumption of Innocence not of Even Odds' (2000) 52 *Cornell L. Rev.* 873.
[12] See Cameron R. Peterson and Lee Roy Beach, 'Man as an Intuitive Statistician' (1967) 68 *Psychological Bulletin* 29, 32.

had a positive mammography in a routine screening. What is the probability that she actually has breast cancer?[13]

Faced with this problem, most people give an answer between 70 and 80 per cent. In fact, the correct answer is 7.8 per cent.[14] Research of this sort has led most psychologists to conclude that we are poor 'intuitive statisticians', and this does not bode well for the use of statistics in the courts. Such conclusions are, however, controversial;[15] for my purposes, one set of criticisms is of particular interest. Some studies show that when the presentation of the information in a problem like the medical diagnosis problem is altered, a much higher proportion of subjects gets the correct answer. This happens, for example, when the information is expressed in a frequency format, such as '10 out of every 1,000 women at age forty who participate in routine screening have breast cancer. 8 of every 10 women with breast cancer will get a positive mammography. . . .'[16] Our ability to reason well when presented with statistics, then, may depend on how the statistical information is represented when we confront it. Some representations enable us to see statistical problems in simpler, more intuitive terms than others. Additionally, some representations remind us of salient features of problems that we might otherwise not attend to.[17] For instance, in the lawyer/engineer problem—where subjects are given a description of a person who sounds like a lawyer, but told that it describes a particular person picked at random from a group comprised of 70 engineers and 30 lawyers, and are asked to give the probability that the description describes a lawyer—the base rate information (the 70:30 ratio) has more impact on subjects' answers when they have *seen* the description drawn at random from descriptions of the whole group.[18]

---

[13] This version of the problem is from Gerd Gigerenzer and Ulrich Hoffrage, 'How to Improve Bayesian Reasoning Without Instruction: Frequency Formats' (1995) 102 *Psych. Rev.* 684, 685.

[14] See ibid. 686. This results from a straightforward application of Bayes' theorem, in which $P(H|E) = P(E|H) P(H)/P(E)$. Where H is 'this woman has breast cancer' and E is 'a positive mammography', $P(H|E) = (0.8 \times 0.01)/(0.01 \times 0.8 + 0.99 \times 0.096) = 0.0776$.

[15] See Jonathan J. Koehler, 'The Base Rate Fallacy Reconsidered: Descriptive, Normative and Methodological Challenges' (1996) 16 *Behavioral & Brain Sciences* 1; Edward Stein, *Without Good Reason: The Rationality Debate in Philosophy and Cognitive Science* (Oxford: Clarendon Press, 1996).

[16] Gigerenzer and Hoffrage, *supra* n. 13, 688. See also Gerd Gigerenzer, 'Ecological Intelligence: An Adaptation for Frequencies' in Denise Dellarosa Cummins and Colin Allen (eds), *The Evolution of Mind* (New York: Oxford University Press, 1998), esp. 22–3; G. Gigerenzer, U. Hoffrage, and A. Ebert, 'AIDS Counselling for Low-Risk Clients' (1998) 10 *AIDS Care* 197; Leda Cosmides and John Tooby, 'Are Humans Good Intuitive Statisticians After All? Rethinking Some Conclusions from the Literature on Judgment Under Uncertainty' (1996) 58 *Cognition* 1.

[17] See G. Gigerenzer, 'The Bounded Rationality of Probabilistic Mental Models' in D. E. Over and K. I. Manktelow (eds), *Rationality: Psychological and Philosophical Perspectives* (London: Routledge, 1993), 289.

[18] See Gerd Gigerenzer, Wolfgang Hell, and Hartmut Blank, 'Presentation and Content: The Use of Base Rates as Continuous Variables' (1986) 14 *Journal of Experimental Psychology: Human Perception and Performance* 513.

How might the general research on statistical reasoning relate to jurors faced with quantified evidence? If jurors reason as people do in the urn problem, one might expect them to be conservative: not updating their probability of guilt sufficiently to reflect the cumulative strength of evidence. If, on the other hand, the medical diagnosis problem is a relevant point of comparison, one would expect jurors to pay insufficient attention to the prior probability of guilt—a process similar to confusing $P(E|H)$ and $P(H|E)$. Looking at the empirical studies that have examined juror processing of probabilistic evidence, it appears that the former bias is dominant. In fact, there is a remarkable degree of consistency between the studies: compared to a Bayesian norm for evidence combination, jurors generally reach conservative estimates of the probability of guilt when confronted with statistical evidence.[19] Given that the principal fear when probabilistic evidence is used is that jurors will give too much weight to it—especially by confusing $P(E|H)$ and $P(H|E)$—this is reassuring. Looking at the studies carefully, however, they do not give too much reason to be complacent.

First, there are always doubts about the external validity of laboratory studies of jurors. There is actually good reason to question the external validity of the juror/probability research: in Schklar and Diamond's study, only 66 per cent of jurors presented with a random match probability of 1 in a billion returned a verdict of guilty.[20] Absent credible evidence of laboratory error or of the defendant having been framed, it is difficult to imagine

---

[19] See William C. Thompson and Edward L. Schumann, 'Interpretation of Statistical Evidence in Criminal Trials: The Prosecutor's Fallacy and the Defense Attorney's Fallacy' (1987) 11 *Law & Hum. Behav.* 167; William C. Thompson, 'Are Juries Competent to Evaluate Statistical Evidence?' (1989) 52 *Law & Contemp. Probs* 9, 30–41; David L. Faigman and A. J. Baglioni, Jr., 'Bayes' Theorem in the Trial Process: Instructing Jurors on the Value of Statistical Evidence' (1988) 12 *Law & Hum. Behav.* 1; Jane Goodman, 'Jurors' Comprehension and Assessment of Probabilistic Evidence' (1992) 16 *Am. J. Trial Advocacy* 361; Brian C. Smith, Steven D. Penrod, Amy L. Otto, and Roger C. Park, 'Jurors' Use of Probabilistic Evidence' (1996) 20 *Law & Hum. Behav.* 49; Angel Carracedo *et al.*, 'Focusing the Debate on Forensic Genetics' (1996) 36 *Science & Justice* 204; F. Taroni and C. G. G. Aitken, 'Probabilistic Reasoning in the Law Part 1: Assessment of Probabilities and Explanation of the Value of DNA Evidence' (1998) 38 *Science & Justice* 165; Jason Schklar and Shari Seidman Diamond, 'Juror Reaction to DNA Evidence: Errors and Expectancies' (1999) 23 *Law & Hum. Behav.* 159. For a review of the early studies, see D. H. Kaye and Jonathan J. Koehler, 'Can Jurors Understand Probabilistic Evidence?' (1991) 154 *J. R. Stat. Soc. (Series A)* 75.

[20] *Supra* n. 19. The experiment included weak non-DNA evidence linking the suspect to the crime; enough, one would have thought, to prove guilt to a very high degree of probability when combined with the DNA evidence. See also Jonathan J. Koehler, Audrey Chia, and Samuel Lindsay, 'The Random Match Probability in DNA Evidence: Irrelevant and Prejudicial' (1995) 35 *Jurimetrics J.* 201, 214–15, reporting studies where 44 per cent of mock jurors presented with a match probability of 1 in a billion returned guilty verdicts. The case sketch included in the article involves weak circumstantial evidence but, considering that the defendant was the victim's husband, the prior should have been quite high: enough to make a not guilty verdict difficult to defend if the match probability was taken seriously. On prior probabilities in cases where D is accused of wife-murder, see I. J. Good, 'When Batterer Turns Murderer' (1995) 375 *Nature* 541.

this happening outside the laboratory.[21] In fact, Schklar and Diamond use results like the one just described to suggest that jurors have expectations about such things as the possibility of planted evidence and laboratory error and that these form the context within which they interpret probabilistic evidence. This is an important point, and it clouds the interpretation of all of the juror/probability studies. I would add, though, that, because acquittals against such overwhelming odds do not seem to be the norm in the real world, the lack of context and explanation in laboratory studies may mean that the statistics presented in them lack weight in the eyes of jurors, and that similar statistics would have a far greater effect on jurors in real trials.

Secondly, although under-weighting of statistical evidence is the general trend in the empirical studies, it is by no means universal. Some subjects in the studies do over-weight statistical evidence, and some fall for the prosecutor's fallacy.[22] Especially significant is Smith *et al.*'s finding that jurors most often over-weighted statistical evidence when their prior probability of guilt was low (the *Adams* scenario).[23]

A further reason for scepticism about the laboratory studies is that they use fairly large match probabilities. Apart from Schklar and Diamond's 1 in a billion, the smallest is the 1 in 10,000 used by Taroni and Aitken,[24] a far cry from the 1 in 200 million reported in *Adams*, which is pretty much the norm for DNA evidence nowadays. It may be that very small match probabilities have a completely—not merely quantitatively—different effect on jurors than the larger figures used in most empirical studies. It is possible that when match probabilities reach the hundreds of millions, jurors simply conclude that the defendant is guilty, and will not allow that exculpatory evidence might suggest otherwise.

---

[21] There is, of course, a well-known example of acquittal in the face of such overwhelming DNA statistics, but in that case there was a plausible argument for framing and laboratory error. See William C. Thompson, 'DNA Evidence in the O.J. Simpson Trial' (1996) 67 *U. Colorado L. Rev.* 827; Darnell M. Hunt, *O.J. Simpson Facts and Fictions: News Rituals in the Construction of Reality* (Cambridge: Cambridge University Press, 1999), 36–9. See also 'DNA Evidence was Not Enough', *The Times*, 6 June 2000.

[22] Most often when the statistical evidence is presented in terms of that fallacy. See Thompson and Schumann, *supra* n. 19; Carracedo *et al.*, *supra* n. 19.

[23] *Supra* n. 19, 73–4. Their explanation of this result—that jurors with low prior probabilities have more room to err—is plausible. If one starts with a relatively high prior probability of guilt, 0.6, say, then even a modest match probability, such as 1 in 100, leads to a posterior probability of guilt of more than 0.99. As the match probability increases, the posterior probability of guilt asymptotes to unity, but few jurors are likely to report a posterior probability of guilt of more than 0.99; they will tend, therefore, to report a posterior probability that gives the impression of their having under-weighted the evidence. In contrast, a juror with a prior probability of guilt of only 0.2 should, on hearing the 1 in 100 statistic, revise her probability to 0.96, and she has more space—that between 0.96 and 1—in which to overshoot the normative value, and thus to give the impression of over-weighting the statistical evidence.

[24] *Supra* n. 20.

I shall return to some of the details of the empirical research below. Having gained an overview of the findings, I now turn to assess the various methods by which probabilistic evidence might be presented in court.

3. LIKELIHOOD RATIOS AND VERBAL CONVENTIONS

In Chapter 3 I noted that likelihood ratios have found favour among some forensic scientists, partly because of their combinatorial qualities. Plainly, jurors are unlikely to have any understanding of just what a likelihood ratio is, so saying that 'the likelihood ratio for the glass evidence is 150' will not be helpful. Instead, the expert can place the likelihood ratio in its proper context, and testify that 'the glass evidence is 150 times more likely if the defendant broke the window than if he did not break the window'. Such testimony conveys an idea of the probative force of the evidence, and respects the $P(E|H)$, $P(H|E)$ distinction. However, although some commentators suggest that testimony in this form will be readily understood by the jury,[25] it is by no means obvious that it will be. We are not used, in our everyday lives, to hearing statements of this sort; it may be obscure to jurors just how the probability of the evidence relates to the probability that the defendant is guilty. Indeed, it has been suggested that jurors may misinterpret such statements and think that they relate to $P(H|E)$. There is some research to support this suggestion.[26]

A more helpful way of expressing likelihood ratios is to stress their multiplicative quality. A glass expert could say, 'whatever your odds were that the defendant was guilty before you heard my evidence, the glass evidence makes those odds 150 times greater'. This, at least, makes it clear what the likelihood ratio means and how it works. But it is unsatisfactory for other reasons. It presumes that the fact-finder is engaged in a process of serial belief-updating—that each time she hears a piece of evidence, her degree of belief in the defendant's guilt increases or decreases. This may be psychologically implausible;[27] it is also impractical. Pieces of evidence presented

---

[25] See Franco Taroni and Colin Aitken, 'Interpretation of Scientific Evidence' (1996) 36 *Science & Justice* 290, 291; Bernard Robertson and Tony Vignaux, 'DNA Evidence on Appeal—II' [1997] *NZLJ* 247, 249.

[26] See Jonathan J. Koehler, 'On Conveying the Probative Value of DNA Evidence: Frequencies, Likelihood Ratios, and Error Rates' (1996) 67 *U. Col. L. Rev.* 859, 879–80; Christopher R. Wolfe, 'Information Seeking on Bayesian Conditional Problems: A Fuzzy-Trace Theory Account' (1995) 8 *J. Behav. Decision Making* 85. Among the juror/probability studies, the most significant finding is Thompson and Schumann's. When statistical evidence was presented in the form of the conditional probability $P(E|H_D)$, 22 per cent of subjects committed the prosecutor's fallacy, compared with only 4 per cent when the evidence was presented as a frequency. *Supra* n. 19, 174.

[27] See, generally, Lola L. Lopes, 'Two Conceptions of the Juror' in Reid Hastie (ed.), *Inside the Juror: The Psychology of Juror Decision Making* (Cambridge: Cambridge University Press, 1993).

in a trial are often interdependent: knowing about one piece of evidence affects the value of another. If jurors are going to multiply pieces of evidence together, they need to wait until the end of the trial, when the dependency relations among the pieces of evidence can be worked out. It is difficult to see a way round this problem.[28] But even if it is ignored, other difficulties remain. Suppose, as in *Adams*, that the prosecution presents only DNA evidence. How, then, should the jury conceptualize its prior belief in guilt? Moreover, the very idea of multiplying the value of pieces of evidence together may not make much sense to jurors, especially as the non-scientific evidence will not be quantified in anything other than the vaguest terms.

There is a rather more natural way of translating the multiplicative nature of likelihood ratios into testimony. Evett has come up with a verbal scale which can be used to describe the degree of support the expert evidence provides for a hypothesis: a likelihood ratio between 1 and 10 would be said to provide 'limited support', one between 10 and 100 'moderate support', one between 100 and 1,000 'strong support', and one over 1,000 'very strong support'.[29] This is a nice solution, and it may provide the most appropriate means of expressing the value of many types of scientific evidence. Nevertheless, this approach has its problems too. Like all of the proposals reviewed so far, it makes a lot of sense once one is familiar with the Bayesian 'prior odds × likelihood ratio = posterior odds' model of evidence evaluation. But to understand the meaning such testimony may have for a jury, one needs to be able to view it from outside the Bayesian paradigm in which it makes obvious sense. Then one can appreciate, I think, that the scientist's testimony might be interpreted as a statement about the posterior odds.[30] Consider the *Adams* scenario, where the non-scientific evidence establishes a good case for Adams' innocence. If the scientist testifies that her evidence provides very strong support for the hypothesis that Adams is the source of the semen, the jury might think that there is a high probability that Adams is guilty whatever the other evidence in the case. The verbal formulation does not quite bring out the multiplicative nature of the

[28] One might tell the jury to wait until the end of their deliberations, work out the prior odds on guilt conditioned on all the non-statistical evidence, and then multiply them by the likelihood ratio. It is doubtful, however, whether jurors could separate out the different items of evidence: their prior odds would probably be affected by their knowledge of the statistical evidence, a form of hindsight bias. See Baruch Fischoff, 'For Those Condemned to Study the Past: Heuristics and Biases in Hindsight' in Daniel Kahneman, Paul Slovic, and Amos Tversky (eds), *Judgment Under Uncertainty: Heuristics and Biases* (Cambridge: Cambridge University Press, 1982). See also David M. Saunders, Neil Vidmar, and Erin C. Hewitt, 'Eyewitness Testimony and the Discrediting Effect' in Sally M. A. Lloyd-Bostock and B. R. Clifford (eds), *Evaluating Witness Evidence* (Chichester: John Wiley, 1983), 68–74.

[29] I. W. Evett, 'Towards a Uniform Framework for Reporting Opinions in Forensic Science Casework' (1998) 38 *Science & Justice* 198, 201.

[30] Some lawyers seem to have interpreted it in this manner. See J. A. Lambert and I. W. Evett, 'The Impact of Recent Judgments on the Presentation of DNA Evidence' (1998) 38 *Science & Justice* 266, 270.

likelihood ratio, and the effects of its combination with low prior odds. Aside from this problem of ambiguity, the verbal formulations have another flaw. A likelihood ratio can be as large as you like—with DNA evidence, likelihood ratios in the hundreds of millions are not uncommon, and we can expect them to get larger in the future—but the verbal scale peaks at 'very strong support'. With such figures, Evett concedes, 'words seem inadequate'.[31] It might be thought rather dishonest not to tell the jury just how incredibly strong the DNA evidence is in a case such as *Adams*. 'The only solution— to which I come reluctantly', Evett writes, 'may be to settle for presenting the number without verbal comment.'[32]

There is another criticism of the verbal equivalents of likelihood ratios, but it is not one, I think, that cuts much ice. It is that the verbal expressions are imprecise.[33] That is true, but it is by no means clear what the value of precision is in this context. If I am told that the likelihood ratio for the expert's evidence is 134, then I have a precise figure—I know that the likelihood ratio is not 133, or 135. But knowing the likelihood ratio with such precision does not do me much good, unless I also have a sharp figure for my prior odds. If all I have in mind is a feeling that it is unlikely that the defendant is guilty, having a precise value for the scientific evidence will not be of much use: knowing that the evidence provides strong support for the hypothesis of guilt will be as helpful as anything to me.[34] It happens, though, that there are ways of getting jurors to put more precise figures on their prior odds. I now turn to consider them.

4. Quantifying Prior Odds

A more robust way of getting jurors to understand the relationship between prior and posterior odds is to encourage them to think in terms of quantified

[31] I. W. Evett, 'Interpretation: A Personal Odyssey' in C. G. G. Aitken and D. A. Stoney (eds), *The Use of Statistics in Forensic Science* (Chichester: Ellis Horwood, 1991), 21.

[32] Ibid. For a means of dealing with extremely large likelihood ratios verbally, see C. G. G. Aitken and F. Taroni, 'A Verbal Scale for the Interpretation of Evidence' (1998) 38 *Science & Justice* 279. The scheme, however, involves the quantification of prior odds—it is only the effect of the likelihood ratio on the prior odds that is expressed verbally—and is therefore subject to the criticisms developed in the following section.

[33] See Bernard Robertson and G. A. Vignaux, *Interpreting Evidence: Evaluating Forensic Science in the Courtroom* (Chichester: John Wiley, 1995), 57 ('the only way to express the relative strength of pieces of evidence that is not open to misinterpretation is to use numbers'); National Research Council, Committee on DNA Forensic Science: An Update, *The Evaluation of Forensic DNA Evidence* (Washington DC: National Academy Press, 1996), 195.

[34] There is another way in which the verbal conventions might be said to be imprecise. Probability expressions gain some of their meaning from context (see Thomas S. Wallsten and David V. Budescu, 'Comment' (1990) 5 *Statistical Science* 23, 24). It is easier to understand what the verbal conventions mean when they are seen together, and one knows that they form a range from 'limited' to 'strong' support. It might therefore be wise for the expert to explain to the jury that 'limited support' is the lowest category of evidence strength, and that it differs from 'moderate' and 'strong' support.

prior odds. One way of achieving this is to present them with a Bayes' table.[35] Suppose the likelihood ratio is 1,000; the following table shows its effect on a variety of prior odds:

Prior Odds	Posterior Odds
1 to 10	100 to 1
1 to 5	500 to 1
1 to 1	1,000 to 1
5 to 1	5,000 to 1
10 to 1	10,000 to 1

The table need not be in terms of odds; it can use percentage probabilities, which are probably easier for lay people to get to grips with. The table can be used as a basic illustration, to give the jury some idea of the relationship between prior and posterior odds.[36] Alternatively, the jury can be invited to quantify its prior odds in order to work out precise posterior odds. The latter creates difficulties similar to those noted in relation to the presentation of the likelihood ratio as a multiplier. There are other problems, too. The quantification of the prior odds may be affected by knowledge that there is relatively powerful scientific evidence against the defendant;[37] or the jury may simply pick the posterior odds that fit its intuition about the case, and then rationalize the prior odds on a *post hoc* basis. Basically, unless the jury can be made to give a firm grounding to the prior odds, use of a Bayes' table rests on too flimsy a foundation for one to be complacent about its use in a criminal trial. This makes the former approach, which avoids explicit quantification of the prior odds, look attractive. But unless the jury has some idea what its prior odds may be, it is not evident that just seeing a Bayes' table will teach it very much. A final problem is that the empirical research suggests that such tools have little impact on jurors.[38]

---

[35] See Michael O. Finkelstein and William B. Fairley, 'A Bayesian Approach to Identification Evidence' (1970) 83 *Harv. L. Rev.* 489, 502; Donald A. Berry and Seymour Geisser, 'Inference in Cases of Disputed Paternity' in Morris H. DeGroot, Stephen E. Fienberg, and Joseph B. Kadane (eds), *Statistics and the Law* (New York: John Wiley, 1986); Stephen E. Fienberg, Samuel H. Krislov, and Miran L. Straf, 'Understanding and Evaluating Statistical Evidence in Litigation' (1995) 36 *Jurimetrics J.* 1, 19–20. A form of this presentation is also endorsed in Ian W. Evett and Bruce S. Weir, *Interpreting DNA Evidence: Statistical Genetics for Forensic Scientists* (Sunderland, MA: Sinauer, 1998), 245, and Ian W. Evett, Lindsey Foreman, Graham Jackson, and James A. Lambert, 'DNA Profiling: A Discussion of Issues Relating to the Reporting of Very Small Match Probabilities' [2000] *Crim. LR* 341, 352–3. For criticism, see Craig R. Callen, 'Bayesian Models as Arguments' in J. F. Nijboer and J. M. Reijntjes (eds), *Proceedings of the First World Conference on New Trends in Criminal Investigation and Evidence* (Lelystad: Koninklijke Vermande, 1997).

[36] See David H. Kaye, 'DNA Evidence: Probability, Population Genetics, and the Courts' (1993) 7 *Harv. J. L. & Tech.* 101, 167–8.

[37] See the sources cited *supra* n. 28.

[38] See Faigman and Baglioni, *supra* n. 19, 7–14; Smith *et al.*, *supra* n. 19, 78. Cf. Carracedo *et al.*, *supra* n. 19.

There is a way of attempting to get the jury to formulate prior odds in a more careful manner, and this was in fact used in *Adams*. During the trial, the defence called as an expert witness a statistician who instructed the jury on how it might use Bayes' theorem to analyse all of the evidence in the case. Owing to deficiencies in the judge's summing up, Adams appealed; his conviction was quashed and a retrial ordered. At the retrial the defence, with the agreement of the prosecution, presented the jurors with a questionnaire which was intended to elicit from them the probabilities required to use Bayes' theorem to analyse the case. The probabilities could then be inserted into an equation at the end of the questionnaire, and the probability of Adams' guilt calculated. Reconvicted, Adams again appealed, largely on the basis that the judge had not treated the questionnaire with sufficient gravity; this time the appeal was dismissed. During both appeals, the Court of Appeal expressed considerable disapproval of the use of Bayes' theorem, commenting in the second appeal that the Bayesian approach was 'a recipe for confusion, misunderstanding and misjudgment'[39] and that 'in cases such as this, lacking special features absent here, expert evidence should not be admitted to induce juries to attach mathematical values to probabilities arising from non-scientific evidence adduced at the trial'.[40] These slights of Bayesian analysis, which had been described by the expert as 'the only logically sound and consistent approach to considering situations such as this',[41] drew considerable criticism from statisticians.[42]

Recall the task the jury faced in *Adams*: somehow to weigh the powerful DNA evidence against evidence pointing towards Adams' innocence and to relate the result to the criminal standard of proof. One aspect of the problem is that, even without the exculpatory evidence, one needs to understand that the posterior probability of innocence may not be 1 in 200 million. The way that this is often explained in this sort of case is to highlight the size of the population of possible culprits (the 'suspect population'). In *Adams*, for example, the defence drew attention to the fact that around 150,000 men between the ages of 18 and 60 lived within ten miles of the crime-scene (the complainant had said that her attacker spoke with a local accent). Allowing that the culprit did not necessarily come from that area, it was suggested that this gave prior odds on Adams' guilt of 1 to 200,000. It is probably difficult to get the jury to appreciate the importance of the $P(E|H)$, $P(H|E)$ distinction without giving examples of this sort, and suggesting, in some way, how they impact on the posterior odds. It is understandable, then, that the defence took the unusual approach it did in the

[39] *Adams (No. 2), supra* n. 9, 384.   [40] Ibid. 384–5.

[41] *Adams, supra* n. 9, 471.

[42] See Robert Matthews, 'Rape Case Ruling Undermines Faith in Juries', *New Scientist*, 8 June 1996, 7; B. Mahendra, 'Bayes Watch' (1996) 146 *New LJ* 1815; Peter Hawkins and Anne Hawkins, 'Lawyers' Probability Misconceptions and the Implications for Legal Education' (1998) 18 *Legal Studies* 316, 331–2.

Adams trials. It may well have seemed that this was the only hope of gaining Adams' acquittal.

During the first appeal, the Court of Appeal made a number of criticisms of the Bayesian approach. Those criticisms are not very convincing, and I shall not discuss them here.[43] Instead, I shall discuss the three most cogent criticisms that I can think of. The first is proposed by Callen.[44] Callen draws a parallel with the Chinese room argument, famously used by Searle to conclude that 'syntax is not sufficient for semantics'.[45] It could be said that the conclusion of Callen's variation is that 'calculation is not sufficient for inference'. Most of the work we do when we engage in inference, he points out, consists in structuring evidence; in forensic contexts, this appears to involve attempting to find hypotheses that account for the evidence, and thinking of relevant factors that may affect the degree of fit between evidence and hypothesis.[46] In *Adams*, this work was done by the expert, leaving only quantification and calculation to the jury. It is possible, then, that the expert would have left out critical aspects of the problem, which might then be overlooked—a point similar to Tribe's argument that the use of Bayes' theorem in criminal cases could lead to 'soft variables', such as the possibility that the defendant was framed, being neglected.[47] The expert in *Adams*, for example, did not include laboratory error as a relevant variable in his structuring of the evidence.[48] That does not mean, though, that this possibility would have been passed over. To the extent that they thought it relevant, jurors may have factored it into the quantification of the DNA evidence. The same goes for several of the other probabilities the jury would have had to address had it undertaken the Bayesian analysis: the questions posed were at a sufficient level of generality that jurors could still carry out their own micro-structuring of the evidence within the macro-structure provided by the expert.[49] Nevertheless, the point remains that the Bayesian

---

[43] For a detailed analysis, see Mike Redmayne, 'Presenting Probabilities in Court: The DNA Experience' (1997) 1 *Int. J. Ev. & Pr.* 187, 204–9. See also Bernard Robertson and Tony Vignaux, 'DNA on Appeal' [1997] *NZLJ* 210.

[44] Craig R. Callen, '*Adams* and the Person in the Locked Room', *International Commentary on Evidence*, <http://www.law.qub.ac.uk/ice> (posted August 1998).

[45] See, e.g., John R. Searle, *The Mystery of Consciousness* (London: Granta, 1997), 11–15.

[46] See Nancy Pennington and Reid Hastie, 'The Story Model for Juror Decision Making' in Reid Hastie (ed.), *Inside the Juror: The Psychology of Juror Decision Making* (Cambridge: Cambridge University Press, 1993).

[47] Laurence H. Tribe, 'Trial by Mathematics: Precision and Ritual in the Legal Process' (1971) 84 *Harv. L. Rev.* 1329, 1361–5.

[48] As Callen observes, some commentators suggest that this is a crucial variable in DNA cases. See, e.g., Jonathan J. Koehler, 'Why DNA Likelihood Ratios Should Account for Error (Even When A National Research Council Report Says They Should Not)' (1997) 37 *Jurimetrics J.* 425.

[49] For example, during the second appeal the Court of Appeal (*supra* n. 9, 382) observed that the questionnaire did not include a box for the difficulty the complainant would have had identifying her attacker (she saw him only briefly, and was called on to make an identification some two years after the rape). All the same, these difficulties were obviously relevant to an evaluation of her evidence, and could have been factored into the likelihood ratio for that evidence.

analysis does seem to change the nature of the jury's task significantly, and that, by focusing attention on certain issues, it may cause others to be ignored. It seems that much of our ordinary reasoning takes place at an implicit, pre-conscious level. The process of trying to capture all of the relevant variables in a formal model may be unsuccessful, resulting in worse, rather than better, decision-making.[50]

A second criticism of the use of Bayes' theorem in *Adams* is that the process of attaching probabilities to the evidence is not easy. Consider the alibi provided by Adams' girlfriend. The general question the jury was invited to answer was 'what is the chance that whichever witness gives the alibi evidence would give that kind of evidence?'[51] This needed to be broken down into two questions—reflecting H_P and H_D—'[h]ow likely is whatever evidence on the alibi the jury hear if he is guilty' and 'how likely is that sort of evidence if he is innocent?'[52] If one accepts that these are meaningful questions to ask—and not everyone would[53]—they are still difficult questions to answer. You might well think that the answer to the second question is a very high probability, for if the alibi is true, you would certainly expect the girlfriend to give alibi evidence. But that misconstrues the question, which is asking about the probability that someone like Adams would have an alibi supported by his girlfriend if he were innocent. Not every innocent person has an alibi. Note, though, that the question is not quite about the proportion of innocent people who have alibis: the specific type of alibi is relevant. Had Adams's girlfriend testified that she and Adams were swimming under Tower Bridge at the time of the rape, the incredibility of the alibi would score it a low probability on the hypothesis that Adams was innocent. Note also that you should not concentrate too precisely on the specifics of Adams's alibi: in the grand scheme of things, the probability that Adams would have been with that particular person on that particular night is tiny. What is being asked is a question about 'that sort of alibi evidence' where 'sort' is neither too specific nor too general. It can be appreciated, then, that it may be very difficult for those who do not have a feel for Bayesian analysis to get to grips with what the questions demand. Even if they manage to, they may not feel much confidence in the answers they give. After all, most of us do not know an awful lot about alibi probabilities.

The third criticism of the task the defence wanted the jury to undertake in *Adams* is the most fundamental. It is that, even had the jury undertaken

[50] See Jonathan St. B. T. Evans and David E. Over, *Rationality and Reasoning* (Hove: Psychology Press, 1996), esp. 45: 'people will tend to be better at achieving their goals when they are relying on basic, preconscious processes . . . than when relying on the explicit use of representations in their conscious reasoning, where their cognitive constraints can be serious.' On this theme, see also Robert Nozick, *The Nature of Rationality* (Princeton: Princeton University Press, 1993), 76–81.

[51] *Adams, supra* n. 9, 475.   [52] Ibid.

[53] The question is whether it is meaningful to assign probabilities to unique events. The view that it is not is well expressed in Steven Pinker, *How the Mind Works* (London: Penguin, 1998), 349–51. See also Cosmides and Tooby, *supra* n. 16, 2–9.

a Bayesian analysis of the case, and performed it well, the result it got may have been of little help to it. During the first trial, the defence introduced the Bayesian analysis during its examination in chief, and in the process it suggested certain figures as answers to the questions, stressing that these were examples only, it being for the jury to come up with its own figures. The figures suggested by the defence led to the conclusion that the odds on Adams' guilt were 55 to 1, meaning that it was 55 times more probable that Adams was guilty than that he was innocent. Suppose the jury did the analysis and came up with a similar figure: what might it make of it? The jury's task is to decide whether the prosecution has proved beyond reasonable doubt that Adams is guilty: how can it relate the posterior odds to 'beyond reasonable doubt'? One can convert the odds into a percentage probability of guilt. The resulting 98 per cent probability may be more meaningful than the statement of odds, but it is hardly any clearer how the figure relates to beyond reasonable doubt.[54] It is no answer to say that the interpretation of 'reasonable doubt' is for the jury, and that, therefore, it must decide by itself whether—to put it crudely—a 2 per cent doubt is a reasonable doubt. That is a trite point; the real problem is how to relate probabilities to concepts, such as reasonable doubt, that we normally think of in non-probabilistic terms. We *can* think about the criminal standard of proof in probabilistic terms, and Bayesian decision theory provides a coherent framework for doing so,[55] but few people are used to that sort of analysis. There is a larger point here. The way people think about evidence in criminal cases is probably well described by the explanation-based decision-making explored by Pennington and Hastie.[56] It is not easy to mix that sort of thinking with Bayesian decision theory. The point is not that forensic proof can only be described in terms of one or the other; it is, rather, that decision theory and explanation-based decision-making are rather like the two views of a Necker cube. They provide different schemas for interpreting evidence or, to draw on Gigerenzer's work,[57] different representations of it. We think more naturally in terms of explanation-based decision-making, but that does not mean we cannot learn Bayesian decision theory. In *Adams*, however,

[54] In fact, it seems that jurors do sometimes discuss the beyond reasonable doubt criterion in probabilistic terms. See Warren Young, Neil Cameron, and Yvette Tinsley, *Juries in Criminal Trials: A Summary of the Research Findings* NZLC PP37 (Wellington: New Zealand Law Commission, 1999), 53. But the discussions the authors report appear to be rather crude attempts to quantify the standard of proof which may not have had much impact on decision-making. Further, these blunt attempts at quantification (with some jurors setting the criminal standard at 50 per cent) do not inspire much confidence in juries relating a posterior probability derived from an *Adams* type process to beyond reasonable doubt.

[55] See, generally, D. H. Kaye, 'Clarifying the Burden of Persuasion: What Bayesian Decision Rules Do and Do Not Do' (1999) 3 *Int. J. Ev. & Pr.* 1. The process involves assigning utilities to guilty and not guilty verdicts, given the truth of H_P and H_D.

[56] See Pennington and Hastie, *supra* n. 46; Nancy Pennington and Reid Hastie, 'Reasoning in Explanation-Based Decision Making' in P. N. Johnson-Laird and Eldar Shafir (eds), *Reasoning and Decision Making* (Oxford: Blackwell, 1994).

[57] See Gigerenzer, *supra* n. 17.

the defence wanted the jury to switch to Bayesian analysis without providing it with a way of interpreting the criminal standard of proof from within
that framework.

5. FREQUENCIES

All of the ways of presenting statistical evidence in court examined so far
have been based on the likelihood ratio. These ratios are said to have important combinatorial properties. They do: the problem is that it is difficult to
get the jury to think of the other evidence in a case in terms that can easily
be combined with them. However, lay decision-makers may find frequencies
easier to understand than likelihood ratios; frequencies may also be easier
to combine with other evidence when one is not thinking about the whole
case in probabilistic terms. That is the implication of some of the research
reviewed above, and it is lent a little plausibility by evolutionary psychology.[58]

One should be cautious, though, about presuming that the results of research
on the medical diagnosis problem—where frequency presentations do seem
to improve decision-making—map directly onto the situation of the jury in
a case such as *Adams*. In the medical diagnosis problem all of the evidence
is in statistical terms, whereas it is not in cases involving statistical evidence.
There is only a little research exploring the effect of frequentist presentations on jury decision-making. This suggests that the mode of presentation
makes a difference in terms of the outcome of the decision-making process,
but it is not clear that the outcomes in frequency formats are closer to
the Bayesian norm which is taken to be the right answer.[59] Thompson and
Schumann did, however, find that the prosecutor's fallacy was less common
when statistics were presented as frequencies than when conditional probabilities were used.[60]

The Court of Appeal's decision in *R. v. Doheny, R. v. Adams*[61] means
that frequency presentations are now favoured by the English courts. On
this approach, an expert presenting DNA evidence in court should

give the jury the random occurrence ratio—the frequency with which the matching
DNA characteristics are likely to be found in the population at large. Provided that
he has the necessary data, and the statistical expertise, it may be appropriate for
him then to say how many people with the matching characteristics are likely to be
found in the United Kingdom—or perhaps in a more limited relevant sub-group,
such as, for instance, the Caucasian, sexually active males in the Manchester area.

---

[58] See Gigerenzer and Hoffrage, *supra* n. 13; Cosmides and Tooby, *supra* n. 16.
[59] See Koehler, *supra* n. 26, 880–3; Taroni and Aitken, *supra* n. 19.
[60] *Supra* n. 19, 174. See also the results of research by Koehler reported in *The Times Higher Educational Supplement*, 20 February 1998, 9.
[61] [1997] 1 Cr. App. R. 369.

This will often be the limit of the evidence which he can properly and usefully give. It will then be for the jury to decide, having regard to all the relevant evidence, whether they are sure that it was the defendant who left the crime stain, or whether it is possible that it was left by someone else with the same matching DNA characteristics.[62]

When summing up, the Court suggested, the following direction from the judge might be appropriate:

Members of the jury, if you accept the scientific evidence called by the Crown, this indicates that there are probably only four or five white males in the United Kingdom from whom that semen stain could have come. The defendant is one of them. If that is the position, the decision you have to reach, on all the evidence, is whether you are sure that it was the defendant who left that stain or whether it is possible that it was one of the other small group of men who share the same DNA characteristics.[63]

What a *Doheny* direction requires, then, is that the DNA evidence should be presented in terms such as 'the probability that a person chosen at random from the suspect population would have this DNA profile is 1 in x'. The expert or the judge, however, should not leave it at this. The jury's attention should also be drawn to the number of other people in the suspect population expected to have the DNA profile. This is doubtless an effective way of steering the jury away from confusing $P(E|H)$ and $P(H|E)$. It also appears to get around the problem of combining the DNA evidence with the other evidence. All the work the DNA evidence does is directed at cutting down the suspect population to just a few individuals. The DNA can then be disregarded, leaving the jury the task of deciding whether the other evidence against the defendant is sufficient to single him out among a small number of individuals. This can be achieved by using a relatively natural process of explanation-based decision-making.

A number of problems remain. Consider a case with a match probability of 1 in 1,000 and a suspect population of 1,000. Under *Doheny*, this invites the direction that 'there is probably only one person in the population from whom the stain could have come'. Even if there was no other evidence against the suspect, one would expect a jury to convict in such a case. On a Bayesian analysis, however, the posterior odds on guilt would be even—only a 50 per cent probability of guilt.[64] This outcome is rather counter-intuitive, and it is worth understanding why it occurs. The match probability indicates how many people with the DNA profile one would expect to find in the suspect population; the figure—one—is, however, only an expectation. It is the most probable number of people in the population

[62] [1997] 1 Cr. App. R. 374. The term 'random occurrence ratio' is a judicial neologism. The court is obviously referring to a match probability; probabilities, however, are not ratios.
[63] Ibid. 375.
[64] The prior odds $(P(H_P|I)/P(H_D|I))$ are 1/999, the likelihood ratio is 999/1, giving posterior odds of 1/1.

who have the DNA profile. But the probability that there is more than one person in the population with the profile is in fact quite high—around 63 per cent.[65] In this example, then, the word 'probably' in the judge's direction is misleading, for there is probably *more than* one person in the population with the profile. This is a general problem with the *Doheny* direction: it tends to convert expectations into precise figures.

A related problem is that the *Doheny* direction only works well with relatively large match probabilities. The appellants in *Doheny* had been tried in the early 1990s, when match probabilities did not approach the tiny values common today. The problem is that, once the match probability outstrips the size of the suspect population, the expectation will be that there are no other people in the population with the DNA profile. Consider applying *Doheny* to *Adams*, where the prosecution presented a match probability of 1 in 200 million. We would have to direct the jury about the probability that someone else in the population shares the DNA profile: in *Adams*, for example, around a 20 per cent probability that there is another person in the United Kingdom with the profile. This may be a workable solution, though it will not be easy for a jury to weigh up any exculpatory evidence against such a probability. The Bayesian analysis in *Adams* makes the prior/posterior odds relationship clear, the *Doheny* direction does not.

How to choose the suspect population? This is a third problem with *Doheny*—though the issue arises in *Adams*, too. It will be in the interests of the prosecution to keep the suspect population as small as possible, in the interests of the defence to make it large. Sometimes they may be able to agree, at others the size of the population will be a disputed issue. Ideally, it is perhaps a jury question, especially if there is disagreement.[66] There is something interesting happening here—the line of thought I am pursuing suggests that it would be appropriate to ask the jury to decide whether the perpetrator lived in the same street, city or country as the victim. We do not normally expect jurors to think in terms of a population of possible

---

[65] Where N is the size of the relevant population and P is the match probability, the probability that one or more other people possess the profile is $1 - (1 - 1/P)^{N-1}$ (see National Research Council, *supra* n. 33, 137). So in the example the calculation is $1 - (1 - 1/1,000)^{999}$ = 0.63.

[66] For the view that experts should not make assumptions about the suspect population, see David A. Stoney and John I. Thornton, 'Author's Response' (1988) 33 *J. Forensic Sci.* 11, 12. In fact, it is not altogether obvious that the definition of the suspect population is best left to the jury. It is possible to use crime statistics to suggest certain plausible priors for particular defendants: see K. A. J. Walsh, J. S. Buckleton, and C. M. Triggs, 'Assessing Prior Probabilities Considering Geography' (1994) 34 *J. Forensic Sci. Soc.* 47; C. Triggs, K. A. J. Walsh, and J. S. Buckleton, 'Assessing Probabilities Considering Eyewitness Evidence' (1995) 35 *Science & Justice* 263. If we are thinking of asking experts to take into account the probability that a person standing three feet from a breaking window would have x fragments of glass transferred to his clothing, or the number of pairs of shoes the average burglar has, why not allow them to consider the probability that the perpetrator lives x miles from the crime-scene?

perpetrators and to use this, effectively, to provide an initial probability of the defendant's guilt—even though this might appear to be an appropriate consideration in any case where identity is the principal issue. We are asking the jury a new kind of question, and expecting it to think of the defendant in an unfamiliar way—as though he has been plucked at random from the suspect population and shares an equal prior probability of guilt with all of its members. There must therefore be some doubt as to whether the jury really will adopt the way of formulating the problem we have presented it with. 'Habitual methods of reasoning are based largely on tacit processes, beyond conscious control', Evans and Over suggest. 'Hence, they will not easily be modified by presentation of verbal instructions.'[67] While this comment relates to subjects in psychological experiments—jurors may have more motivation to conform to judicial instructions—it cannot be presumed that simply telling jurors to think of the defendant as one among a small group will really have much impact on their reasoning.[68]

A final problem with the *Doheny* direction connects to the earlier discussion of the Bayesian turn in forensic science. Likelihood ratios have certain advantages over other ways of conveying the value of forensic science evidence, because they enable the forensic scientist to take into account the improbability of finding the evidence given the truth of H_P—a consideration that may weaken otherwise incriminating evidence. This would be the case where, for example, more fragments of glass are found on the suspect's clothes than expected, or where the results of DNA evidence are surprising given the presumed number of contributors to a stain.[69] In such cases, it is claimed, 'there is no sensible alternative'[70] to using likelihood ratios. That may be an exaggeration. One can certainly attempt to explain to the jury that certain inconsistencies in the evidence undermine H_P; one might even present modified frequencies to the jury to reflect the diminished force of the evidence.[71] These solutions are certainly not as neat as using a likelihood ratio—and modified frequencies are unlikely to find favour with scientists—but they should not be dismissed out of hand.

---

[67] *Supra* n. 50, 20.

[68] For a case that implies that jurors do not perceive defendants in *Doheny* type cases as having a very small prior probability of guilt, see *R. v. Lashley* CA 9903890 Y3 (8 February 2000). The *Doheny* direction left Lashley as one of around seven men sharing the crime-scene profile. There was no other evidence against him—not even geographical proximity to the crime-scene. Nevertheless, the jury convicted. See also *R. v. Smith* CA 9904098 (8 February 2000).

[69] See the discussion in Ch. 3.

[70] Evett and Weir, *supra* n. 35, 225. See also Bernard Robertson and G. A. Vignaux, 'Explaining Evidence Logically' (1998) 148 *New LJ* 159, 160 ('the frequency will only produce a correct answer where one suspect is compared with one mark').

[71] One way of achieving this would be to work out an initial (Level I) likelihood ratio without conditioning on specific information about the case. A second (Level II) likelihood ratio would then be calculated with that information taken into account. The first likelihood ratio would be divided by the second and the frequency modified by dividing by this product.

6. ERROR RATES

The preceding sections of this chapter have hopefully brought out the core of the presentation problem. In this section and the following one, I look at slightly more complex issues that add further twists to the problem of presenting statistical evidence to juries in a comprehensible manner. One aspect of DNA evidence that has attracted considerable debate concerns the relationship between the match probability and $P(E|H_D)$. It is tempting to assume that the latter term is just the match probability—the probability that a person picked at random from the relevant population will match the crime-scene trace. This may not be the case for a number of reasons. Some of these are brought into focus by thinking carefully about E. The evidence the jury hears is that the defendant's DNA matches the crime-scene DNA, but *hearing* this evidence is not the same as knowing that the two samples match. If the laboratory made a mistake during the analysis of the DNA, perhaps contaminating the crime-scene DNA with the sample from the defendant, then the jury might hear that there was a match when the defendant was not the source of the crime-scene DNA. Other subtleties in the evidence appear when H_D is scrutinized. In the last example I presumed an H_D along the lines of 'the defendant is not the source of the crime-scene DNA', but another hypothesis of interest to the fact-finder is 'the defendant did not have contact with the crime-scene'. This hypothesis can be true even when the defendant is the source of the crime-scene DNA—if, for example, the evidence was planted,[72] or if a dishonest police officer switched the crime-scene DNA for a sample taken from the defendant.

Rather than focusing on these latter possibilities, most debate has concentrated on the possibility of error during the laboratory profiling process. That is largely because some proficiency tests conducted on forensic science laboratories in the United States have found relatively large false positive rates for DNA profiling—around 2 per cent.[73] No figures are available for England, although there are anecdotes of errors that would be relevant.[74]

---

[72] How can one plant DNA? '[T]here are already anecdotes of New York prostitutes starting a market in used condoms, apparently so that the buyers can use the contents to divert suspicion': Philip Kitcher, *The Lives to Come: The Genetic Revolution and Human Possibilities* (London: Allen Lane, 1996), 179. See also Thompson, *supra* n. 21.

[73] See Richard Lempert, 'After the DNA Wars: Skirmishing with NRC II' (1997) 37 *Jurimetrics J.* 439, 448. As Lempert observes, it is no easy matter to interpret error rates, and the significance of these figures is open to debate.

[74] See 'DNA Database Under Fire After Samples Mix-Up', *The Independent*, 22 October 1995, reporting a false match 'caused by a technician mixing up two test tubes'. However, the story also notes the practice within the Forensic Science Service of sending DNA matches derived from the offender database to a second laboratory for confirmatory testing. See also David J. Balding and Peter Donnelly, 'How Convincing is DNA Evidence?' (1994) 368 *Nature* 285, 286 (mis-labelling of a DNA sample sent for re-testing), and the less serious errors reported in 'DNA Expert Admits Mistake in Link to Killer', *The Guardian*, 25 January 1997 (expert pressing wrong button on computer during statistical analysis); 'Faults Found on Met Police Database' (1995) 145 *New LJ* 1439 (computer errors on statistical database).

Taking the 2 per cent figure for illustrative purposes, its significance, some suggest, is that it provides a ceiling for $P(E|H_D)$. With a match probability of 1 in 100,000, $P(E|H_D) = (0.00001 + 0.02) - (0.00001 \times 0.02) = 0.0200098$.[75] The laboratory error rate, therefore, dominates the conditional probability that concerns the jury in all cases where it is larger than the match probability. This obviously has implications for the figures presented to the jury, and the way they are presented.

One option is to present the jury with both the match probability (or a likelihood ratio based on it) and the laboratory error rate. There is some empirical evidence that weighs against this option. In a mock juror study, Koehler *et al.* compared subjects in three conditions.[76] In the first, subjects received both a small match probability (one in a billion) and an error probability. In the second, subjects were not informed of the match probability, but only of the 2 per cent figure, representing the combined match probability and error rate. Subjects in a third condition received just the match probability. It was found that subjects in the first condition convicted the defendant about as often as those in the third, and much more frequently than those in the second. One interpretation of this finding is that subjects did not understand that the error probability formed a ceiling for $P(E|H_D)$. Given the general research on probabilistic reasoning,[77] this result is not surprising, and several commentators have argued that jurors therefore should only be presented with a statistic—such as the 2 per cent figure in the example—that accounts for the probability of laboratory error.

There are a number of significant criticisms of this proposal.[78] One of the purposes of laboratory proficiency tests is to improve testing procedures. When a laboratory discovers that it has made a mistake on a test, it is likely to try to locate the cause of the error and to take steps to ensure that it does not re-occur. Acknowledged errors in the past, therefore, decrease the probability of future errors. This is just one facet of a larger problem, i.e. relating error rates established in proficiency tests to error probabilities in specific cases, which are the probabilities of interest to jurors. The error probability depends, for example, on the care with which the profiling process was conducted (perhaps there is evidence that it was conducted

---

[75] Those who find the mathematics obscure might prefer to think of the problem in terms of Koehler *et al.*'s analogy (see *supra* n. 20, 211). Suppose a baseball player is very good at throwing the ball—always getting it within a few yards of the base he is aiming at—but not so good at collecting (fielding) the ball after it has been hit into the field. If his error rate for throwing is 1 in 1,000, but for fielding it is 2 in 100, then it is the latter we should attend to if we want to know his chances of performing well at his next attempt, because in order to throw the ball he must first field it.

[76] *Supra* n. 20, 211–19.

[77] It seems that people often combine probability figures by averaging them, a strategy that would over-weight $P(E|H_D)$ so long as the error rate was larger than the match probability. See, e.g., Lola L. Lopes, 'Procedural Debiasing' (1987) 64 *Acta Psychologica* 167.

[78] See National Research Council, *supra* n. 33, 85–7; Margaret A. Berger, 'Laboratory Error Seen Through the Lens of Science and Policy' (1997) 30 *UC Davis L. Rev.* 1081.

extremely carefully, or perhaps a confirmatory test was conducted at a second laboratory).

A study by Schklar and Diamond is also relevant to the error rate problem.[79] Like Koehler *et al.*, these authors found that mock jurors did not appear to combine error probabilities and match probabilities in the normatively appropriate manner (even when they received instructions on how to do so). However, they also found that subjects did not take the figures provided to them in the study at face value. Subjects came to the study with their own expectations about error probabilities (as well as about the possibility of intentional tampering with DNA samples), and their own estimations of what error probabilities and match probabilities 'really' were after hearing all of the evidence tended to differ from those provided by the experts.

Together with questions about the relevance of error rates to $P(E|H_D)$, Schklar and Diamond's study casts some doubt on the wisdom of presenting combined error/match probability statistics to jurors. The combination strategy, it would seem, prevents jurors from using their own estimates of error rates to modify match probabilities. However, if the fears that juries will be unduly swayed by very small match probabilities are credible, the alternative is hardly more palatable, because it involves revealing the small match probability to the fact-finder in the knowledge that the limiting effect of the error probability will not be fully understood. Further, if the DNA statistics were presented in terms of the probability that a match would be mistakenly reported when the defendant was innocent, jurors would be alerted to the fact that error rates had been taken into account. The more appropriate solution, it seems to me, is to combine the figures. Although that provides the jury with less information, the information (the probability of *hearing* the DNA evidence given H_D) is more relevant and, given the predominant fear, less likely to mislead. That still leaves, of course, the problem of estimating the probability of error in a particular case.[80] That is difficult to do, but no more difficult, one would have thought, than assigning values to some of the very subjective probabilities involved within the Bayesian framework, such as the transfer and persistence probabilities in the glass evidence example discussed in Chapter 3. Proficiency tests evidently provide a starting point but, given the argument that such tests work to reduce error rates, it may be that a defensible value will be somewhat smaller than that determined in a proficiency test. A similar elicitation process to that used in glass cases could be used to gain a probability of error from the expert.[81] The basic point is that, as match probabilities become very small (consider the 1 in 200 million in *Adams*), so it becomes more difficult to believe that they are not significantly undermined by the probability of error. As Berry

[79] *Supra* n. 19.
[80] For one solution to the problem, see Lempert, *supra* n. 73, 453–4.
[81] See I. W. Evett, 'Criminalistics: The Future of Expertise' (1993) 33 *J. Forensic Sci. Soc.* 173, 175–7.

observes, when a probability is extremely small, events of low probability, such as laboratory error, 'rise to the surface and become dominant'.[82] It is only appropriate, then, for experts to think through the implications of error rates, and to factor these into $P(E|H_D)$.

7. SPECIFYING ALTERNATIVE HYPOTHESES: RELATIVES IN DNA CASES

One way of responding to the laboratory error problem is to shift the responsibility of exploring error rates to defendants. If experts present unmodified match probabilities in court, defendants are, of course, free to raise the possibility of laboratory error and to explain its significance to the jury, just as they are free to raise the possibility that the police planted the evidence. There are several reasons, though, why the analogy with planted evidence is inapt. Laboratory performance is more intimately associated with the individualizing power of DNA evidence than is police behaviour, scientists are better placed to assess its probability, and there are more meaningful statistics on its prevalence. In addition, the thought that the prosecution in a criminal case has exaggerated the strength of its evidence is distasteful, and the 'leave it to the defence' response too cavalier, given that some defence counsel might not appreciate the significance of error probabilities. There is, though, a more general issue here, which involves how we decide which possibilities experts should take into account when estimating the strength of scientific evidence.

One aspect of this problem surfaced during the discussion of glass evidence in Chapter 3. There it was seen that the exact terms of H_P and H_D could have a significant effect on the probative value of glass found on a suspect's clothes, but that if the expert lacked information about, say, the distance from the window the offender was standing when it was broken, she could restrict her evidence to source probabilities (Level I). In some circumstances, however, this may not circumvent the problem caused by the informational vacuum. Where DNA evidence is concerned, assessment of the hypothesis 'the blood did not come from the defendant' is affected by what is presumed about the offender. This is because the probability of finding another DNA profile like the defendant's varies among different racial groups. It also varies dramatically when the offender is presumed to be a close relative of the defendant. The general problem here is that the greater the degree of relatedness between suspect and offender, the more probable it is that their DNA profiles will match.[83]

---

[82] Donald A. Berry, 'Comment' (1994) 9 *Statistical Science* 252, 253.

[83] This can usefully be conceptualized by thinking of the denominator of the likelihood ratio in the following terms: $P(O = PX|H_D, D = PX, I)$. It is known that the defendant has profile X ($D = PX$) and this implies that, if H_D is true, the offender has profile X also. By including $D = PX$ in the conditioning for $O = PX$, I am emphasizing that $P(O = PX)$ may be affected by information that $D = PX$. Where O and D are related, knowing that $D = PX$ increases $P(O = PX)$.

The problem can be conceptualized in the following manner. The denominator of the likelihood ratio—($P(E|H_D, I)$—involves assuming that the defendant is not the source of the crime-scene DNA, but an innocent defendant will not often be in the position of being able to suggest that some specific other person is the source. H_D should therefore be thought of, not as a single hypothesis, but as a disjunction of many mutually exclusive hypotheses. In theory, it is possible to specify one hypothesis for every single member of the suspect population. On consideration of some of these specific hypotheses, the denominator will be very small and the likelihood ratio, therefore, very large (this will tend to be the case when the hypothesis involves a member of a different racial group to the defendant). On other hypotheses, the denominator will be larger, being at its largest when the offender is presumed to be closely related to the defendant—a brother, say. Obviously, unless the suspect population is exceptionally small, it will be impractical to work out the likelihood ratio for each possible offender, just as it will be impractical to present them all to the jury. Instead, the expert might try to combine the effect of the various possible relationships between suspect and offender in a single likelihood ratio. The denominator of this likelihood ratio can be thought of as:[84]

$$P(E|S, I) = \sum_{k=1}^{j} P(E|S, k)\, P(k)$$

where S represents the suspect's DNA profile and k the relationship between suspect and offender in a population of j individuals. $P(k)$ denotes the prior probability of the relationship between suspect and offender, i.e. the probability, based on the non-DNA evidence, of relationship k between suspect and offender.[85]

---

[84] See John. F. Y. Brookfield, 'The Effect of Relatedness on Likelihood Ratios and the Use of Conservative Estimates' (1995) 96 *Genetica* 13, 16.

[85] The symbol 'Σ' means sum. In the equation it denotes the adding together of the probabilities of finding the evidence for each person in a population of j individuals, from the first ($k = 1$) to the jth, weighted by their priors.

A less technical explanation of what is going on here proceeds as follows. Imagine a household containing five people: X, his father, two brothers, and a cousin. Suppose that a stranger staying in the house has been found dead in his room, and that X's DNA is found to match blood found under the stranger's fingernail. The probability that X is the killer depends, among other things, on the probability that the DNA of one of the other occupants of the house would also match this trace. Suppose that the relevant calculations indicate that the probability of a match between X's DNA and his brothers' is 0.1; his father's 0.05; and his cousin's 0.025. What also needs to be taken into account is that one of these people may be a more plausible suspect than the others. If one of the brothers had a grudge against the stranger, as well as ready access to his room, then it is more probable that the offender will match X's DNA than if none of the other occupants had the slightest reason or opportunity to kill the stranger. This is what the equation attempts to capture through the expression $P(k)$. The equation takes these independent grounds for suspicion into account by weighting the individual match probabilities (0.1, 0.05, 0.025) by the probability that each of the occupants committed the crime.

The problem caused by a consideration of the relationship between the defendant and the offender is not just one of added complexity, it is also that the denominator of the likelihood ratio includes $P(k)$, a variable that is affected by the non-scientific evidence, and this is not usually considered the scientist's domain. In a case where relatives are suspects, Evett notes, 'the import of the scientific evidence cannot be detached neatly from the other evidence. Like it or not, to assess his evidence it is necessary for the scientist to gain some idea of how the court is thinking in relation to [the hypothesis that a relative is the offender].'[86] This is not a problem that can reasonably be ignored, because if the suspect population contains siblings of the defendant, the effect can be significant. Evett gives an example where a likelihood ratio in the thousands would be reduced to around four if the defendant and his brother were considered to be the only suspects.[87]

One way of responding to the problem of siblings is to choose a reasonable size for the suspect population, N, and then to presume that every member of the population has an equal prior probability of guilt, this being the reciprocal of the population size (i.e. $1/N$). This assumption has the effect of holding $P(k)$ constant for all siblings in the suspect population. In a large population, $P(k)$ will then be sufficiently small that the presence of siblings in the suspect population may make little difference to the likelihood ratio. There are two problems with the assumption of equal priors. First, there are a number of reasons why the prior probability of guilt of the defendant's siblings may be substantially greater than $1/N$. Evidence that picks out the defendant as a suspect could also pick out his siblings, who may share his appearance, lifestyle, and relationship to the victim. As the $P(k)$ for each sibling increases, so will their combined effect on the likelihood ratio. A second problem is that even if $P(k)$ is just $1/N$, the effect of siblings may still be significant. '[T]he relevant issue', Balding and Donnelly note, 'is not whether or not there is reason to suspect the defendant's siblings, but the strength of the evidence against them relative to the strength of the non-DNA evidence against the defendant.'[88] In the *Adams* scenario, where there is no non-DNA evidence against the defendant, it may be reasonable to assign $1/N$ to the probability that the defendant is guilty, and then the presence of siblings in the population may be sufficient to justify an acquittal even if there is no more reason to suspect them than other members of the suspect population.[89]

[86] I. W. Evett, 'Evaluating DNA Profiles in a Case Where the Defence is "It Was My Brother"' (1992) 32 *J. Forensic Sci. Soc.* 5, 12.

[87] Ibid. 7–8. See also *Adams (No. 2), supra* n. 9, 379 (noting that a match probability of 1 in 200 million would be reduced to 1 in 220 if a brother was considered as the alternative suspect).

[88] David J. Balding and Peter Donnelly, 'Inferring Identity from DNA Profile Evidence' (1995) 92 *Proc. Nat. Acad. Sci. USA* 11741, 11744.

[89] See ibid. See also David J. Balding, 'Errors and Misunderstandings in the Second NRC Report' (1997) 37 *Jurimetrics J.* 469, 474.

There are other ways of dealing with the siblings problem than attempting to work out a likelihood ratio that incorporates $P(k)$. One is to eliminate the defendant's siblings by profiling them. Understandably, this solution is favoured by scientists,[90] but it will not always be workable. Unless there is evidence to inculpate a sibling, the police will not be able to obtain a sample from him without consent, and he and the defendant may have a mutual interest in his remaining an unknown quantity in the case. Another solution is to disaggregate the likelihood ratio and to present more than one match probability to the jury. In practice, forensic scientists in England give probabilities 'for individuals in the same and different racial groups from the suspect depending on the circumstances and, if requested, also provide figures for close blood relations'.[91] The advantage of this approach, for the expert, is that $P(k)$ can be ignored. The probability that an individual in each of the, say, Caucasian, Asian, Afro-Caribbean, first cousin and sibling groups would share the defendant/crime-scene profile can be presented, and it can be left to the jury to appreciate that the prior probability of someone from each of these groups having committed the crime varies. What the jury should also appreciate—though it may not—is that the defendant's prior may vary as a function of $P(k)$. For example, a juror who thinks that the prior for a particular sibling is large is presuming that there is some reason to suspect the sibling more than other members of the population. Absent specific evidence that inculpates the sibling but not the defendant, however, parity of reasoning implies that the defendant's prior will be equally high. It will not generally be appropriate to consider that a sibling's prior is 0.05 but that the defendant's is $1/N$, where N is some large number.

Most commentators agree that it is appropriate to present more than one match probability to the jury.[92] It will be appreciated that this rather complicates the task of presenting DNA evidence to juries whatever method of presentation is chosen. Consider, for example, how one might incorporate the match probability for siblings in the *Doheny* approach. If there are siblings in the suspect population, it might be appropriate to factor that information into the calculation of the number of people in the population expected to share the defendant's profile. However, because *Doheny* assumes a uniform prior of $1/N$ for all members of the suspect population, that approach cannot then account for the possibility that a sibling's prior may be significantly large. What also require consideration are the circumstances in which the effect of siblings will be considered relevant to the match probability. Some proposals for dealing with siblings require that there be evidence against, or suspicion of, a sibling before the probability of their

---

[90] See Evett, *supra* n. 86, 14; Brookfield, *supra* n. 84, 16.

[91] Lindsay A. Foreman, Adrian F. Smith, and Ian W. Evett, 'Bayesian Analysis of DNA Profiling in Forensic Identification Applications' (1997) 160 *J. R. Stat. Soc. (Series A)* 429, 469.

[92] See, e.g., Balding and Donnelly, *supra* n. 88, 11743; N. E. Morton, 'The Forensic DNA Endgame' (1997) 37 *Jurimetrics J.* 477, 479.

having a matching profile is taken into account.[93] The English practice is to give a figure for siblings only when requested. Some commentators find this unsatisfactory, pointing out the possible correlation between defendant and sibling priors,[94] as well as the fact that defendants may be reluctant to raise the possibility that a sibling committed the crime.[95] In addition, defendants may lack effective representation. There are parallels here with arguments about laboratory error; both issues raise more general questions about the relationship between the heavy burden of proof placed on the prosecution and the expert's duty to consider scientifically significant hypotheses. I suggested above that it seemed inappropriate to leave the laboratory error problem to defendants if it was likely to have significant effects on the match probability. As with laboratory error, the sibling effect is intimately connected to the match probability, which suggests that it should be considered as a matter of course. However, without information from defendants, who are best placed to know about the number of siblings in the suspect population, scientists will find it difficult to do so.[96] The solution might be to require the police to enquire about the presence of siblings in the suspect population in cases that involve DNA evidence.

8. Precision and Pragmatism

The presentation problem is a difficult one. It is possible to criticize all of the proposals put forward, and, when the dust settles, it is not obvious that there is any best solution. That is partly because the empirical evidence available is so poor. For those reasons, I do not have any very clear proposals to make on the subject. I want, instead, to suggest a way of rethinking the problem, by questioning some of the assumptions that drive the debate. At this point, what is required is to take a step back in order to consider some of the turns the argument in this chapter has taken. I started out by asking what seemed to be a simple question: what is the best way of presenting statistical evidence to a jury? I ended up considering whether jurors should be encouraged to consider the size of the suspect population, to combine error rates and match probabilities, and even whether they should be

[93] See National Research Council, *supra* n. 33, 113.

[94] See Richard Lempert, 'Comment: Theory and Practice in DNA Fingerprinting' (1994) 9 *Statistical Science* 255, 256–7; Lempert, *supra* n. 73, 457–8.

[95] See David J. Balding, Peter Donnelly, and Richard A. Nichols, 'Comment: Some Causes for Concern About DNA Profiles' (1994) 9 *Statistical Science* 248, 249. For a case where the presence of siblings looks to cause particular problems—ignored by the court—see *Smith, supra* n. 68. Smith was not connected to the crime, other than through geographical proximity and a DNA match. He had thirteen siblings.

[96] Brookfield does, however, suggest a way in which the number of close relatives in the suspect population might be calculated. See J. F. Y. Brookfield, 'The Effect of Relatives on the Likelihood Ratio Associated with DNA Profile Evidence in Criminal Cases' (1994) 34 *J. Forensic Sci. Soc.* 193, 196.

instructed in Bayesian probability theory. Why on earth do these come to look like sensible options when statistics are used in court? What drives the process of escalation, I suspect, is the allure of precision. By modelling the jury's decision-making process one can calibrate precisely the impact that a match probability should have on a rational fact-finder. It is then natural to look for ways of implementing the model. As the search for ways of doing this proceeds, a simple fact may be overlooked: that the degree of precision that is aimed for cannot really be achieved within the context of trial by jury. Perhaps the culprit here is probability theory: using it to model the jury's task may have actually ended up distorting the presentation problem, rather than helping to provide a solution to it.

The best solution to the presentation problem may be to use Evett's verbal conventions. These have the advantage of being compatible with the Bayesian approach, as well as seeming to be easily comprehensible. There is some concern that they may be open to misinterpretation, and that this will be significant in cases where the prior odds are low. But Bayesian modelling of the juror's decision task may have exaggerated this problem. The way to generate concern over low prior odds is to posit a large suspect population and to suggest that the defendant should be seen as a person plucked at random from that population, having a prior probability of guilt the same as that of all other members of the suspect population. In other words, to suggest that if the crime was committed in a city with population X, the odds against the defendant being the criminal are X to one. Note that this argument applies to all cases where identity is in issue—not just cases involving statistical evidence. However, we would probably find it odd if jurors did see defendants in such cases as 'random men' and, if asked to justify her view of the defendant as a non-random man, a juror would doubtless explain that the defendant was certainly *not* plucked at random from the population and placed in the dock. This would be the case even if, during the trial, the prosecution presented no evidence to explain how the defendant first came to the attention of the police. After all, the juror might reason, the police must have had some grounds for suspecting the defendant in the first place—perhaps his prior record, or some other inadmissible evidence.

An obvious response to this is that such thinking should not be accepted, because it cuts against the presumption of innocence. But I am not convinced that it does. Some Bayesians do interpret the presumption of innocence as requiring that everyone in a particular population, including the defendant, have a uniform, tiny, prior probability of guilt at the start of a trial,[97] but,

---

[97] See, e.g., Richard Lempert, 'The New Evidence Scholarship: Analyzing the Process of Proof' in Peter Tillers and Eric D. Green (eds), *Probability and Inference in the Law of Evidence: The Uses and Limits of Bayesianism* (Dordrecht: Kluwer, 1988), 77; comments of D. H. Kaye and David J. Balding, in Ronald J. Allen *et al.*, 'Probability and Proof in *State v. Skipper*: An Internet Exchange' (1995) 35 *Jurimetrics J.* 277, 293; Friedman, *supra* n. 11.

even if one accepts this description of the presumption,[98] it is not necessarily right to describe the juror as falling foul of it, unless she is thinking in probabilistic terms.[99] A juror employing explanation-based decision-making should not automatically be criticized for seeming to break a norm of probabilistic decision-making. The juror might, though, be said to be ignoring the presumption of innocence in another way, by judging the defendant on the basis of evidence that has not been formally admitted at trial.[100] No juror, however, can come to the trial without any knowledge of how the world works, and simply seeing the defendant as a non-random person does not appear to be especially pernicious. If the juror speculated that the defendant had come to the attention of the police on the basis of his prior record, the criticism that she was taking bad character into account might have more bite. But again, presuming that the defendant was known to the police before being suspected of the present crime does not necessarily offend the character evidence rule, which seems to me to be directed at drawing rather more specific propensity inferences against the defendant.[101] If these arguments

<hr/>

[98] Cf. Tribe, *supra* n. 47, 1371: '[t]he presumption retains force not as a *factual* judgment, but as a *normative* one—as a judgment that society *ought* to *speak* of accused men as innocent, and *treat* them as innocent, until they have been properly convicted after all they have to offer in their defense has been carefully weighed. The suspicion that many are *in fact* guilty need not undermine either this normative conclusion or its symbolic expression through trial procedure, so long as jurors are not compelled to articulate their prior suspicions of guilt in an explicit and precise way' (original emphasis).

[99] Or at least in the probabilistic terms adopted by her critics. For probabilistic conceptions of the presumption of innocence that do not require the rather artificial assumption of uniform probability within a suspect population, see Simon Blackburn, 'Review of *The Probable and the Provable*' (1980) 44 *Synthese* 149; James Logue, *Projective Probability* (Oxford: Clarendon Press, 1995), 152–3.

[100] See John Henry Wigmore, *Evidence in Trials at Common Law*, rev. James H. Chadbourn (Boston: Little, Brown, 1981), Vol. 9, 230. Wigmore suggests that the presumption of innocence 'cautions the jury to put away from their minds all the suspicion that arises from the arrest, the indictment, and the arraignment, and to reach their conclusion solely from the evidence adduced'. Cf. Adrian A. S. Zuckerman, 'Law, Fact or Justice?' (1986) 66 *Boston U.L. Rev.* 487, 503–4. Zuckerman argues that the presumption does not require the jury to 'ignore the common-sense implications of the evidence'. Discussing *R. v. Abadom* [1983] 1 All ER 364, a case where part of the evidence against the defendant was the fact that he had incriminating glass on his shoes, he suggests that it was proper for the jury not to believe that 'the accused was chosen at random to have his shoes examined'. For criticism of Zuckerman's views on *Abadom*, see Richard D. Friedman, 'Generalized Inferences, Individual Merits and Jury Discretion' (1986) 66 *Boston U.L. Rev.* 509, 512–13 ('a conviction on such hypothesized evidence . . . is invalid'). See further Friedman, *supra* n. 11, 879–83.

[101] The ban on character evidence is often said to apply to a particular type of reasoning, rather than a type of evidence, that reasoning being 'propensity reasoning', which probably involves reasoning that, because the defendant has committed crimes on previous occasions, he has a propensity to commit crime (or a particular sort of crime). Although it is not terribly clear just what sort of reasoning falls within this category (see Mike Redmayne, 'A Likely Story!' (1999) 19 *Ox. J. Leg. Stud.* 659), the juror would not appear to be explicitly engaging in propensity reasoning. That her reasoning can be reconstructed in terms of a propensity inference (she might be said to be thinking that the defendant's prior record renders him more likely than other people to have committed the present crime) might, though, convince some that it falls within the exclusionary principle. My own view, though, is that attempts to base the exclusionary rule on a particular type of reasoning are bankrupt. Cf. I. H. Dennis, *The Law of Evidence* (London: Sweet & Maxwell, 1999), 594–600.

are right, Bayesian analyses of jury decision-making that rely on low prior odds describe the jury's task neither realistically nor normatively. If they are wrong, then there is a problem in implementing the presumption of innocence in many more cases than those involving statistical evidence.

This line of thought takes some of the force out of certain criticisms of methods of presenting statistical evidence to juries. To return to Evett's verbal conventions, there is said to be a possibility that verbal expressions such as 'very strong evidence' will be misinterpreted, but this is not such a telling problem if cases with low prior odds are rare. The other serious criticism of verbal conventions is that the proposed expressions have too low a ceiling: 'very strong evidence' or even 'extremely strong evidence' cannot capture the tiny match probabilities associated with DNA evidence. That is a cogent criticism only if jurors are likely to be able to conceptualize the evidential impact of match probabilities such as 1 in 100,000 or 1 in 200 million. But it may be that such small probabilities make little sense to most lay people and that, beyond a certain threshold, their impact on decision-makers is such that there is no real difference between them.[102] If so, there is little point in presenting them to jurors if a phrase such as 'very strong evidence' is easier to understand and to combine with other evidence. If, however, it is thought that 'very strong evidence' is too weak a phrase for some of the smallest probabilities, there is an alternative, which is for the expert to testify that he is certain, or sure, that the DNA profile came from the defendant.

This last suggestion is controversial, because it appears to trample over the distinction between $P(E|H)$ and $P(H|E)$. Nevertheless, it has been accepted for some considerable time in the domain of fingerprinting.[103] On the fingerprint model an examiner who sees enough points of similarity between two fingerprints becomes subjectively convinced that they were made by the same person. Why not permit the same process with DNA profiles? The FBI, in fact, has instituted a policy for doing just this, though only when the match probability reaches 1 in 260 billion.[104] One reason why there is caution about this policy is, ironically, because the statistical basis of DNA profiling is better understood than that of fingerprinting. This means that extreme probabilities can be quantified; it also means that the framework of assumptions underlying very small match probabilities is relatively transparent, and it can be seen that such figures currently rely on hypotheses that have not been tested. 'We cannot carry out experiments to investigate

---

[102] While the empirical research finds that posterior odds generally increase as the match probability decreases, the correlation is often very small. See, especially, Goodman, *supra* n. 19, 372; Thompson, Brittan, and Schumann, discussed in Thompson, *supra* n. 19; Taroni and Aitken, *supra* n. 19.

[103] See Ch. 3 § 3.

[104] 'DNA Fingerprinting Comes of Age' (1997) 278 *Science* 1407. For discussion, see D. J. Balding, 'When Can a DNA Profile be Regarded as Unique?' (1999) 39 *Science & Justice* 257; B. S. Weir, 'Are DNA Profiles Unique?' in *The Ninth International Symposium on Human Identification* (Madison, WI: Promega Corp., 1998).

the robustness of the independence assumptions inherent in a match probability as small as 1 in 260 billion,' Evett and Weir observe. 'The number is heavily dependent on subjective judgment.'[105]

A further criticism of conclusive DNA identifications is that 'certain' is thought to mean 'belief with probability one' which, it is suggested, involves the scientist saying that the match probability is so small 'that no amount of contrary evidence will shake me from the opinion that the crime sample was left by the defendant'.[106] The problem with this criticism is that it is made from a certain probabilistic perspective, where certainty means probability one, and probability one is all but impossible.[107] But it should not be presumed that experts are talking about probabilistic certainty when they say they are certain, and surely not that this is what jurors will interpret them as meaning. People all the time say they are certain of things to which they would not assign probability one if they understood just what probability one meant.[108] It is quite possible, then, that if a scientist said that, based solely on her interpretation of the scientific evidence, she was certain, or sure, that the DNA in the crime-scene stain was left by the defendant, jurors would still be prepared to acquit the defendant if there was sufficient exculpatory evidence. The judge could emphasize the fact that acquittal was still an option by saying, as in the *Buckley* direction for fingerprints, that 'the expert's opinion is not conclusive and that it is for the jury to determine whether guilt is proved in the light of all the evidence'.[109] Alternatively, the expert could be restricted to a phrase such as 'virtually certain'. There is surely no more reason to believe that jurors will inevitably convict in this situation than there is to believe that they will inevitably convict when presented with a match probability of 1 in 200 million, or a likelihood ratio of 200 million.

If the value of trace evidence was not expressed numerically, much pressure would also be released from the error rates debate. What drives the argument for a combined error/match probability statistic is the intuition that it is rather dishonest to present tiny match probabilities to juries when they are dwarfed by error probabilities. And, because match probabilities are quantified, it is felt that the probability of an error in a particular case must also be quantified. That there is no good way of doing that is what engages much of the criticism of the combination proposal.[110] If DNA evidence was just described as 'very strong evidence' then, unless there was

---

[105] Evett and Weir, *supra* n. 35, 244.   [106] Ibid. 241.

[107] A good example of this sort of thinking is Ward Edwards' remark that 'no real-world proposition has probability 1; I would not assign probability 1 to the proposition that my name is Edwards', in 'Comment' (1986) 66 *Boston U.L. Rev.* 623, 623.

[108] There is empirical evidence to support this intuition: see Frederick Mosteller and Cleo Youtz, 'Quantifying Probabilistic Expressions' (1990) 5 *Statistical Science* 2. In a review of studies of the interpretation of probabilistic expressions, the authors found that 'certain' was interpreted as covering a probability range from 91 to 98 per cent.

[109] *R. v. Buckley, The Times*, 12 May 1999.   [110] See Berger, *supra* n. 78, 1086–92.

reason to believe that the error probability was very high, error probabilities could be ignored. Admittedly, on the certainty model there might still be some concern that laboratory error was being ignored by juries. But, because it is doubtful that juries will treat certain identifications as implying probability one, and because it seems that juries have their own expectations about error probabilities, the case for presenting error probabilities is weakened. If there was evidence that error rates were relatively high, that would count against adopting the certainty model in the first place, and not necessarily in favour of presenting quantified error probabilities to juries.[111]

The possibility that the suspect population contains close relatives of the defendant is a further possible criticism of the certainty model. It creates difficulties even under probability models. Two ways of dealing with the problem suggest themselves. First, one might permit the expert to talk only in terms of 'very strong evidence' when there are close relatives in the suspect population. Alternatively, the expert could state that if there was a possibility of a relative having committed the crime, she would no longer be certain that the defendant was the source of the DNA.

9. THE DATABASE PROBLEM

The solutions to the problem of presenting statistical evidence in the courts just outlined may not be appropriate in every case. Part of the argument hinged on the claim that the jury does not, and should not, usually see the defendant as a person selected at random from the population. There are, however, cases where it is more or less correct to see the defendant as a 'random man', and these pose special problems. England now has a DNA database that enables the DNA from crime-scene stains to be compared to the DNA profiles of large numbers of suspects and convicted offenders. This enables suspects to be located and brought to trial solely on the basis of a match with a crime-scene profile.[112] Apart from the fact that they have

---

[111] It would not, though, rule it out, and it may be that it is easier for juries to comprehend the impact of an error probability on a 'certain' identification than on a small match probability. See Lempert, *supra* n. 73, 467.

[112] This is a slight simplification. Defendants linked to a crime through a database search must have been convicted or suspected of a previous crime, which, in the broad sense of the word, is evidence that they have committed the present crime. However, because one can be the subject of a database search when only having committed (or having been suspected of) some rather minor crime, different in character to the present crime, and all that is being presumed is that 'the defendant was located through a database search', this will be fairly weak evidence. For an example, see 'Rapist Gets Life Ten Years On After DNA Test', *The Times*, 24 August 1999 (suspect in rape case located after an unconnected motoring incident).

Other facts about the DNA database bring home the possibility of seemingly impressive random matches. See 'Mismatch Calls DNA Tests into Question', *USA Today*, 8 February 2000, reporting a database match with a match probability of 1 in 37 million which was considered coincidental. Although the headline—and accompanying story—is alarmist, random matches of this sort are to be expected the larger the database gets and the longer it is used. FSS

been convicted or suspected of another crime—which under the legislation need not be a serious crime—such people may be brought to trial when there really is no other evidence against them: no 'form' for the type of offence they have been arrested for, nor any other inadmissible evidence. In database cases, though, it remains unlikely that the jury will view the defendant as a random man, even though it would be appropriate to do so.[113] This is not just because the jury may consciously speculate that there is some inadmissible evidence linking the defendant to the crime; it is also because people generally find it difficult to see the events that occur to them as random. Recall that, in the lawyer/engineer experiment, there is evidence that subjects only start to consider the description as being taken at random from the group when given a specific cue.[114] We seem to have a propensity to see events as patterned rather than as the result of chance.[115] One solution to the problem would be to let the jury know that the defendant is only on trial because he was picked out in a database search, but that approach is disfavoured because it would alert the jury to the defendant's criminal record.[116]

Database cases have created considerable discussion because it has been argued that DNA evidence in database cases is weaker than in non-database cases, and that the weakening effect of the database search should be incorporated in the match probability presented to the jury.[117] Those who see the problem from a Bayesian perspective, however, do not agree that

scientists report that they expect 'to get between 100–200 adventitious matches a year, i.e. "innocent" by chance matches between an individual on the database and a crime scene stain'. D. J. Werrett and R. Sparkes, '300 Matches Per Week—The Effectiveness and Future Development of DNA Intelligence Databases—Parts 1 and 2' in *The Ninth International Symposium on Human Identification, supra* n. 104.

[113] See *Lashley*; *Smith*, both *supra* n. 68.

[114] See Gigerenzer *et al.*, *supra* n. 18. The authors found that just *telling* subjects that the description was taken at random from the group had less effect than letting subjects *see* the description taken at random from among the group. See also Evans and Over, *supra* n. 50, 101–2, who suggest that, in the lawyer/engineer problem, '[t]he mere presentation of these pieces of information in the wording of instructions will not produce an internalised belief of the kind common to much real-world reasoning.' Thus, while Donnelly and Friedman suggest that counsel can alert the jury to the fact that a database case is a low prior odds case, by drawing attention to the lack of incriminating evidence and the possibility that other people would match the profile, I am not convinced that this will be effective. See Peter Donnelly and Richard D. Friedman, 'DNA Database Searches and the Legal Consumption of Scientific Evidence' (1999) 97 *Mich. L. Rev.* 931, 959.

[115] See Thomas Gilovich, Robert Vallone, and Amos Tversky, 'The Hot Hand in Basketball: On the Misperception of Random Sequences' (1985) 17 *Cog. Psychol.* 295; Richard Dawkins, *Unweaving the Rainbow: Science, Medicine and the Appetite for Wonder* (London: Allen Lane, 1998), 145–79.

[116] Although the DNA database scenario is novel, the problem has previously arisen with identifications from mug-shots and fingerprint records, where it has been held that the jury should not be alerted to the manner of identification. See *R. v. Lamb* (1979) 71 Cr. App. R. 198; *R. v. Bleakley* [1993] Crim. LR 203; *R. v. Allen* [1996] Crim. LR 426.

[117] See National Research Council, *supra* n. 33, 133–5, 161; N. E. Morton, 'The Forensic DNA Endgame' (1997) 37 *Jurimetrics J.* 477, 487–93.

the search erodes the match probability.[118] Part of the disagreement on this issue may be due to the fact that in a database case we tend to characterize the defendant as a random man, sharing a low prior probability of guilt with the rest of the relevant population, whereas in non-database search cases we do not.[119] It follows from my arguments that this is in fact a reasonably sensible distinction: there is a difference between the defendant in the database case and the defendant picked out by other evidence. It is one, moreover, that will not be apparent to the jury unless it is informed about the database search, a solution that causes other problems.[120] It seems, then, that cases where there is only a database-generated match linking the defendant to the crime require special measures.[121] Presenting the jury with a watered-down match probability, or likelihood ratio, is one response—though a very crude one. A more appropriate solution is to tackle the root of the problem, and to bring home to the jury the fact that the prior odds against the defendant are low. Both a *Doheny* direction and the Bayesian analysis presented in *Adams* are ways of achieving this.

I was critical earlier of both the *Doheny* and *Adams* approaches to the presentation problem; those criticisms are still valid, but there comes a point where they are not overwhelming. During the second *Adams* appeal, defence counsel argued that once the prosecution had introduced statistical evidence, the defence had a right to explain Bayesian analysis to the jury, in order to demonstrate the effect of the non-scientific evidence on the posterior probability.[122] That argument has considerable force: small match probabilities are difficult to interpret and to combine with other evidence, and in database cases the jury needs to understand both why the prior odds may be low and why this is significant. A *Doheny* direction may be the most appropriate solution, in that it is simpler for the jury to apply. But the *Adams* approach demonstrates more clearly the relationship between prior and posterior odds. Especially in cases involving exculpatory evidence and very small match probabilities, that relationship is crucial. Notwithstanding the

---

[118] See David J. Balding and Peter Donnelly, 'Evaluating DNA Profile Evidence When the Suspect is Identified Through a Database Search' (1996) 41 *J. Forensic Sci.* 603; Donnelly and Friedman, *supra* n. 114.

[119] See Mike Redmayne, 'The DNA Database: Civil Liberty and Evidentiary Issues' [1998] *Crim. LR* 437, 449.

[120] See n. 116, *supra*.

[121] What if D was located through a database search, but there is some non-database evidence against him—his vague similarity to an eyewitness description, say? In a case like that, I would think that special measures are still required. However, more and more evidence could be added to this hypothetical scenario, until I would concede that it should be treated like a non-database case. The lack of a clear dividing line leaves my argument in some difficulty. I can only suggest a pragmatic approach, requiring special measures when there is a good argument that any rational assessment of the prior odds would have them very low. The demarcation problem does not convince me that there is no distinction to be made between database and non-database cases, any more than the difficulty of identifying the point where small numbers become large numbers persuades me that all numbers are small.

[122] *Supra* n. 9, 380.

difficulties involved in assigning probabilities to evidence, and in interpreting the posterior odds that result from the Bayesian analysis, the defence's strategy in *Adams* seems a legitimate one to use. At least, the defence should have the opportunity to pursue it if it wants to. Outlawing it, as the Court of Appeal has done, appears to underestimate the difficulty of *Adams*-type cases, a difficulty that is borne principally by the defence.

There is another way of dealing with the database problem, which is for the defence simply to tell the jury that there is no evidence against the defendant other than the DNA evidence because he was located through a database search. That strategy may not be as bad for the defence as it at first sounds. For one thing, it is probably the most effective way to get the jury to think about the defendant as a random man. While *Adams* and *Doheny* both attempt to impress upon jurors the fact that there is a large suspect population, they may not be influenced by such arguments, thinking instead that there is some undisclosed evidence linking the defendant to the crime. There will obviously be fears that the jury will view the defendant in a bad light once it knows he has a previous conviction. But if the conviction is for some minor offence, different in kind to the one with which the defendant is now charged, it may not prejudice the defendant at all.[123]

10. OTHER EVIDENCE TYPES

Much of the discussion in the preceding sections has concentrated on DNA cases. The Bayesian approach can be applied to other types of trace evidence, and some commentators have urged that all trace evidence be presented using likelihood ratios.[124] What of such arguments? There are good reasons for the use of likelihood ratios: they allow a number of significant variables to be incorporated within a single assessment of evidence strength. Putting aside doubts about the subjective nature of some of the probabilities involved, they do seem to be the most appropriate means of expressing the strength of evidence. However, given the difficulty that lay people are likely to have in interpreting likelihood ratios, there is every reason to keep them out of court. Evett's verbal conventions provide a suitable alternative. Given the characteristics of most types of trace evidence, it seems that the expression 'very strong support' will not create the 'too low a ceiling' problems that it does with DNA evidence.

---

[123] Research conducted for the Law Commission found that mock jurors 'rated the defendant as significantly *less* likely to have committed the crime with which he was charged if they were told that he had a recent dissimilar conviction than under the base [control] condition' (original emphasis). See Law Commission, *Evidence in Criminal Proceedings: Previous Misconduct of a Defendant—A Consultation Paper*, Law Com. Con. Paper No. 141 (London: Stationery Office, 1996), 329.

[124] See Franco Taroni and Colin Aitken, 'Forensic Science at Trial' (1997) 37 *Jurimetrics J.* 327, 336–7.

Fingerprints, however, are an exception. Even in the absence of good statistical models for fingerprint comparison, many believe that the likelihood ratio for a sixteen-point fingerprint match is huge.[125] If that is correct, then the expression 'very strong support' may be unsatisfactory, just as it may be for the smallest DNA match probabilities. The certainty model, then, is probably appropriate. But it may not always be. English courts have accepted fingerprint evidence on less than sixteen points of similarity[126] and, with the abandonment of the sixteen-point standard, matches on eight points, and fewer, may come to be presented in the courts. This inevitably reopens the issue of how to present such evidence. In *R. v. Charles*,[127] the Court of Appeal heard argument that a direction along the lines of *Doheny* should be developed for fingerprint evidence. It was not impressed by the idea, but it seems that it did not really grasp the parallel with DNA. With fingerprint evidence, a *Doheny* direction is even more problematic than it is with DNA, because the number of people in the suspect population who would match the crime-scene print can only be guessed. The most appropriate solution, again, seems to be to switch to verbal expressions such as 'very strong support'. Unfortunately, the absence of a convincing statistical model means that it is hard to tell where experts should draw the lines between 'strong support', 'very strong support', and certainty. It may well be best to leave this to the expert's judgement, but it is important, at least, that fingerprint experts become familiar with the issues, and understand the limitations of the certainty model once the sixteen-point standard has been abandoned.

Fingerprint evidence can also raise database problems:[128] there now exists in England a national fingerprint database, against which crime-scene prints can be matched. Once more, the lack of a statistical model for fingerprint comparison makes it difficult to assess just how problematic this is. With a sixteen-point match, the very low prior odds in a database case may

---

[125] See David A. Stoney, 'Fingerprint Identification: Scientific Status' in David L. Faigman, David H. Kaye, Michael J. Saks, and Joseph Sanders (eds), *Modern Scientific Evidence: The Law and Science of Expert Testimony* (St Paul: West Publishing, 1997), Vol. 2, 66. Note, though, the important distinction between the individuality of fingerprints and the ability of examiners to classify them so as never to attribute a print from one person to another person. On this general point, see David A. Stoney, 'Source Individuality Versus Expressed Individuality' (1988) 33 *J. Forensic Sci.* 1295. See also 'Yard in Fingerprint Blunder', *The Times*, 6 April 1997.

[126] See, e.g., *R. v. Charles* CA 9800104 Z2 (17 December 1998); *Reid v. DPP* QBD CO2493/95 (26 March 1996).

[127] Ibid.

[128] See David A. Stoney and John I. Thornton, 'A Critical Analysis of Quantitative Fingerprint Individuality Models' (1986) 31 *J. Forensic Sci.* 1187, 1201–2, 1209, 1215. Fingerprint evidence also poses problems when there are relatives in the suspect population. Although even identical twins do not have matching fingerprints (because fingerprints are affected by unpredictable variations in cell growth), the prints of relatives are more similar to each other than those of non-relatives (see Stephen M. Stigler, 'Galton and Identification by Fingerprints' (1995) 140 *Genetics* 857). Ideally, this should be factored into a conclusion about the strength of fingerprint evidence.

be insignificant, and the certainty model, therefore, still satisfactory. There must come a point, however, where it will be appropriate to alert the jury to the fact that the defendant should be considered to be a random man. Here, the argument parallels that for DNA evidence, and the *Doheny* or *Adams* approach may be called for. The fact that no one knows whether this will occur at ten points, eight points, or some lower number, suggests that the courts should proceed with caution in such cases.

11. CONCLUSION

While the issues discussed in this chapter have received relatively little attention from legal commentators, they are, I think, both conceptually and practically, some of the more difficult ones currently facing the courts. I have assessed most of the suggested ways of presenting statistical evidence to the jury that have been proposed; all of them are subject to criticism. Instead of trying to choose between these methods, I have suggested another way of thinking about the problem, which involves lowering our sights some-what. Perhaps justice really is less precise than chemistry: perhaps we just cannot expect a lay decision-maker to understand the precise impact that a match probability of 1 in 200 million should have on her prior odds. Telling the jury that the evidence provides very strong support for the prosecution's case, or that the expert is certain that the defendant was its source, may be the best we can do.

A slightly different way of thinking about the problem is this: DNA evidence is very different from other types of evidence. We have not had statistics like 1 in 200 million used in court before, and it may be foolish to expect people to understand exactly what they mean. If DNA statistics highlight the bounded rationality of our trial process, the limits on the ability of forensic science to improve our decision-making, then that should be no great surprise. DNA evidence has also become different from other types of evidence (except, perhaps, fingerprints) in another way. Database searches allow us to try defendants who are incriminated only by a DNA match. Unless they are informed of the way the defendant was located, it is unlikely that jurors will fully appreciate that such defendants should be viewed as people randomly selected from the suspect population. It will require some work to persuade jurors to change their representation of the defendant. Either *Doheny* or *Adams* provides a reasonable solution: it should be left to the defence to decide which it prefers.

Given that they cut against much of the commentary on the presentation problem, some readers may be wondering how seriously they should take the solutions I have put forward. As I have said, they are intended partly as an attempt to get us to think about the problem in a different way. It would certainly be nice if we could get jurors to appreciate the impact that a likelihood ratio of 200 million should have on their decision-making, but, given the difficulty of getting them to quantify their prior odds, we should not expect that they ever will. If we accept this, and lower our expectations, some of the criticisms of the methods of presenting statistics in court that I have reviewed lose much of their force. The *Doheny* direction can be criticized, but if it is treated as a rough and ready solution to a difficult problem, rather than as a perfect one, it stands up fairly well. In the final analysis, however, all of the proposals in this area are badly under-determined by the empirical evidence, and no one can put forward any particular solution with much confidence. Of my proposals, I will say only that I take them to be as well supported by the empirical evidence as any others. Under-determination by empirical evidence is, of course, no novelty in criminal evidence. Despite valiant research efforts, we do not know very much about how jurors process character or hearsay evidence, for example. We therefore proceed with caution. It is sometimes claimed that this attitude displays a lack of respect for the jury, and it may be that my arguments in the later sections of this chapter will be interpreted in a similar way.[129] But the claim is easily flipped, perhaps more so with statistics than with character and hearsay evidence. Our caution may in fact bespeak respect for the jury's limited competence, an unwillingness to burden it with tasks that it is not suited to performing. Precision is, and will remain, beguiling, but its pursuit should not blind us to our limitations.

[129] See, e.g., Mirjan R. Damaška, *Evidence Law Adrift* (New Haven: Yale University Press, 1997), 29.

5

The Admissibility of Expert Evidence: (1) Evidentiary Reliability

This chapter and the following one examine the rules of evidence governing the admissibility of expert evidence in criminal trials. The discussion in the present chapter concentrates on the ways in which English evidence law does, or might, set reliability standards for the scientific techniques that form the basis of expert testimony in the courts. In Chapter 6 the discussion turns away from reliability to address the rules governing the subject matter of expert testimony, particularly those rules that tend to exclude evidence offered by psychiatrists and psychologists. The focus of these chapters, then, is exclusionary rules of evidence. These rules attempt to improve adjudicative fact-finding by keeping information from the jury.

1. The Admissibility of Expert Evidence in English Law

Although the concern in this chapter is evidentiary reliability, the rules on the admissibility of expert evidence first need to be reviewed *en masse* in order to bring those rules governing reliability into sharper focus. There is a body of rules that might be termed the law of expert evidence.[1] Some of these rules are procedural, such as those governing the pre-trial disclosure of expert evidence.[2] Others are general rules of evidence: the rule against hearsay, for example, applies to expert evidence, and may be used to exclude it.[3] The discretion to exclude evidence that is more prejudicial than probative might also provide a basis for exclusion.[4] There are also admissibility rules that apply exclusively to expert evidence. Expert evidence may be excluded if it concerns a topic on which the court is able to form its own

---

[1] See, generally, Tristram Hodgkinson, *Expert Evidence: Law and Practice* (London: Sweet & Maxwell, 1990).

[2] See Magistrates' Court (Advance Notice of Expert Evidence) Rules 1997 (SI 1997 No. 705); Crown Court (Advance Notice of Expert Evidence) Rules 1987 (SI 1987 No. 716). Failure to comply with the rules may lead to expert evidence being ruled inadmissible.

[3] See, generally, Law Commission, *Evidence in Criminal Proceedings: Hearsay and Related Topics*, Law Com. No. 245 (London: Stationery Office, 1997), 135–43.

[4] *R. v. Sang* [1980] AC 402.

judgement,[5] or, possibly, if it concerns the 'ultimate issue' which the court must decide.[6] Exclusion might also result from a purported expert's lack of expertise on the topic on which she is giving evidence.[7] In short, there are a number of rules that can be used to exclude expert evidence.

None of these rules, however, speaks directly to the central area of concern in this chapter: the reliability of expert evidence.[8] Is an expert witness therefore permitted to base her evidence on a technique or theory of dubious validity? Not necessarily. It is possible that the body of rules outlined above is sufficient to exclude unreliable expert evidence.[9] The closest thing to a reliability-based rule in English law is the rule that an expert must have appropriate qualifications. The leading case is *R. v. Silverlock*,[10] in which a solicitor, whose expertise was said to be based on his business experience as well as his own independent study, was permitted to give opinion evidence on handwriting identification. His lack of formal training was not taken to disqualify him. In order to give expert evidence, the court held, a witness must be *peritus* (skilled), '[b]ut we cannot say that he must become peritus in the way of his business or in any definite way. The question is, is he peritus? Is he skilled? Has he an adequate knowledge?'[11] At first sight, there is a troubling circularity to this: the test for expertise appears to be expertise. However, given the wide range of areas of knowledge that may be relevant to litigation, and the different ways in which knowledge about them may be gained, this pragmatic approach is largely appropriate. A court might need to hear evidence about the value of property,[12] about drug paraphernalia,[13] or about the literary merit of an allegedly obscene book.[14] Australian courts have attempted to lay down stricter criteria for expertise, such as the requirement of academic training, but this has only proved problematic.[15]

Despite the merits of the *Silverlock* test, it would be naïve to suppose that it offers any guarantee of evidentiary reliability. '[F]ailure to query more than

---

[5] *R. v. Turner* [1975] QB 834.

[6] *R. v. Theodosi* [1993] RTR 179. The ultimate issue rule and the rule in *Turner* are considered in Ch. 6.

[7] *R. v. Silverlock* [1894] 2 QB 766. The rule also applies where a person who has been allowed to give expert evidence goes beyond her area of expertise: *R. v. Inch* (1989) 91 Cr. App. R. 51.

[8] 'Reliability' is a rather vague term and it might be thought appropriate to define it precisely. However, the term is frequently used in discussions of evidence and I take it to have a commonly understood, if rather imprecise, meaning. When, later in the chapter, precision becomes more important, I offer a definition. In the scientific literature it is common to distinguish 'reliability' from 'validity' (see, e.g., Stuart A. Kirk and Herb Kutchins, *The Selling of DSM: The Rhetoric of Science in Psychiatry* (New York: De Gruyter, 1992), 28–32); for the purposes of this chapter, however, I generally use the terms interchangeably.

[9] See Hodgkinson, *supra* n. 9, 133–4.

[10] *Supra*, n. 7. See also *R. v. Oakley* [1979] RTR 417.   [11] Ibid. 771.

[12] *English Exporters (London) Ltd* v. *Eldonwall Ltd* [1973] 1 All ER 726.

[13] *R. v. Barker* (1988) 34 A. Crim. R. 141.

[14] Obscene Publications Act 1959, s. 4(2) permits expert evidence on this topic.

[15] See *Clark* v. *Ryan* (1960) 103 CLR 486; *Weal* v. *Bottom* (1966) 40 ALJR 436; *Nickisson* v. *R.* [1963] WAR 114.

qualifications at the courthouse door', it has been claimed, 'leads inevitably to the admission of invalid science.'[16] 'The most essential prerequisite to improvement' in the treatment of expert evidence, Strong writes, 'is judicial recognition that reliability attaches to the general propositions used by the expert, and not to the expert personally or to the expert's field of special-ization.'[17] The solicitor in *Silverlock* would still pass the test in that case, though today one might be surprised to find a person with no formal qualifications giving handwriting evidence. Worse still, an astrologer could pass the *Silverlock* test.

The limitations of relying on *Silverlock* in cases involving evidence of dubi-ous reliability are illustrated by the Court of Appeal's decision in *R. v. Robb*,[18] a case that I shall use as the foundation for the discussion in this chapter. In this kidnapping case, a lecturer in phonetics had been called by the pro-secution to give his opinion that the voice heard on tape-recordings of ransom demands was the defendant's. The expert's technique was based on auditory comparison alone; he agreed with the observations of the defence that '[t]he great weight of informed opinion, including the world leaders in the field, was to the effect that auditory techniques unless supple-mented and verified by acoustic analysis were an unreliable basis of speaker identification.'[19] He conceded that '[h]e had conducted no experiments or tests on the accuracy of his own conclusions.'[20] The court, however, held that his evidence had been correctly admitted. It relied on his being a qualified phonetician with experience in the task he had undertaken. He had been consulted, it was said, in a number of cases where voice identification was in issue, and he had testified 'on some 25 occasions, on each of which the court's decision had been consistent with his opinion'.[21] Further, 'on the facts of this case at least he was not shown to be wrong'.[22] His expertise in phonetics and his track record in the courts, then, were sufficient to establish the admissibility of his opinion, despite his minority view, his failure to test his technique, and the fact that expertise in phonetics does not map directly onto expertise in voice identification. The only conces-sion to the existence of a duty to exclude unreliable expert evidence was the observation that 'the evidence of an astrologer, a soothsayer, a witch-doctor or an amateur psychologist'[23] should not be admitted.

The fact that the rule in *Silverlock* is poorly suited to ensuring the reliability of expert evidence, however, does not mean that English courts are powerless to exclude bad science. The trial judge's decision to admit the evidence in *Robb* had been appealed on the basis of section 78 of the

---

[16] David L. Faigman, Elise Porter, and Michael J. Saks, 'Check Your Crystal Ball at the Courthouse Door, Please: Exploring the Past, Understanding the Present, and Worrying about the Future of Scientific Evidence' (1994) 15 *Cardozo L. Rev.* 1799, 1814.

[17] John William Strong, 'Language and Logic in Expert Testimony: Limiting Expert Testimony by Restrictions of Function, Reliability, and Form' (1992) 71 *Oregon L. Rev.* 349, 369 (footnote omitted).

[18] (1991) 93 Cr. App. R. 161.   [19] Ibid. 165.   [20] Ibid.
[21] Ibid.   [22] Ibid. 166.   [23] Ibid. 164.

Police and Criminal Evidence Act 1984 (PACE). Under this section, evidence adduced by the prosecution may be excluded 'if it appears to the court that . . . the admission of the evidence would have such an adverse effect on the fairness of the proceedings that the court ought not to admit it'. If evidence is unreliable, then it can be said that it might be unfair to admit it.[24] In fact, section 78 has been used to exclude DNA evidence on at least two occasions when its reliability has been challenged.[25] Another possibility is that prosecution evidence of dubious validity might be excluded under the discretion to exclude evidence that is more prejudicial than probative.[26]

Section 78 of PACE and the prejudicial/probative discretion, however, apply only to prosecution evidence.[27] If dubious expert evidence is adduced by the defence, and none of the rules described above can be applied to it, there appears to be no rule that could be used to exclude it.[28] That this lacuna has not been exploited more often by defendants may be due to the other rules, outlined above, being sufficiently flexible to do the work of a reliability rule.[29] Nevertheless, at some stage those rules must prove unequal to the task.

Even ignoring the lack of an exclusionary rule for unreliable expert evidence presented by the defence, there is still an argument that the present rules are unsatisfactory. First, section 78 was not designed to apply to expert evidence, and it gives courts little guidance as to when such evidence is ripe for rejection. A rule applying specifically to expert evidence might do a better job. Secondly, a specific reliability rule would make it easier for parties to challenge unreliable expert evidence adduced by their opponents. Not only would it—to speak metaphorically—give them a hook upon which to hang their arguments, it would also allow the courts to facilitate challenges to expert evidence through explicit allocation of the burden of proof. The unsatisfactory state of the present law in this respect is illustrated by the fact that defendants wishing to challenge expert evidence adduced by the prosecution seem to bear the burden of proof;[30] or at least, given the absence of explicit rules, an informal burden of proof. In *Robb*, for example, although the Court

[24] See Peter Mirfield, *Silence, Confessions and Improperly Obtained Evidence* (Oxford: Clarendon Press, 1998), 131–3, 140–1.

[25] *R. v. Borham* (unreported, Central Criminal Court, 3 November 1992); *R. v. Hammond* (unreported, Central Criminal Court, 7 December 1992). *Hammond* is discussed in William Bown, 'DNA Fingerprinting Back in the Dock', *New Scientist*, 6 March 1993, 14. See also N. Coleman, 'A View From the Bar' (1994) 34 *J. Forensic Sci. Soc.* 113.

[26] This discretion was recognized in *Sang, supra* n. 4. There may also be a common law discretion to exclude unreliable evidence independently of *Sang*, but its scope is unclear and it has only ever been applied to confession evidence: see *R. v. Miller* [1986] 1 WLR 1191.

[27] See *R. v. Lobban* [1995] 1 WLR 877.

[28] In some cases it might also be argued that unreliable expert evidence is irrelevant. If a technique is as likely to produce a particular result if the defendant is guilty as if he is innocent, then evidence based on the technique would have a likelihood ratio of 1: it would be irrelevant. The pragmatic character of the legal test for relevance may also mean that, where defence expert evidence has a likelihood ratio only just greater than 1, it could still be excluded.

[29] In Ch. 6 I argue that the rule in *Turner* is often responsive to reliability concerns.

[30] See Beverley Steventon, *The Ability to Challenge DNA Evidence*, Royal Commission on Criminal Justice Research Study No. 9 (London: HMSO, 1993), 37.

of Appeal observed that 'if the Crown are permitted to call an expert witness of some but tenuous qualifications the burden of proof may imperceptibly shift and a burden be cast on the defendant',[31] it did seem to connive at a burden shift when it remarked that 'the appellant had ample opportunity to meet and rebut Dr. Baldwin's evidence, if he could'.[32] Other commentators have remarked on a similar process in appeals involving challenges to scientific evidence.[33] Given the resource imbalance that exists between defence and prosecution (which, if anything, is greater than normal where scientific evidence is concerned), this is problematic.

In this chapter I argue that English law should create a reliability-based exclusionary rule for expert evidence.[34] A proposal to create a new exclusionary rule of evidence should not be made lightly. There already exists a good number of exclusionary rules, and their complexity and difficulty are notorious. They impose a considerable burden on trial judges and give rise to a large number of appeals. So it is worth asking, at the outset, whether there is any evidence that such a rule is needed. It is easy to point to the well-known miscarriage of justice cases of the 1970s where unreliable scientific evidence played an important role in securing convictions.[35] It is possible—though, it must be admitted, by no means certain—that a reliability-based exclusionary rule could have prevented this from occurring, or at least that it would have made the post-conviction appeals easier for the appellants.[36] There are, though, current examples of courts admitting expert evidence of questionable validity. *Robb* provides one. Four others are worth mentioning. First, stylometry, a technique used to investigate disputed authorship, has been used to contest the authenticity of confessions and has been admitted by the Court of Appeal on at least two occasions.[37] Both the technique's underlying theory and its ability to produce meaningful results have been contested.[38] Secondly, expert evidence based on handwriting

---

[31] *Supra* n. 18, 166.   [32] Ibid. 167.

[33] See Richard Nobles, David Schiff, and Nicola Shaldon, 'The Inevitability of Crisis in Criminal Appeals' (1993) 21 *Int. J. Soc. L.* 1.

[34] The proposal is not novel: see Peter Alldridge, 'Recognising Novel Scientific Techniques: DNA as a Test Case' [1992] *Crim. LR* 687. For other expressions of concern about English law in this area, see John Jackson, 'Trial Procedures' in Clive Walker and Keir Starmer (eds), *Justice in Error* (London: Blackstone Press, 1993), 139; Paul Roberts, 'The Admissibility of Expert Evidence: Lessons From America' (1996) 4 *Expert Evidence* 93; id., 'Tyres With a "Y": An English Perspective on *Kumho Tire* and its Implications for the Admissibility of Expert Evidence', *International Commentary on Evidence*, <http://www.law.qub.ac.uk/ice/> (posted July 1999); Penney Lewis and Alastair Mullis, 'Delayed Criminal Prosecutions For Childhood Sexual Abuse: Ensuring a Fair Trial' (1999) 115 *LQR* 265, 288.

[35] See, generally, Alec Samuels, 'Forensic Science and Miscarriages of Justice' (1994) 34 *Med. Sci. Law* 148.

[36] See Nobles *et al.*, *supra* n. 33; Richard Nobles and David Schiff, *Understanding Miscarriages of Justice* (Oxford: Oxford University Press, 2000), 173–215.

[37] See Bernard Robertson, G. A. Vignaux, and Isobel Egerton, 'Stylometric Evidence' [1994] *Crim. LR* 645; Jolyon Jenkins, 'Scientific Laws?', *New Statesman & Society*, 16 July 1993, 30.

[38] See the papers in (1992) 1 *Expert Evidence* 79–99; R. A. Hardcastle, 'Forensic Linguistics: Determination of Authorship' (1993) 33 *J. Forensic Sci. Soc.* 95; id., 'CUSUM: A Credible Method for the Determination of Authorship?' (1997) 37 *Science & Justice* 129.

identification is commonly presented in criminal trials.[39] Although the comparison of handwriting has grown as a serious discipline since the days when *Silverlock* was decided, the available empirical evidence raises doubts about the ability of experts to perform the task any better than lay people.[40] A third example is evidence based on the diagnosis of battered woman syndrome (BWS), which has been presented in a number of English trials.[41] The research on BWS has been subjected to considerable criticism.[42] The testimony of those who claim to have recovered memories of sexual abuse provides a fourth illustration.[43] Although this testimony is not in itself expert evidence, its reliability depends upon an assessment of the scientific evidence for the phenomena of repression and recovery,[44] about which there is considerable controversy.[45]

Evidently, examples such as these do not prove that a new exclusionary rule provides an appropriate solution. Ultimately, the argument will be that the adoption of a reliability-based exclusionary rule for expert evidence would implement existing evidence law principles. But that is to jump ahead. I shall begin by examining the rules governing the admissibility of expert evidence in other common law jurisdictions, in order to provide a broader perspective on the issues.

2. ADMISSIBILITY RULES IN CANADA, AUSTRALIA, AND NEW ZEALAND

Admissibility rules in other Commonwealth jurisdictions reflect many of the features of English law. There is no explicit reliability-based rule. Instead, courts have relied on a miscellany of other rules that can be applied to

[39] Featuring in around 7 per cent of Crown Court cases. See Michael Zander and Paul Henderson, *Crown Court Study*, Royal Commission on Criminal Justice Research Study No. 19 (London: HMSO, 1993), 85.

[40] See D. Michael Risinger, Mark P. Denbeaux, and Michael J. Saks, 'Exorcism of Ignorance as a Proxy for Rational Knowledge: The Lessons of Handwriting Identification Expertise' (1989) 137 *U. Pa. L. Rev.* 731; D. Michael Risinger with Michael J. Saks, 'Science and Non-Science in the Courts: *Daubert* Meets Handwriting Identification Expertise' (1996) 82 *Iowa L. Rev.* 21. Cf. Andre A. Moenssens, 'Handwriting Identification Evidence in the Post-*Daubert* World' (1997) 66 *UMKC L. Rev.* 251; Mark P. Denbeaux, D. Michael Risinger, and Michael J. Saks, ' "Brave New" Post-*Daubert* World—A Reply to Professor Moenssens' (1998) 29 *Seton Hall L. Rev.* 405.

[41] See, e.g., *R. v. Emery* (1993) 14 Cr. App. R. (S.) 394; *R. v. Howell* [1998] 1 Cr. App. R. (S.) 229.

[42] See Donald Alexander Downs, *More than Victims: Battered Women, the Syndrome Society, and the Law* (Chicago: University of Chicago Press, 1996), 76–99, 138–81. BWS is discussed in more detail in Ch. 6 § 9.

[43] What appear to be recovered memories were admitted in *R. v. H.* CA No. 99/0111 Z4 (25 November 1999).

[44] See *State v. Hungerford* 697 A. 2d 916, 920–1 (1997).

[45] See, e.g., Martin Conway (ed.), *Recovered Memories and False Memories* (Oxford: Oxford University Press, 1997); Stephen Porter, John C. Yuille, and Darrin R. Lehman, 'The Nature of Real, Implanted, and Fabricated Memories for Emotional Childhood Events: Implications for the Recovered Memory Debate' (1999) 23 *Law & Hum. Behav.* 517.

expert evidence in order to secure the exclusion of unreliable evidence.[46] Nevertheless, the question of reliability has received more attention in these countries than in England, and a few developments deserve attention.

Freckelton, an Australian commentator, has identified a rule—which he terms the 'field of expertise rule'—that can be used to address reliability concerns.[47] However, as he and other writers note, the scope and status of the rule remain opaque.[48] The rule has been expressed in terms of whether the subject matter on which expert evidence is adduced 'is such as to be the proper subject of expert testimony'[49] or a 'recognized field of specialist knowledge'.[50] The putative rule might be thought of as a logical extension of the rule in *Silverlock*: it recognizes that expert skills can be developed in some areas but not in others. As such, it represents a direction in which English law may develop.[51] Creatively applied, the rule might be a useful tool for screening expert evidence (if the requirement of *recognized* knowledge is emphasized, much dubious science might be caught), but it is far from satisfactory. A field of expertise rule shares the flaws of *Silverlock* in that it emphasizes expertise rather than reliability. The rule is perhaps better suited to policing the division of expertise between the expert and the trier of fact (by limiting expert testimony to those subjects about which the trier of fact lacks expert knowledge), rather than to screening out bad science.

The other significant trend in Australia, Canada, and New Zealand has been the adoption, by various courts at various times, of versions of admissibility rules based on United States case law.[52] Most significant has been the use, by some Canadian courts, of the latest United States authority, *Daubert* v. *Merrell Dow Pharmaceuticals, Inc.*[53] However, *Daubert* still has

---

[46] See Ian R. Freckelton, *The Trial of the Expert* (Melbourne: Oxford University Press, 1987), 63; David Paciocco, 'Evaluating Expert Evidence for the Purpose of Determining Admissibility: Lessons from the Law of Evidence' (1994) 27 CR (4th) 302, 309–12.

[47] Ibid. 55–67. See also Ian R. Freckelton, 'Judicial Attitudes Toward Scientific Evidence: The Antipodean Experience' (1997) 30 *UC Davis L. Rev.* 1137, 1189–204.

[48] Ibid. 59, 65; Stephen J. Odgers and James T. Richardson, 'Keeping Bad Science Out of the Courtroom—Changes in American and Australian Expert Evidence Law' (1995) 18 *UNSW Law J.* 108, 113. In the Federal jurisdiction and in New South Wales, any such rule may have been abrogated by Section 79 of the 1995 Evidence Acts. Section 79 conditions the admissibility of expert evidence simply on the expert's possessing 'specialised knowledge'; one court has held that this rules out any field of expertise requirement: *B. and R. and the Separate Representative* [1995] FLC 92–636, p. 82, 415.

[49] *R.* v. *Gilmore* [1977] 2 NSWLR 935, 939.

[50] *Eagles* v. *Orth* [1976] Qd R. 313, 320.

[51] *Robb, supra* n. 18, 164 refers to the 'field . . . in which expertise may exist', though no reference is made to Australian law.

[52] See, e.g., *R.* v. *Medvedew* (1978) 6 CR 3d 185; *R.* v. *Gilmore, supra* n. 46.

[53] 113 S. Ct 2786 (1993). For Canadian approval, see *R.* v. *Murrin* (1999) 181 DLR (4th) 320. Previous Canadian cases had taken steps in the direction of *Daubert* by suggesting multi-criterial tests for the admissibility of expert evidence: see, e.g., *R.* v. *Johnston* (1992) 69 CCC (3d) 395.

not received recognition at Supreme Court level in Canada.[54] Flirtation with American admissibility rules has rarely been a consistent practice in the Commonwealth, and courts have often expressed suspicion of United States law, arguing that experience in that jurisdiction shows that the rules are flawed.[55] Some of these decisions have been criticized on the ground that they demonstrate a misunderstanding of the relevant rules.[56] It will be easier to judge the merits of the United States approach once it has been examined in more detail.

3. ADMISSIBILITY RULES IN THE UNITED STATES

In the United States, attempts to develop a rule that will exclude expert evidence that is unreliable, while admitting reliable evidence, have generated a large amount of case law and a huge secondary literature. Before surveying the major trends in the law and commentary, one general observation should be made. In recent years, the development of admissibility rules for expert evidence in the United States has been driven by 'toxic tort' litigation, such as the cases involving the claim that the morning sickness drug Bendectin causes birth defects and that silicon-gel breast implants cause connective tissue disorder.[57] Here, the primary issue is causation and the evidence proffered is often statistical. The litigation is also fairly politicized.[58] The courts have, however, tended to apply the principles developed in toxic tort cases to criminal litigation. One should be cautious about drawing lessons from case law that tends not to distinguish between civil and criminal litigation to English law, where the distinction is more pronounced.

Until the 1920s, the rules governing the admissibility of expert evidence in the United States were similar to those in England: admissibility was based on expertise.[59] Then, in *Frye* v. *United States*,[60] the District of Columbia Court of Appeals held that expert evidence based on a primitive lie detector test was inadmissible. In a much-quoted passage, the court commented that:

Just when a scientific principle or discovery crosses the line between the experimental and the demonstrable stages is difficult to define. Somewhere in this twilight zone

---

[54] The closest the Canadian Supreme Court has come to adopting a reliability-based admissibility rule for scientific evidence is *R.* v. *Mohan* (1994) 89 CCC (3d) 402. This case suggested that an enquiry into reliability formed a part of the determination of relevance.

[55] See David E. Bernstein, 'Junk Science in the United States and the Commonwealth' (1996) 21 *Yale J. Int'l L.* 123, 141, 147, 156, 159.

[56] Ibid.

[57] See Michael D. Green, *Bendectin and Birth Defects* (Philadelphia: University of Pennsylvania Press, 1996); Marcia Angell, *Science on Trial: The Clash of Medical Evidence and the Law in the Breast Implant Case* (New York: W. W. Norton, 1996).

[58] See Peter H. Schuck, 'Multi-Culturalism Redux: Science, Law, and Politics' (1993) 11 *Yale L. & Policy Rev.* 1.

[59] See Faigman *et al.*, *supra* n. 16, 1803–5.   [60] 293 F. 1013 (1923).

the evidential force of the principle must be recognized, and while the courts will go a long way in admitting expert testimony deduced from a well-recognized scientific principle or discovery, the thing from which the deduction is made must be sufficiently established to have gained general acceptance in the particular field in which it belongs.[61]

These two sentences became the basis for a rule requiring the exclusion of expert evidence based on (novel[62]) scientific techniques that are not generally accepted by the scientific community. Although it was not until the 1970s that the rule was commonly applied,[63] the *Frye* test became the dominant admissibility rule for expert evidence until the Supreme Court's 1993 decision in *Daubert* v. *Merrell Dow Pharmaceuticals, Inc.*[64] While that decision ended *Frye*'s reign in the federal jurisdiction, a number of States continue to apply the *Frye* test to expert evidence.[65]

   The influence of *Frye* may be due, in part, to its intuitive appeal. '[T]he requirement of general acceptance in the scientific community', one court has claimed, 'assures that those most qualified to assess the general validity of a scientific method will have the dominant voice.'[66] In fact, the general acceptance requirement does no such thing, because indeterminacies in the delimitation of the relevant scientific community,[67] in the required degree of acceptance,[68] in the method of determining general acceptance,[69] in the definition of what must be accepted,[70] and in the interpretation of

---

[61] 293 F. 1013. 1014.

[62] Courts and commentators often presume that *Frye* applies only to novel scientific techniques. *Frye* itself does not explicitly restrict scrutiny to such techniques, and the logic of such a restriction has been questioned. See James E. Starrs, '*Frye* v. *United States* Restructured and Revitalized: A Proposal to Amend Federal Evidence Rule 702' (1987) 115 FRD 92, 94–7; id., 'There's Something about Novel Scientific Evidence' (1999) 28 *Southwestern U.L. Rev.* 417.

[63] See Lee Loevinger, 'Science as Evidence' (1995) 35 *Jurimetrics J.* 153, n. 19.

[64] 113 S. Ct 2786 (1993). References in the text are to 125 L. Ed. 2d 469 (1993).

[65] See Heather G. Hamilton, 'The Movement from *Frye* to *Daubert*: Where Do the States Stand?' (1998) 38 *Jurimetrics J.* 201.

[66] *United States* v. *Addison* 498 F. 2d 741, 743 (1974).

[67] Moenssens gives the example of spectrographic voice identification, suggesting that the relevant scientific community would include linguists, psychologists, engineers, and those who conduct the tests. Andre E. Moenssens, 'Admissibility of Scientific Evidence—An Alternative to the *Frye* Rule' (1984) 25 *William & Mary L. Rev.* 545, 548–9. Despite this, admissibility was often conditioned on the say-so of practitioners—the same few in each case. The trend was halted in *People* v. *Kelly* 549 P. 2d 1240 (1976), where a requirement that the accepting community be disinterested was added to the *Frye* test. See also *People* v. *Williams* 164 Cal. 2d Supp. 858, 862 (1958), limiting the relevant community to 'those expected to be familiar with [the] use of the technique in question', and *Coppolino* v. *State* 223 So. 2d 68 (1968), recognizing a community consisting of a single scientist.

[68] See *People* v. *Young* 391 NW 2d 270, 288 (1986): 'there are no general criteria to decide if there has been general acceptance. Because it is impossible to find unanimous agreement in any field, the courts have been hard pressed to find the appropriate number of experts who must have accepted the technique as reliable.'

[69] See Paul C. Giannelli, 'The Admissibility of Novel Scientific Evidence: *Frye* v. *United States*, a Half-Century Later' (1980) 80 *Colum. L. Rev.* 1197, 1215–19.

[70] See ibid. 1211–15.

'scientific'[71] ensure that judges applying *Frye* are left with considerable room to manoeuvre. It was problems such as these that led courts and commentators in other jurisdictions to be sceptical about developing a stricter approach to the scrutiny of expert evidence.

Within the United States, *Frye* also met a more basic challenge, aimed at what might be termed its underlying philosophy. The *Frye* test erects an evidentiary hurdle that expert evidence must overcome. In an influential critique, McCormick questioned the logic of this. 'General scientific acceptance', he argued, 'is a proper condition upon the court's taking judicial notice of scientific facts, but not a criterion for the admissibility of scientific evidence.'[72] Instead of subjecting expert evidence to a special admissibility threshold, McCormick suggested, it made better sense to treat it like other evidence; that is, to admit it if relevant, but to exclude it if its probative value was outweighed 'by the familiar dangers of prejudicing or misleading the jury, unfair surprise and undue consumption of time'.[73] This objection to *Frye* is insightful, but this 'relevancy approach'—as it came to be known —may in practice collapse into the test it was designed to replace. To determine whether expert evidence will prejudice or mislead the jury, one needs to assess its reliability; this, in turn, may invite the question whether the technique on which it is based is generally accepted. Indeed, as courts and commentators developed the relevancy approach, they tended to produce lists of factors to be taken into account in determining reliability; one such factor was invariably general acceptance.[74] This 'check-list' approach to admissibility was sometimes referred to as a 'reliability' test.

In 1975, the Federal Rules of Evidence were introduced. These added another angle to debates about the correct approach to the admissibility of scientific evidence. Rule 702 sets out criteria for the admissibility of expert evidence:

If scientific, technical or other specialized knowledge will assist the trier of fact to understand the evidence or to determine a fact in issue, a witness qualified as an expert by knowledge, skill, experience, training, or education, may testify thereto in the form of an opinion or otherwise.[75]

[71] For example, *Frye* was often not applied to the evidence of doctors, psychiatrists, and psychologists: see David McCord, 'Syndromes, Profiles and Other Mental Exotica: A New Approach to the Admissibility of Nontraditional Psychological Evidence in Criminal Cases' (1987) 66 *Oregon L. Rev.* 19, 84–6; Bert Black, 'A Unified Theory of Scientific Evidence' (1988) 56 *Fordham L. Rev.* 595, 647.

[72] Charles McCormick, *Evidence* (St Paul: West Publishing, 1954), 363.

[73] Ibid. 363–4.

[74] See, e.g., *United States* v. *Williams* 583 F. 2d 1194 (1978); *United States* v. *Downing* 753 F. 2d 1224 (1985); Mark McCormick, 'Scientific Evidence: Defining a New Approach to Admissibility' (1982) 67 *Iowa L. Rev.* 879, 911.

[75] Developments in the case law, discussed below, have led to a proposed amendment to rule 702. The amendment is likely to become law in the near future. It reads: 'If scientific, technical, or other specialized knowledge will assist the trier of fact to understand the evidence or to determine a fact in issue, a witness qualified as an expert by knowledge, skill, experience,

Neither the rules nor the notes of the advisory committee that drafted them refer to *Frye*.[76] Attempts by commentators to find a solution to the *Frye* debate in the language of rule 702, however, generated more heat than light.[77] Nevertheless, when, in 1993, the Supreme Court ruled on the admissibility of scientific evidence in federal trials, it was to rule 702 that it turned to determine the issue.

In *Daubert* v. *Merrell Dow Pharmaceuticals, Inc.*,[78] the court held that the lack of reference to *Frye*, coupled with the federal rules' purported 'liberal thrust'[79] towards admissibility, meant that the 'austere'[80] general acceptance test was not good law in the federal courts. The court did not, however, decide that a simple relevancy test should be applied. Instead, it held, judges must perform a 'gatekeeping role',[81] and screen scientific evidence to ensure its reliability before admitting it. The details of the test to be applied were developed through a rather strained exegesis of the first thirteen words of rule 702. Expert testimony must, the court held, be based on 'scientific . . . knowledge' (a reliability criterion); it must also 'assist the trier of fact' (a relevance criterion).[82] Reliability was to be determined with reference to the constituents of scientific knowledge, which were held to include consideration of whether the technique 'can be (and has been) tested'; whether it has been the subject of publication and peer review; the technique's error rate; and whether the technique is generally accepted. These factors, the court stressed, were only guidelines and should not be taken to be exhaustive.[83]

The Supreme Court's judgment in *Daubert* was broadly welcomed by commentators.[84] This in itself says quite a lot about the new admissibility test: the criteria in it appear sufficiently vague to have been interpreted as favourable both by members of the civil plaintiffs' bar (who tend to favour low admissibility standards for scientific evidence) and members of the defendants' bar (who favour stricter standards).[85] The best way to gauge the

training, or education, may testify thereto in the form of an opinion or otherwise, if (1) the testimony is based upon sufficient facts or data, (2) the testimony is the product of reliable principles and methods, and (3) the witness has applied the principles and methods reliably to the facts of the case.' For discussion of this amendment and the background to it, see *Communication from the Chief Justice, the Supreme Court of the United States*, 106th Congress, 2d Session, House Doc. 106–225 (Washington DC: Government Printing Office, 2000).

[76] See Stephen A. Saltzburg and Kenneth R. Redden, *Federal Rules of Evidence Manual* (Charlottesville: Michie, 1977), 414.

[77] See Paul C. Giannelli, '*Daubert*: Interpreting the Federal Rules of Evidence' (1994) 15 *Cardozo L. Rev.* 1999, 2013–14.

[78] *Supra* n. 64.   [79] Ibid. 480.   [80] Ibid.
[81] Ibid. 485.   [82] Ibid. 480–1.   [83] Ibid. 482–4.

[84] See, generally, *Scientific Evidence After the Death of Frye* (Symposium) (1994) 15 *Cardozo L. Rev.* 1745–2249.

[85] See Margaret G. Farrell, '*Daubert v Merrell Dow Pharmaceuticals*: Experts Testify on Expert Testimony' in Larry Kramer (ed.), *Reforming the Civil Justice System* (New York: New York University Press, 1996), 213–14. It was quickly recognized that *Daubert* left important questions unanswered. See, e.g., Margaret A. Berger, 'Evidentiary Framework' in Federal Judicial Center (ed.), *Reference Manual on Scientific Evidence* (Washington DC: Federal Judicial Center, 1994), 44; D. H. Kaye, *Science in Evidence* (Cincinnati: Anderson Publishing Co., 1997), 96–9.

actual effect of *Daubert* would seem to be to look at the case law applying it. This exercise, however, yields few clear answers. This is partly because the points of comparison—the *Frye* and relevancy tests—are so flexible that they could be applied strictly or laxly, depending on the court.[86] It is also because *Daubert* is subject to similarly flexible interpretation. In practice it seems that *Daubert* has been applied in like manner to the previous tests, with some courts using it as a tool to conduct a close review of proffered scientific evidence and others taking a more restrained approach.[87] A few trends, however, are worth noting. *Frye* has continued to exert a strong gravitational pull, even in the federal courts.[88] This is probably due to the inclusion of the *Frye* test within the *Daubert* criteria, as well as to *Frye*'s intuitive appeal and supposed ease of application. Beyond this, in criminal cases *Daubert* has led to a reassessment by some courts of their approach to the admissibility of evidence that had been excluded under *Frye*: polygraph evidence is the prime example.[89] At the same time, some techniques that have long been admitted without question are now in danger of being excluded. These include some forensic identification techniques that do not have a history of empirical validation, such as handwriting identification evidence.[90] *Daubert* may also have played a role in easing the reception of DNA evidence in the courts.[91]

Since *Daubert*, the Supreme Court has considered questions pertaining to expert evidence on two further occasions. The later cases are not a radical departure from *Daubert*—together they are referred to as the *Daubert* trilogy—but they do fill in some of the gaps in that judgment. The decision in *General Electric Co.* v. *Joiner*[92] will receive little attention here. Its principal significance is in deciding that the standard of appellate review of trial court decisions on expert evidence is the deferential 'abuse of discretion'

[86] See Bert Black, Francisco J. Ayala, and Carol Saffran-Brinks, 'Science and Law in the Wake of *Daubert*: A New Search for Scientific Knowledge' (1994) 72 *Texas L. Rev.* 715, 743–5; 'Developments in the Law: Confronting the New Challenges of Scientific Evidence' (1995) 108 *Harv. L. Rev.* 1481, 1490–8.

[87] See Ruth Saunders, 'The Circuit Courts' Application of *Daubert v. Merrell Dow Pharmaceuticals, Inc.*' (1997) 46 *Drake L. Rev.* 407.

[88] See Richard D. Friedman, 'The Death and Transfiguration of *Frye*' (1994) 34 *Jurimetrics J.* 133; Martin L. C. Feldman, 'May I have the Next Dance Mrs *Frye*?' (1995) 69 *Tulane L. Rev.* 793. On state courts' reaction to *Daubert*, see Hamilton, *supra* n. 65.

[89] See, e.g., *United States* v. *Cordoba* 104 F. 3d 225 (1997); *United States* v. *Pulido* 69 F. 3d 192 (1995). See also *United States* v. *Hall* 93 F. 3d 1337 (1996).

[90] See *United States* v. *Starzecpyzel* 880 F. Supp. 1027 (1995). In that case the court decided that, although handwriting evidence failed the *Daubert* test, it should be admitted under FRE 702 as 'technical or other specialized knowledge'. See also *United States* v. *Velasquez* 64 F. 3d 844 (1997) (handwriting evidence); *Williamson* v. *Reynolds* 904 F. Supp. 1529 (1995) (voice identification) and, generally, Erica Beecher-Monas, 'Blinded by Science: How Judges Avoid the Science in Scientific Evidence' (1998) 71 *Temple L. Rev.* 55.

[91] See David L. Faigman, 'Making the Law Safe for Science: A Proposed Rule for the Admission of Expert Testimony' (1996) 35 *Washburn LJ* 401, 418. This claim is hard to verify, because *Daubert* entered the scene just as the balance of scientific opinion was starting to tip in favour of the reliability of DNA evidence.

[92] 522 US 136 (1997).

standard.[93] More significant is the decision in *Kumho Tire Co., Ltd* v.
Carmichael.[94] Rather paradoxically, this decision might be said to have made
Daubert both more and less flexible. Some courts had taken to classifying
certain forms of expert evidence as technical or experience-based expertise,
rather than as scientific knowledge—thus avoiding the words in FRE 702
that were the foundation for the reasoning in *Daubert*, and, therefore,
dodging the *Daubert* criteria too.[95] *Kumho* clarifies *Daubert*'s compass: the
Daubert criteria apply to all forms of expertise. But in the process of tighten-
ing *Daubert*'s grip on expert evidence, the Supreme Court also loosened
it, for it emphasized that the *Daubert* criteria must be applied flexibly in
all cases. This provides courts with a little more leeway when applying
Daubert. I shall return to *Kumho*, and its implications, later in the chapter.

4. ASSESSING THE TESTS: GENERAL ACCEPTANCE OR SCIENTIFIC SOUNDNESS?

This brief review of United States law suggests that the impact of different
admissibility standards should not be exaggerated. No test will ensure that
unreliable scientific evidence will not find its way into the courtroom.[96] Nor
does there seem to be an awful lot to choose between the different tests.
Nevertheless, the rules do at least focus attention on the need to examine
the reliability of scientific evidence and to exclude such evidence if it is
unreliable: this is the principal distinction between United States and English law in this area. There are also broad distinctions in the underlying
philosophy of the different rules which probably have some effect on case
outcomes. The rules are best viewed as tools: although the rules themselves
cannot determine the manner in which they are used by judges, some forms
of the exclusionary rule may be more useful than others because they
draw attention to questions that should be asked of scientific evidence in
criminal cases. This section explores these broad differences, suggesting that,
at least for criminal cases, *Daubert* is a useful tool for examining the
reliability of expert evidence. The discussion here sets the stage for an
analysis of the general justifications for exclusionary rules.

[93] The other significant point in *Joiner* relates to a rather obscure passage in *Daubert*, which
drew a distinction between an expert's methodology and conclusions, suggesting that judges
should focus on the former (*supra* n. 64, 483). *Joiner* back-pedalled on this point, noting that
'conclusions and methodology are not entirely distinct from one another'. *Supra* n. 92, 146.
The issue is likely to be most significant in civil cases. For critical discussion of *Joiner*, see Michael
J. Saks, 'The Aftermath of *Daubert*: An Evolving Jurisprudence of Expert Evidence' (2000) 40
Jurimetrics J. 229, 231–6.
[94] 119 US 1167 (1999).
[95] See, e.g., *Starzecpyzel*, *supra* n. 90; Michael H. Graham, 'The Expert Witness Predica-
ment: Determining "Reliable" Under the Gatekeeping Test of *Daubert*, *Kumho*, and Proposed
Amended Rule 702 of the Federal Rules of Evidence' (2000) 54 *U. Miami L. Rev.* 317, 325–32.
[96] See Michael J. Saks, 'Merlin and Solomon: Lessons From the Law's Formative
Encounters with Forensic Identification Science' (1998) 49 *Hastings LJ* 1069, esp. 1133–4.

Frye: A Conservative Standard

Behind the *Frye* test is a presumption that some scientific tests exist in a 'twilight zone' when they are 'experimental' rather than 'demonstrable'.[97] Although nothing in the language of *Frye* restricts the application of the test to novel scientific techniques, the evolutionary model of science implicit in *Frye* suggests that new forms of expert evidence should face a time-lag before they are admitted by the courts. This conservative aspect of *Frye* is often criticized: *Frye*, it is thought, may mandate the exclusion of perfectly valid evidence.[98] Yet it is the conservative nature of *Frye* that appeals to many of its supporters.[99] In the wake of *Daubert*, those state courts that have chosen to retain *Frye* have tended to stress the risks of relying on scientific evidence that has no proven track record.[100]

Conservatism, however, is not a virtue in itself. Why is it considered desirable where expert evidence is concerned? A common justification for *Frye*'s conservatism is the claim that juries are overawed by scientific evidence,[101] presumably meaning that they will give it massive probative value and pay no heed to any doubts expressed about its reliability. There is, however, almost no evidence to support this claim; rather, the little evidence we have about juror reactions to scientific evidence tends to undermine it.[102] A more reasonable claim is that, if the reliability of scientific evidence is challenged, jurors will find it difficult to make a reasonable assessment of the issues owing to the complex nature of scientific evidence. If this is true, though, it might provide a general justification for strict scrutiny of challenged expert evidence rather than a justification for a conservative approach to 'experimental' scientific evidence. For that reason, the empirical evidence on jury assessment of expert testimony is examined below.

[97] *Supra* n. 60, 1014.

[98] See Edward J. Imwinkelried, 'Attempts to Limit the Scope of the *Frye* Standard for the Admission of Scientific Evidence: Confronting the Real Cost of the General Acceptance Test' (1992) 10 *Behav. Sci. & Law* 441.

[99] See, e.g., Paul C. Giannelli, 'In Defense of *Frye*' (1983) 99 FRD 202, 206. Giannelli limits his comments to criminal cases.

[100] See, e.g., *People* v. *Leahy* 882 P. 2d 321, 330–1 (1994); *State* v. *Carter* 524 NW 2d 763, 777–80 (1994).

[101] See, e.g., the much quoted assertion in *United States* v. *Addison*, *supra* n. 66, 744: scientific evidence may 'assume a posture of mystic infallibility in the eyes of a jury of laymen'.

[102] A commonly cited example is an experiment in which Loftus found that mock jurors were more willing to convict on the basis of eyewitness testimony than on a fingerprint identification: Elizabeth Loftus, 'Psychological Aspects of Courtroom Testimony' (1980) 347 *Annals NY Acad. Sci.* 27. For other evidence on this issue, see Shari Seidman Diamond and Jonathan D. Casper, 'Blindfolding the Jury to Verdict Consequences: Damages, Experts, and the Civil Jury' (1992) 26 *Law & Soc. Rev.* 513, esp. 539–44, 557–58; Jason Schklar, 'DNA Evidence in the Courtroom: A Social-Psychological Perspective' in Michael Freeman and Helen Reece (eds), *Science in Court* (Aldershot: Ashgate, 1998); Edward J. Imwinkelried, 'The Standard for Admitting Scientific Evidence: A Critique from the Perspective of Juror Psychology' (1982) 28 *Villanova L. Rev.* 554; Rita James Simon, *The Jury and the Defense of Insanity* (New Brunswick: Transaction Publishers, 1999) (orig. 1967) 78–96, 217–18.

There may be better defences of *Frye*'s conservatism than the argument that jurors will be overawed. One is that the time-lag between the development of a technique and its reception by the courts ensures that there will be a minimum reserve of experts who are knowledgeable about it and who can therefore attest to its reliability—or otherwise.[103] This is a more reasonable justification, although it should be noted that, because *Frye* challenges are usually only mounted when experts have come forward to criticize evidence, it does not seem to work well in practice.[104] There is a considerable degree of interaction between the courts and the scientific community,[105] and sometimes it is only the use of scientific evidence in court that will encourage scientists to challenge it; yet, without challenges by scientists, courts will be given the impression that general acceptance exists.

There is a further defence of *Frye*'s conservatism which, while difficult to articulate, may explain some of the attraction the test holds. One difficulty with traditional defences of *Frye* is that they often involve the claim that novel scientific techniques are, by definition, unreliable. There is no good reason to believe, however, that novel scientific techniques are especially unreliable, nor that their reliability will be improved by the time-lag. What the passage of time may ensure is that more becomes known about a technique: even if a technique's reliability is not enhanced over time, the amount of information available to the courts, on which they can make reasoned judgements about reliability, should increase. The focus here is not on the validity of the evidence proffered, but on our epistemic attitude towards it. As the amount of evidence about a technique builds up, we can be more confident in the judgements we make about it.[106] This epistemic issue may be linked to broader principles of fairness. 'Every individual', Nozick claims, has 'the right that information sufficient to show that a procedure of justice about to be applied to him is reliable and fair . . . be made publicly

---

[103] See *Commonwealth* v. *Lykus* 327 NE 2d 671, 677 (1975) ('the application of [*Frye*] protects the parties by assuring a reserve of experts who may be needed to testify').

[104] DNA evidence provides an example. In the United States, DNA evidence was never ruled inadmissible during the first year and a half of its use, even though it was then that the technique was most vulnerable. Once scientists became aware of the assumptions underlying DNA statistics, challenges were frequent and the evidence was excluded on a number of occasions. See, e.g., David H. Kaye, 'The Admissibility of DNA Testing' (1991) 13 *Cardozo L. Rev.* 353, 357. A similar story can be told about the use of DNA evidence in England, where it was first used in 1986, and first excluded in 1992.

[105] The 'co-construction' of law and science is a theme of Jasanoff's. See Sheila Jasanoff, *Science at the Bar: Law, Science, and Technology in America* (Cambridge, MA: Harvard University Press, 1995).

[106] I have suggested that the concept of 'second order uncertainty' captures this aspect of *Frye*. See Mike Redmayne, 'Expert Evidence and Scientific Disagreement' (1997) 30 *UC Davis L. Rev.* 1027, 1075–7 (Feldman's concept of 'deep uncertainty' is similar: Heidi Li Feldman, 'Science and Uncertainty in Mass Exposure Litigation' (1995) 74 *Texas L. Rev.* 1). This article also uses the example of DNA evidence to show how decisions to exclude evidence can prompt further research on it, thus increasing our knowledge about it.

available or made available to him.'[107] The time-lag helps to ensure that such information will be available.

Strict Scrutiny and Jury Competence

Calls for the strict scrutiny of scientific evidence (whether the tool for scrutiny be *Frye*, *Daubert*, or some other reliability test) are usually premised on the assumption that juries are poorly suited to assessing expert evidence when there are doubts about its reliability. In contrast, McCormick's relevance approach might be thought to be based on faith in the ability of juries to make rational decisions about scientific evidence. The Court of Appeal's judgment in *Robb* displays a similarly confident attitude. There is some empirical evidence that may enable us to judge which is the better view.

General studies of jury trials have tended not to raise concerns about scientific evidence.[108] Some studies have specifically examined juror responses to scientific evidence and other types of complex evidence.[109] The principal conclusions are that: jurors are relatively confident of their ability to assess expert evidence;[110] they are aware of how the adversarial context affects expert evidence and tend to give most weight to experts who present accessible testimony and give firm conclusions;[111] they sometimes consider

[107] Robert Nozick, *Anarchy, State, and Utopia* (Oxford: Blackwell, 1974), 102. Nozick's discussion of adjudicative procedures occurs in the context of an attempt to justify the application of such procedures to those who argue that they have never agreed to any social contract imposing them—part of a wider attempt to show how a minimal, coercive state might emerge from a 'state of nature'. Nevertheless, this idea that those subjected to adjudicative procedures should be able to make a reasoned assessment of their fairness seems to have broader application.

[108] See, e.g., Harry Kalven and Hans Zeisel, *The American Jury* (Chicago: University of Chicago Press, 1966), 137-9, 149-62; Warren Young, Neil Cameron, and Yvette Tinsley, *Juries in Criminal Trials: A Summary of the Research Findings*, NZLC PP37 (Wellington: New Zealand Law Commission, 1999), 25-6; Zander and Henderson, *supra* n. 39, 176-7, 206-7.

[109] An excellent review of the literature is Richard Lempert, 'Civil Juries and Complex Cases: Taking Stock after Twelve Years' in Robert E. Litan (ed.), *Verdict: Assessing the Civil Jury System* (Washington DC: The Brookings Institution, 1993). For other general reviews, see Imwinkelried, *supra* n. 92; Daniel W. Shuman, Anthony Champagne, and Elizabeth Whitaker, 'Juror Assessments of the Believability of Expert Witnesses: A Literature Review' (1996) 36 *Jurimetrics J.* 371; Joe S. Cecil, Valerie P. Hans, and Elizabeth C. Wiggins, 'Citizen Comprehension of Difficult Issues: Lessons From Civil Jury Trials' (1991) 40 *Am. U.L. Rev.* 727; Larry Heuer and Steven D. Penrod, 'Jury Decision-Making in Complex Trials' in Ray Bull and David Carson (eds), *Handbook of Psychology in Legal Contexts* (Chichester: John Wiley, 1995); Michael S. Jacobs, 'Testing the Assumptions Underlying the Debate About Scientific Evidence: A Closer Look at Juror "Incompetence" and Scientific "Objectivity"' (1993) 25 *Connecticut L. Rev.* 1083; Joseph Sanders, *Bendectin on Trial: A Study of Mass Tort Litigation* (Ann Arbor: University of Michigan Press, 1998), ch. 5; Neil Vidmar, 'The Performance of the American Civil Jury: An Empirical Perspective' (1998) 40 *Ariz. L. Rev.* 849, 854-66.

[110] See Zander and Henderson, *supra* n. 39, 206-7; J. Cecil, E. Lind, and G. Bermant, *Jury Service in Lengthy Civil Trials* (Washington DC: Federal Judicial Center, 1987), 27.

[111] See Neil Vidmar, *Medical Malpractice and the American Jury: Confronting the Myths About Jury Incompetence, Deep Pockets, and Outrageous Damage Awards* (Ann Arbor: University of Michigan Press, 1995), 141, 158; American Bar Association, *Jury Comprehension*

paradigmatically rational criteria such as expert reasoning, impartiality, and qualifications;[112] they vary in their ability to cope with complex evidence, but a group of twelve people is likely to contain some who can perform the task well and who will give guidance to less able jurors;[113] and they sometimes fail to appreciate the cogency of criticisms levelled at scientific evidence.[114]

Two pieces of jury research are worth a little more attention. One fairly intuitive hypothesis about juror processing of expert evidence, which finds some support in the social psychology literature on persuasion, is that juror response will be a function of complexity.[115] As expert evidence becomes more complicated, it is thought that jurors will shift from evaluating the content of the testimony to rely instead on peripheral indicia of its value, such as the expert's apparent expertise or attractiveness (some research, for example, has found that jurors report considering the appearance of experts when evaluating their evidence[116]). Cooper, Benedict, and Sukel tested this theory in a laboratory study and found some support for it.[117] Where expert testimony was not especially complex, juror response to two experts was not affected by the fact that one had more impressive credentials than the other. Credentials did seem to affect evaluation, however, when more complex testimony was presented. A second important study—involving 1,022 prospective jurors—was conducted by Diamond and Casper. The research explored juror response to different forms of expert testimony; some subjects engaged in group deliberation, the results of which were recorded. The authors concluded that:

even when . . . testimony is arcane, complex and difficult to follow, jurors make conscientious and often successful efforts to deal with the substance of what they hear, and their decisions reflect such activity. . . . The responses to expert testimony

in Complex Cases (Chicago: American Bar Association, 1989), 40–3; Anthony Champagne, Daniel Shuman, and Elizabeth Whitaker, 'An Empirical Examination of the Use of Expert Witnesses in American Courts' (1991) 31 *Jurimetrics J.* 375; Daniel W. Shuman, Elizabeth Whitaker, and Anthony Champagne, 'An Empirical Examination of the Use of Expert Witnesses in the Courts—Part II: A Three City Study' (1994) 34 *Jurimetrics J.* 193.

[112] See Vidmar, *supra* n. 111, 175–8; Daniel W. Shuman, Anthony Champagne, and Elizabeth Whitaker, 'Assessing the Believability of Expert Witnesses: Science in the Jury Box' (1996) 37 *Jurimetrics J.* 23.

[113] American Bar Association, *supra* n. 111, 16, 22; Neil Vidmar, 'Are Juries Competent to Decide Liability in Tort Cases Involving Scientific/Medical Issues? Some Data From Medical Malpractice' (1994) 43 *Emory LJ* 885.

[114] See Joseph Sanders, 'From Science to Evidence: The Testimony on Causation in the Bendectin Cases' (1993) 46 *Stanford L. Rev.* 1, esp. 27–60.

[115] See Paul Rosenthal, 'Nature of Jury Responses to the Expert Witness' (1983) 28 *J. Forensic Sci.* 528; Note, 'The *Frye* Doctrine and Relevancy Approach Controversy: An Empirical Evaluation' (1986) 74 *Geo. LJ* 1769, 1783–6.

[116] See Rosenthal, ibid.; Champagne *et al.* and Shuman *et al.*, both *supra* n. 111.

[117] Joel L. Cooper, Elizabeth A. Bennett, and Holly L. Sukel, 'Complex Scientific Testimony: How do Jurors Make Decisions?' (1996) 20 *Law & Hum. Behav.* 379. The study did not involve any group deliberation; such deliberation might be presumed to have had an ameliorating effect.

we observe [*sic*] . . . suggest that jurors play an active role in assimilating and assessing testimony. Jurors did not simply adopt the view of a witness they rated high on expertise, using apparent expertise as a peripheral cue that the expert must be correct. . . . Rather, consistent with deeper processing of information . . . the jurors appeared to consider and evaluate the content of what the expert was presenting, and were less likely to be persuaded if they did not feel they understood it.[118]

Rather than scrutinizing studies of jury reaction to technical evidence, one might try to use more general knowledge about jury decision-making as the basis for informed speculation about how expert evidence will be processed. The available research suggests that jurors may assess expert evidence on the basis of the other evidence presented to them during a case. Support for this comes from two sources. First, studies suggest that assessments of the probative value of evidence are interdependent. Jurors cannot neatly compartmentalize evidence: proponent's evidence *x* will be deemed more probative than it might otherwise be if a juror has already heard proponent's evidence *y* and deemed it highly probative.[119] Secondly, there is considerable support for an 'explanation-based' or 'story' model of juror decision-making.[120] One might speculate that jurors use the explanatory schemata that they have already constructed in order to assess expert evidence. If there is conflicting expert evidence, the jury may interpret it as lending support to the explanation it already finds most plausible.[121] A graphic illustration of this sort of process is provided by Schklar. In one experiment he found that 'background attitudes about the causes of sexual assault appear to be related to the degree to which people interpret an inclusionary DNA match report as incriminatory evidence'.[122] What this 'holistic' model of evidence processing suggests is that sometimes evidence that deserves little weight may be used to lend support to a verdict favoured by other evidence.

On the basis of the available research, then, there are grounds for limited scepticism about the ability of jurors to understand and effectively assess scientific evidence. If we had better research from which to draw conclusions, however, it seems unlikely that it would provide decisive reasons for favouring one approach to admissibility rather than another. This is

---

[118] Diamond and Casper, *supra* n. 102, 557–8.

[119] See David M. Saunders, Neil Vidmar, and Erin C. Hewitt, 'Eyewitness Testimony and the Discrediting Effect' in Sally M. A. Lloyd-Bostock and Brian R. Clifford (eds), *Evaluating Witness Evidence* (Chichester: John Wiley, 1983); Jonathan D. Casper, Kennette Benedict, and Jo L. Perry, 'Juror Decision Making, Attitudes and the Hindsight Bias' (1989) 13 *Law & Hum. Behav.* 291.

[120] See Nancy Pennington and Reid Hastie, 'The Story Model for Juror Decision Making' in Reid Hastie (ed.), *Inside the Juror: The Psychology of Juror Decision Making* (Cambridge: Cambridge University Press, 1993).

[121] See Willem A. Wagenaar, Peter J. van Koppen, and Hans F. M. Crombag, *Anchored Narratives: The Psychology of Criminal Evidence* (Hemel Hempstead: Harvester Wheatsheaf, 1993), 179–80; Richard Lempert, 'Experts, Stories, and Information' (1993) 87 *Nw. U.L. Rev.* 1169, 1176. Sanders, *supra* n. 109, 130–41.

[122] Schklar, *supra* n. 102, 118.

partly due to the limitations of even large quantities of well-conducted jury research.[123] But even convincing evidence of juror incompetence would leave open the possibility that better presentation of expert testimony,[124] or significant attempts to educate the jury on the issues about which it must make decisions,[125] would improve decision-making. More fundamentally, however, the nature of the problem posed by expert evidence limits the relevance of the empirical research. Where doubts are expressed about the reliability of expert evidence, it is sometimes the case that the scientific community itself is divided on the issue. Sometimes that is because a technique, or its forensic use, is relatively new, and the research record does not enable any conclusion about its ability to be drawn with great confidence. However good a decision-maker the jury is, it is certainly not in a position to make a better decision on such a question than anyone else.[126] This suggests that the focus on jury competence is somewhat misplaced. What is just as important is our general approach to regulating the admissibility of evidence that carries with it the risk of error. I return to this question below.

Strict Scrutiny and Judicial Competence

Strict scrutiny of expert evidence might be justified by credible research showing that jurors have difficulty telling good science from bad; but if judges experience similar difficulties, there is little point asking *them* to scrutinize the evidence thoroughly. Most judges, after all, cannot be expected to be especially scientifically literate. This point was made forcefully by Chief Justice Rehnquist in his concurring judgment in *Daubert*. Rehnquist was concerned that trial judges would be required to become 'amateur scientists'[127] in order to carry out the gatekeeping task outlined by the majority. Therefore, while agreeing that the Federal Rules of Evidence abrogated *Frye*, he dissented from that part of the judgment setting out the indicia of reliability to be used by judges performing their gatekeeping role.

One might argue, however, that, given Rehnquist's concern, this was just the wrong approach. He would have preferred to say nothing at all about the indicia of good science. The majority at least gave some guidance to the trial judges who have to decide whether or not to admit expert testimony.

[123] See Richard O. Lempert, 'Civil Juries and Complex Cases: Let's Not Rush to Judgment' (1981) 80 *Mich. L. Rev.* 68, 106–30.
[124] See, e.g., Joseph Sanders, 'From Science to Evidence: The Testimony on Causation in the Bendectin Cases' (1993) 46 *Stan. L. Rev.* 1, 60–85; id., 'Scientific Validity, Admissibility, and Mass Torts After *Daubert*' (1994) 78 *Minn. L. Rev.* 1387, 1435–40.
[125] See Ronald J. Allen and Joseph S. Miller, 'The Common Law Theory of Experts: Deference or Education?' (1993) 87 *Nw. U.L. Rev.* 1131; Edward J. Imwinkelried, 'The Next Step in Conceptualizing the Presentation of Expert Evidence as Education: The Case for Didactic Trial Procedures' (1997) 1 *Int. J. Ev. & Pr.* 128.
[126] See, generally, Scott Brewer, 'Scientific Testimony and Intellectual Due Process' (1998) 107 *Yale LJ* 1535.
[127] *Supra* n. 64, 487.

If the factors outlined really are hallmarks of good science, judges have been provided with considerable help in sorting the good science from the bad. Still, it may be that, even with the *Daubert* guidelines, judges are not well placed to decide whether the methodology on which expert evidence is based is sound.[128] Concerns such as these have prompted some commentators to defend *Frye* on the grounds that it, at least, can be applied by non-scientists.[129]

It is difficult to assess this criticism of *Daubert*. Certainly, it appears over-generalized: the case law reveals some sophisticated applications of the *Daubert* criteria to complex evidence.[130] It may also be possible to give judges a general grounding in scientific methodology with relatively little effort on their part, as some publications claim to do.[131] In any case, it is rather disingenuous to defend *Frye* on the grounds that it demands no knowledge of scientific methodology. After all, one will not usually find, in the scientific literature, lists of scientists who accept or reject various types of evidence.[132] Rather, if there is any relevant literature, it will consist of articles supporting or criticizing a technique. When assessing this literature, or the claims of a critical expert, a judge ideally needs some knowledge of scientific methodology in order to gauge the significance of the criticisms made.[133] The choice is not between easy *Frye* and difficult *Daubert*; it is between strict and lax scrutiny.

Admissibility Standards and the Nature of Science

In order to judge the soundness of an admissibility test for scientific evidence, one needs to know something about the nature of the science to which it will be applied. In *Daubert*, the Supreme Court even went so far as to dabble in the philosophy of science. In the section of the judgment outlining the indicia of good science, the court claimed that:

[128] See Paul S. Milich, 'Controversial Science in the Courtroom: *Daubert* and the Law's Hubris' (1994) 43 *Emory LJ* 913.

[129] See Brian Leiter, 'The Epistemology of Admissibility: Why Even Good Philosophy of Science Would not Make for Good Philosophy of Evidence' [1997] *BYUL Rev.* 803.

[130] See, e.g., *State v. Porter* 698 A. 2d 739 (1997). An English example is *Reay and Hope v. British Nuclear Fuels Plc* (1994) 5 Med. LR 1.

[131] See Federal Judicial Center, *supra* n. 79; Kenneth R. Foster and Peter W. Huber, *Judging Science: Scientific Knowledge and the Federal Courts* (Cambridge, MA: MIT Press, 1997). For the argument that judges do not need to become amateur scientists in order to apply *Daubert*, see David L. Faigman, *Legal Alchemy: The Use and Misuse of Science in Law* (New York: W. H. Freeman, 1999), 64, 197–201.

[132] For an exception, see Saul M. Kassin, Phoebe C. Ellsworth, and Vicki L. Smith, 'The "General Acceptance" of Psychological Research on Eyewitness Testimony: A Survey of the Experts' (1989) 44 *Am. Psychol.* 1089.

[133] See Samuel R. Gross, 'Substance and Form in Expert Testimony: What *Daubert* Didn't Say' in Kramer, *supra* n. 85, 245.

Ordinarily, a key question to be answered in determining whether a theory or technique is scientific knowledge that will assist the trier of fact will be whether it can be (and has been) tested. 'Scientific methodology today is based on generating hypotheses and testing them to see if they can be falsified; indeed, this methodology is what distinguishes science from other fields of human inquiry.' Green, at 645. See also C. Hempel, Philosophy of Natural Science 49 (1966) ('[T]he statements constituting a scientific explanation must be capable of empirical test'); K. Popper, Conjectures and Refutations: The Growth of Scientific Knowledge 37 (5th ed. 1989) ('[T]he criterion of the scientific status of a theory is its falsifiability, or refutability, or testability' (emphasis deleted)).[134]

The problems involved in using falsifiability as a criterion for demarcating science from non-science are legion. It is too demanding a criterion: most existential statements (for example, 'there are atoms', 'there is a missing link') are not obviously falsifiable,[135] and some disciplines commonly thought of as scientific might no longer qualify if the test were taken seriously.[136] Conversely, falsification is also too weak a criterion: the claims of astrologers, psychics, and water diviners are all falsifiable, yet few would want to call them scientific.[137] The fact that the theories are typically underdetermined by observational evidence also poses significant problems for falsificationism.[138] It is not surprising, then, that *Daubert* has been criticized for 'rest[ing] on a basic misunderstanding of the history and philosophy of science'.[139]

While the Supreme Court can be criticized for presuming that falsification can do the work of demarcating science from non-science, its critics can be criticized for failing to understand the work that *Daubert* is meant to do. As I read it, *Daubert* lays down standards for the admissibility of expert evidence. Although references to science occur in the judgment,

[134] *Supra* n. 64, 482–3, citing Michael D. Green, 'Expert Witnesses and Sufficiency of Evidence in Toxic Substances Litigation: The Legacy of Agent Orange and Bendectin Litigation' (1992) 86 *Nw. U.L. Rev.* 643.

[135] See Larry Laudan, 'The Demise of the Demarcation Problem' in *Beyond Positivism and Relativism: Theory, Method and Evidence* (Boulder: Westview Press, 1996), 218.

[136] See Alan Chalmers, *Science and Its Fabrication* (Milton Keynes: Open University Press, 1990), 18. Chalmers suggests that physics would not qualify. For similar criticism, see Philip Kitcher, *Abusing Science: The Case Against Creationism* (Cambridge, MA: MIT Press, 1982), 42–5.

[137] See Laudan, *supra* n. 135.

[138] See Robert Klee, *Introduction to the Philosophy of Science: Cutting Nature at its Seams* (New York: Oxford University Press, 1997), 72–3. While this claim is logically true (no theory, by itself, can entail an observation), it is in practice less problematic than it is sometimes made out to be. Faced with an observation that cannot be reconciled with a favoured theory, few scientists will go so far as to 'plead hallucination'. See Philip Kitcher, *The Advancement of Science: Science Without Legend, Objectivity Without Illusions* (New York: Oxford University Press, 1993), 247–56.

[139] Adina Schwartz, 'A "Dogma of Empiricism" Revisited: *Daubert v. Merrell Dow Pharmaceuticals, Inc.* and the Need to Resurrect the Philosophical Insight of *Frye v. United States*' (1997) 10 *Harv. J.L. & Tech.* 149, 152. For similar criticisms, see G. Edmond and D. Mercer, 'Recognising *Daubert*: What Judges Should Know About Falsificationism' (1997) 5 *Expert Evidence* 29; Ronald J. Allen, 'Expertise and the *Daubert* Decision' (1994) 84 *J. Crim. L. & Criminol.* 1157, 1169–73.

the word 'science' is only playing the role of a proxy for 'reliable', because what *Daubert* is really trying to do is lay down standards for deciding when evidence is reliable enough to be admitted. This does not let the Supreme Court entirely off the hook: as I have stated, the fact that a theory can be tested (e.g. astrology) is not really a good way of deciding whether it is reliable. Nor does the fact that a theory *has been* tested tell us whether it is reliable: the theory of phlogiston has (literally) been tested to death.[140] This suggests, then, that it would be better to read the first sentence in the passage quoted above as follows: 'Ordinarily, a key question to be answered in determining whether a theory or technique is scientific knowledge that will assist the trier of fact will be whether it has been tested, and, if so, whether the tests show that the theory is valid or the technique reliable.'

This has led, by a roundabout route, to an important point. I want to suggest that a requirement that expert evidence be tested (and, it goes without saying, that the results of the tests are favourable) should form a crucial part of an admissibility test for expert evidence in criminal cases. In the discussion of the merits of *Frye*, it emerged that the time-lag might play the valuable role of generating more information about the reliability of a technique, and that such information would fulfil an important epistemic end by enabling courts to make judgements about reliability with more confidence. But that would only tend to occur if the technique was tested during the time-lag; it is therefore testing, rather than the time-lag, that is doing the important work here. A 'testedness' requirement would fulfil this function of *Frye*, but more directly. In other important contexts, a requirement of testedness would perform far better than *Frye*. *Frye* looks for general acceptance in a scientific community. In most scientific communities, this would be a good means of assessing the validity of a theory, provided that the theory was of sufficient interest within the community.[141] *Frye* works poorly, however, when applied to one of its main constituencies: forensic science. Take the example of DNA profiling.[142] When first developed, it was of little interest outside the forensic science community and it was used in the courts before the theories underlying it were shown to be valid—at least, to the satisfaction of some scientists. General acceptance, therefore, was a poor means of determining the reliability of DNA profiling: only those using it were interested in it, and those using it presumed it to be reliable. Nevertheless, DNA profiling was exceptional in that, when scientists in the wider community became aware of the assumptions its proponents were making, there was a reasonably large pool of scientists with knowledge of the relevant areas—such as population genetics—who were able to subject

---

[140] See Kitcher, *supra* n. 138, 98–103.

[141] See ibid. ch. 8. Sometimes, however, science develops in such a way that controversial claims lose their significance for a scientific community. For an example, see Eliot Marshall, 'Disputed Results Now Just a Footnote' (1996) 273 *Science* 174.

[142] See, generally, Redmayne, *supra* n. 106, 1047–62.

it to close scrutiny. Where many other forensic science techniques are concerned, however, scientists outside the forensic science community are neither interested nor knowledgeable enough to scrutinize the techniques.[143] The claims of handwriting experts, forensic odontologists, and experts on hair and voice identification simply do not interest most scientists, and have been subjected to little empirical validation.[144] Yet within their own domains, these techniques are generally accepted. This is one of the principal failings of *Frye*, and is one of the reasons why it has not prevented dubious evidence from being admitted in United States courts.[145] A testedness requirement would, in theory, do a far better job of screening out unreliable evidence.

5. Justifying the Adoption of a Reliability-Based Admissibility Rule

The Logic of Exclusionary Rules

The discussion of United States law has given some idea of the type of rule that might be adopted in England to exclude unreliable scientific evidence. It has not, however, shown that English courts should adopt such a rule. To do that, the purposes of admissibility rules in criminal trials need to be examined. Such an examination, though, cannot be carried out in the abstract. It is not hard to imagine a trial process that made no use of admissibility rules, leaving all doubts about the reliability of evidence to the trier of fact. That, however, is not the approach taken by English courts. The analysis needs, therefore, to be situated within a general understanding of the purposes of admissibility rules in English law. This is no simple task, because the purposes of those rules are not clearly understood. This is due, I suspect, to the fact that most admissibility rules have multiple, overlapping purposes.[146] It will be easiest to examine the logic of admissibility rules by referring to two examples which, I shall argue, bear some similarity to rules excluding unreliable scientific evidence. These are the rules excluding unreliable confession evidence[147] and the rule excluding evidence used for hearsay purposes.

---

[143] See further Ch. 2 § 3.

[144] See Saks, *supra* n. 96. For a general attack on the unscientific nature of forensic science, see William C. Thompson, 'A Sociological Perspective on the Science of Forensic DNA Testing' (1997) 30 *UC Davis L. Rev.* 1113.

[145] See Saks, ibid.; Paul C. Giannelli, ' "Junk Science": The Criminal Cases' (1993) 84 *J. Crim. L. & Criminol.* 105.

[146] For a discussion in respect of one rule, see Christopher B. Mueller, 'Post-Modern Hearsay Reform: The Importance of Complexity' (1992) 76 *Minn. L. Rev.* 367.

[147] Principally section 76(2) of the Police and Criminal Evidence Act 1984. The test in section 76 is actually best described as a 'hypothetical unreliability' test, because a confession will be excluded if obtained 'in consequence of anything . . . which was likely . . . to render [it] unreliable . . . notwithstanding that it may be true'. In practice, however, it usually functions like a plain reliability test, and the thinking behind it is largely that unreliable confessions should not be admitted.

The English criminal justice system is committed to using lay people as fact-finders. In the Crown Court, this means trial by jury. Trial by jury has a number of significant characteristics. Juries are passive decision-makers: they have little control over the evidence presented to them.[148] The jury decision-making process is largely unconstrained; it is presumed, however, that jury verdicts are based on good reasoning. If there is evidence that the decision-making process was affected by factors likely to undermine rational decision-making,[149] or if the decision is plainly against the weight of evidence,[150] the jury's verdict will be quashed. A further point about jury decision-making is that it is decision-making under risk. That is, because the jury can never be completely sure about what happened, there will be an element of uncertainty in its verdict.

While the rules of evidence do little to control the jury's reasoning process—a jury is not usually told, for example, how to weigh evidence or to settle disputes between witnesses, this being left to common sense—the rules do regulate the way the jury deals with risk. The principal example is the law on the burden and standard of proof which holds that, subject to certain exceptions, the jury should not find the defendant guilty unless the prosecution has proved guilt beyond reasonable doubt. This rule ensures that the prosecution bears a greater risk of error than the defence: it is a risk allocation rule. Some admissibility rules can also be viewed as risk allocation rules. The rules excluding unreliable confession evidence apply almost exclusively to the prosecution:[151] they therefore protect defendants from the risk that a jury will believe a false confession to be true, and place on the prosecution the risk that the jury will not hear about a true confession. The discretion to exclude evidence thought to be more prejudicial than probative only applies to prosecution evidence.[152] It, too, can be seen as a risk allocation rule.

Not all admissibility rules can easily be viewed as risk allocation rules, however.[153] The rule against hearsay, for example, applies equally to

---

[148] See C. R. Callen, 'Inference From the Secondary Evidence of Ordinary Witnesses and Scientific Experts' in J. F. Nijboer and J. M. Reijntjes (eds), *Proceedings of the First World Conference on New Trends in Criminal Investigation and Evidence* (Lelystad: Koninklijke Vermande, 1997), 37. This is not to say that juries are passive in all respects: for example, they critically examine the evidence presented to them. See Diamond and Casper, *supra* n. 102, esp. 515–17.

[149] See, e.g., *R. v. Young* [1995] 2 Cr. App. R. 379. Cf. *R. v. Gough* [1993] 2 All ER 724; *Gregory v. United Kingdom* (1997) 25 EHRR 577; *Sander v. United Kingdom, The Times*, 9 May 2000. The scope for quashing such verdicts, however, is greatly reduced by the refusal of the courts to enquire into what happens in the jury room: see J. C. Smith, 'Is Ignorance Bliss? Could Jury Trial Survive Investigation?' (1998) 38 *Med. Sci. Law* 98.

[150] See Criminal Appeal Act 1968, s. 2. The Court of Appeal is, however, generally reluctant to use this power: see Rosemary Pattenden, *English Criminal Appeals 1844–1994* (Oxford: Clarendon Press, 1996), 129–53.

[151] But see *Myers v. DPP* [1997] 3 WLR 552.   [152] *R. v. Lobban, supra* n. 27.

[153] For an analysis of admissibility rules that interprets them all in terms of risk allocation, see Alex Stein, 'The Refoundation of Evidence Law' (1996) 9 *Can. J. L. & Juris.* 279.

prosecution and defence.[154] But if the rule does not allocate risk, what is its function? An obvious suggestion is that, because hearsay evidence is unreliable, it is excluded to prevent the fact-finder from returning a mistaken verdict. But before accepting that explanation, some careful analysis is called for, starting with the concept of unreliability itself. To this point, I have been using a concept of unreliability without explaining just what is meant by it. There is certainly nothing aberrant about this: most writing on evidence treats the concept of reliable and unreliable evidence as unproblematic. However, it is occasionally pointed out that 'reliable' has no clear meaning,[155] and sometimes it seems as though the term might collapse into other common evidentiary terms: the reliability of evidence, it might be thought, is just its probative value;[156] or, perhaps, unreliable evidence is actually irrelevant.[157] *Daubert* itself has been said to use the word in two different ways.[158] Despite these problems, I think the common use of the term does have a coherent, if unarticulated, meaning, which treats 'reliable' as a synonym of 'dependable' or 'trustworthy'. Nevertheless, we lack well-developed conceptual tools for talking about the reliability, or dependability, of evidence, so it is worth engaging in some theoretical groundwork that will provide a better grasp of these notions.

Likelihood ratios offer the best conceptual tool for thinking about the strength of evidence. To understand reliability it helps, following Goldman,[159] to introduce a distinction between two types of likelihood ratio: subjective and objective. Subjective likelihood ratios are composed of subjective probabilities, or likelihoods, while objective likelihood ratios contain objective ones. Subjective probabilities are those probabilities that a person will assign to terms such as $P(E|H)$ given her background information; within the Bayesian scheme there is nothing controversial about them. But the idea that there exist objective probabilities—such as a specific objective probability for $P(E|H)$—is. Under the Bayesian scheme, probability can be seen as a measure of uncertainty, and the idea that there exist 'true' or 'better' probabilities is arguably incoherent. 'Crucially', Brookfield asserts, 'a

---

[154] In theory, at least: see *R. v. Turner* (1975) 61 Cr. App. R. 67, 88. It is possible that, in practice, police and prosecutors have access to more hearsay evidence than does the defence, and that they are therefore hit more harshly by the rule. Then again, the statutory exceptions to the rule probably benefit the prosecution more than defendants. See, generally, Andrew L.-T. Choo, *Hearsay and Confrontation in Criminal Trials* (Oxford: Clarendon Press, 1996), 41, 143–62.

[155] See Bernard Robertson and G. A. Vignaux, *Interpreting Evidence: Evaluating Forensic Science in the Courtroom* (Chichester: John Wiley, 1995), 7–8.

[156] For an interpretation of this sort, in the context of hearsay evidence, see Richard D. Friedman, 'Thoughts From Across the Water on Hearsay and Confrontation' [1998] *Crim. LR* 697, 700.

[157] The House of Lords decision in *R. v. Blastland* [1986] AC 41 seems to me to come close to this definition.

[158] See Graham, *supra* n. 95, 336–8.

[159] Alvin I. Goldman, *Knowledge in a Social World* (Oxford: Clarendon Press, 1999), 115–23.

statement of probability is, by its nature, a statement of partial knowledge, so it is paradoxical to imply that in principle we cannot calculate the probability of an event without further empirical knowledge.'[160] If, for example, E is a piece of testimony from witness W, and H is the hypothesis that W is telling the truth, then if we had perfect knowledge of all the factors affecting $E|H$ we would (assuming determinism) know whether H was true, and would not waste our time talking about probabilities. Despite these problems, the concept of objective likelihoods is useful; it also has intuitive appeal, for, as Goldman observes, 'in testimony cases it looks as if jurors . . . work hard at trying to get *accurate* estimates of . . . probabilities, which seems to presume objective facts concerning such probabilities'.[161] If one is, understandably, cautious about the coherence of the idea of objective probabilities, the concept can be operationalized in terms of effectively used background information, the best available estimate, or a well-informed, unbiased observer[162]—anything, really, that gets across the idea that some probabilities are better than others.

The point of insisting on a distinction between objective and subjective likelihood ratios is that it allows a workable definition of reliability. Evidence is unreliable when the fact-finder's subjective likelihood ratio for the evidence departs from the objective likelihood ratio. This conceptualization suggests why courts might wish to exclude unreliable evidence. If the fact-finder's subjective likelihood ratio for a piece of evidence differs from its objective value, this may lead to too large or too small a revision in her estimate of the defendant's guilt.[163] This, however, is a rather unconvincing basis for the justification of reliability-based exclusionary rules. Under the definition of reliability just given, *all* evidence is presumptively unreliable, because it would take remarkable faith in fact-finders to believe that their subjective likelihood ratios will often match the objective ones. In any case, it is not obvious that the gap between objective and subjective likelihood ratios will be especially damaging to the fact-finding process. It may be that, so long as both objective and subjective likelihood ratios point in the same direction (i.e. that they are both greater than or less than one), the fact-finder will be led closer to an objective final probability of guilt than she would otherwise be.[164] After all, excluding evidence is a drastic option. The reason why the general rule is that we admit all relevant evidence is that

---

[160] John Brookfield, 'Law and Probabilities' (1992) 355 *Nature* 207, 207.

[161] *Supra* n. 159, 117 (original emphasis).

[162] See, generally, William A. Dembski, *The Design Inference: Eliminating Chance Through Small Probabilities* (Cambridge: Cambridge University Press, 1998), 67–88.

[163] Goldman, *supra* n. 159, 294. It is worthwhile to note another part of the theoretical background of Goldman's analysis: he offers a proof that, where subjective likelihoods match objective ones, Bayesian belief revision leads to an expected increase in truth possession (at 115–23). This, then, underlines the value in using objective likelihoods.

[164] Ibid. 295.

we believe that relevant evidence helps the fact-finder to ascertain the truth; the exclusion of evidence may thwart this end.

In spite of these problems, it may be possible to salvage a rationale for excluding unreliable evidence—one that fits our intuitive justifications—from the thrust of the analysis so far. If it looks as though the divergence between objective and subjective likelihood ratios for an item of evidence will be large, then there would be fairly good reasons for thinking that admitting the evidence would distort the fact-finding process. Confessions provide a good example. We suspect that a confession will, typically, receive a very powerful subjective likelihood ratio.[165] But where we have reason to believe that the objective likelihood ratio is much smaller—where, for example, the defendant who confessed is suggestible—we fear that admitting the evidence will unduly distort the fact-finding process. The problem with this sort of analysis, Goldman points out, is twofold. First, we usually do not have very good information about what either the subjective or objective likelihood ratios for various sorts of evidence are. Secondly, even if we have reasonable intuitions about the likelihood ratio values—as is the case with confessions—it would seem that a sensible approach would be to encourage the fact-finder to moderate her subjective likelihood ratio by warning her, for example, about the danger of false confessions. This strategy would avoid the information loss associated with exclusionary rules. Thus, Goldman concludes, 'the veritistic rationale for exclusion—the misestimation rationale—rests on shaky ground'.[166]

Goldman's analysis is enlightening, but it misses some important points. First of all, his model implies that decision-making will always be improved by access to relevant evidence. But 'people do not have zero costs of absorbing and analyzing evidence', Posner points out. They consequently 'encounter problems of overload'.[167] Additionally, evidence may sometimes engender cognitive illusions. 'Keeping evidence from the jury', therefore, 'is an alternative to what might otherwise be time-consuming and ineffectual efforts at enlarging and debiasing the jury's cognitive capacities.'[168] These are rather like the traditional concerns captured by the language of FRE 403, which some commentators—pre-*Daubert*—suggested provided a suitable basis for policing the admissibility of expert evidence.[169] A second point about

---

[165] For empirical evidence, see Saul M. Kassin and Katherine Neumann, 'On the Power of Confession Evidence: An Experimental Test of the Fundamental Difference Hypothesis' (1997) 21 *Law & Hum. Behav.* 469.

[166] *Supra* n. 159, 295.

[167] Richard A. Posner, 'An Economic Approach to the Law of Evidence' (1999) 51 *Stanford L. Rev.* 1477, 1523.

[168] Ibid.

[169] Rule 403 reads: 'Although relevant, evidence may be excluded if its probative value is substantially outweighed by the danger of unfair prejudice, confusion of the issues, or misleading the jury, or by considerations of undue delay, waste of time, or needless presentation of cumulative evidence.' Writers such as McCormick, *supra* n. 72, argued that this provided the best basis for exclusion of expert evidence. See also Margaret A. Berger, 'A Relevancy Approach to Novel Scientific Evidence' (1988) 26 *Jurimetrics J.* 245.

Goldman's analysis is that, by focusing on individual likelihood ratios, it sets up a rather hermetic model of evidence evaluation. As I observed above, pieces of evidence may—through the sort of cognitive illusion referred to by Posner—interact with one another.[170] Admitting expert evidence for a party might make the rest of her evidence look stronger; and obviously weak evidence admitted for a party may end up looking stronger when it is seen alongside the rest of her evidence.

There are, thirdly, more fundamental concerns about Goldman's model. By using likelihood ratios to conceptualize juror judgements, he is working on the assumption that jurors reason probabilistically. That is, that faced with, say, a disputed confession, they will temper their degree of belief in its worth to reflect their doubts about its validity. But jurors may, instead, reason categorically. Rather than using degrees of belief, they may rely on the simpler tripartite structure of believe/do not believe/withhold judgement. Doubts about the confession may affect the probability of their deciding to believe it, but not the evidentiary power they accord it once they have made the 'believe' decision. Goldman himself has argued that belief is sometimes best described as categorical;[171] one advantage of categorical belief, which makes it a plausible model of our doxastic attitudes, is that it makes it easier to keep track of a large number of interdependent pieces of evidence.[172] In certain respects, there is not all that much difference between the probability and categorical models. As I have described the latter, probability plays a role: there is a certain likelihood that a piece of evidence will be believed.[173] Perhaps Goldman's subjective likelihood ratios could be remodelled along these lines. But the assumption that jurors reason categorically—an assumption that the legal system seems to make[174]—does appear to have two

---

[170] See, generally, Sanders, *supra* n. 109, 130–41.

[171] Alvin I. Goldman, *Epistemology and Cognition* (Cambridge, MA: Harvard University Press, 1986), 324–43.

[172] See Gilbert Harman, 'Positive Versus Negative Undermining in Belief Revision' in Hilary Kornblith (ed.), *Naturalizing Epistemology*, 2nd edn (Cambridge, MA: MIT Press, 1994) (essay orig. 1986).

[173] This could be conceptualized as the 'resilience threshold' for belief in a piece of evidence. What may well play a role in overcoming this threshold is the extent to which other evidence available to the juror supports the hypothesis the evidence is being used to prove. This categorical model, then, reinforces the dangers posed by the non-hermetic nature of evidence evaluation—the second point made above.

[174] I cannot offer much more than intuition here. We tend to talk of 'fact-finding', not of assigning probabilities to pieces of evidence. The adversarial presentation of evidence involves advocates arguing that witnesses are telling the truth or are mistaken, not that they probably are: it is reasonable to assume that jury deliberations take a similar form. Of course, that this is how we talk does not necessarily mean that this is how we reason: see Richard E. Nisbett and Timothy DeCamp Wilson, 'Telling More Than We Can Know: Verbal Reports on Mental Processes' (1977) 84 *Psychol. Rev.* 231. However, Pennington and Hastie's 'story model', *supra* n. 120, does seem to involve something like categorical reasoning. Another bit of evidence comes from a study that found that mock jurors gave no weight at all to hearsay evidence, rather than discounting its weight on account of hearsay dangers, as they had been instructed to do: see Peter Miene, Roger C. Park, and Eugene Borgida, 'Juror Decision Making and the Evaluation of Hearsay Evidence' (1992) 76 *Minn. L. Rev.* 683, 693.

implications for the Goldman model. First, if fact-finder belief is categorical, the strategy of warning the fact-finder not to put too much weight on a piece of evidence looks to be ruled out. A second point follows from this: if the error to which unreliability speaks is believing evidence that should not be believed, the misestimation gap looks to be larger and therefore to have more drastic consequences for the fact-finding process. This suggests that courts should take particular caution when evidence is outcome-determinative (for example, a full confession or the disputed evidence in *Robb*), because then a decision to believe it delivers a mistaken verdict. This analysis, I think, fits our intuitions about the exclusion of some types of evidence. Where a confession has a reasonable probability of being false, a court will be reluctant to admit it, even if the possibility that the defendant confessed falsely can be emphasised during the trial. This is because, if the fact-finder decides to believe a false confession, the consequences will be dire.

What comes out of the analysis to this point is that reliability-based exclusionary rules can make good sense, especially where powerful evidence is involved. But the analysis so far is not the whole story; there are two further aspects of exclusionary rules that deserve attention. First of all, there is the modern elaboration of the best evidence principle, expounded by Nance.[175] The effect of many exclusionary rules, Nance suggests, should be understood, not in terms of their effect at the moment of application—say, a trial taking place today—but in terms of their long-term effects—effects on future trials. The exclusion of a piece of evidence may not make much sense in terms of today's trial, for it will deprive the jury of probative information. However, without a rule excluding, for example, hearsay, litigants will have little incentive to look for and present original sources of evidence as opposed to hearsay sources; they will also have more incentive to present fabricated hearsay.[176] In the long run, then, the hearsay rule may help to ensure that courts get the best evidence more often, even if it means that they forgo the best available evidence in individual cases. This might, therefore, lead to a long-term increase in verdict accuracy.

A second addition to the basic analysis of reliability-based exclusionary rules is suggested by Callen.[177] Drawing on Gricean semiotics, Callen argues that a court's decision to admit evidence may indicate to the jury that the evidence is sufficiently trustworthy to be relied upon. The idea is that the jury may think that it would not have been given the evidence if it was not reasonably reliable. While this theory may underestimate the extent to which jurors realize that litigants have an incentive to present dubious

---

[175] Dale A. Nance, 'The Best Evidence Principle' (1988) 73 *Iowa L. Rev.* 227.

[176] For the application of Nance's theory to hearsay, see Dale A. Nance, 'Commentary: A Response to Professor Damaška—Understanding Responses to Hearsay: An Extension of the Comparative Analysis' (1992) 76 *Minn. L. Rev.* 459.

[177] Craig R. Callen, 'Hearsay and Informal Reasoning' (1994) 47 *Vanderbilt L. Rev.* 43.

evidence, and also to distort the evidence they present as much as possible,[178] it offers an important insight into the logic of exclusionary rules by high-lighting the responsibility courts bear for the quality of evidence presented to juries. It may be that part of the underlying philosophy of exclusionary rules is an intuition that it is better for a jury to make a mistake because of evidence that it has not been presented with, than because of evidence that has been admitted and which the jury has relied on. It might be said that rules such as the hearsay rule perform a risk allocation function, but that here risk is not being shifted from one party to another, but from one locus of decision-making (the jury) to another (the courts). 'Rule-based decision-making', Schauer observes, 'relinquishes aspirations for complete optimization in order to guard against significant decision-maker error, and in doing so reflects the necessarily risk-averse aspect of rule-based decision-making.'[179] In the context of an exclusionary rule of evidence, there might be good reasons for preferring court (rule-based) error to jury error. Jury decision-making is largely uncontrolled. If we let unreliable evidence go to the jury, we can never be sure that the verdict was not a product of reliance on evidence that should not have been relied upon. But if we do not give the jury the evidence, we know that it cannot have caused the decision. To be sure, the verdict may still have been in error, and the error may have been avoided had the jury been given the unreliable evidence. But I suspect this second type of error is rather less salient to a court—it is quite difficult to talk of errors being caused by evidence not given—and that the strategy of keeping unreliable evidence from the jury may reflect common attitudes to risk.[180] More importantly, a preference for court error shows a degree of respect for the jury. It is often remarked that it is odd that we trust juries to make momentous decisions, but then display a large degree of distrust in them by shielding them from much relevant evidence.[181] But by doing so, it might be argued, we are shielding the jury from making difficult deci-sions about evidence it is not well placed to judge. This strategy may even improve the way the jury reasons about the rest of the evidence presented

---

[178] For expert evidence, at least, there is good evidence that jurors are aware of the implica-tions of the adversarial context. See the sources cited at n. 111 *supra*. But it seems plausible that awareness of adversarial bias is most likely to be engaged when prosecution and defence present conflicting expert evidence. When evidence is only led by, say, the prosecution, jurors are more likely to presume that evidence comes with the court's warrant.

[179] Frederick Schauer, *Playing by the Rules: A Philosophical Examination of Rule-Based Decision-Making in Law and in Life* (Oxford: Clarendon Press, 1991), 154–5.

[180] People tend to be more averse to risks they perceive they cannot control than to those they think they can: see Paul Slovic, 'Perception of Risk' (1987) 236 *Science* 280. Although the analogy is not perfect, I suspect risk aversions of this sort may play a part in explaining exclusionary rules. The analogy I have in mind is along these lines: I would feel worse if I gave X a gun and he shot someone (whom he might have shot anyway by getting a gun elsewhere) than if I refused to give him a gun and he was unable to save someone's life (which he might have been able to do had he had a gun).

[181] See, e.g., Mirjan R. Damaška, *Evidence Law Adrift* (New Haven: Yale University Press, 1997), 29.

to it. 'Jurors have no monetary incentives to weight evidence carefully,' Posner observes. 'By screening from them evidentiary materials that would make their job even more difficult and thus require them to exert greater uncompensated mental efforts without any compensation, the rules of evidence reduce jurors' costs and so improve their product.'[182]

These arguments, particularly those in the last paragraph, may not provide especially strong justifications for reliability-based exclusionary rules. But they do, I think, pick out many aspects of the philosophy underlying such rules. What emerges from this discussion is that exclusionary rules are rather subtler than they are sometimes taken to be. What should also be coming into focus is how an exclusionary rule for scientific evidence might be justified. I now turn directly to this task.

Justifying the Exclusion of Expert Evidence

Expert witnesses occupy a special position in court. They are allowed to testify on topics that lay witnesses would not be permitted to address.[183] Further, expert testimony will often be on a subject, such as identity, so central to the trial as to be outcome-determinative. *Vis-à-vis* the jury, experts are also placed in a special position, because most jurors will not be able to use their everyday knowledge to evaluate the expert's claims closely. It is reasonable to suppose that jurors will defer to the opinions of experts more than to the testimony of lay witnesses.[184] These features of expert evidence put an onus on the courts to make some inquiry into the reliability of the expert testimony.

The reason why experts are permitted to give evidence on issues that lay witnesses would not be permitted to address is that their judgements

---

[182] Posner, *supra* n. 167, 1523.

[183] This statement is rather vague, because it reflects the difficulty of pinning down just what it is that distinguishes lay from expert witnesses. Perhaps it is worth digressing here in an attempt to pinpoint it. The fact/opinion distinction cannot do the work. For one thing, the distinction is hazy (see John A. Andrews and Michael Hirst, *Criminal Evidence*, 3rd edn (London: Sweet & Maxwell, 1997), 727–30). Further, lay people are sometimes permitted to give opinion evidence (see ibid.) and much expert evidence falls on the fact side of the line. Another option is that the expert does not have to observe the facts of the case personally. But that will not do the work either—think of character witnesses. There would also be problems in defining the 'facts of the case': does the police officer who questions a suspect observe the facts of the case? What does distinguish the expert seems to be this: the police officer and the lay witness give evidence that tries to put the juror in their shoes, to see what they saw, hear what they heard, etc. They relate their sense data, plus some basic opinions, which the juror can be left to make sense of. The expert goes a step further, because she relies on more sophisticated interpretation of sense data. The bloodstain becomes a spray pattern; the two fingerprints match; the bars on the autoradiograph become a DNA profile. The rather banal conclusion, then, is that experts rely on specialized knowledge. Evidently, this will not always lead to a very sharp distinction between expert and lay witnesses. Plainly, too, this model will not work for all types of expert: the statistician called to challenge the statistical model used by the prosecution does not fit neatly into it in terms of interpreting sense data—but the core idea of specialized knowledge does still seem to be the distinguishing factor.

[184] See Lempert, *supra* n. 121.

are presumed to be trustworthy. This can be shown by comparing those situations where lay witnesses are permitted to give opinion evidence. Two examples are the opinion that a person was drunk,[185] and the opinion that a car was speeding.[186] These are topics on which lay people are presumed to be able to form sound opinions. The presumption of soundness makes sense of admitting evidence that a jury is likely to defer to. Deferring to the opinions of others, especially experts, is not particularly suspect; such epistemic deference is a common feature of our cognitive lives.[187] Nevertheless, when we take decisions of particular importance, we can be expected to take some steps to ensure that we are deferring to sound judgement. Given that the jury is a passive fact-finder, it seems that it falls to the court to screen expert testimony to ensure that jurors will not be put in the position of deferring to unsound opinions.

This much suggests that courts have a duty to make some inquiry into the soundness of expert evidence before it reaches the jury.[188] To this point, however, the analysis has rested on the rather naïve assumption that experts will not be scrutinized by the parties in court. If there are doubts about the reliability of expert testimony, it might be argued that the evidence should go to the jury, so long as its potential shortcomings have been drawn to the jury's attention. Drawing on parallels with hearsay and confession evidence, it becomes apparent that this strategy would not fit well with the general approach that English law takes to unreliable evidence.

One reason why hearsay evidence does not go to the jury is that, because the declarant cannot be cross-examined, it is thought that the jury is not in a good position to make a judgement about the probative value of the evidence. Expert evidence is different, because the expert can be cross-examined in front of the jury. Nevertheless, parallels remain. The jury will probably not gain as much from the cross-examination of an expert as it would from an ordinary witness, because ordinary credibility cues would be unlikely to tell the jury much about the reliability of the expert's evidence.[189] While skilful cross-examination and the presentation of opposing expert testimony can bring out the limitations of expert evidence, the jury may find it difficult to judge just how significant any criticisms are, in the same way that informing the jury about hearsay dangers may not

---

[185] *R. v. Davies* [1962] 3 All ER 97.   [186] *Swain* v. *Gillette* [1974] RTR 446.

[187] See Alvin I. Goldman, 'Epistemic Paternalism: Communication Control in Law and Society' in *Liaisons: Philosophy Meets the Cognitive and Social Sciences* (Cambridge, MA: MIT Press, 1992); Jerry A. Fodor, 'The Dogma that Didn't Bark (A Fragment of Naturalized Epistemology)' in Hilary Kornblith (ed.), *Naturalizing Epistemology*, 2nd edn (Cambridge, MA: MIT Press, 1994) (essay orig. 1991), 210–11. For a more general treatment, see C. A. J. Coady, *Testimony: A Philosophical Examination* (Oxford: Clarendon Press, 1992); cf. Elizabeth Fricker, 'Telling and Trusting: Reductionism and Anti-Reductionism in the Epistemology of Testimony' (1995) 104 *Mind* 393.

[188] The courts' responsibility to ensure the quality of expert testimony was recognized in *R. v. Inch* (1990) 91 Cr. App. R. 51, 54.

[189] See Stephen A. Salzburg, '*Frye* and Alternatives' (1983) 99 FRD 208, 211–12.

enable it to judge the impact of those dangers on a particular piece of hearsay evidence. I have already developed some parallels between expert and confession evidence in the previous section. Both can be outcome-determinative, and that points towards exclusion because the risk involved in admitting the evidence may be great. The reason for excluding evidence in such circumstances is captured by the familiar probative value/prejudicial effect discretion.

When expert evidence is viewed through the lens of the best evidence principle, the reasons for excluding it begin to look stronger than they are for excluding hearsay and unreliable confessions. When hearsay evidence is tendered, exclusion might be justified in terms of long-term incentives. Even so, a court might understandably be reluctant to exclude hearsay if it suspects that, on this occasion, the hearsay proponent could not have presented better evidence. In other words, the proponent may be a victim of circumstance rather than of her own poor preparation for trial. With confessions, the long-term effects of exclusion may be that police officers will become more careful about questioning suspects. However, given the exigencies of crime investigation, there are limits to what the police can do to improve the quality of confession evidence. The need to question suspects effectively and the difficulty of assessing their suggestibility combine to produce a form of evidence that will always have a degree of unreliability. In contrast, when expert evidence is excluded owing to reliability concerns, the proponent may be able to improve the quality of the evidence in the future. This is most obvious when the proponent is the state, which is in a good position to carry out further research on a technique or theory. Whether or not the research undertaken shows the evidence to have been valid, something valuable will have been achieved: an increased knowledge base on which to judge the probative value of the evidence when proffered in the future. Note, however, that this reasoning only applies with force to the state, which is a repeat player, and therefore has both the incentives and resources to carry out research on the expert evidence it uses. Although experts employed by the defence may be encouraged to test their theories in order to testify in court, they may simply not be prepared to, while defendants, as one-off litigants, will be genuine victims of circumstance unless there already exists better evidence that they could use to prove their point.

The arguments presented here cannot establish that every legal system should adopt a reliability-based exclusionary rule for expert evidence. What I suggest they do show, however, is that it is inconsistent for the English legal system to apply reliability-based exclusionary rules to hearsay and confession evidence, while not applying one to expert evidence. What now needs to be considered is the form the exclusionary rule should take.

It will be apparent from the earlier discussion that I think that *Daubert* is a better rule than the others found in United States jurisprudence. *Daubert* is not perfect—I quibbled above with the reference to falsifiability—

and much depends on how it is applied in practice. But it is clear that any rule in this area will be indeterminate. The advantage of *Daubert* is that it focuses on the key question of scientific validity, and, especially if the idea of 'testedness' is taken seriously, identifies important indicia of validity for forensic science techniques. The most pertinent criticism of the *Daubert* test is that it requires judges to decide issues about the validity of scientific evidence, issues that they may find difficult. This problem should not be under-estimated. Many English judges only sit on the bench part-time, and they might find it even harder than their American counterparts to develop a degree of scientific literacy. This, though, is not a knock-down criticism. One response is that, if the courts are going to rely on expert opinion testimony as a means of determining criminal liability, they have some responsibility to ensure that the testimony is reliable. The analysis in Chapter 2 suggests that expert testimony is being used increasingly in criminal litigation; the techniques used may also be becoming more complex. Consequently, one would only expect that judges will have to adapt to this trend by gaining the knowledge that would enable them to assess such evidence critically. A second response is that *Daubert* itself holds some of the solutions to the problem. If all judges were fully versed in scientific methodology, there would probably be little need for any explicit admissibility rule for scient-ific evidence. We could simply rely on the probative value/prejudicial effect discretion, leaving it to judges to gauge the degree of evidential support for the technique in question. The advantage of *Daubert* is that it identifies for judges some of the crucial factors. What is more, those factors can be applied flexibly. For example, one of the *Daubert* factors, general acceptance, could be used as an escape route for a judge flummoxed by the question whether a series of tests had shown a technique to be reliable. Though that solution—in effect, the application of *Frye*—would not be optimal, it would at least be preferable to the current *laissez-faire* attitude taken by English courts.

6. *ROBB* RECONSIDERED

In order to tease out and clarify some of the implications of my proposal it will be helpful to return to *Robb*,[190] the voice identification case considered at the beginning of this chapter. There, the Court of Appeal relied on the expert's being a well-credentialled phonetician in order to justify the trial court's decision to admit his testimony. How might a court applying some-thing like the *Daubert* test have decided the case?

The first point to note is that the burden of proof on the issue would have been clarified. Under *Daubert*, the prosecution would have had to prove,

---

[190] *Supra* n. 18.

on the balance of probabilities, that the technique passed the test.[191] The prosecution would have had to show that the evidence was based on sound scientific methodology, with reference to the criteria of testing, error rate, peer-review and publication, and general acceptance. It was admitted that the expert had 'conducted no experiments or tests on the accuracy of his conclusions'.[192] Is that a good reason for excluding the evidence? Consider the implications of using evidence that has not been tested. Neither judge, jury nor expert have any idea how accurate the expert's conclusions are. We do know that the expert is confident of his own abilities, but that tells us little, especially as overconfidence in one's own abilities is a well-known judgemental bias.[193] We also know that the expert is a phonetician with good credentials, but that only tells us that he is an expert on speech processes and, we might presume, the analysis of speech sounds. That does not mean that he is able to come to accurate conclusions on voice identification.[194] There would be two ways in which we might become more confident about his identification ability. The first would be to investigate the validity of the theory of voice identification which, presumably, involves presumptions about inter- and intra-personal variation in speech. If inter-personal variation is great, and if intra-personal variation is not great, then we would have some reason to be confident about the expert's ability to form a reliable opinion about the identity of the voices he compared.[195] The second way would be to test the expert by giving him a sample of voices from multiple sources, with some voices represented by more than one recording. If he succeeded in matching voices from the same source and distinguishing voices from different sources, we would have good reasons for being confident about his judgement. It would also be helpful to know how difficult the test was, which might be estimated by giving the same sample to non-experts; if they scored as well as the expert, his testimony would have little value. The virtue

---

[191] *Supra* n. 64, 480. I discuss the appropriate standard of proof for prosecution and defence below.

[192] *Supra* n. 18, 165.

[193] See, generally, Stuart Sutherland, *Irrationality: The Enemy Within* (London: Constable, 1992), 236–56. For evidence that scientists rate evidence that agrees with their theories more highly than other evidence, see Jonathan J. Koehler, 'The Influence of Prior Beliefs on Scientific Judgments of Evidence Quality' (1993) 56 *Organizational Behavior and Human Decision Processes* 28.

[194] One review of voice identification ability endorses the common sense assumption that '[a] practical knowledge of phonetics is . . . likely to improve speaker recognition', but notes that 'this has not been studied explicitly'. Richard Hammersley and J. Don Read, 'Voice Identification in Humans and Computers' in Siegfried Ludwig Sporer, Roy S. Malpass, and Guenter Koehnken (eds), *Psychological Issues in Eyewitness Identification* (Mahwah, NJ: Lawrence Erlbaum, 1996), 142. There are some reasons to be cautious of such assumptions. Studies of training in facial recognition have produced no good evidence that training improves identification ability, which implies that, for some recognition tasks, holistic assessment performs as well as atomistic assessment. See M. M. Woodhead, A. D. Baddeley, and D. C. Simmonds, 'On Training People to Recognize Faces' (1979) 22 *Ergonomics* 333.

[195] The evidence suggests that intra-personal variation can be as large as inter-personal variation. See Hammersley and Read, *supra* n. 194, 124.

of a test like this would be twofold. Not only would we start to have good reasons for deferring to the expert's judgement (if he performed well), but we would also gain some idea of the probative value of his evidence by looking at the number of false positives and false negatives from the test. In *Daubert*'s terms, we would have some idea of his error rate.

As it was, the jury in *Robb* had to reach a conclusion without such information. The expert had been cross-examined by the defence; this highlighted that he was not using a generally accepted voice identification technique. The court noted that, consequently, it would not have been surprising had the jury 'conclude[d] that they should receive his evidence with caution or that they should place little or no reliance on it'.[196] As has been stressed, it cannot be said, in the abstract, that this is a bad way of dealing with the problem. Even within the context of the English criminal trial, it fits with the way much evidence is treated. The testimony of lay witnesses frequently conflicts, but the jury is left to decide whom to believe, which is no easy task.[197] But leaving the question of the credibility of the expert's testimony in *Robb* to the jury does conflict with the approach English law takes to confession and hearsay evidence which, unlike lay testimony, the jury cannot be expected to assess effectively using ordinary credibility cues. To appreciate this point, think how odd it would sound were the Court of Appeal to say: 'given that the confession was not recorded, it would not be surprising had the jury concluded that they should place little or no reliance on it'.[198] The strategy in *Robb* fits poorly with the way in which the courts respond to unreliable evidence in parallel contexts.

To argue that the evidence in *Robb* should have been excluded is not to express a general scepticism about jury decision-making ability. The argument, rather, is that the jury has very little information with which to make an informed decision about the voice expert's evidence. If it does choose to rely on the evidence, this will be through deferring to the expert's authority on an issue there is no good reason to think the expert is an authority on. Yet, to draw on Callen's theory, the jury might be forgiven for thinking that, given that the evidence had been admitted, it did have a reasonable degree of reliability.

Despite all this, one might still be cautious about concluding that the evidence in *Robb* should have been excluded. Although the jury had to make a difficult decision, the evidence on which it had to base its judgement was not especially complex and the defence's criticisms of the expert evidence were easy to understand. This was not a case where the expert was using technical apparatus that might have lent an aura of precision to his evidence.

[196] *Supra* n. 18, 166.
[197] See, generally, George Fisher, 'The Jury's Rise as Lie Detector' (1997) 107 *Yale LJ* 575.
[198] Or, similarly, 'given that the declarant was not available for cross-examination, it would not be surprising had the jury concluded that they should place little or no reliance on the hearsay evidence.'

He was quite explicit that all he did was listen to the two recordings, which lends credence to the Court of Appeal's supposition that the jury was unlikely to place great weight on his evidence. This leads to an aspect of *Daubert*'s application to expert evidence not yet considered: whether it should be applied to 'non-scientific' or 'technical' expert evidence.

7. THE SCIENTIFIC/TECHNICAL DISTINCTION

The Supreme Court's decision in *Daubert* left a number of questions un-answered. Foremost among them was how the *Daubert* factors relate to the wording of rule 702 of the Federal Rules of Evidence, which refers to 'scientific, technical or other specialized knowledge'. In *Daubert*, the court developed the new admissibility test by emphasizing the words 'scientific . . . knowledge', a strategy that implies that different standards might apply to non-scientific expert evidence. If that were the case, there would need to be a credible way of drawing a distinction between scientific and non-scientific knowledge. There would then be the question of what admissibility standards should be applied to the latter. The Supreme Court has now addressed these questions. In *Kumho Tire Co., Ltd v. Carmichael*,[199] it held that the *Daubert* factors should be applied to all expert evidence, but that in all cases they should be applied flexibly.

An English case, *R. v. Browning*,[200] provides a nice example of the dif-ficulties in this area. In that case one question was whether the defendant, who drove a Renault 25, had crossed the Severn Bridge at a particular time. Video-recordings from cameras on the bridge were available, and during Browning's appeal there was some argument as to whether a Renault 25 could be seen in certain rather unclear images from the recordings. The experts who gave evidence on this matter included the president of the Renault Owner's Club and a Renault employee who had driven 23 different Renault 25s. Their Renault-identifying abilities had never been tested, much less subjected to peer-review or accorded a specific error rate. At face value, their expert testimony fails the *Daubert* test and should have been excluded. Yet that would be unwelcome. Such people have gained expertise through their experience and can give useful opinions to the courts. It is easy to think of more mainstream examples, too. Pathologists have considerable experience in diagnosing causes of death and interpret-ing wounds, but often refer to their skills as being more of an art, based on experience, than a science.[201] *United States* v. *Starzecpyzel*[202] provides

[199] 119 US 1167 (1999).
[200] [1995] Crim. LR 227. The comments that follow are based on a transcript from LEXIS.
[201] See Roger Smith, 'Forensic Pathology, Scientific Expertise and Criminal Law' in Roger Smith and Brian Wynne (eds), *Expert Evidence: Interpreting Science in the Law* (London: Routledge, 1989).
[202] 880 F. Supp. 1027 (1995).

another illustration. In that case the prosecution presented testimony from a handwriting expert to establish that a signature had been forged. On appeal it was ruled that the evidence failed the *Daubert* test. Nevertheless, the court held the evidence rightly admitted as technical or specialized knowledge that would be helpful to the jury. The decision in *Starzecpyzel* has drawn considerable criticism from some commentators who suggest that the court abused the *Daubert* standard and let in unreliable testimony.[203]

There are many reasons why rigorously tested expertise may not be available to a court in a particular area. It is just not very surprising that Renault identification has failed to attract the attention of the scientific community. The problem facing the court, however, was at least amenable to investigation through scientific methodology. Indeed, something along these lines did occur, because the experts obtained film of a Renault 25 taken from a similar distance to the car in the video film in order to compare its appearance. Some of the questions that pathologists must answer, however, cannot easily be studied in this manner. No one is going to volunteer to be the subject in an experiment to test whether a certain sort of stab wound was caused by a certain sort of blow with a certain sort of knife. Other issues, though, such as how quickly body temperature drops after death, can be studied more easily. At other times, phenomena that are amenable to testing may prove too complex for certain sorts of scientific theorizing. Handwriting and fingerprints, for example, are extremely variable. This creates problems of classification, making it difficult to develop statistical models in these disciplines.[204] Voice identification probably faces similar difficulties. Nevertheless, if a person claims to be able to identify common sources from different samples of handwriting, or from different fingerprints, that claim can be tested, as was seen in the discussion of *Robb*.

How, then, should the courts respond to these problems? It would certainly be helpful if a clear dividing line could be drawn between scientific and technical knowledge. Some courts and commentators have attempted to establish one. Renaker, for example, suggests that the concept of an 'explanative theory' is the key to the distinction:

[The] cases demonstrate that even when the expert states an opinion, courts find in effect that testimony characterized as specialized knowledge involves the application not of an explanative theory but of a 'helpful practical skill derived from . . . training and experience.' In contrast to this 'purely practical' expertise, an expert witness testifying to scientific knowledge provides theoretical expertise. The scientific

[203] See Risinger with Saks, *supra* n. 40.
[204] See David A. Stoney, 'What Made Us Ever Think We Could Individualize Using Statistics?' (1991) 31 *J. Forensic Sci. Soc.* 197; I. W. Evett, 'Interpretation: A Personal Odyssey' in C. G. G. Aitken and D. A. Stoney (eds), *The Use of Statistics in Forensic Science* (Chichester: Ellis Horwood, 1991), 20.

knowledge expert applies an explanative theory to draw a conclusion about facts in the case, to 'predict back' from an outcome to determine causation.[205]

Others, while not relying on the concept of an explanative theory, have made similar distinctions. Technical knowledge, it is suggested, is based on experience; it is subjective and not 'criticizable'.[206] There are valuable ideas here, but ultimately they fail to make a workable distinction. The Renault experts in *Browning* arguably relied upon an explanatory theory. They noted that, because Renault 25s have a wrap-around rear windscreen, one would expect a large rear window to be visible on the video-recording if the disputed vehicle was indeed a Renault 25. Another problem is that some identification techniques that may give extremely valuable and powerful evidence, and which one would wish to be subjected to rigorous standards, may rest on subjective judgement developed through experience, and may employ no explanatory theories.[207] This may well be the position with hand-writing and fingerprint identification. In fact, subjective evaluation and the use of tacit knowledge is probably a rather common feature of science.[208]

It is not surprising that efforts have been made to develop a test for distinguishing scientific from technical expertise. Although *Daubert* contains a lot of good sense, the judgment suggests that the key to regulating expert testimony rests on working out what makes science scientific. This, in turn, depends on finding a distinction between science and non-science, a quest that is, in all probability, doomed to failure.[209] What is more feasible, though, is indicating the criteria that make certain knowledge claims particularly reliable, a task *Daubert* performs rather well. Given all this, there

[205] Teresa S. Renaker, 'Evidentiary Legerdemain: Deciding When *Daubert* Should Apply to Social Science Evidence' (1996) 84 *Cal. L. Rev.* 1657, 1668 (footnotes omitted).

[206] See David E. Bernstein, ' "Non-Scientific" Experts: What Degree of Judicial Scrutiny Should They Face?', Washington Legal Foundation, Critical Legal Issues Working Paper Series No. 89 (1998). See also Edward J. Imwinkelried, 'The Next Step After *Daubert*: Developing a Similarly Epistemological Approach to Ensuring the Reliability of Nonscientific Expert Testimony' (1994) 15 *Cardozo L. Rev.* 2271.

[207] See I. W. Evett, 'Criminalistics: The Future of Expertise' (1993) 33 *J. Forensic Sci. Soc.* 173; id., 'Expert Evidence and Forensic Misinterpretations of the Nature of Exact Science' (1996) 36 *Science & Justice* 118. While underlining the importance of experience, Evett emphasizes that 'an expert only becomes such . . . when he has shown in repeated tests under controlled conditions that his judgment is up to the standards that a criminal justice system expects.' Ibid. (1993) 174.

[208] For example, Evett and Weir claim that ' "objective science" can exist only within the framework of subjective judgment'. Ian W. Evett and Bruce S. Weir, *Interpreting DNA Evidence: Statistical Genetics for Forensic Scientists* (Sunderland, MA: Sinauer, 1998), 217; see also Peter Donnelly and Richard D. Friedman, 'DNA Database Searches and the Legal Consumption of Scientific Evidence' (1999) 97 *Mich. L. Rev.* 931, 971–8. On the role of intuitive judgement in science, see, generally, H. M. Collins, *Changing Order: Replication and Induction in Scientific Practice* (Chicago: University of Chicago Press, 1992), esp. ch. 3; and for an application to forensic science, Harry Collins and Trevor Pinch, *The Golem at Large: What You Should Know About Technology* (Cambridge: Cambridge University Press, 1998), 152–3.

[209] See Laudan, *supra* n. 135; Kitcher, *supra* n. 138, 197–8.

is something to be said for the Supreme Court's decision in *Kumho Tire*, which at least did not attempt to draw a scientific/technical distinction. That judgment, however, may prove to have thrown the baby out with the bathwater because, in emphasizing the flexibility of the *Daubert* standards, it may have opened the door to more unreliable evidence.[210]

A better approach would be to establish the *Daubert* criteria, particularly that of testing, as the norm. The problem is then to come up with principles that could govern the admissibility of expert evidence that does not satisfy *Daubert*. There is nothing wrong with experience-based expertise, such as that used in *Browning*. But if this sort of expertise is admitted too readily, it may provide an escape route for unreliable evidence. Further, the incentives to test forensic science techniques, which I have argued are an important rationale for a testedness standard, will be diluted. It seems, therefore, that two principles should govern experience-based expertise. One is a best evidence principle. Faced with experience-based testimony, a court should ask whether there exists better evidence; in other words, evidence based on a technique that has been tested.[211] Because there is no scientific research on Renault 25 identification, we should be inclined to accept the best evidence there is. The court, though, should also ask a more difficult question: whether, given the importance of the evidence in litigation, the testing of the technique used or the abilities employed could be expected. The idea here is to create an incentive to test evidence if it is going to be a mainstay of criminal litigation. If vehicle identification from blurred video pictures were to become a common issue in criminal trials, we would expect the development of better evidence than the untested opinions of those familiar with various makes of car. Given that the research would not be particularly difficult to carry out, the courts should demand more reliable evidence.[212]

In addition to the best evidence principle, courts should also ask other questions about experience-based expert evidence, which are best summarized under the familiar test of whether evidence is more prejudicial than probative. This would involve examining the importance of the evidence in the case. Potentially outcome-determinative evidence should obviously be treated with caution. In *Browning*, the Renault identification was not the central issue in the trial: even if there had been clear evidence that the

---

[210] For an example of *Daubert*'s post-*Kumho* flexibility, see *United States* v. *Paul* 175 F. 3d 906 (1999); cf. *United States* v. *Rutherford* (2000) US Dist. LEXIS 4519.

[211] See, e.g., Nance's discussion of *People* v. *Park* 380 NE 2d 795 (1978), in which a sheriff's testimony that a substance smelt, felt, and looked like cannabis was held inadmissible. 'The weakness of the Sheriff's testimony', Nance observes, 'seems less important than the problems of missing evidence, in this case scientific evidence.' Dale A. Nance, 'Missing Evidence' (1991) 13 *Cardozo L. Rev.* 831, 847.

[212] See, to similar effect, David L. Faigman, 'The Evidentiary Status of Social Science Under *Daubert*: Is it "Scientific," "Technical," or "Other" Knowledge?' (1995) 1 *Psychol., Pub. Policy, & Law* 960, 974–5.

car was a Renault 25, it might not have been Browning's. Had the identification of the car been the fulcrum of the trial, however, there would be more reason to treat the evidence with caution. In such a situation it might even have been appropriate to arrange tests of the expert's Renault-identifying abilities. Another factor to be considered here is the likely impact of the evidence on the jury. One intuition underlying the application of laxer standards to experience-based expert testimony is that the jury will put less weight on it than it would on 'scientific' expert testimony. It is reasonable to presume that a jury would not have been unduly impressed by the Renault experts in *Browning*. Fingerprinting and handwriting identification, however, which are known to be vocational skills, almost certainly will have a far greater impact on the jury.[213] A further, related, factor that should be considered is the extent to which the experiential expert can explain the basis of her opinion to the jury. Recall that one of the *Browning* experts was able to explain one of the theories on which he relied: that the wrap-around rear window of a Renault 25 would produce a distinctive shape on the video. That is something that the jury can easily check for itself. In contrast, had the expert simply said, 'I've driven Renaults for twenty years, I know one when I see one', the jury is being asked simply to defer to his expertise. Claims such as that should be treated with caution. Experts will usually have insights into their perceptual abilities which they are able to articulate.[214] In addition, an appeal to experiential authority tends to render cross-examination by the opponent meaningless,[215] a factor to be weighed on the prejudicial side of the scales. Finally, there may be ways in which courts can limit the prejudicial effect of expert testimony. The experts in *Browning*, for example, could have been permitted to explain to the jury the identifying features of a Renault 25, but not to offer an opinion on whether the car in question actually was a Renault 25. Since the demise of the ultimate issue rule,[216] I suspect that limitations on the form of expert testimony have been under-used. Yet such limitations can be valuable.[217] In the Renault example, the prejudicial effect of the testimony would be limited; at the same time, the expert would be forced to articulate the basis on which any identification would be made.

The decision in *Starzecpyzel*[218] illustrates how these rather convoluted principles might be applied in practice. In that case, a handwriting

[213] See Strong, *supra* n. 17, 318–19.

[214] There may be exceptions. For example, a musician asked whether a particular note is a middle C could be expected to give a reliable answer, but perhaps not to explain the criteria she used in forming her judgement. The example is from Paul M. Churchland, 'Perceptual Plasticity and Theoretical Neutrality: A Reply to Jerry Fodor' in *A Neurocomputational Perspective: The Nature of Mind and the Structure of Science* (Cambridge, MA: MIT Press, 1989) (essay orig. 1988), 268–9. Churchland's analysis suggests that such perceptual fine-tuning may be fairly common. But there are ways of testing even such perceptual judgements: see Kitcher, *supra* n. 138, 226.

[215] See Bernstein, *supra* n. 206.   [216] See the discussion in Ch. 6, § 7.
[217] See Strong, *supra* n. 17, 369–79.   [218] *Supra* n. 90.

identification expert was allowed to opine that a particular signature had been forged. The court observed that handwriting identification expertise has a poor research record and that those studies which have been undertaken suggest that the evidence is not very reliable. For those reasons, the evidence failed the *Daubert* test. Nevertheless, the evidence was still admitted under the 'technical knowledge' limb of rule 702 because it was thought that the prejudicial effect of the testimony could be controlled through careful jury instructions, and because the expert was considered able to offer valuable information about the questioned signature. For example, the expert had examined 224 genuine examples of the signature and this had enabled him to form an opinion about the extent of natural variation in the subject's handwriting. As the court noted, this was not a task that the jury could feasibly undertake by itself. The expert would, it seems, have been able to explain the nature of such variation during examination-in-chief and cross-examination. It appears reasonable, therefore, to have admitted evidence on this topic.[219] What is more difficult to defend is the court's decision to have allowed the expert to express an opinion about the genuineness of the signature. Given that there was little evidence that handwriting experts can make such judgements reliably, it would have been preferable to exclude that opinion, rather than admitting it but instructing the jury to treat it with caution.[220]

Finally, consider, once more, the decision in *Robb*. The report gives few details of the form the expert's testimony took, but most of the factors point towards exclusion. First, there is better evidence available: computer-based voice recognition techniques that have a known error rate.[221] Secondly, testing is feasible but has not been carried out, even though, as the court noted, the expert had testified in 25 other trials and had been consulted in over 200 investigations. Thirdly, cross-examination would not have allowed the jury to come to an informed opinion about the value of the evidence, because its value rested on untested assumptions about the expert's perceptual abilities. A factor in favour of admissibility might have been that the expert was able to explain the features of the two speech samples on which he based his judgement.[222] Even so, one cannot draw a conclusion of identity from

---

[219] Cf. Faigman, *supra* n. 131, 77–8.

[220] The strategy of allowing expert testimony on the general characteristics of handwriting, but excluding an opinion on identity, has been adopted in *Rutherford*, *supra* n. 210; *United States* v. *Santillan* (1999) US Dist. LEXIS 21611; *United States* v. *Hines* 55 F. Supp. 2d 515 (2000). See also *United States* v. *Van Wyk* 83 F. Supp. 2d 515 (2000).

[221] See Hammersley and Read, *supra* n. 194.

[222] According to the report, the expert 'described the features of the human voice to which he paid attention. He testified that he had found no significant difference between the voices on the disputed tape and the voice on the control tape. Had he found differences he could no doubt have identified the differences. But if one concludes that A is indistinguishable from B, having identified the features one has considered, one can do no more.' *Supra* n. 18, 166. Which, of course, is specious: having compared the two coins in my pocket and found them indistinguishable, I do not conclude that they are the same coin.

similarity without knowing how common the features in question are, so such an explanation would have limited value. All this is to say that the decision to admit the evidence was mistaken.

8. Procedural Issues

The proposed adoption of a new exclusionary rule for expert evidence raises questions about the burden of proof the proponent of expert evidence should face in order to satisfy a court that her evidence should be admitted. These questions have received relatively little extended discussion in the United States.[223] In *Daubert*, the Supreme Court simply observed that rule 104 of the Federal Rules of Evidence would apply; that rule requires proof on the balance of probabilities by the proponent.[224] *Daubert*, however, was a civil case, and it might be thought that a higher standard of proof is appropriate in criminal litigation. Moreover, some American commentators have suggested that different burdens of proof should be applied to the prosecution and defence in criminal cases.[225]

In English law, when the admissibility of evidence is in issue, its proponent usually bears a burden of proof, being proof beyond reasonable doubt for the prosecution and proof on the balance of probabilities for the defence.[226] This appears to be an appropriate approach to expert evidence. There are potential problems, however. Most admissibility questions involve evidence, such as confessions and dying declarations, that is admitted on a one-off basis. The asymmetrical burdens of proof do not, therefore, produce visibly odd results. With scientific evidence, though, the possibility arises that the different burdens will create a situation where a form of expert evidence, such as testimony based on stylometry, would be admissible for the defence but not for the prosecution. Some commentators are critical of such asymmetrical results.[227] The appropriate response to this criticism is, I think, to ignore it. Asymmetrical admissibility would be the result of a well-established rule of evidence, and the fact that the results of varied admissibility standards would become visible is not a particularly good reason for changing the rule.

Another potential criticism is that some expert evidence, which is currently adduced by defendants, would become vulnerable to exclusion. Possible

---

[223] But see Margaret A. Berger, 'Procedural Paradigms for Applying the *Daubert* Test' (1994) 78 *Minn. L. Rev.* 1345.

[224] *Supra* n. 64, 480.

[225] See Giannelli, *supra* n. 69, 1245–50; Schwartz, *supra* n. 139, 229–35. See also Andrew Ligertwood, *Australian Evidence*, 3rd edn (Adelaide: Butterworths, 1998), 460.

[226] See Colin Tapper, *Cross and Tapper on Evidence*, 8th edn (London: Butterworths, 1995), 189–90.

[227] See Robertson and Vignaux, *supra* n. 155, 189–90; Alex Kozinski, 'Brave New World' (1997) 30 *UC Davis L. Rev.* 997, 1010.

examples are testimony on battered woman syndrome and testimony based on stylometry. It could be argued that the exclusion of such evidence is unacceptable, because defendants should have the right to present evidence that may satisfy a jury of their innocence.[228] The United States Supreme Court has taken some tentative steps in this direction. It has recognized that defendants have a right to present relevant evidence but that that right is restricted. Relevant defence evidence may be excluded by a rule of evidence so long as its effects are not 'arbitrary or disproportionate to the purposes they are designed to serve';[229] effects will be arbitrary or disproportionate when exclusion of evidence has 'infringed a weighty interest of the accused'.[230] In practice, these caveats, which allow the exclusion of unreliable evidence, rob the right of much of its force.[231] Such restrictions on the right to present exculpatory evidence do, however, seem to be justified. Earlier I suggested that evidence law carries a commitment to rational decision-making. This commitment justifies oversight of the quality of evidence presented to the jury. To be sure, excluding unreliable expert evidence proffered by defendants means that those defendants will bear a risk of error: perhaps the evidence really is reliable, or far more reliable than is thought. But defendants already bear a risk of error (the beyond reasonable doubt requirement does not require certainty), and nothing in the logic of evidence law prevents courts from increasing that risk by applying rules that have a sound purpose. Of course, we might wish to favour defendants by building some asymmetry into admissibility rules, and there will always be arguments about just how much asymmetry there should be. The asymmetrical standards of proof with which English law settles admissibility questions is an example of how admissibility rules favour defendants; they seem entirely appropriate as a means of regulating the admissibility of expert evidence.

9. Conclusion

This chapter has taken the form of a long and rather complex argument for the adoption of a reliability-based exclusionary rule for expert evidence in English law. It may therefore be helpful to review the ground covered. English law is not bereft of tools for the exclusion of unreliable scientific evidence. I have suggested, however, that current law is inadequate because no

---

[228] See Katherine Goldwasser, 'Vindicating the Right to Trial by Jury and the Requirement of Proof Beyond a Reasonable Doubt: A Critique of the Conventional Wisdom About Excluding Defense Evidence' (1998) 86 *Geo. LJ* 621. See also Roger Leng, 'Losing Sight of the Burden of Proof? A Challenge to Symmetrical Assumptions about Admissibility' in Ian Madelin (ed.), *Admissibility of Evidence in Criminal Trials* (Windsor: St George's House, 1999).
[229] *Rock* v. *Arkansas* 483 US 44, 56 (1987).
[230] *United States* v. *Scheffer* 523 US 303, 307–8 (1998).
[231] See Mike Redmayne, '*United States v Scheffer*: An English Perspective', <http://www.law.umich.edu/thayer/schef.htm> (posted May 1998).

burden of proof is explicitly placed on the proponent of scientific evidence, and because current rules give little guidance to judges on the factors to take into account when reviewing scientific evidence. I also made a case for a new rule from a different direction, by drawing on analogies with existing reliability-based exclusionary rules. The use of analogies with existing rules may, of course, mean that my argument is based on rather flimsy foundations. After all, the hearsay rule is the subject of considerable criticism.[232] There are, however, few absolutes in evidence law, and new rules need to be established with reference to existing ones. Nevertheless, even if the hearsay rule is abolished (which is unlikely), the reasons for excluding unreliable scientific evidence seem to me to be stronger than the reasons for excluding hearsay. We have less reason to believe in the ability of the jury to assess scientific evidence appropriately. We also have more reason to believe that the results of exclusion will be more beneficial in the long run. At least as regards the prosecution, exclusion should encourage the testing of techniques on which expert evidence is based.[233]

I have not offered an explicit formulation of the exclusionary rule that I am arguing for, nor do I intend to. Any such rule is probably best formulated in terms of guidelines. I have argued, though, that the rule should be based on the *Daubert* standards, excised of their demarcationist pretensions. I have also suggested a set of criteria that can be used to assess the admissibility of expert evidence that fails to satisfy the *Daubert* standard.

Considerable emphasis has been placed on the importance of testing the techniques on which expert evidence is based. That is because, as far as the sort of evidence used in criminal litigation is concerned, testing has a number of virtues. It is the only way we can gain reliable knowledge about the value and the limitations of expert evidence. Unless the information gained through testing is available, a jury will often be left in the position of having to defer blindly to an expert's claims. Most forensic science techniques can be tested without undue difficulty, and the state is in an ideal position to perform tests. Bearing that in mind, the justification for the proposed rule can be summed up in the words of Maurice J in *R. v. Lewis*:

whenever the Crown wishes to rely upon forensic evidence the prosecutor has a clear duty, not just to his client, the Crown, but to the trial judge and the jury to acquaint them, in ordinary language, . . . with those aspects of the expert's discipline and methods necessary to put them in a position to make some sort of evaluation of the opinions he expresses. Where the evidence is of a comparatively novel kind, the duty

---

[232] See Friedman, *supra* n. 156; John D. Jackson, 'Hearsay: The Sacred Cow that Won't Be Slaughtered?' (1998) 2 *Int. J. Ev. & Pr.* 166. I am not aware, however, of any criticism of the policy of excluding unreliable confession evidence (as opposed to the rules that have developed to implement that policy).

[233] Although it is difficult to trace causes in this area, exclusionary rules do seem to have had some effect on the amount of research conducted on various scientific techniques in the United States. See, generally, Saks, *supra* n. 96.

resting on the Crown is even higher: it should demonstrate its scientific reliability. It is not an answer to considerations that dictate these things be done to say the defence may draw it out on cross-examination; that is an abdication of the Crown's primary function in a criminal prosecution.[234]

To put the point more bluntly: if the state does not test the scientific evidence with which it seeks to convict defendants, it should forfeit the right to use it.

[234] (1987) 29 A. Crim. R. 267, 271.

6

The Admissibility of Expert Evidence: (2) The Rule in R. v. Turner

In the preceding chapter I suggested that the lack of development of a reliability-based exclusionary rule for expert evidence in English law might be due, in part, to the existence of other rules that can do the requisite work. In this chapter I examine one of those other rules in detail. I have chosen to refer to this area of law as the rule in *R. v. Turner*.[1] This may imply that *Turner* contains a single, easily stated rule. It will soon be seen that it does not. The chief merit of the rather vague title that I have chosen is that it avoids associating *Turner* with any specific principle.[2]

The rule in *Turner* is used principally to exclude the evidence of psychologists and psychiatrists,[3] typically on the grounds that their evidence cannot contribute anything of value to the jury's deliberations. Implicitly, then, the rule is concerned with issues central to the law of criminal evidence: issues about the role of the jury and about how admissibility rules are connected to the wider ends of criminal justice.

1. *R. v. Turner*: First Principles

Lord Justice Lawton's judgment in *R. v. Turner* contains some well-known passages, quoted with approval[4] and disapproval[5] in numerous cases and

---

[1] [1975] 1 QB 835.

[2] For example, Freckelton reformulates the *Turner* rule as the 'common knowledge rule'. This marginalizes important aspects of the case law. See Ian R. Freckelton, *The Trial of the Expert* (Melbourne: Oxford University Press, 1987), 38–54.

[3] For an exception, see Mark Stephens and Peter Hill, 'The Role and Impact of Journalism' in Clive Walker and Keir Starmer (eds), *Miscarriages of Justice: A Review of Justice in Error* (London: Blackstone Press, 1999), 273.

[4] See, for example, Lord Taylor, 'The Lund Lecture' (1995) 35 *Med. Sci. Law* 3, 7. Lord Taylor's admiration for the judgment in *Turner* can also be seen in his judicial pronouncements: see, e.g., *R. v. Masih* [1986] Crim. LR 395; *R. v. Heaton* [1993] Crim. LR 593.

[5] See, for example, Fiona E. Raitt, 'A New Criterion for the Admissibility of Scientific Evidence: The Metamorphosis of Helpfulness' in Helen Reece (ed.), *Law And Science: Current Legal Issues Volume 1* (Oxford: Oxford University Press, 1998), 156; Katherine O'Donovan, 'Law's Knowledge: The Judge, The Expert, The Battered Woman, and Her Syndrome' (1993) 20 *J. Law & Soc.* 427, 430.

articles. Quoting those passages out of context is unhelpful;[6] I therefore begin with a close analysis of the case that will not only place Lawton LJ's dicta in context, but also highlight some aspects of the evidence in *Turner* that seem to have gone unnoticed.

Terence Turner was charged with the murder of a girl whom he had repeatedly struck with a hammer while they were sitting in a car. At trial his defence was provocation, but this failed and he was convicted of murder. He appealed on the ground that the judge had wrongly excluded the evidence of a psychiatrist he had called. Turner testified at trial, and his account of events leading up to the killing was that the girl, whom he was deeply in love with, had confessed to him that, during his recent stay in prison, she had slept with other men and had become pregnant by one of them. On hearing this, Turner claimed, he picked up a hammer that was down by the side of his seat. 'It was never in my mind to do her any harm,' he said, 'I did not realize what I had in my hand.'[7] This account laid a plausible basis for the defence of provocation.[8] It was, however, challenged by the prosecution. Although the report does not specify the prosecution's theory of the case, this was presumably that the killing, rather than being a sudden response to revelations from the girl, had a degree of premeditation.

The relevance of the disputed psychiatric evidence needs to be assessed against this background. The psychiatrist's report concluded that Turner was not suffering from any mental illness; but it did contain the following observations:

[The defendant's] homicidal behaviour would appear to be understandable in terms of his relationship with [the victim] which . . . was such as to make him particularly vulnerable to be overwhelmed by anger if she confirmed the accusation that had been made about her. If his statements are true that he was taken completely by surprise by her confession he would appear to have killed her in an explosive release of blind rage. His personality structure is consistent with someone who could behave in this way.[9]

At trial, defence counsel suggested that the evidence was relevant (*a*) to help the jury to accept as credible the defendant's account of what happened, and (*b*) to tell them why he was provoked. On appeal it was suggested that the report was relevant because it helped to establish (*c*) lack of intent, (*d*) that the defendant was likely to be easily provoked, and (*e*) that his account of events was likely to be true. As to (*c*), Lawton LJ simply observed that

---

[6] See Paul Roberts, 'Will You Stand Up In Court? On the Admissibility of Psychiatric and Psychological Evidence' (1996) 7 *J. Forensic Psychiatry* 63.

[7] *Supra* n. 1, 838.

[8] Provocation is governed in part by the Homicide Act 1957, s. 3, but this is subject to substantial interpretation by the case law.

[9] Quoted in *supra* n. 1, 839.

'[i]ntent was not a live issue in this case'.[10] Ground (*b*) is ambiguous. It may refer to the reason why Turner supposedly lost his temper, i.e. because he was deeply in love; if so, it is relevant to what is referred to as the gravity of provocation. Alternatively, (*b*) might be another means of expressing (*d*), that is, it might be relevant to Turner's degree of self-control. On either interpretation, there is a problem: in 1975 provocation was governed by *Bedder* v. *DPP*,[11] under which the defendant's actions had to be compared to those of a reasonable person sharing none of his characteristics, so that neither (*b*) nor (*d*) appears to have been relevant to a material fact.[12] That conclusion, however, ignores another way in which (*d*) may have been relevant: call this argument *d'*. We have noted that the prosecution was denying Turner's version of the circumstances surrounding the killing. If Turner was easily provoked, then that arguably supports his account of events. The argument goes like this: people who are short-tempered are more likely to lose their temper at any particular point in time than people who are not short-tempered. Turner was short-tempered, therefore he may have lost his temper on the night in question. The evidence of irascibility is relevant because it takes Turner above the loss of temper base-rate. This argument is sound, but although *d'* establishes that the evidence is relevant, it does not suggest that the evidence would have any significant effect on the fact-finder's reasoning. Even if Turner is twice as likely as the ordinary person to lose his temper, that still does not make it very likely that he lost his temper on the night in question.[13] In fact, looking at the psychiatrist's statement as quoted

[10] Quoted in *supra* n. 1, 840. However, given that the prosecution had to prove intent beyond reasonable doubt, and that the defendant's account raised lack of intent, this conclusion is difficult to defend.

[11] [1954] 2 All ER 801. The law was later changed in *R. v. Camplin* [1978] AC 705.

[12] In fact, in so far as it was relevant to Turner's level of self-control, admitting the evidence would have been counter-productive for the defence because it would have suggested that his response was *not* that of a reasonable person.

[13] To express the point I am trying to make a little more technically: if the fact-finder approaches the case like a Bayesian, and starts from a low prior probability for loss of temper, then, although the irascibility evidence will double the odds on loss of temper, no one will be very impressed by that because the probability that Turner lost his temper will remain low. If there is other evidence of loss of temper, such as Turner's testimony, the irascibility evidence will no longer be very important: it will be swamped by other, more powerful evidence. It will have little impact because it would not be conditionally independent of that evidence. In short, under *d'* the evidence lacks pragmatic relevance.

If this remains obscure, the point can be put in a simpler way. Suppose you know that I am apt to lose my temper whenever I see litter being dropped. That will not make you believe that I lost my temper yesterday—unless you have some reason to believe that I saw litter dropped. If I tell you that 'yesterday I lost my temper because I saw litter dropped', that will not make you believe that I lost my temper much more than my saying simply 'yesterday I lost my temper'; the litter is playing a minor role, perhaps only adding plausible colour to the story. Things may be a little different in the *Turner* scenario: the psychiatrist gives evidence that Turner will lose his temper under certain conditions and you know independently that Turner may have been in those conditions, because he was spending time with his girlfriend (rather like your knowing that I live in an area where I am prone to see littering). Nevertheless, you are still dependent on Turner for part of the story (the girl's confession), and Turner's direct evidence about losing his temper is still likely to play the major role in the inferential chain.

in the judgment, this does not appear to have been quite the argument on which the evidence was tendered. Rather than suggesting that Turner is just short-tempered, the psychiatrist's conclusion appears to be that he is particularly susceptible to a certain form of provocation: a girlfriend's admission of infidelity. But note that Turner's being susceptible to such provocation does not make it more likely that the victim said anything that would have angered him; *that* must be established independently of Turner's susceptibility. This does, though, point to a third argument for the relevance of the evidence: argument *d''*. There is independent evidence—Turner's testimony —that the girl said something that may have riled him. It is possible that the jury will find this story plausible, but not believe that her confession led to Turner losing his temper. *d''* is an argument for the conditional relevance of the evidence: given that the girl confessed to sleeping with other men, evidence that Turner is short-tempered makes it more probable that he did lose his temper. Under *d''* the evidence is relevant, and it is—initially— plausible to believe that the jury will reason in such a way as to make it relevant. To put it a little more formally: if the psychiatrist testifies that Turner is twice as susceptible as the ordinary person, then, *if we believe that the girl did confess to him*, the psychiatrist's evidence has a likelihood ratio of two (hearing the evidence makes it seem twice as likely that Turner lost his temper than it seemed before). There is a complicating factor, however. A juror who is inclined to believe that part of Turner's account relating to the girl's confession may well be inclined to believe that part of his account relating to his loss of temper; if so, *d''* appears to lose its probative value because, if you believe that Turner lost his temper, learning that he is the sort of person likely to lose his temper will not really make you believe it more. As an argument for the relevance of the evidence, *d''* has a self-refuting tendency, because the condition precedent to relevance (believing Turner) erodes its probative value.

This leads, finally, to (*a*) and (*e*): the claims that the psychiatrist's evidence will help the jury to believe Turner's account. I have touched on ways in which the psychiatrist's evidence may support Turner's account in my analysis of *d'* and *d''*. There may be others. Perhaps the psychiatrist concluded that Turner was telling the truth. To the extent that he was a good judge of credibility, his opinion on Turner's evidence would have probative value. However, the passage from the psychiatrist's report quoted above suggests that he could add nothing on this issue beyond arguments *d'* and *d''*. He wrote: '[i]f his statements are true that he was taken completely by surprise by her confession he would appear to have killed her in an explosive release of blind rage.'[14] This is couched as a conditional probability, and one does not need to be an expert in probability theory to realize that, if Turner's statement is true, he did indeed kill in an explosion of blind rage,

---

[14] *Supra* n. 1, 839.

because that is just what Turner himself said. The psychiatrist's statement is tautologous. The statement that Turner's 'personality structure is consistent with someone who could behave in this way'[15] is barely more helpful. It may be relevant on an argument similar to d' and d'', but the statement highlights the problems of the phrase 'consistent with', which simply means 'not incompatible with'. The personality structure of all but the most phlegmatic members of the population may be consistent with the sort of attack Turner carried out, but that tells us little about their guilt. In this context, the fact of consistency only takes on substantial probative value when the characteristics of the majority of the population are known to be *inconsistent* with the behaviour in question.

In sum, so far as one can tell from the judgment of the Court of Appeal, the psychiatrist's proposed testimony was almost completely irrelevant to material issues at trial. Under d' it possesses probative value, but not in a way that is likely to affect the jury's reasoning. Under d'' it is relevant if the fact-finder is inclined to believe that the girl confessed, but not that Turner lost his temper.

I have subjected the evidence in *Turner* to this close analysis for a number of reasons. First, because once the extent to which the proposed psychiatric evidence lacked probative value is understood, the Court of Appeal's judgment is much easier to defend on the facts. In terms of its outcome, *Turner* was an easy case. This provides a second reason for the detailed analysis: it cautions against interpreting some of the dicta in *Turner* too widely. Thirdly, the relevance of testimony offered by psychiatrists and psychologists is not always obvious, and the sort of close analysis I have undertaken will frequently be necessary—though, as will be seen, it is often ignored. This leads to a fourth reason, which is that the basic structure of the arguments for the relevance of the *Turner* evidence will recur in other cases; this introduction to *Turner* is a preparation, therefore, for some of what is to come.

Having established a good understanding of the psychiatrist's proposed testimony, and of the ways in which it might have been relevant to issues at the trial, I want next to assess Lawton LJ's justifications for excluding the evidence. The starting point for his analysis is, as it should be, the relevance of the evidence. He states that the evidence was relevant because '[a] quick-tempered man will react more aggressively to an unpleasing situation than a placid one.'[16] This suggests that the argument for admissibility was d'', but Lawton LJ does not note the rather precarious nature of this argument. With the relevance of the evidence supposedly established, Lawton LJ asks whether the evidence was admissible on the rules governing opinion evidence:

[15] *Supra* n. 1, 839.   [16] Ibid. 841.

The foundation of these rules was laid by Lord Mansfield in *Folkes* v. *Chadd* (1782) 3 Doug. K.B. 157 and was well laid: the opinion of scientific men upon proven facts may be given by men of science within their own science. An expert's opinion is admissible to furnish the court with scientific information which is likely to be outside the experience and knowledge of a judge or jury. If on the proven facts a judge or jury can form their own conclusions without help, then the opinion of an expert is unnecessary. In such a case if it is given dressed up in scientific jargon it may make judgment more difficult. The fact that an expert witness has impressive scientific qualifications does not by that fact alone make his opinion on matters of human nature and behaviour within the limits of normality any more helpful than that of the jurors themselves; but there is a danger that they may think it does.[17]

Having laid down these principles of admissibility, Lawton LJ's next step is to apply them to the proffered psychiatric evidence. He identifies the core of the expert's evidence as being that Turner 'had had a deep emotional relationship with the girl which was likely to have caused an explosive release of blind rage when she confessed her wantonness to him'.[18] This, he concludes, is not admissible because it deals with a matter:

well within ordinary human experience. We all know that both men and women who are deeply in love can, and sometimes do, have outbursts of blind rage when discovering unexpected wantonness on the part of their loved ones; the wife taken in adultery is the classic example of the application of the defence of provocation. . . . Jurors do not need psychiatrists to tell them how ordinary folk who are not suffering from any mental illness are likely to react to the stresses and strains of life. It follows that the proposed evidence was not admissible to establish that the defendant was likely to have been provoked.[19]

At this point, a slight ambiguity in Lawton LJ's reasoning becomes apparent. I have assumed so far that he is addressing *d″*. *d″* is, however, essentially an argument for the relevance of the evidence to the credibility of Turner's account of what happened on the night in question. But Lawton LJ goes on to remark that:

The same reasoning applies to [the evidence's] suggested admissibility on the issue of credibility. The jury had to decide what reliance they could put upon the defendant's evidence. He had to be judged as someone who was not mentally disordered. This is what juries are empanelled to do. The law assumes they can perform their duties properly. The jury in this case did not need, and should not have been offered, the evidence of a psychiatrist to help them decide whether the defendant's evidence was truthful.[20]

There is, of course, a distinction between evidence going to the credibility of X's account and evidence going to the credibility of X: habitual liars

---

[17] Ibid.
[18] Ibid. As I hope has been made clear, it would be better to say '*if* she confessed her wantonness to him'.
[19] Ibid. 841–2.   [20] Ibid. 842.

can tell the truth, and evidence independent of their credibility can help to establish that they are telling the truth on a particular occasion. This may be the distinction that Lawton LJ is making when he separates evidence showing that Turner was 'likely to have been provoked' from evidence relevant to his credibility. If so, it is still rather puzzling, because although defence counsel argued that the psychiatrist's evidence was relevant to establish that Turner's account of events was likely to be true, nothing suggests that the psychiatrist would have gone further, and given evidence that was directly relevant to Turner's credibility, such as an assertion that he believed that Turner was telling the truth. Indeed, the psychiatrist was careful to point out that his conclusions were based *on the assumption that* Turner's statements were true. It is possible, then, that when Lawton LJ refers to evidence showing that Turner was likely to have been provoked, he is using 'provoked' as a term of art and has in mind argument *d*: that the evidence shows that Turner's reaction was that of a reasonable person. But, given the law on provocation in 1975, this does not look to be a legitimate argument.

What, then, is one to make of Lawton LJ's reasoning? As regards the disputed evidence, his conclusions are sound. Under argument *d*, jurors certainly do not need psychiatrists to describe the likely reactions of the defendant, because their task is to decide whether his reaction was that of a reasonable person. This task is normative rather than inferential, and no evidence from a psychiatrist can properly help them with it. Under argument *d'*, the evidence was, to all intents and purposes, irrelevant. That leaves argument *d''*. Even if it is granted that the evidence is relevant—after all, it is possible that the jury will believe that the girl confessed to Turner but not that he lost his temper—it is fair to say that the psychiatrist could add little that would help the jury. As Lawton LJ points out, the jury could be expected to know that an explosion of rage was a possible reaction to the girlfriend's revelation. All the psychiatrist could add was that Turner was in a category of people who might react in this manner. Again, the jury can be presumed to know that some people are more vulnerable to unwelcome revelations than others; the psychiatrist's opinion that Turner was in this category would have added little to their knowledge, and virtually nothing that could not have been brought out by cross-examining Turner himself.

Inherent in this reasoning is an assumption that relevance *per se* is not sufficient to establish the admissibility of expert evidence. In Lawton LJ's judgment, exclusion is justified by stressing the negative effects of admissibility. It is not immediately clear, however, just what dangers would be involved in admitting the psychiatrist's evidence. The most significant observation is that: '[t]he fact that an expert witness has impressive scientific qualifications does not by that fact alone make his opinion on matters of human nature and behaviour within the limits of normality any more helpful than that of the jurors themselves; but there is a danger that they may think it does.'[21] The danger seems to be, then, that the jury will disregard their own everyday knowledge of human behaviour when deciding what happened in the car, and rely solely on the psychiatrist's observations. In the context of *Turner*, though, it is not obvious that this is a significant danger. If the psychiatrist had testified that Turner was likely to have been provoked had the girl confessed, then (unless, perhaps, it treated the psychiatrist's evidence as creating a reasonable doubt) the jury would still have had to rely on other evidence—such as Turner's testimony—when deciding whether Turner actually had been provoked. On this analysis, the danger posed by the testimony would only be great if there were grounds for scepticism about the psychiatrist's ability to make judgements about Turner's likely behaviour. What is important in this situation, then, is the dubious basis of the expert's judgement rather than the fact that it coincides with an area of juror expertise.

There is another, and, I would suggest, more significant, way in which admitting the psychiatrist's evidence might have been dangerous. The evidence was not, at the time, relevant to the legal test of provocation. Perhaps there was a danger that the jury might have thought it was. The psychiatrist's opinion could have undermined the objective standard of the law of provocation through the jury's taking the defendant's emotional immaturity into account when considering whether his response to the girl's conduct was reasonable. Although one might argue that the jury should be trusted not to use the evidence inappropriately, the danger may not be insignificant. The jury is a passive fact-finder; lacking control over the presentation of evidence, it may presume that any evidence the court has allowed it to hear is relevant.[22] Where, as in *Turner*, it is difficult to work out just what a piece of evidence is relevant to, it is not inconceivable that the jury will connect the evidence with the issue it most obviously relates to: the defendant's ability to conform himself to the standard of self-control set by the criminal law. Even if the jury did not consciously apply the expert evidence to this standard, its consideration of the issue might have been affected by what may well have been an appeal to its emotions on defence counsel's part. I shall refer to this as the danger of 'normative distortion'.

I am all too aware that this analysis of the *Turner* rule is still bogged down in foundational issues, but one important point should now be emerging: an application of the rule may involve balancing the probative value of expert evidence against its potentially adverse effect on the jury's fact-finding and law-applying functions. Indeed, Roberts has argued that the rule is best understood in this manner and that, when it is, it will be seen that *Turner*

---

[21] *Supra* n. 1, 841.
[22] See, generally, Craig R. Callen, 'Hearsay and Informal Reasoning' (1994) 47 *Vanderbilt L. Rev.* 43.

involves the application of general evidentiary principles rather than a rule crafted specifically for application to expert evidence.[23] Important though this insight is, it is potentially troubling. In England the *Turner* rule has been applied almost exclusively to defence evidence, and the exclusion of relevant defence evidence is not a practice that is easy to justify. Although some common law jurisdictions possess a rule excluding evidence the probative value of which is outweighed by 'the danger of . . . confusion of the issues, or of misleading the jury, or of considerations of undue delay, waste of time or needless presentation of cumulative evidence'[24] (all excellent reasons for excluding the *Turner* evidence), English law may not recognize such a rule.[25] Although the discretion in *Sang*[26] excludes unduly prejudicial prosecution evidence, it was seen in the previous chapter that there is no explicit equivalent for defence evidence. If relevant defence evidence is excluded when it infringes no explicit exclusionary rule, this is likely to be due to its being classified as irrelevant under the pragmatic test of legal relevance which, on some accounts, already involves a consideration of the factors mentioned above.[27] Explicit balancing of the probative value of defence evidence against its tendency to waste time, or even to confuse the issues, would evidently be controversial. Nevertheless, when these factors are considered under the guise of legal relevance there may be a tendency for the careful evaluation of logical relevance and probative value to be ignored (as I have suggested it was in *Turner*). In the discussion to follow, I shall draw attention to the balancing aspect of the *Turner* rule. But, having regard to both the difficulty of justifying the sort of balancing that might be carried out and the fact that such an exercise fits poorly with the current rules regulating the admissibility of defence evidence in English law, I shall also stress that evidence which falls victim to the balancing process is nearly always, as in *Turner*, of minimal probative value, and that often the dangers of admitting it would be significant.

While understanding the *Turner* rule in terms of a balancing process connects it to general evidentiary strategies, there may be reasons why it is

---

[23] *Supra* n. 6.

[24] United States Federal Rule of Evidence 403. There are similar provisions in Australian law: see Evidence Act 1995 (Cth), s. 135.

[25] The lack of a clear rule in this area is well illustrated by the rather conflicting statements of the Law Commission in two recent reports. In *Evidence in Criminal Proceedings: Previous Misconduct of a Defendant*, Law Com. Con. Paper No. 141 (London: HMSO, 1996), paras 10.15, 10.81, the Commission identifies rules allowing the exclusion of evidence that may cause delay and confusion (citing *A.-G.* v. *Hitchcock* (1847) 1 Ex. 91 and *Hollingham* v. *Head* (1858) 4 CB (NS) 388), and suggests that they should be applied more widely. Yet in *Evidence in Criminal Proceedings: Hearsay and Related Topics*, Law Com. No. 245 (London: Stationery Office, 1997), paras 11.16–11.17, it reports on the (negative) views received on a proposal to *introduce* a rule allowing courts to exclude evidence for almost identical reasons.

[26] *R.* v. *Sang* [1980] AC 402.

[27] See, generally, Andrew L.-T. Choo, 'The Notion of Relevance and Defence Evidence' [1993] *Crim. LR* 114; Rosemary Pattenden, 'The Discretionary Exclusion of Relevant Evidence in English Civil Proceedings' (1997) 1 *Int. J. Ev. & Pr.* 361.

easier to justify the exclusion of expert evidence than other types of evidence. The fear that juries will be especially impressed by expert evidence is often trotted out (as it was in *Turner*: 'they may think it does'). But I would also suggest a less obvious reason. Suppose that, rather than calling a psychiatrist, Turner had called an eyewitness who had seen the killing take place from some distance away in bad light. The witness testifies that he thinks that Turner's version of events is true. Like the psychiatrist's evidence, this has rather low probative value. But Turner cannot be blamed for that: that is just the way events turned out. Admitting the eyewitness evidence will not encourage other defendants to go out looking for poor quality eyewitness evidence. But admitting the psychiatrist's evidence would tend to suggest that there was a precedent, that other defendants have the right to call psychiatrists to testify about the likelihood of their reacting in a certain manner. The point is a best evidence point:[28] the long-term effects of admitting the psychiatric evidence will be more pernicious than the long-term effects of admitting the eyewitness evidence.

By this point in the chapter, readers may be expecting some explanation of just what the 'rule in *R. v. Turner*' is. I hope that I have said enough about Lawton LJ's judgment to show that it is sufficiently opaque that it cannot be taken to establish any rule or rules. What the judgment does provide, though, is a number of themes that have been developed in other cases; these themes often provide good reasons for excluding expert evidence. It is to them that the discussion in this chapter will now turn. Beyond introducing some of these themes, I hope by now to have established a mode of analysis that is crucial to understanding the law in this area. That analysis requires paying attention to first principles by always asking: 'what, exactly, is the expert evidence relevant to, why is it relevant, and how much probative value does it have?'

2. NORMATIVE DISTORTION

In *Turner*, one reason for excluding the psychiatrist's evidence was that it had the potential to distort the law on provocation that the jury had to apply. The expert evidence of psychiatrists and psychologists frequently presents this danger, and this sometimes explains why such evidence is excluded. Occasionally, however, courts are not alert to just what is going on, and allow psychiatric and psychological evidence to alter substantive criminal law. In order fully to understand the problem of normative distortion, it will be helpful briefly to consider the legal foundations of criminal responsibility and the ways in which notions of responsibility employed by psychologists may differ from them.

---

[28] See, generally, Dale A. Nance, 'The Best Evidence Principle' (1988) 73 *Iowa L. Rev.* 227.

In conventional criminal law theory, responsibility attaches to an actor who engages in prohibited conduct with a particular mental state. D commits the crime of murder when he causes death (prohibited conduct) intentionally (mental state). Liability may not attach to D, however, if he has a valid defence: for instance, intentional killing is not unlawful if done for the purposes of self-defence. The point to stress is that an enquiry into why D acted, or why his mental state was formed, is generally not called for.[29] It may be that D decided to kill because he was drunk, because he was deranged, or because he was coerced, but by themselves such factors will not prevent an ascription of criminal liability to D. A drunken, deranged or coerced intent is, after all, still an intent. Yet it is the causes of human action that often concern psychologists. One example is the range of psychological research that suggests that human behaviour is often attributable to situational factors rather than to the character of the actor. The results of this research are largely consistent, as well as counter-intuitive, to the extent that the term 'fundamental attribution error' has been coined by psychologists to refer to the naïve tendency to attribute human action to character rather than to external causes.[30] This research is impressive and interesting—but that does not make it relevant to criminal responsibility. The claim that the external causation of D's actions should affect his criminal responsibility, Morse suggests, might be termed the 'fundamental psycholegal error'.[31] It is only in rare circumstances, as where a claim of duress or provocation can be made, that external causation affects responsibility. Even in these cases situational causation *per se* is insufficient to excuse the actor: there is usually a requirement that D acted as a reasonable person would have done. What is more, the external pressures to act which arise in these situations are well enough understood by folk psychology that expert evidence will rarely enlighten jurors.

Some examples will help to clarify these points. In *Turner*, defence counsel claimed that the psychiatrist's evidence would establish why Turner lost his self-control. Presuming that Turner did lose his self-control, the evidence may well have explained why he did; but this was not a material issue, just as establishing why Turner was sitting in the car with the girl in the first place was immaterial. A more graphic example is provided by *R. v. Kingston*.[32] Here, the defendant was charged with the indecent assault of a

[29] For a defence of this practice of excluding considerations of motive from criminal responsibility, see Antony Duff, 'Principle and Contradiction in the Criminal Law: Motives and Criminal Liability' in Antony Duff (ed.), *Philosophy and the Criminal Law: Principle and Critique* (Cambridge: Cambridge University Press, 1998).

[30] See R. Nisbett and L. Ross, *Human Inference: Strategies and Shortcomings of Social Judgment* (Englewood Cliffs: Prentice-Hall, 1980), 122–7. For a critical analysis of the psychological literature in this area, see Roger C. Park, 'Character at the Crossroads' (1998) 49 *Hastings LJ* 717, 728–38.

[31] Stephen J. Morse, 'The "Guilty Mind:" Mens Rea' in D. K. Kagehiro and W. S. Laufer (eds), *Handbook of Psychology and Law* (New York: Springer, 1992), 223.

[32] [1995] 2 AC 355.

minor. He argued that he would not have given in to his paedophiliac urges had his drink not been spiked by a third party who wanted to blackmail him. The House of Lords was prepared to concede that this was true, but, because Kingston had still intended to do what he did, this explanation of his actions was held to be of no relevance to his criminal responsibility.[33] Turning to a third example, in a critical review of the *Turner* case law, Mackay and Colman[34] refer to an attempt made to introduce psychological evidence in *R. v. Neeson*.[35] The events forming the basis of the trial had taken place when a car driven by two British soldiers had driven into a crowd attending the funeral of a man who had been killed at an earlier IRA funeral. The crowd had attacked the car, and assaulted and killed the soldiers. The defendants in *Neeson* had been charged with offences such as causing grievous bodily harm, false imprisonment, criminal damage, and affray. The expert evidence would have drawn attention to situational factors explaining the apparently irrational group behaviour witnessed during the attack.[36] The trial judge excluded the evidence—rightly, it would seem. The question for the court was not whether the average person caught up in the crowd would have acted as the defendants did, but whether the defendants had the requisite *mens rea* for the offences with which they were charged.[37] Even the most extreme compulsion fails to negate *mens rea*: the bank cashier ordered by the gunman to hand over the bank's money still intends to hand it over. Only if the group behaviour amounted to duress (which, in English law, requires a threat of death or serious bodily harm) would it excuse the intentional criminal action (which explains why the bank cashier would not be guilty of aiding and abetting the robbery). The psychological evidence in *Neeson*, then, appears to have been irrelevant.

The basic point here is that a careful analysis of the law will sometimes reveal that psychological evidence has no bearing on criminal responsibility. Furthermore, if an indulgent judge admits the evidence, there is a risk of confusing the jury in its law-applying task. Once this is understood, the decisions in a number of the English cases applying the *Turner* rule are easy to justify. Sometimes the fact that expert evidence is excluded because it is

---

[33] The evidence would have been relevant to establish his degree of culpability, but that was an issue for the judge at the sentencing stage.

[34] R. D. Mackay and Andrew M. Colman, 'Excluding Expert Evidence: A Tale of Ordinary Folk and Common Experience' [1991] *Crim. LR* 800, 805.

[35] Unreported, Belfast Crown Court 1990, discussed in ibid. 806.

[36] The defendants' behaviour was said to have lacked the 'deliberation, reflection and self-monitoring associated with normal behaviour'; ibid.

[37] See, generally, Note, 'Feasibility and Admissibility of Mob Mentality Defenses' (1995) 108 *Harv. L. Rev.* 1111. *Neeson* was tried in a Diplock court, i.e. by a judge sitting without a jury. Perhaps that counts in favour of admissibility. The principle remains, though, that the evidence was not relevant to the fact-finding stage of the trial. In jurisdictions where there is a tendency to mix guilt-determination and sentencing considerations, there is a better argument for admissibility. This may explain the decisions recounted in Andrew M. Colman, 'Crowd Psychology in South African Murder Trials' (1991) 46 *Am. Psychol.* 1071.

irrelevant is obvious, as in *Coles*,[38] where the objective test of recklessness plainly meant that evidence of the defendant's inability to appreciate risks was irrelevant. At other times, however, judges have failed to draw attention to the fact that the primary basis for exclusion is irrelevance. Instead, they have relied on comments about helpfulness and normality, giving the impression that the courts are unduly dismissive of psychiatric and psychological evidence. Thus the judge in *Neeson* held that the psychological evidence dealt with matters 'which are part of the sum of human experience and knowledge and are readily recognisable by ordinary people',[39] an assertion that is difficult to defend. English case law provides several other examples. In *R v. Roberts*,[40] Watkins LJ ruled that expert evidence was inadmissible on the deaf defendant's response to provocation, opining that:

The jury . . . must have been all too painfully aware of the appellant's handicaps and the effect they had or were likely to have on his mental state in stressful circumstances. No amount of medical evidence could, in our view, have served to further enlighten them as to that.[41]

This statement goes too far. The psychiatrist had experience of the behaviour of the prelingually deaf, including their tendency to irrational explosions of anger, facts which one would presume were not known to the jury. It would have been far better to have ruled that, given that defence counsel seemed to be arguing that the expert evidence was admissible on the issue of the defendant's tendency to lose his self-control, it was simply irrelevant, because the jury's task was to measure the defendant's behaviour against that of a reasonable person with normal levels of self-control.[42] In *Strudwick and Merry*[43] the second defendant had attempted to call the evidence of a psychologist and a psychiatrist at her trial for child cruelty.[44] The expert evidence would have been to the effect that Merry was psychologically damaged owing to her own abuse as a child, and that this might explain her failure to protect her daughter from Strudwick's abuse. The Court of Appeal, citing *Turner*, held that there 'was nothing in the case which a jury would be unable to deal with unaided by the experts'.[45] A better basis for the decision would have been that, given that the *mens rea* of the offence required only that Merry be aware of or not care about her child's need for medical aid,[46] the precise reason why she was indifferent to her children did not matter.

---

[38] [1995] 1 Cr. App. R. 157.   [39] Quoted in Mackay and Colman, *supra* n. 34, 806.
[40] [1990] Crim. LR 122.   [41] *R. v. Roberts*, LEXIS transcript.
[42] That seems to have been the law at the time of the trial. However, in later cases the Court of Appeal has departed from strict objectivism in provocation: see *R. v. Smith* [1999] 1 Cr. App. R. 256; *R. v. Campbell* [1997] 1 Cr. App. R. 199.
[43] (1994) 99 Cr. App. R. 326.
[44] Contrary to section 1(1) of the Children and Young Persons Act 1933.
[45] *Supra* n. 43, 332.   [46] *R. v. Sheppard* [1981] AC 394.

In *Roberts* and *Strudwick* the failure of the courts carefully to analyse the relevance of the expert evidence had no effect on case outcome: the evidence was properly excluded, and the precise reason for exclusion is, perhaps, none too important. Other cases, however, suggest that insufficient attention to the relevance of expert evidence can be dangerous, because normative distortion may lead to a *de facto* change in the law. This can be illustrated by examining the effect that evidence of battered woman syndrome (BWS) has had on the law governing self-defence. The Canadian Supreme Court's decision in *R. v. Lavallee*[47] serves as an example. Although the court in *Lavallee* has been criticized for failing to scrutinize the scientific credentials of BWS and for admitting expert evidence based largely on hearsay (issues I shall examine later), those aspects of its decision which address the law of self-defence, and the relevance of BWS to it, have generally been praised.[48] However, a close reading of the decision reveals that here, too, the Supreme Court went astray.

Lavallee shot her partner Rush in the back as he was walking away from her. The background to the killing shows that she had a plausible claim of self-defence: Rush had used violence against her on a number of occasions. On the night of the killing there had been a party at their house. Towards the end of the evening he had hit her and threatened to beat her further when their guests left. Section 34 of the Canadian Criminal Code establishes self-defence as a defence to a killing performed to repel an assault if D kills 'under reasonable apprehension of death or grievous bodily harm' and if D 'believes on reasonable and probable grounds that he cannot otherwise preserve himself from death or grievous bodily harm'. To show that she met those requirements, a psychiatrist gave evidence about the effects of BWS on Lavallee. Some of this evidence related to the cycle of violence that is said to characterize the battering relationship; this was used to indicate that Lavallee met the first limb of section 34. Assuming the validity of the BWS theory of battering relationships, this was probably unobjectionable.[49] The evidence suggested that Lavallee had experienced cycles of violence, contrition, and tension-building followed by further violence, and that the night of the killing had been preceded by a tension-building phase. She could therefore read the situation as one in which Rush would shortly inflict grievous harm upon her. It is in linking BWS to the second limb of section 34, however, that normative distortion becomes apparent. The psychiatrist used the BWS notion of 'learned helplessness' to suggest that Lavallee believed that she 'could not otherwise preserve herself'—by leaving the house, for example.

[47] (1990) 55 CCC (3d) 97.

[48] See Paul Roberts, 'Expert Evidence in Canadian Criminal Proceedings: More Lessons from North America' in Reece, *supra* n. 5, 195; Aileen McColgan, 'In Defence of Battered Women who Kill' (1993) 13 *Ox. J. Leg. Stud.* 508.

[49] One might, however, question whether expert evidence was needed to make the point. The psychiatrist was describing a basic inductive inference from past to future violence, a process with which jurors could be expected to be familiar.

When it came to why Lavallee did not try to leave when she realized that her life would be in danger later in the evening, the Supreme Court quoted the psychiatrist's observations at trial:

Well, I think this is a reflection of what I've been talking about, this ongoing psychological process, her own psychology and the relationship, that she felt trapped. There was no out for her, this learned helplessness, if you will, the fact that she felt paralyzed, she felt tyrannized. She felt, although there were obviously not steel fences around, keeping her in, there were steel fences in her mind which created for her an incredible barrier psychologically that prevented her from moving out.[50]

The Supreme Court held that evidence of this sort was properly admitted to 'assist the jury in assessing the reasonableness of [Lavallee's] belief that killing her batterer was the only way to save her life'.[51] The emphasis in the passage just quoted, however, is on Lavallee's *distorted* perceptions, and it is difficult to understand how distorted perceptions can be reasonable. One might respond that, if Lavallee's distorted perceptions had been caused by the battering relationship, they were reasonable in the sense that she was not at fault for having them. Explaining the aetiology of her belief does not, however, render it objectively reasonable, any more than a Vietnam veteran's wartime experiences render objectively reasonable his belief that his local Vietnamese shopkeeper is a threat to his life.[52] The beliefs of both may be understandable, but they are pathological and do not qualify the actor for self-defence under Canadian law.[53] Moreover, the distinction between reasonable and unreasonable beliefs drawn by Canadian law is important, because it reflects a sound distinction between justification and excuse. Those who believe that their lives are under threat owing to a belief which, given the information available to them, is reasonable, have a justification for killing. Those who kill after forming unreasonable beliefs may only claim excuse.[54] If this distinction is ignored, then *any* delusional belief would qualify the actor for self-defence.[55]

I shall return to BWS evidence later, analysing two of the English cases in which it has been held to be relevant. But now I turn to another of the themes in the *Turner* case law.

---

[50] *Supra* n. 47, 124.   [51] Ibid. 126.

[52] See *State* v. *Cocuzza* (1981), discussed in James Q. Wilson, *Moral Judgment* (New York: Basic Books, 1997), 34. On defences used by Vietnam veterans, see also David McCord, 'Syndromes, Profiles and Other Mental Exotica: A New Approach to the Admissibility of Nontraditional Psychological Evidence in Criminal Cases' (1987) 66 *Oregon L. Rev.* 19, 64–6.

[53] Note that in jurisdictions where the belief that triggers self-defence need not be reasonable, this objection does not hold: see the discussion of BWS in *R.* v. *Oakes* [1995] 2 NZLR 673, 676.

[54] On this distinction, see Robert F. Schopp, *Justification Defenses and Just Convictions* (Cambridge: Cambridge University Press, 1998), 120–34. Cf. B. Sharon Byrd, 'Putative Self-Defense and Rules of Imputation in Defense of the Battered Woman' in Leo Katz, Michael S. Moore, and Stephen J. Morse (eds), *Foundations of Criminal Law* (New York: Oxford University Press, 1999) (essay orig. 1994).

[55] Subject to the prosecution's ability to prove insanity beyond reasonable doubt.

3. DISPROVING MENS REA

In the preceding section I argued that some of the psychological and psychiatric evidence offered to the courts is simply irrelevant, and that courts would do well to exclude it on this ground. That expert evidence is being offered at all on the sorts of issues just discussed implies that some lawyers and experts fail to grasp the basic fact that psychological compulsion does not affect *mens rea*. This does not mean, though, that expert evidence can never be relevant to *mens rea*; one finds occasional cases where expert evidence is legitimately offered on the abilities of defendants to form intentions or to foresee consequences. An example is *Toner*,[56] where the defendant was charged with the attempted murder of his wife and with wounding his son with intent to cause grievous bodily harm. Shortly before the attacks, Toner had supposedly broken a forty-one-day fast, and he wished to call medical evidence to show that this might have caused a hypoglycaemic trance. The trial judge had excluded this evidence on the ground that it did not provide a sufficient evidential basis for a defence of automatism; consequently, counsel had not been able to pursue with the doctor the possibility that the defendant had lacked *mens rea* (intent) for the crimes. The Court of Appeal held that the defence should have had the opportunity of exploring the effect of hypoglycaemia on Toner's intentions at the time. Given that the prosecution bore the burden of proving the defendant's *mens rea*, this was a sensible conclusion, even though the court admitted that the medical evidence provided only the most tenuous basis for inferring lack of intent.

In other cases where, like *Toner*, diminished responsibility or insanity is not in issue, attempts to use psychiatric evidence to disprove intent have been thwarted at the admissibility stage. In *Chard*,[57] psychiatric evidence on the intentions of a person not suffering from diminished responsibility was held inadmissible. In its emphasis on jury competence with respect to the mental states of normal people, Roskill LJ's judgment prefigures *Turner*:

one purpose of jury trials is to bring into the jury box a body of men and women who are able to judge ordinary day-to-day questions by their own standards, that is, the standards in the eyes of the law of theoretically ordinary reasonable men and women. That is something which they are well able by their ordinary experience to judge for themselves. Where the matters in issue go outside that experience and they are invited to deal with someone supposedly abnormal, for example, supposedly suffering from insanity or diminished responsibility, then plainly in such a case they are entitled to the benefit of expert evidence. But where, as in the present case, they are dealing with someone who by concession on the medical evidence was entirely normal, it seems to this Court abundantly plain, on first principles of the admissibility of expert evidence, that it is not permissible to call a witness, whatever his personal experience, merely to tell the jury how he thinks an accused man's mind

---

[56] (1991) 93 Cr. App. R. 382.   [57] (1971) 56 Cr. App. R. 268.

—assumedly a normal mind—operated at the time of the alleged crime with reference to the crucial question of what that man's intention was. As I have already said, this applicant was by concession normal in the eyes of the law.[58]

Evidence on the intentions of a defendant who was not mentally ill was also excluded in *Reynolds*.[59] In *Coles*,[60] although the principal reason for exclusion was that the evidence was irrelevant, the court also held that, '[u]nless some factor of the mental health or psychiatric state of the defendant is raised',[61] expert evidence on the defendant's capacity for foresight was inadmissible. In *Masih*[62] the defendant was charged with rape, a crime requiring proof of the defendant's knowledge of, or recklessness as to, the victim's lack of consent. Despite Masih's low IQ, counsel was not permitted to call psychiatric evidence on his ability to appreciate the victim's lack of consent.

These decisions are harder to defend than those discussed in the previous section. The evidence is clearly relevant to a material fact (*mens rea*) that the prosecution bears the burden of proving. Might there still be a danger of normative distortion? These are not cases where the jury may think that the defendant ought to be excused owing to situational pressures: the cases just involve defendants who, for various reasons, may not have formed the requisite mental state. Whether *mens rea* exists is a factual, not a normative, question,[63] and the evidence is unlikely to play on the jury's sympathies. What the passage from *Chard* suggests has happened is that the notorious one-time rule that a man is presumed to have intended the natural consequences of his actions has been transmuted into a rule of evidence.[64] That is hardly a desirable state of affairs.[65] This is not, however, to suggest that the evidence offered in these *mens rea* cases is unproblematic. The problem with it, though, stems from the incredible conclusions drawn by some of the experts, rather than from any general principle about the admissibility of expert evidence on issues of culpability. In *Chard*, the psychiatrist had concluded that 'what does seem clear to me in the light of this man's personality was that there was no mens rea on his part to commit murder at any time that evening'.[66] In *Reynolds*, the psychiatrist had formed the opinion that the

---

[58] (1971) 56 Cr. App. R. 270–1.   [59] [1989] Crim. LR 220.
[60] [1995] 1 Cr. App. R. 157.
[61] Ibid. 168. See also *R. v. Stephenson* [1979] QB 695.   [62] [1986] Crim. LR 395.
[63] A counter-argument is that the exclusion of expert evidence on the mental states of normal people reflects a normative commitment to behaviourism and folk psychology in *mens rea* definitions. However, even if such a commitment exists, exceptions such as *Toner* suggest that it is not sufficiently strong to found the sort of bright line rule that *Turner* has sometimes been taken to establish.
[64] In *DPP v. Smith* [1961] AC 290 the rule was said to have the status of an irrebuttable inference (subject to evidence of mental abnormality), but any such rule has been abrogated by section 8 of the Criminal Justice Act 1967. See, generally, Edward Griew, 'States of Mind, Presumptions and Inferences' in Peter Smith (ed.), *Criminal Law: Essays in Honour of J.C. Smith* (London: Butterworths, 1987).
[65] See the discussion in *Schultz v. R.* [1982] WAR 171.
[66] *Supra* n. 57, 269–70. Worse still, counsel wished to cross-examine the psychiatrist on Chard's *inability* to form any intent to kill or do grievous bodily harm.

defendant, who had hit the victim fifteen times with a hammer while he was taking money from the till in the shop in which he worked, had not intended to harm her. Although Reynolds had admitted to him that he grabbed the hammer 'to knock out his victim', the psychiatrist did not think 'that at any point the thought of physically injuring [the victim] crossed his mind . . . she was seen as nothing more than an obstacle lying between himself, the money and the planned future'.[67] Perhaps the psychiatrist genuinely thought that Reynolds did not realize that hitting someone repeatedly on the head with a hammer in order to knock them out was virtually certain to do them harm. A better explanation of his conclusion, however, as well as of the psychiatrist's opinion in *Chard*, is that he was confusing intention and desire.

The report in *Masih* contains few details of the psychiatrist's evidence, other than that he had concluded that the defendant had a low IQ. Given the facts of the case, it is unlikely that the jury would have thought that this suggested that he had not appreciated the victim's lack of consent. Nevertheless, it was certainly relevant to the issue, and it is hard to defend the decision to exclude the evidence on the grounds that the jury were well placed to judge his ability to draw a conclusion of this type. Nor does the process of balancing the advantages of admitting the evidence against its disadvantages suggest a different result. If effectively controlled by the judge, the evidence was unlikely to confuse the jury. Furthermore, it would have been difficult for defence counsel to draw out Masih's low intellectual abilities on direct examination: expert evidence was probably the only effective means of doing so. The Court of Appeal justified excluding the evidence on the ground that Masih was mentally normal: although he was in the bottom 3 per cent of the population, he was two points above the level of subnormality (drawn at 70: Masih's IQ was 72). As several commentators have noted, this seems an unduly narrow line to draw.[68]

When it comes to establishing lack of *mens rea*, then, the interpretation of *Turner* as establishing a normal/abnormal rule is unsatisfactory. Given that the prosecution bears the onus of proving *mens rea* beyond reasonable doubt, rules limiting the ability of defendants to show lack of *mens rea* raise serious criminal justice issues. It is true that psychiatric evidence on culpability will sometimes be hard to credit and will often be of low probative

---

[67] *Reynolds*, LEXIS transcript.

[68] See, e.g., Rosemary Pattenden, 'Conflicting Approaches to Psychiatric Evidence in Criminal Trials: England, Canada and Australia' [1986] *Crim. LR* 92; Marc Beaumont, 'Psychiatric Evidence: Over-Rationalising the Abnormal' [1988] *Crim. LR*. 290. Of course, a line of sorts has to be drawn somewhere, and wherever it is drawn it will appear arbitrary. The best way of phrasing the objection to *Masih* is that drawing a bright line at the level used by psychiatrists for certain classificatory purposes prevents a more pragmatic, context-sensitive approach. There are similarities here to the match/no match approach to identification evidence in forensic science, which produces a 'fall-off-the-cliff' effect. See the discussion in Ch. 3 § 1.

value. These facts might provide reasons for exclusion in some cases, but equally they will not be difficult to expose on cross-examination. Moreover, 'no *mens rea*' claims in cases like *Chard* are unlikely to be taken seriously by jurors. Fears of unjustified acquittals, therefore, are almost certainly misplaced.[69]

4. Expert Evidence and Confessions

The *mens rea* cases paint a picture of the Court of Appeal clinging to one version of the *Turner* rule—a strictly drawn distinction between normal and abnormal defendants—and, in the process, reaching some dubious decisions. When it comes to expert evidence on the reliability of confessions, however, this distinction has been abandoned, and a more pragmatic approach is apparent.

The Court of Appeal's reassessment of the rules in this area began in *R.* v. *Raghip*; *R.* v. *Silcott*; *R.* v. *Braithwaite*.[70] The Court heard expert evidence on the reliability of Raghip's confession, which showed that Raghip had a low IQ (74), that he was suggestible, and that his level of social functioning was that of a ten-year-old. During a previous appeal, expert evidence had been excluded by Taylor CJ who, relying on his own judgment in *Masih*, had concluded that '[t]he jury were in as good a position, if not better than the psychologist to judge how amenable this young man was to suggestion.'[71] The Court of Appeal now held that this was wrong: 'we are not attracted to the concept that the judicial approach [to the admissibility of confessions] should be governed by which side of an arbitrary line, whether at 69/70 or elsewhere, the IQ falls.' In future trials, judges should decide the question of admissibility 'upon the facts of the case before [them] unfettered by any borderline or cut off point or classification of intelligence'.[72] This approach was endorsed in *R.* v. *Ward*: 'on the authorities as they now stand . . . the expert evidence of a psychiatrist or a psychologist may properly be admitted if it is to the effect that a defendant is suffering from a condition not properly described as mental illness, but from a personality disorder so severe as properly to be categorised as mental disorder.'[73] These decisions establish that expert psychological evidence can properly be admitted on the issue of the reliability of a confession—something which,

[69] See, generally, Stephen J. Morse, 'Undiminished Confusion in Diminished Capacity' (1984) 75 *J. Crim. L. & Criminol.* 1, 5–20.

[70] *The Times*, 9 December 1991.

[71] Quoted in *R.* v. *Raghip*, LEXIS transcript. For another case where the rule in *Turner* was used to exclude evidence on a defendant's tendency to confess falsely, see *R.* v. *Weightman* [1991] Crim. LR 204. That decision might be defended on its facts, because the accused's having a histrionic personality was admitted by the prosecution and had already been attested to by her probation officer. The expert could probably have added little.

[72] Ibid.   [73] [1993] 1 WLR 619, 690.

it seems, had already become the practice of some judges prior to its endorsement in *Raghip*.[74] In that case the court emphasized 'that nothing we say in this judgment is intended to reflect upon the admissibility of psychiatric or psychological evidence going to the issue of the defendant's mens rea'.[75] The distinction makes a degree of sense: where expert evidence is admitted on the factors that may have led an innocent defendant to confess, there are few dangers of normative distortion. However, in so far as this caveat is intended to distinguish *Raghip* and *Ward* from *Turner*, it fails, because in the latter the expert evidence was not tendered primarily on Turner's *mens rea* but on an issue of fact: whether or not he lost his temper at all.

One can detect in *Ward* a tendency to remove one arbitrary line only to draw another, using the concept 'personality disorder so severe as properly to be categorized as mental disorder'. The strict application of this criterion would actually have led to the exclusion of the evidence in *Raghip*, because there the defendant was afflicted by a low mental age and IQ with concurrent high suggestibility, factors that do not seem to add up to a 'personality disorder'.[76] Because abnormal suggestibility will not always be accompanied by a personality disorder, a strict application of the dictum in *Ward* might have unfortunate effects. It is not surprising, then, that the Court of Appeal has had to redraw the boundary of admissibility again. The test now is not whether the defendant's abnormality amounts to a personality disorder, but whether the abnormality 'might render the confession or evidence unreliable'.[77] The urge to create a cut-off point has not altogether disappeared: as well as an abnormal disorder, there must be a 'very significant deviation from the norm'.[78] Nevertheless, this threshold is now so vague that it will probably prove innocuous.

Before leaving this topic, one further case calls for scrutiny. At first sight, *R. v. Heaton*[79] is open to criticism on the grounds that the Court of Appeal was applying the *Ward* criteria too crudely. Expert evidence on suggestibility was held to be rightly excluded, as there was 'no suggestion of mental handicap or retardation'.[80] A closer examination, though, reveals a far better reason for excluding the evidence: the psychiatrist had merely noted

[74] A number of decisions are cited in that judgment.
[75] *Raghip*, LEXIS transcript. These words were quoted with approval in *Ward, supra* n. 73, 690.
[76] See also *R. v. Everett*, CA, 29 July 1988.
[77] *R. v. O'Brien, Sherwood and Hall, The Times*, 16 February 2000 (quotation from Casetrack transcript). See also *R. v. Roberts* CA 96/3593/S1 (19 March 1998); *R. v. Walker* [1998] Crim. LR 211.
[78] Ibid.   [79] [1993] Crim. LR 593.
[80] *R. v. Heaton*, LEXIS transcript. Although those with low IQs and borderline retardation tend to be particularly suggestible, suggestibility is by no means confined to such people. See, generally, Gisli Gudjonsson, *The Psychology of Interrogations, Confessions and Testimony* (Chichester: John Wiley, 1992), 131–64.

his 'impression' that Heaton was 'a very suggestible individual'. Taylor CJ observed:

Unless the medical evidence sought to be introduced on an issue of this kind is truly based upon some scientific data or expert analysis outside the experience of the judge and jury, a mere impression, even of a highly qualified doctor, that the defendant 'is not exceptionally bright' or that he is 'very suggestible', will not be admissible for the reasons set out by Lawton LJ [in *R. v. Turner*].[81]

This is a potentially important reinterpretation of Lawton LJ's influential judgment. For the first time the Court of Appeal is explicitly basing its decision not on the jury's assumed competence in respect of normal people, but on the fact that the expert's opinion lacks an identifiable expert basis. The psychiatrist, it seems, had administered no tests to the defendant in order to gauge his suggestibility; this was simply an impression he had formed during an interview with the defendant. It is arguable, then, that he had no sounder basis for forming an opinion than did the judge and jury, who were able to observe the defendant and to listen to the interview tapes. On this analysis, the expert was not speaking as an expert, and had no right to give opinion evidence to the court. This may well have provided a sound reason for excluding the evidence in *Chard*, *Reynolds*, and in *Turner* itself. In each of these cases, it appears that the psychiatrist had formed an opinion based largely on an interview with the defendant, without obviously employing any expert skills.

5. JURY COMPETENCE, REDUNDANCY, AND HELPFULNESS

The principal component of the *Turner* rule is usually taken to be that experts may only give evidence on topics 'outside the experience and knowledge of a judge or jury'. On one view, this is a sensible requirement. However, as has frequently been pointed out, it is potentially problematic. Psychologists, in particular, often study everyday human behaviour, but they may develop valuable, sometimes counter-intuitive, knowledge about it.[82] Indeed, I have argued that too coarse an application of this part of the *Turner* rule leads to decisions, like that in *Masih*, that are not easy to defend. Other common law jurisdictions have tended to move away from a strict application of the 'outside the jury's experience' rule.[83] In the United States, for instance, FRE 702 sets a 'helpfulness' standard. According to the Advisory

---

[81] *Heaton*, LEXIS transcript.

[82] See Mackay and Colman, *supra* n. 34; R. D. Mackay and Andrew M. Colman, 'Equivocal Rulings on Expert Psychological and Psychiatric Evidence: Turning a Muddle Into a Nonsense' [1996] *Crim. LR* 88.

[83] For Australia, see *R. v. Murphy* (1988) 167 CLR 95; *R. v. Hoogwerf* (1992) 63 A. Crim. R. 302. For Canada, see Roberts, *supra* n. 48. For New Zealand, see *R. v. Decha-Iamsakun* [1993] 1 NZLR 141, 146–8; Law Commission (New Zealand), *Evidence: Reform of the Law*, Report 55, Vol. 1 (Wellington: Law Commission, 1999), 23–4.

Committee on the rules, the best way to decide whether testimony will be helpful is to ask 'whether the untrained layman would be qualified to determine intelligently and to *the best possible degree* the particular issue without enlightenment from those having a specialized understanding of the subject involved in the dispute'.[84]

A helpfulness test is certainly an improvement on the present wording in *Turner*, but for present purposes I prefer to use the word 'redundant' to describe evidence that is properly excluded under this head, and to call this part of the *Turner* rule the 'jury competence' limb. My caution about the term 'helpful' is due to the fact that it is insufficiently precise: it might be taken to incorporate issues about reliability and complexity, as well as redundancy. For analytical purposes, it is preferable to keep these issues separate. The discussion so far has hopefully made one point clear: where expert evidence has been excluded for good reason, the reason is rarely that the evidence is redundant. Expert evidence offered to the courts may be of low probative value, as in *Turner*, or it may be irrelevant, as in *Strudwick*. Hardly ever, though, is it completely redundant.

6. *Turner* Revisited: Credibility and Hearsay

I now need to return to Lawton LJ's judgment to draw attention to two further reasons for excluding expert evidence that have not figured in the discussion so far. One of these points was mentioned briefly in the discussion of *Turner* that began this chapter. Turner's counsel argued that the psychiatrist's evidence was relevant to his client's credibility and it was held inadmissible on this ground, Lawton LJ commenting: '[t]he jury in this case did not need, and should not have been offered, the evidence of a psychiatrist to help them decide whether the defendant's evidence was truthful.'[85] I noted that this part of the judgment was puzzling because, although counsel may have misled the judge through his reference to admissibility on credibility, it did not seem that the psychiatrist did offer any testimony on Turner's credibility—at least, not directly. The psychiatrist's evidence was only relevant to credibility in the manner that almost all defence evidence is: because it supported the defendant's version of events.

This ambiguity in the notion of credibility highlights the need to define credibility more precisely. There are a number of kinds of credibility that are relevant to the evaluation of testimony, but here I shall make only a fairly coarse distinction between two broad types. Both are aspects of 'overall credibility', defined as whether, on a particular occasion, a particular

---

[84] Advisory Committee's commentary on rule 702, in Stephen A. Saltzburg and Kenneth R. Redden, *Federal Rules of Evidence Manual*, 2nd edn (Charlottesville: Michie, 1977), 414 (quoting Mason Ladd, 'Expert Testimony' (1952) 5 *Vand. L. Rev.* 414, 418).

[85] *Supra* n. 1, 842.

person is telling the truth. Suppose I tell you that yesterday I saw Elvis Presley crossing Oxford Street. That claim is incredible. Now suppose I tell you that I saw Jones (a mutual friend of ours) crossing Oxford Street yesterday: that is credible. I shall term this type of credibility 'factual credibility'. Technically, it relates to the prior probability of the assertion;[86] less technically, to the plausibility of the account. Now imagine that you know me to be a dreadful liar: you will tend to treat any claim I make, whether it relates to Elvis Presley or to Jones, with suspicion. This is 'personal credibility'. On the other hand, you may know me to be scrupulously honest but very short-sighted. This too would give you reason to doubt my claim about Jones, as would my poor memory or habitual drunkenness. Factors such as these can be incorporated in the concept of personal credibility, but it is worth noting that there are conceptually distinct aspects of personal credibility: those relating to mendacity and those relating to perceptual reliability.

The psychiatrist's testimony in *Turner* appears to have related only to factual credibility. It did so, however, on the basis of arguments d' and d''. Although it was also excluded on these arguments, this was because it was thought to be evidence on an area of jury competence, not because it might have contributed to the assessment of Turner's credibility. Any rule that did exclude evidence of factual credibility would be absurd, because it would exclude testimony from a passenger in Turner's car who supported his version of events.[87] It would therefore be best to ignore that part of Lawton LJ's judgment which relates to credibility: it is either fundamentally misconceived or *obiter*, and any restriction on expert evidence relating to credibility should be derived independently of it.

There is a further aspect of the judgment in *Turner*, one that has not been considered at all so far. Lawton LJ noted that:

all the facts upon which the psychiatrist based his opinion were hearsay save for those which he observed for himself during his examination of the defendant such as his appearance of depression and his becoming emotional when discussing the deceased girl and his own family. It is not for this court to instruct psychiatrists how to draft their reports, but those who call psychiatrists as witnesses should remember that the facts upon which they base their opinions must be proved by admissible evidence. This elementary principle is frequently overlooked.[88]

---

[86] See Mike Redmayne, 'Standards of Proof in Civil Litigation' (1999) 62 *Modern L. Rev.* 167, 185–7. This is best viewed as a subjective probability: thus your firm belief that Elvis Presley is alive, or that Jones was out of town yesterday, will affect your analysis of the factual credibility of my assertion.

[87] If there had been such a witness, it would certainly be odd to describe his evidence as supporting Turner's credibility rather than as direct evidence that Turner was provoked. It would also be wrong for the fact-finder to use the evidence to support both, because that would involve double-counting the evidence (effectively giving it twice the weight it deserves). Note, however, that, having used the evidence in support of one, the fact-finder can deduce the other.

[88] *Supra* n. 1, 840.

It was therefore held to be incumbent on defence counsel to establish the facts on which the expert's opinion was based during examination-in-chief. To be precise, the facts on which the expert's opinion was based were not hearsay, because the hearsay rule is a 'rule of use'[89] and only applies to out of court assertions that are tendered in court as evidence of their truth.[90] This does not prevent an expert from relying on out of court assertions as the basis for an opinion. Nevertheless, expert evidence based on such assertions will often be the functional equivalent of hearsay, because if the fact-finder relies on the expert's opinion she will also be relying (at one remove) on the truth of the out of court assertions. Additionally, if the expert recounts the out of court assertions on which her opinion is based, the jury may use the evidence for a hearsay purpose.[91]

The hearsay limb of the rule in *Turner* is now well established:

A doctor may not state what a patient told him about past symptoms as evidence of the existence of those symptoms because that would infringe the rule against hearsay, but he may give evidence of what the patient told him in order to explain the grounds on which he came to a conclusion with regard to the patient's condition.[92]

The correct approach, then, is for the judge to warn the jury that, to the extent that the expert's opinion is based on out of court statements that are not supported by direct evidence, it should be aware that it is based upon a 'flimsy or non-existent foundation'.[93] Some commentators go so far as to argue that, where there is no admissible evidence to support the expert's opinion, the opinion is entitled to no weight, and is therefore inadmissible.[94] Given, however, that the rationale for excluding hearsay evidence is not that it is entitled to no weight, but that the jury may give it too much weight, and that the only substantial hearsay danger is that of insincerity, this proposal probably goes too far. All the same, expert evidence based on hearsay raises both analytical and procedural problems.[95] I return to them later.

---

[89] See, generally, Philip McNamara, 'The Canons of Evidence—Rules of Exclusion or Rules of Use?' (1986) 10 *Adelaide L. Rev.* 341.

[90] See *Wilband* v. *The Queen* (1967) 2 CCC 6, 11: expert evidence 'is not evidence of the truth of the [second-hand] information but evidence of the opinion formed on the basis of that information'.

[91] There is evidence that jurors will use the evidence in this manner, even if warned not to: see Regina A. Schuller, 'Expert Evidence and Hearsay: The Influence of "Secondhand" Information on Jurors' Decisions' (1995) 19 *Law & Hum. Behav.* 345.

[92] Rupert Cross, *Evidence*, 5th edn (London: Butterworths, 1979), 446, approved in *R.* v. *Bradshaw* (1985) 82 Cr. App. R. 79, 83.

[93] *Bradshaw*, loc. cit.

[94] R. J. Delisle, '*Lavallee*: Expert Opinion Based on "Some Admissible Evidence"—*Abbey* Revisited' (1990) 76 CR (3d) 366, 369; Rosemary Pattenden, 'Expert Opinion Evidence Based on Hearsay' [1982] *Crim. LR* 85, 87–8.

[95] See, generally, Pattenden, ibid.; Edward J. Imwinkelried, 'A Comparativist Critique of the Interface Between Hearsay and Expert Opinion in American Evidence Law' (1991) 33 *Boston Coll. L. Rev.* 1; Peter Wardle, '*R.* v. *Abbey* and Psychiatric Opinion Evidence: Requiring the Accused to Testify' [1984] *Ottawa L. Rev.* 116.

To this point, I have been attempting to develop an exposition of the rule in *Turner* by examining discrete aspects of the case law. Although this has allowed me to highlight various reasons for excluding expert evidence (some good, some bad), it might play down the fact that these discrete reasons are commonly intertwined and that in some cases the exclusion of expert evidence is best understood as a response to its multiple failings.[96] In the remainder of this chapter I shall continue to highlight separate themes in the *Turner* case law, but I shall also draw attention to the blurred boundaries between them. A first step in this direction can be taken by pausing here to note the interrelation of the 'credibility', 'hearsay', and 'jury competence' heads of exclusion. Consider again the evidence on intention in *Chard* and *Reynolds*. The discussion of those cases concluded with the observation that the experts may not have been using any special skills to form their opinions about the defendants and that this might justify exclusion of their evidence under the jury competence argument. The evidence in *Chard* and *Reynolds* also falls foul of the hearsay argument because it is based on what Chard and Reynolds said, and this needs to be established by direct evidence. It is therefore entitled to little weight. Note, though, that it falls foul of the hearsay argument to just the extent that it falls foul of the jury competence argument: that is, to the extent that the expert is not using special skills. If the expert administered a test to the defendant to establish his level of cognitive functioning, then he would have been using the defendant's responses for non-hearsay purposes while at the same time performing a task that the jury could not. The credibility argument overlaps to a similar extent. The jury may infer from the expert's evidence that he believes that the defendant is telling the truth (i.e. that he did not intend to kill) and it may be impressed by this. But, again, the expert is doing no more than what the jury itself can do by listening to the defendant testify; only if special skills are used would the jury have good reasons for inferring the defendant's credibility from the expert's testimony.[97]

7. Expert Evidence and Credibility

I have suggested that *Turner* should not be taken to establish any rule about the admissibility of expert evidence on a witness's credibility. Turning to

---

[96] See, for example, Roberts' analysis of *R. v. Hurst* [1995] 1 Cr. App. R. 82, *supra* n. 6 (discussing three different problems).

[97] This is not to say that psychiatrists and psychologists just listen to people and repeat what they say. Psychiatrists and psychologists can, I am sure, use their expert knowledge to reach sound conclusions based purely on clinical interviews; conclusions, moreover, that lay people could not reach. All I am saying is that to have their evidence admitted in court they need to make it obvious that this is what they are doing; and that the experts in *Chard* and *Reynolds*—as well as those in *Turner* and *Heaton*—did not do so. Consequently, their evidence was vulnerable under multiple heads of exclusion.

other sources, it becomes apparent that expert evidence on credibility is not always excluded. In *Toohey* v. *Metropolitan Police Commissioner* the House of Lords held that, although personal credibility was largely an area of jury competence, there were exceptions:

Human evidence shares the frailties of those who give it. It is subject to many cross-currents such as partiality, prejudice, self-interest and, above all, imagination and inaccuracy. Those are matters with which the jury, helped by cross-examination and common sense, must do their best. But when a witness through physical (in which I include mental) disease or abnormality is not capable of giving a true or reliable account to the jury, it must surely be allowable for medical science to reveal this vital hidden fact to them.[98]

Another exception to a purported rule excluding expert evidence on credibility appears to have been established in the confession cases, examined above. These exceptions are linked by the fact that they all relate to reliability aspects of personal credibility, as opposed to mendacity aspects.

Two recent English cases examine the credibility limb of the *Turner* rule.[99] *R. v. Robinson*[100] concerned the alleged indecent assault of a mentally retarded 15-year-old. The case turned on the reliability of her evidence. During cross-examination of the prosecution's witnesses, defence counsel asked the complainant whether her mother had put words into her mouth; a similar question was asked of the police officer who had interviewed her. At the end of its case the prosecution called an educational psychologist to testify to aspects of the complainant's credibility. She stated that '[the complainant] remembers important matters quite well. . . . She could not adopt ideas from someone else.'[101] The Court of Appeal held that this evidence should have been excluded. 'In our view', it opined, 'the Crown cannot call a witness of fact and then, without more, call a psychologist or psychiatrist to give reasons why the jury should regard that witness as reliable.'[102] It quoted with approval a Canadian case where such credibility bolstering was likened to the ancient practice of oath helping.[103]

The second case is *G. v. DPP*,[104] where the Court of Appeal ruled that the expert evidence of a psychologist, called to cast doubt on the credibility

---

[98] [1965] AC 595, 608. In a later passage, the exception was defined in less strict terms: '[m]edical evidence is admissible to show that a witness suffers from some disease or defect or abnormality of mind that affects the reliability of his evidence' (at 609). Given the improbability of any witness being *incapable* of giving a true or reliable account, this is surely a better way of expressing the rule.

[99] A third relevant case is *Bernal and Another* v. *R.* (Privy Council, 28 April 1997). See Graeme Broadbent, 'Polygraph Evidence in Jamaica—The Door Left Ajar' (1998) 62 *J. Crim. L.* 585. The reasoning in *Bernal* is open to criticisms similar to those developed below.

[100] [1994] 3 All ER 346.   [101] Ibid. 350.   [102] Ibid. 352.

[103] *R.* v. *Kyselka* (1962) 133 CCC 103. The Canadian Supreme Court has also drawn parallels with oath helping in its influential decision in *R.* v. *Béland and Phillips* (1987) 43 DLR (4th) 641.

[104] [1997] 2 All ER 755.

of two child witnesses, had been properly excluded during the re-hearing of the case in the Crown Court (the case was heard without a jury). The court accepted that the evidence, which dealt with the reliability of interviews with the children, was 'a legitimate area for expert evidence, although [it] will be of much greater value to a jury with no knowledge of this topic than to a magistrate or judge who may have great experience of it'.[105] One reason for excluding the evidence, therefore, was that the psychologist had told the court little that it did not know and had pointed to few details about the interview record which would not have been brought out by counsel. The court also referred to larger reasons for excluding this sort of evidence, quoting from its judgment in *R. v. Davies*:

It is fundamental that experts must not usurp the function of the jury in a criminal trial. Save in particular circumstances, it is the task of the jury to make judgements on the questions of reliability and truthfulness. Particular circumstances arise when there are characteristics of a medical nature in the make-up of the witness, such as mental illness, which would not be known to the jury without expert assistance. Those circumstances do not arise in the case of ordinary children who are not suffering from any abnormality. It may well be open to parties in a particular case to call general expert evidence in relation to the Cleveland [child interviewing] guidelines and, for example, to tell the jury that over interviewing [*sic*] as a matter of generality has been shown by expert research to have a much more adverse effect on children than on adults but the witness cannot express an opinion whether a particular child witness is a reliable or truthful witness. That is precisely the province of the jury in a criminal case, or the judge when considering the admissibility of evidence. . . .[106]

The expert evidence in *G*., the court concluded, 'almost wholly usurps [the] function of the court'.[107] These credibility cases raise so many issues that, before proceeding to analyse the reasoning in them, it will be helpful to clear the ground by briefly considering three related areas of the law.

Oath Helping

That evidence resembles a form of trial which has long since fallen into desuetude, and which is now regarded as irrational, might be a good reason for its exclusion; but only if the resemblance is strong. The connection between expert evidence on credibility and the practice of oath helping, or compurgation, is not. In the days of compurgation, the concepts of evidence and trial were very different to our modern ones. '[I]n old times', Maitland writes, 'proof was not an attempt to convince the judges, it was an appeal to the supernatural.'[108] The oath sworn by a compurgator was not evidence in the

---

[105] [1997] 2 All ER, 759.
[106] *R. v. Davies* CA, 3 November 1995, quoted in ibid. 759–60.   [107] Ibid. 760.
[108] F. W. Maitland, *Equity, also, the Forms of Actions at Common Law; Two Courses of Lectures* (Cambridge: Cambridge University Press, 1909), 309.

modern sense; it did not 'touch the issue'[109] but appealed to divine intervention. This was reflected in the forms compurgation took:

> If a defendant on oath and in a set form of words will deny the charge against him,
> and if he can get a certain number of other persons (compurgators) to back his denial
> by their oaths, he will win his case. If he cannot get the required number, or they
> do not swear in the proper form, 'the oath bursts,' and he will lose.[110]

From our modern perspective, this certainly appears irrational.[111] But when
an expert gives evidence about a witness's factual or personal credibility,
this will presumably utilize her expertise to interpret credibility cues in the
witness's behaviour or in the assertions she makes. The comparison with
compurgation is unconvincing.[112]

Credibility Rules

The rules governing the use of evidence to prove credibility are complex.
Briefly, defendants who testify are permitted to call evidence of good character, and if they do so judges should instruct the jury that this is relevant
both to their propensity to commit crime and to their personal credibility.[113]
The law was once that such evidence was relevant *primarily* to credibility.[114]
Beyond this, evidence on credibility is restricted by the rule against evidence
on collateral issues. The purpose of this rule is to exclude evidence of low
probative value in order to save time and money and to prevent the jury
from becoming confused and distracted. This is a laudable purpose, but the
'bluntness'[115] of the collateral issues rule means that important evidence may
sometimes be caught by it; as a matter of logic, it would be preferable to
confront directly the probative value and potential prejudicial effect of each
piece of evidence.[116] The unsatisfactory nature of the rule is reflected in the
fact that there exist exceptions to it. *Toohey* establishes one. It is also

---

[109] Julius Stone, rev. W. A. N. Wells, *Evidence: Its History and Policies* (Sydney:
Butterworths, 1991), 5.

[110] Sir William Holdsworth, *A History of English Law*, 3rd edn (London: Methuen, 1922),
Vol. 1, 305 (footnotes omitted).

[111] For a nuanced account of the rationality of oath helping, see Mirjan Damaška, 'Rational
and Irrational Proof Revisited' (1997) 51 *Cardozo J. Int. & Comp. L.* 25, 29–31.

[112] Credibility experts bear a little more similarity to trial by witness, described in Holdsworth, *supra* n. 110, 302–5, and it is possible that this is what courts and commentators have
in mind when they draw comparisons between experts and oath helpers. Witnesses were
'persons produced by plaintiff or defendant to swear a belief in his tale' (ibid. 302), but the
differences between them and credibility experts are still marked. '[T]hese bands of witnesses
were treated as formal tests. Their testimony was not weighted, but, provided they told a
consistent tale, their numbers were balanced one against another and the party whose band
of witnesses was the more numerous won' (ibid. 303).

[113] *R. v. Vye* [1993] 1 WLR 471.   [114] *R. v. Bellis* [1966] 1 WLR 234.

[115] See N. E. Simmonds, 'Bluntness and Bricolage' in Hyman Gross and Ross Harrison (eds),
Jurisprudence: Cambridge Essays (Oxford: Clarendon Press, 1992).

[116] See, generally, A. A. S. Zuckerman, 'Relevance in Legal Proceedings' in William Twining
(ed.), *Facts in Law* (Wiesbaden: Franz Steiner, 1983).

recognized that there are trials in which credibility becomes a central issue.[117]

In addition to these basic rules, evidence that is said to be relevant to the defendant's personal credibility may be admitted by a triggering event. If the defendant 'puts his character in issue' by claiming he is of good character, or by casting imputations on the character of a prosecution witness, or by giving evidence against a co-defendant, then evidence of his previous convictions can be admitted for the purpose of undermining his credibility.[118]

Ultimate Issues

The reference in *G.* to the expert's usurping the function of the court is reminiscent of the rule that 'it is not competent in any action for witnesses to express their opinions upon any of the issues, whether of law or fact, which the Court or a jury has to determine'.[119] The 'ultimate issue rule' was abolished in civil cases by section 3 of the Civil Evidence Act 1972. Its status in criminal cases is uncertain: although abolition was proposed by the Criminal Law Revision Committee,[120] this proposal never reached the statute books. Criminal courts have recognized that the rule is honoured most often in the breach,[121] but it has never been specifically abrogated and courts occasionally appear to rely on it to justify the exclusion of evidence.[122] While credibility is not an ultimate issue in the sense of being a 'material' or 'constitutive' fact, credibility determinations are often outcome-determinative, and might, therefore, be thought to be ultimate issues in this sense. This seems to have been the position taken by various civil courts that have excluded expert testimony about the truthfulness of child witnesses on the grounds that such evidence usurps the role of the court.[123] In *Re M. and R. (minors) (sexual abuse: expert evidence)*[124] the Court of Appeal drew attention to the provisions of the Civil Evidence Act, and held that it had been wrong to exclude expert evidence on credibility in those cases.

---

[117] *R. v. Funderburk* [1990] 2 All ER 482, 491.

[118] Criminal Evidence Act 1898, s. 1(f).

[119] *Joseph Crosfield & Sons (Ltd) v. Techno-Chemical Laboratories Limited* (1913) 29 TLR 378, 379.

[120] Criminal Law Revision Committee, *Eleventh Report (General)* (London: HMSO, 1972), para. 63.

[121] *DPP v. A. and B.C. Chewing Gum Ltd* [1968] 1 QB 159, 164; *Stockwell* (1993) 97 Cr. App. R. 260, 265–6.

[122] In *R. v. Theodosi* [1993] RTR 179, 184, the Court of Appeal held that one reason why certain observations of an accident investigator should have been excluded was that he was 'usurping the function of the jury and answering the very question which it was the jury's and only the jury's province to decide'. For another—obscurely reasoned—decision that may draw on the ultimate issue rule, see *R. v. Jeffries* [1997] Crim. LR 819.

[123] *Re S. and B. (minors) (child abuse: evidence)* [1990] 2 FLR 489; *Re F.S. (minors)* [1996] 1 FCR 666; *Re N. (a minor) (sexual abuse; video evidence)* [1996] 4 All ER 225; cf. the more nuanced discussion in *Re K. (minors) (alleged sexual abuse: evidence)* [1996] 2 FCR 425.

[124] [1996] 4 All ER 239. See John Jackson, 'Ultimate Issues: The Cheshire Cat Strikes Again!' at <http://www.law.umich.edu/thayer/ultimate.htm> (visited 19 March 1998).

Whether in civil or criminal cases, the ultimate issue prohibition makes little sense.[125] If an expert can offer relevant and reliable evidence, it should generally be admitted. In cases heard without a jury, the claim that expert evidence will usurp the court's role is silly: it implies that the judge, having admitted the evidence, will be overcome by an irresistible urge to decide the case solely on the basis of the expert evidence, regardless of its merits. The claim hardly makes more sense in jury trials, because the judge can impress upon the jury that it is for it to make the ultimate decision based on all the evidence.[126] Put simply, 'usurpation' claims rely on the spurious assumption that giving evidence on an issue is the same as deciding that issue. Nevertheless, the belief that experts should not offer opinions on ultimate issues is a resilient one and, like the villain in a Hollywood thriller, the ultimate issue rule has proved remarkably difficult to kill off.[127] Its effects are usually not especially pernicious, because expert evidence on ultimate issues often lies beyond the witness's expertise, and it is frequently irrelevant. Ultimate issue opinions might, therefore, be excluded on those grounds instead. However, if courts are to avoid excluding evidence that will help them to make better decisions, they should make these reasons explicit rather than rely on a rule with no good justification.

G. And *Robinson* Re-Examined

Having dealt with these related matters, I return to the decisions in G. and *Robinson*. The evidence in G. was rightly excluded, but not because it usurped the function of the court. It should have been excluded on a simple balancing exercise: it was time-consuming, potentially confusing, and told the court little it could not work out for itself.

The decision in *Robinson* is not so easy to justify. First of all, it is not clear that the decision can be distinguished from cases such as *Toohey*[128] and *Ward*,[129] where expert evidence on credibility was admitted. On this point, the court appears to have endorsed the appellant's arguments:

in a proper case, evidence from a psychiatrist or psychologist may be admissible to show that a witness is unreliable or a confession is unreliable. But [the appellant] points out that there is no case in which psychiatric or psychological evidence has been admitted to boost, bolster or enhance the evidence of a witness for the Crown or indeed of any witness. He submits that it is for the jury to assess the reliability

---

[125] See, generally, J. D. Jackson, 'The Ultimate Issue Rule: One Rule Too Many' [1984] *Crim. LR* 75; McCord, *supra* n. 52, 73–6.

[126] The way the court slips from 'answer' to 'decide' in the quotation from *Theodosi*, *supra* n. 122, nicely illustrates the fallacy involved here. The expert may *answer* the question, but only the jury can *decide* it.

[127] See Jackson, *supra* n. 124; Rick Brown, 'Limitation of Expert Testimony on the Battered Woman Syndrome in Homicide Cases: The Return of the Ultimate Issue Rule' (1990) 32 *Arizona L. Rev.* 665.

[128] *Supra* n. 98.   [129] *Supra* n. 73.

and persuasiveness of witnesses and it cannot be right to allow evidence, however expert, to suggest to the jury that they should believe a witness of fact.[130]

The final sentence obviously cannot do the work of distinguishing *Toohey* and *Ward*. Is there, then, a valid distinction between evidence undermining reliability and that bolstering it? It does not seem so. The claim that bolstering credibility is suspect is in fact largely incoherent. Recall that in *Robinson* the defence had drawn attention to the fact that the complainant might have been influenced by others, even if it did not suggest that she was lying. There was therefore a good argument that the evidence was 'rehabilitative' of the reliability[131] aspect of her personal credibility. But even had the defence not made those suggestions, the evidence is still properly described as rehabilitative of credibility rather than credibility boosting. All the expert did was testify that the complainant had a good memory and was not suggestible; logically, that would only have been relevant to her credibility if the fact-finder had been thinking that she *was* suggestible or forgetful. Testimony cannot be bolstered unless it is already regarded as weak; but if it is regarded as weak, there is legitimate space for the expert evidence to work in. Perhaps there is an argument about relevance here: the evidence is not relevant because the complainant's credibility was not impugned. But, as the court noted, '[t]he case turned crucially on the reliability of the complainant';[132] any jury thinking carefully about finding the defendant guilty would surely have scrutinized her evidence with care. The expert evidence seems, therefore, to have been only too relevant.[133] Consequently, the argument that the evidence should only have been admitted after being triggered by a defence attack on the witness's credibility does not really hold up.[134] Nor are there convincing parallels with the situations in which credibility evidence may be triggered under section 1(f) of the Criminal Evidence Act 1898. In so far as they can be justified at all, those rules can be defended as a means of preventing the trial from

---

[130] *Supra* n. 100, 351.

[131] The mendacity aspect of her personal credibility—on which there is probably good reason to be cautious about admitting expert evidence—does not seem to have been in issue, and nothing the expert said appears to have addressed it.

[132] *Supra* n. 100, 352.

[133] For a similar situation, see *Funderburk*, *supra* n. 117. There is another parallel with *Funderburk*, in that in both cases the evidence might be said to be relevant, not because it rebuts a claim made by the opposing side, but because it will rebut something that it is reasonable to speculate the jury will be thinking. In *Funderburk*, no claim was made that the victim was a virgin before the alleged rape; but her description of the rape carried this implication, and this made her virginity a relevant issue. See also *R.* v. *S.M.S.* [1992] Crim. LR 310.

[134] Cf. John Norris and Marlys Edwardh, 'Myths, Hidden Facts and Common Sense: Expert Opinion Evidence and the Assessment of Credibility' (1995) 38 *Crim. LQ* 73; *R.* v. *J.* (1994) 75 A. Crim. R. 523.

degenerating into a mud-slinging contest,[135] but there was no question of that in *Robinson*.

Nevertheless, there are objections to the expert evidence in *Robinson*. One problem is that the defence should have had a right to rebut the expert evidence by further evidence of its own; because the testimony had caught it unawares it was not able to do so and this caused an imbalance in the proceedings. Had the defence been able to have an expert interview the complainant and testify on her credibility, there would be no unfairness objection to allowing the prosecution's expert to testify on credibility. One might, though, worry instead about the unseemly prospect of conflicting expert evidence on the credibility of a key witness. Is this a serious objection to expert credibility testimony? In itself it is not; but it does point to the real problem here, which is the reliability of expert evidence on credibility. Where expert evidence is unreliable, expert conflict is likely. In *Robinson* the expert testified that the complainant 'could not adopt ideas from someone else'. It is difficult to believe that this categorical statement can be true, and it would not have been difficult for the defence to find an expert to challenge it. It would surely have been better not to admit it in the first place.

8. RE-EXAMINING THE CREDIBILITY TABOO

In the previous section I dealt rather bluntly with some of the reasons given to justify excluding expert evidence on credibility in criminal trials. There were good reasons for this: a number of the justifications for the exclusionary policy do not stand up to close scrutiny. The fact remains, however, that courts in common law jurisdictions are reluctant to admit expert evidence touching directly on a defendant's credibility.[136] Now that some of the bad reasons for the credibility taboo have been discarded, I re-examine the issues with an eye to wider policy concerns.

---

[135] The rules cannot easily be justified on the grounds that previous convictions are relevant to personal credibility, unless one reasons through factual credibility by relying on the ('forbidden') inference that the defendant has a propensity to commit crime. See Richard D. Friedman, 'Character Impeachment Evidence: Psycho-Bayesian [!?] Analysis and a Proposed Overhaul' (1991) 38 *UCLA L. Rev.* 637; Susan Marlene Davies, 'Evidence of Character to Prove Conduct: A Reassessment of Relevancy' (1991) 27 *Crim. L. Bull.* 504, 521.

[136] Canadian law is discussed below; the High Court of Australia has recently moved the law in a similar direction to that described for Canada: *Farrell* v. *The Queen* [1998] HCA 50. For the United States, see *State* v. *Kim* 645 P. 2d 1330 (1982) and *State* v. *Batangan* 799 P. 2d 48 (1990), and, generally, Christopher B. Mueller and Laird C. Kirkpatrick, *Evidence* (Boston: Little, Brown, 1995), 733–4. For New Zealand, see *R.* v. *B. (an accused)* [1987] 1 NZLR 362; *R.* v. *Accused* [1989] 1 NZLR 715. These cases have been partially overruled by Evidence Act 1908, s. 23G, which allows limited expert testimony on credibility-related features of children under 17. See *R.* v. *S.* [1995] 3 NZLR 674; also Law Commission, *supra* n. 83, 25–6.

The Canadian law is a convenient place to begin. In *R. v. Béland and Phillips*,[137] the Supreme Court held polygraph evidence to be inadmissible, largely because of fears about admitting evidence on credibility. That decision has remained influential, but later cases have allowed that it will sometimes be appropriate to admit expert evidence touching on credibility. In *R. v. Marquard*,[138] a case involving an allegation of an aggravated assault on a young child, the court considered the admissibility of the testimony of the doctor who had examined her when she was taken to hospital. The doctor had been allowed to testify about general characteristics exhibited by abused children, and the reasons why they might lie about the origins of their injuries. 'It is a fundamental axiom of our trial process', the court held, 'that the ultimate conclusion as to the credibility or truthfulness of a particular witness is for the trier of fact, and it is not the proper subject of expert opinion.'[139] Nevertheless:

> while expert evidence on the ultimate credibility of a witness is not admissible, expert evidence on human conduct and the psychological and physical factors which may lead to certain behaviour relevant to credibility, is admissible, provided the testimony goes beyond the ordinary experience of the trier of fact.[140]

Such evidence, limited to the general characteristics of groups of witnesses and not extending to specific conclusions about a particular witness, is sometimes referred to as 'social framework' or 'group character' evidence.[141] What characterizes this type of testimony is that the expert, rather than giving direct evidence, gives 'meta-evidence' intended to supply the fact-finder with contextual information that will improve her evaluation of the other evidence presented to her. In the context of credibility evidence, the significance of the concept is that the expert will generally testify about factual credibility rather than personal credibility. One difficulty with this approach is that it may be difficult to decide whether a particular expert has overstepped the mark. This is graphically illustrated by *Marquard* itself, where the majority and minority disagreed on this very point. Subsequently, in *R. v. R. (D.)*,[142] the Supreme Court re-affirmed the admissibility of group character evidence on credibility, but its members again disagreed on whether the evidence that had been given at trial fitted that description.[143] The way in which expert testimony in cases involving children's evidence is adduced probably adds

---

[137] (1987) 43 DLR (4th) 641.   [138] (1993) 85 CCC (3d) 193.

[139] Ibid. 228.   [140] Ibid. 229.

[141] See John Monahan and Laurens Walker, 'Judicial Use of Social Science Research' (1991) 15 *Law & Hum. Behav.* 571, 581 (social framework); Robert P. Mosteller, 'Syndromes and Politics in Criminal Trials and Evidence Law' (1996) 46 *Duke LJ* 461, 462 (group character).

[142] (1996) 107 CCC (3d) 289.

[143] It is worth noting that L'Heureux-Dubé J dissented in both cases, holding the evidence in *Marquard* admissible, but that in *R. v. R. (D.)* inadmissible. This implies that the difficulty in identifying true group character evidence is not due to differing conceptions of what group character is, but reflects difficulties of classification in individual cases.

to the difficulty of drawing a sharp distinction. Often the expert called to testify will have examined the victim and drawn the conclusion of abuse. Shoehorning her evidence into the group character format will do little to hide this fact from the jury, especially as the expert may also be giving evidence of the indicia of abuse found during her examination. Further, in drawing conclusions about the provenance of, say, a child's injuries, the expert will often have drawn conclusions about the credibility of any story told to her by the child; her testimony will be shot through with conclusions about the child's credibility whether or not she makes them explicit. In fact there is a danger that, by emphasizing form rather than content, the group character rule will inhibit proper scrutiny of the foundations of the expert's evidence: often questions of the sort 'why did you think the child was telling the truth?' will be the most effective.[144]

Faced with the difficulty of drawing the group character line, one might lean either towards allowing direct evidence on credibility, or towards excluding all evidence touching on credibility. Choosing the former course, Berger argues that '[w]e should face the fact that [group character] evidence in the sex abuse cases is about credibility, abandon the cliché that experts may not testify about credibility and concentrate on examining the proffered testimony to determine whether this is the unusual kind of case in which the expert could assist the jury in assessing the witness's veracity.'[145] Others, however, are more cautious. Roberts, who, like Berger, is sceptical of the ability to draw a bright line around group character, is reluctant to sanction any evidence on credibility. This leads back, then, to asking whether there are good reasons for the credibility taboo.

In *Marquard* the Supreme Court observed that ultimate conclusions about credibility are for the jury. This seems to be ultimate issue reasoning, which, I have suggested, there is reason to be sceptical of. Berger makes the point nicely: 'even though it is indisputable that "determinations of credibility are for the jury," the conclusion that, therefore, a witness may never express an opinion about another witness's credibility is no more logically warranted than to deduce that because the jury is the trier of fact a witness may never express an opinion about a factual matter.'[146] Might this be too dismissive? Although there is a logical distinction between evidence and decision-making, it can be argued that expert evidence carries more authority than other evidence and that, therefore, juries will be so inclined to agree with experts that the equation of evidence with decision-making is warranted. Perhaps the fact that credibility is a difficult issue lends extra

---

[144] See Margaret A. Berger, '*United States* v. *Scop*: The Common-Law Approach to an Expert's Opinion About a Witness's Credibility Still Does Not Work' (1989) 55 *Brooklyn L. Rev.* 559, 612, 620.

[145] Ibid. 614.

[146] Ibid. 591 (footnote omitted). See also Michael W. Mullane, 'The Truthsayer and the Court: Expert Testimony on Credibility' (1991) 43 *Maine L. Rev.* 53.

weight to this concern; as the majority in *Marquard* observed, 'credibility is a notoriously difficult problem, and the expert's opinion may be all too readily accepted by a frustrated jury as a convenient base upon which to resolve its difficulties'.[147] There are two responses to these concerns. First, the very fact that jurors possess common knowledge about credibility puts them in a good position to come to their own conclusions; they may therefore be more sceptical about an expert's testimony on credibility than about testimony on a more esoteric issue, such as DNA profiling. Some support for this contention comes from the studies of jury reactions to polygraph evidence, which have generally found that juries are not over-whelmed: they draw their own conclusions about credibility, not always agree-ing with the polygrapher's verdict.[148] Secondly, if the expert really is an expert on the matters she testifies about, then she does have authority on credibility, and it would be reasonable to defer to her judgement.

There is another way of expressing the objection to expert testimony on credibility. Such testimony, it is sometimes said, 'invades the province of the jury'.[149] Although most courts treat this phrase as though it means the same thing as 'usurps the function of the jury',[150] it does bear a slightly different interpretation. This is that we have decided that credibility determinations are for the jury and we simply will not permit expert aid, whether or not it would be helpful, and whether or not it would usurp the jury's function in any way. Admitting expert evidence might give the impression that we no longer absolutely trusted jury credibility judgements, and that would be a bad thing. Or perhaps the verdicts of courts will be less 'acceptable' to the community if they appear to be based on expert credibility determina-tions.[151] I do not find it easy to articulate the reasoning that may be involved here, but Roberts has picked up on it. Discussing the equation of polygraphy with oath helping made in *Béland*, he argues that 'polygraphy *does* resemble compurgation inasmuch as neither is compatible with the traditional conception of a criminal trial'.[152] He proceeds to quote McIntyre J in that case:

It is a basic tenet of our legal system that judges and juries are capable of assessing credibility and reliability of evidence. . . . I would seek to preserve the principle that in the resolution of disputes in litigation, issues of credibility will be decided by human triers of fact, using their experience of human affairs and basing judgment upon their

---

[147] *Supra* n. 138, 228.
[148] See Edward J. Imwinkelried, 'The Standard for Admitting Scientific Evidence: A Critique from the Perspective of Juror Psychology' (1982) 28 *Villanova L. Rev.* 554, 567–8.
[149] See, for example, *United States* v. *Brown* 501 F. 2d 146, 150 (1974) (holding expert evidence on eyewitness identifications inadmissible).
[150] See McCord, *supra* n. 52, 73–7.
[151] I am thinking here of Nesson's arguments: see Charles R. Nesson, 'The Evidence or the Event? On Judicial Proof and the Acceptability of Verdicts' (1985) 98 *Harv. L. Rev.* 1357.
[152] *Supra* n. 48, 212.

assessment of the witness and on consideration of how an individual's evidence fits into the general picture revealed on a consideration of the whole of the case.[153]

Roberts goes on to draw a parallel between the rule excluding expert testimony on credibility and a body of fundamental rules of procedural law— such as trial by jury, the presumption of innocence, and the right to legal advice—which 'cannot be watered down, much less abandoned, by judges in ordinary criminal proceedings'.[154] In *Marquard*, he suggests, the Supreme Court 'renegotiat[ed] the boundaries of procedural law'.[155]

This line of thinking, I admit, helps explain the resilience of the credibility taboo. All the same, I am not sure what to make of it. It seems to me that the argument continues to rest on the assumption that juries will automatically defer to expert judgements on credibility, for only then would we really replace trial by jury with trial by expert. Moreover, other sorts of expert evidence have the potential substantially to affect jury decision-making. Courts admit DNA evidence which is very cogent and, more often than not, outcome-determinative. DNA evidence has enormous implications for the credibility of any explanation offered by the defendant; yet no one argues that DNA evidence redraws the boundaries of procedural law.[156] To be sure, DNA evidence is probably rather more reliable than a psychiatrist's conclusions about the credibility of witnesses. But that only suggests that reliability concerns, rather than *Turner* rule factors, are the driving force here.

I suspect, too, that the boundaries of procedural law are more flexible than Roberts's analysis might suggest. English courts admit expert evidence on the reliability of confessions—essentially a credibility issue. Indeed, in the United States such evidence has been excluded at trial on the grounds that it would 'invade the prerogative of the jury'.[157] In contrast, many United States jurisdictions accept polygraph evidence as well as expert evidence on

---

[153] *Supra* n. 137, 654, 656.   [154] *Supra* n. 48, 218.

[155] Ibid. 215. To similar effect, see Steven I. Friedland, 'On Common Sense and the Evaluation of Witness Credibility' (1989–90) 40 *Case Western Reserve L. Rev.* 165.

[156] For an argument that comes close, see Mirjan R. Damaška, *Evidence Law Adrift* (New Haven: Yale University Press, 1997), 143–52. Damaška argues that the 'creeping scientization of factual inquiry' may lead to momentous transformations of fact-finding systems, comparable to those that 'occurred in the twilight of the Middle Ages, when magical forms of proof retreated before the prototypes of our present evidentiary technology' (at 143, 151). While I am sympathetic to the view that the increasing use of expert evidence poses challenges to legal systems, the changes that are likely to result do not seem to me to be so far-reaching. While the decline of magical forms of proof may have been accompanied by an epistemological shift to what has been termed a 'Galilean style' of reasoning (see Ian Hacking, 'Language, Truth and Reason' in Martin Hollis and Steven Lukes (eds), *Rationality and Relativism* (Cambridge, MA: MIT Press, 1982)), the practice of deferring to experts on technical questions seems to raise no greater epistemological issue than the practice of deferring to one's watch on the question of what time it is: see Jerry A. Fodor, 'The Dogma That Didn't Bark (A Fragment of Naturalized Epistemology)' in Hilary Kornblith (ed.), *Naturalizing Epistemology*, 2nd edn (Cambridge, MA: MIT Press, 1994) (essay orig. 1991), 210–11. This is not to deny that the problem of certifying expertise raises difficult issues.

[157] *United States* v. *Hall* 93 F. 3d 1337 (1996).

eyewitness testimony,[158] evidence that would almost certainly be excluded in England. The Canadian courts have admitted credibility testimony in cases involving child witnesses, albeit limited by the group character format. English civil courts have gone even further, allowing specific conclusions on credibility, but even group character evidence looks to be forbidden in the criminal courts. It is difficult to discern any pattern here; the exceptions to the credibility taboo that have developed have an almost random quality to them. But, to take just one example, I suspect that the confession exception has developed in England in part because the criminal justice system has a guilty conscience over false confessions, and in part because of the development of credible expertise on confessions.[159] A commitment to 'procedurally legitimate' verdicts may exist; but it exists always in tension with other values, such as a commitment to accurate fact-finding. Whenever it is thought that expert evidence can contribute to that aim, courts will face immense pressure to admit it. That, surely, is a good thing.

All this is to say that there are no good reasons for the blanket exclusion of expert evidence on credibility. But that is not to say that courts should readily admit credibility evidence. They should only do so if they think the evidence has reasonable probative value and is reliable, or if its unreliability can be brought home to the jury. I suspect that Wagenaar *et al.* are correct when they claim that 'valid expertise on the trustworthiness of witnesses does not exist',[160] but at the end of the day that depends on the scientific evidence that credibility experts can muster.[161] It would certainly be rash to claim that such expertise could never exist, and I shall not commit myself to any view here.

Earlier, I considered the Canadian Supreme Court's attempt to limit the form of expert testimony on credibility and raised questions about its workability. Despite the problems of the group character/specific credibility evidence distinction, there may be limits on form that would be useful when experts offer testimony on areas close to an ultimate issue. In Chapters 3 and 4 I discussed the Bayesian presentation of expert evidence, which involves a distinction between $P(E|H)$ and $P(H|E)$, and suggested that

---

[158] See James R. McCall, 'Misconceptions and Reevaluation—Polygraph Admissibility After *Rock* and *Daubert*' [1996] *U. Ill. L. Rev.* 363; Roger B. Handberg, 'Expert Testimony on Eyewitness Identification: A New Pair of Glasses for the Jury' (1995) 32 *Am. Crim. L. Rev.* 1013. Eyewitness evidence is discussed in more detail in § 10 below.

[159] See Gudjonsson, *supra* n. 80.

[160] Willem A. Wagenaar, Peter J. van Koppen, and Hans F. M. Crombag, *Anchored Narratives: The Psychology of Criminal Evidence* (Hemel Hempstead: Harvester Wheatsheaf, 1993), 196.

[161] For research suggesting that experts may have something to offer on credibility, see Eric Shepherd and Anna Mortimer, 'Identifying Anomaly in Evidential Text' in Anthony Heaton-Armstrong, Eric Shepherd, and David Wolchover, *Analysing Witness Testimony: A Guide for Legal Practitioners and Other Professionals* (London: Blackstone Press, 1999); Amina Memon, Aldert Vrij, and Ray Bull, *Psychology and Law: Truthfulness, Accuracy and Credibility* (London: McGraw-Hill, 1998), chs 1 and 2.

there were good reasons for experts giving evidence in terms of the former rather than the latter. Enforcing the distinction in cases where expert evidence is offered on credibility might dissolve some of the concerns expressed by courts. First, it would mean that experts never gave evidence in the form 'in my opinion, X was telling the truth/has been abused'. This, in turn, would make juries less likely simply to substitute the expert's judgement for their own. Secondly, it would force experts to be more precise about the foundation for their evidence. In a child abuse case, the expert might testify in terms such as 'the evidence provides fair/good/strong support for a conclusion of abuse'.[162] When pressed, she would need to point to factors that were more likely to be found in abused children than in non-abused children. To take a specific example: in *Robinson*, the expert would have been permitted to testify that the complainant possessed characteristics supporting the conclusion that she would not adopt ideas from someone else. If pressed, she would need to identify the characteristics and support the opinion with evidence that they were more common in non-suggestible children than in suggestible children.

If evidence were to be given in the form just suggested, it might still be obvious to a jury that the expert believed the witness. But that would no longer matter so much, because there would no longer be especial concern about credibility evidence. In addition, the jury would be able to hear specific reasons for the expert's believing the witness and would therefore have solid grounds for accepting her evidence if it chose to do so. A possible objection to this proposal is that experts might rarely be in a position to know that certain characteristics are more common in abused than non-abused children. But if that were the case, the expert would have no grounds for drawing a conclusion of abuse and should not be giving evidence at all.[163] The Bayesian format encourages rigorous thinking, and that can be no bad thing.

At this point in the chapter, I hope that the *Turner* rule has been thoroughly dismantled. It should be clear that the rule contains a number of components, some valuable—such as concerns about normative distortion —others less so—such as the credibility taboo. The concluding part of this chapter now turns to two case studies of issues on which expert evidence is or might be given, and examines the arguments for excluding or admitting

---

[162] For a more detailed discussion of how Bayesian analysis maps onto testimony in child abuse cases, see Thomas D. Lyon and Jonathan J. Koehler, 'The Relevance Ratio: Evaluating the Probative Value of Expert Testimony in Child Sexual Abuse Cases' (1996) 82 *Cornell L. Rev.* 43.

[163] For an all too rare recognition of this point in the case law, see *R. v. F.* (1995) 83 A. Crim. R. 502, 507–9. As was seen in Ch. 5 § 7, there are exceptions to this: we can have good reasons for trusting an expert's judgement even when she cannot articulate the basis on which it is made. It does not seem to me that this model would apply to the assessment of the credibility of children, if only because the expert would have had no good way of calibrating her judgement against known examples of true and false testimony.

the evidence. The examples chosen are evidence on battered woman syndrome and on eyewitness identification. The principal purpose of this is illustrative: I want to show how the *Turner* concerns function in practice, and how they can be picked apart and analysed in specific contexts. The case studies also demonstrate how the reliability and validity of scientific research varies depending on the purposes for which it is used.[164] The primary aim is not, therefore, to reach firm conclusions about whether these types of evidence should be admitted by English courts. However, one can only gain a full understanding of the *Turner* concerns by considering the strengths and weaknesses of these types of evidence, so the discussion will inevitably suggest some answers to the admissibility questions.

9. EXPERT EVIDENCE ON BATTERED WOMAN SYNDROME

Battered woman syndrome (BWS) evidence has already made an entrance in the earlier discussion of *Lavallee*. There it was shown that a careful analysis of the evidence highlighted the danger of its causing normative distortion. BWS evidence has been used in a number of trials in England.[165] Before examining two of the cases, I describe BWS evidence and the criticisms that have been levelled at it in a little more detail.

It is not easy to give a clear definition of BWS. The use of the word 'syndrome' implies that BWS consists of identifiable psychological symptoms caused by an abusive relationship. Proponents of BWS commonly draw on the work of Lenore Walker, who identifies two components of the syndrome: learned helplessness and the cycle of violence.[166] Walker developed the concept of learned helplessness from research showing that dogs repeatedly subjected to electric shocks lost the inclination to escape from further shocks, even when given the opportunity. She hypothesized that women subjected to abuse might lose the will to resist, and that this might explain the initially surprising fact that some women stay in abusive relationships. The cycle of violence theory posits that abuse typically follows a cycle, in which there is a tension-building phase, followed by a battering incident, followed in turn by a period of loving contrition. The cycle has twofold significance: first, like learned helplessness, it may help explain why women stay in violent relationships. Secondly, it may provide an explanation for the fact that some abused women attack their partners during a lull in the violence. The suggestion is that these women can predict that they will be subjected to further violence in the future.

---

[164] See, generally, Mosteller, *supra* n. 141.

[165] In addition to the two discussed here, see *R. v. Howell* [1988] 1 Cr. App. R. (S.) 229; *R. v. Grainger* [1997] 1 Cr. App. R. (S.) 369; *R. v. Hobson* [1998] 1 Cr. App. R. 31.

[166] Lenore E. Walker, *The Battered Woman* (New York: Harper & Row, 1979); Lenore E. Walker, *The Battered Woman Syndrome* (New York: Springer, 1984).

In *The Battered Woman Syndrome*,[167] Walker reports research purporting to establish the existence both of learned helplessness among battered women and of the cycle of violence as a characteristic of battering relationships. Her research has been subjected to substantial criticism.[168] Concerns have been expressed about Walker's methodology and about the lack of support her data provide for the theory of BWS.[169] Furthermore, other studies of violent relationships lend little support to Walker's theory. There is some evidence that battered women suffer from depression, and some that they exhibit some symptoms of post-traumatic stress disorder.[170] Rather than examining the research in detail, I shall make a more general point. It is difficult to conduct research to show that violent relationships cause particular symptoms. The ideal way to investigate a hypothesis about the

[167] Ibid.

[168] See, generally, Donald Alexander Downs: *More Than Victims: Battered Women, The Syndrome Society and the Law* (Chicago: University of Chicago Press, 1996), 76–99; 138–81; Robert F. Schopp, Barbara J. Sturgis, and Megan Sullivan, 'Battered Woman Syndrome, Expert Testimony, and the Distinction Between Justification and Excuse' [1994] *U. Ill. L. Rev.* 45, 49–64; David L. Faigman and Amy J. Wright, 'The Battered Woman Syndrome in the Age of Science' (1997) 39 *Ariz. L. Rev.* 67.

[169] See, especially, David L. Faigman, 'The Battered Woman Syndrome and Self-Defense: A Legal and Empirical Dissent' (1986) 72 *Virginia L. Rev.* 619, 626–43. See also Regina A. Schuller and Neil Vidmar, 'Battered Woman Syndrome Evidence in the Courtroom: A Review of the Literature' (1992) 16 *Law & Hum. Behav.* 273.

[170] See Schopp *et al.*, *supra* n. 168, 59–64. For a thorough review of the research, see Regina Schuller and Patricia A. Hastings, 'Battered Woman Syndrome: Scientific Status' in David L. Faigman, David H. Kaye, Michael J. Saks, and Joseph Sanders (eds), *Modern Scientific Evidence: The Law and Science of Expert Testimony*, Vol. 1 (St Paul: West Publishing, 1997) and Regina Schuller, 'Battered Woman Syndrome: Scientific Status' in 1999 Pocket Part to ibid. Although this level of detail is not especially relevant to the discussion in the text, the following summarizes these sources, with a few observations of my own. In recent writings, Walker has cast BWS as a type of post-traumatic stress disorder (see Lenore E. A. Walker, 'Understanding Battered Woman Syndrome', *Trial*, February 1995, 30, 32; ead., in 'Symposium: Women and the Law' (1993) 20 *Pepperdine L. Rev.* 1111, 1177). There are problems in equating BWS with PTSD, however. PTSD itself is a poorly defined condition (see, e.g., Rachel Rosser, 'Stress, Personality Disorder and Post-Traumatic Stress Disorder' [1995] *Current Opinion in Psychiatry* 98). A further problem is that the DSM criteria for PTSD list exposure to a stressor as a requirement for diagnosis (see *Diagnostic and Statistical Manual of Mental Disorders*, 4th edn (Washington DC: American Psychiatric Association, 1994), 424–9; also *The ICD-10 Classification of Mental and Behavioural Disorders: Clinical Descriptions and Diagnostic Guidelines* (Geneva: World Health Organisation, 1992), 147–9). This would create problems for diagnostic uses of BWS/PTSD: if a court uses PTSD symptoms as evidence of exposure to violence, it will be bootstrapping, because the PTSD diagnosis will itself depend on a presumption that the woman has been exposed to violence. Additionally, the research finds that many women who have not been exposed to violent relationships have PTSD symptoms, and that some women who have been victims of violence do not. Reliance on PTSD, therefore, will create considerable numbers of false positives and false negatives. If some equivalent to BWS is looked for without relying on PTSD, problems remain. Schuller and Hastings, at 373, conclude that 'a range of studies document a host of psychological problems or symptomology that can be identified among battered women. There does not appear, however, to be a single profile that captures the impact of abuse on a woman. Rather the research demonstrates that "battered women's diverse psychological realities are not limited to one particular profile" '. (Quoting Mary Ann Dutton, 'Understanding Women's Response to Domestic Violence: A Redefinition of Battered Woman Syndrome' (1993) 21 *Hofstra L. Rev.* 1191, 1210).

symptoms of abuse would be to take a random sample of women in order
to find those symptoms. If the symptoms were far more common among
battered women than among non-battered women, that would support the
hypothesis. In practice, researchers have used battered women as a sample
population.[171] Even if certain symptoms, such as depression, are common
among battered women, the skewed sample obviously cannot establish that
depression is caused by battering. Put simply, the point is this: it is fairly
easy to do research to show whether symptom x is common among abused
women. It is more difficult to show whether symptom x is caused by abuse:
that would require comparison with a sample of non-abused women. It is
harder still to uncover whether symptom x can be used to diagnose that a
woman has been abused, because even if abuse causes symptom x, symptom
x (like depression) might also be caused by other factors.

In *R. v. Thornton (No. 2)*[172] the Court of Appeal held that BWS was
relevant to the defence of provocation. BWS, it held,

> may be relevant in two ways. First, it may form an important background to what-
> ever triggered the actus reus. A jury may more readily find there was a sudden loss
> of control triggered by even a minor incident, if the defendant has endured abuse
> over a long period, on the 'last straw' basis. Secondly, depending on the medical
> evidence, the syndrome may have affected the defendant's personality so as to
> constitute a significant characteristic relevant (as we shall indicate) to the second
> question the jury has to consider in regard to provocation.[173]

The first ground of relevance is unobjectionable, but it is unclear why BWS
is relevant to the defendant's background. The defendant, it would seem,
has either suffered a long period of abuse or she has not, and her suffering
from the syndrome makes no difference to that fact. A charitable interpretation suggests two possibilities: BWS may provide evidence that D has suffered a long period of abuse. This would require that BWS symptoms are
delineated clearly enough and are sufficiently specific to violent relationships
to allow them to be used in a diagnostic manner. However, even in the United
States, where BWS has widespread admissibility, it is rarely used diagnostic-
ally.[174] Given the state of BWS research, that is not surprising. Alternatively,
the court may mean that if the long period of abuse triggered BWS, BWS
would make D perceive the minor incident as more serious than it would
strike the average person as being, because it would remind her of her
helplessness and low self-esteem. She would therefore be more likely to

---

[171] On the biases that may result from basing a sample on the 'dependent variable', see Gary
King, Robert O. Keohane, and Sidney Verba, *Designing Social Inquiry: Scientific Inference in
Qualitative Research* (Princeton: Princeton University Press, 1994), 128–39.
[172] [1996] 2 All ER 1023.   [173] Ibid. 1030.
[174] See Mosteller, *supra* n. 141, 483–4; Holly Maguigan, 'Battered Women and Self-
Defense: Myths and Misconceptions in Current Reform Proposals' (1991) 140 *U. Pa. L. Rev.*
379, 461–7. Cf. Walker (1993), *supra* n. 170, 1174–5.

lose her self-control than the average person. This is similar to argument *d″* in *Turner* and, as in *Turner*, BWS evidence may not have much probative value when used in this manner. Whether BWS can do the work required of it here depends on how the expert approaches the problem. If she concludes that, because Thornton was in a violent relationship, she must suffer from helplessness and low self-esteem, then she is relying on the research to establish something that it may not do: that battering regularly produces symptoms such as helplessness. Alternatively, the expert may examine Thornton and find that she suffered from feelings of helplessness and low self-esteem. But if that is the case, BWS is doing no work at all, because the jury can be told directly that Thornton so suffered. That her symptoms were caused by the battering is neither here nor there. That is fortuitous, both because of the causal point, and because, as Lawton LJ observed, expert evidence 'dressed up in scientific jargon'[175] may not ease the jury's task; for these reasons, reference to BWS is probably best avoided.

The second ground of relevance—the suggestion that BWS symptoms may form a 'significant characteristic'—is even more problematic. Here the court assumes that BWS is relevant to the objective test of provocation, that is, the jury's decision whether a reasonable person sharing D's characteristics (here BWS) would react as D did. Analytically, it is helpful to divide this question into two parts: (*a*) the gravity of provocation to D and (*b*) the reasonableness of D's response to provocation of that gravity.[176] Despite the promise of an explanation later in the judgment, the court never does explain just why BWS might be relevant to either of these questions. On the then conventional theory of provocation BWS may[177] have been relevant to (*a*) (this is basically argument *d′* in *Turner*, now rendered acceptable by the change in the law wrought by *Camplin*[178]). As suggested above, low self-esteem and helplessness may make provocation graver to D than it would to a non-BWS sufferer,[179] but, again, it seems that the concept of BWS is best avoided here. Additionally, given that, as was seen in the discussion of *Lavallee*, BWS involves cognitive distortion, it might have been helpful if

---

[175] *Supra* n. 1, 841.

[176] If this distinction seems obscure—and its supposed opaqueness has contributed to the difficulties in clarifying the law on provocation—it can be conceptualized in the following manner. Imagine a 10 point gravity of provocation scale. Minor provocation (the bus being late) scores close to 1; grave provocation (violence) close to 10. The juror should put herself in D's shoes—taking all of her characteristics into account—and decide where on the scale the provocation comes. This is the gravity of provocation to D. Then the juror should forget all about D's characteristics and ask, 'how would the reasonable person react to provocation of this gravity?' The answer to this question will indicate whether D's response was reasonable.

[177] The caveat is necessary because relevant characteristics may have been restricted to those about which D had been taunted. See *R. v. Morhall* [1996] AC 90; *Luc Thiet Thuan v. R.* [1996] 2 All ER 1033, 1048.

[178] [1978] AC 705.

[179] This appears to have been how BWS evidence was used in *R. v. Howell* [1998] 1 Cr. App. R. (S.) 229.

the Court of Appeal had examined the relevance of unreasonable mistakes to provocation.[180]

Whether D's characteristics are relevant to (*b*) is controversial, but, at the time *Thornton* was decided, the Court of Appeal may have been assuming that they were.[181] The reason for caution here is that, if all of D's characteristics are taken into account in assessing (*b*), the law's requirement that the response to the provocation be reasonable loses most of its meaning.[182] Ignoring this problem, how might BWS help the jury to answer (*b*)? It is difficult to see how either learned helplessness or the cycle theory can show D's response to have been reasonable.[183] In fact, there is a fundamental contradiction involved in using BWS to show that a violent response was reasonable, because women who become helpless and remain in a battering relationship seem to exhibit a greater degree of self-control than most people.[184]

One does not need to have a terribly sophisticated knowledge of BWS and the criticisms levelled at it to appreciate the problems in the court's reliance on it in *Thornton*. The principal problem, as so often, is a failure to establish the relevance of the evidence to the questions a jury must address. In the second BWS case I consider, similar problems recur. The case, *R. v. Emery*,[185] also illustrates the difficulties caused by attempts strictly to enforce the credibility limb of the *Turner* rule.

Emery and her partner Hedman were tried with offences arising from the death of their child. Each blamed the other for being violent towards the

---

[180] There is some authority for the claim that unreasonable mistakes do not affect provocation: see J. C. Smith and Brian Hogan, *Criminal Law*, 8th edn (London: Butterworths, 1996), 375–6. However, the absence of modern authority and the fact that unreasonable mistakes deprive actors of claims of duress (*R. v. Graham* [1982] 1 All ER 801) raise some doubts about this.

[181] See *R. v. Smith* [1999] 1 Cr. App. R. 256. In *Smith*, 268–9, *Thornton* is one of the cases cited to show that D's characteristics were treated as being relevant to (*b*). I cannot find any clear statement to that effect in *Thornton*. On this question, see also the House of Lords decision in *R. v. Smith* [2000] 3 WLR 654. This decides that D's characteristics *are* relevant to (*b*); the dissenting judgment of Lord Hobhouse contains a close analysis of the Court of Appeal case law which throws doubt on whether the majority's view was ever adopted there, except, perhaps, in *R. v. Campbell* [1997] 1 Cr. App. R. 199.

[182] See, generally, Andrew Ashworth, *Principles of Criminal Law*, 2nd edn (Oxford: Clarendon Press, 1995), 269–73.

[183] If learned helplessness explains why D did not leave the violent relationship, might that be relevant to (*b*)? I am doubtful that it could be. The reason why D failed to leave in the past is irrelevant, and, because provocation requires that D lost her self-control, there is no requirement of withdrawal from the provoking situation. Nevertheless, evidence on why D did not leave might be relevant for other reasons: see below.

[184] The most cogent argument on this question is made by Lord Millett, in *Smith* (HL), *supra* n. 181. Millett suggests that expert evidence would be relevant to show the effect that prolonged exposure to violence would have on the reasonable person. He argues that, by showing that violence wears down its victim's self-control, the evidence would be relevant without the need to accept that D's particular characteristics are relevant to (*b*). In theory, this is a sound argument; the problem with it is that current research does not really portray prolonged exposure to violence as a disinhibitor, in the way that Millett seems to presume it does.

[185] (1993) 14 Cr. App. R. (S.) 394.

child; both were convicted of cruelty to a person under 16 [186] Hedman was also convicted of assault occasioning actual bodily harm, and this suggested that the jury had found that he had actually used violence towards their child while Emery had merely been complicit in it. At trial, Emery had used BWS evidence in an attempt to show that she had ignored Hedman's treatment of the child because she was subjected to duress, the duress being Hedman's regular acts of violence against her. Two experts gave evidence describing the symptoms of BWS.

An initial problem in *Emery* concerns the work the BWS evidence was required to do. Having described the effects of BWS, the experts opined that Emery was a typical example of a BWS sufferer. But for the duress defence to work, it is not enough that Emery has BWS characteristics; those characteristics must also have been *caused* by any duress she was subjected to (contrast the situation in *Thornton*, where what was important was Thornton's characteristics, and their causation was largely irrelevant). So what the jury needs to know is whether BWS characteristics may have any cause other than battering. Put another way, it needs to know how specific BWS characteristics are to battered women, because if the symptoms were caused by something other than battering, Emery has no valid claim of duress. One can only presume that the court thought BWS symptoms were relatively specific to battering.

This is only the start of the difficulties in *Emery*. During the course of their evidence, it seems that the experts recounted to the court what Emery had told them about the violence she had suffered. Concern was expressed that the jury might use the expert evidence to decide whether Emery (who gave evidence at trial) was telling the truth about Hedman's violence towards her. In response, the trial judge carefully instructed the jury that it should decide for itself whether Emery was telling the truth, and only then go on to consider the expert evidence.

The Court of Appeal endorsed the judge's approach, relying on a distinction between the evidence of fact (had Emery been abused?) and the expert evidence. It would, though, have been difficult for the jury to obey the judge's instructions about not using the expert evidence for credibility purposes, because the experts had diagnosed the symptoms of BWS. On the hypothesis that the BWS evidence was relevant in the first place, Emery had BWS, and if Emery had BWS, she had (I am assuming) probably been abused. If she had been abused, of course, she was telling the truth about Hedman's violence. In other words, the BWS diagnosis was relevant to factual credibility, and could be used to support Emery's credibility just as the psychiatrist's evidence in *Turner* supported Turner's credibility under arguments *d'* and *d''*.

---

[186] Contrary to Children and Young Persons Act 1933, s. 1.

I stated earlier that the credibility limb of the *Turner* rule was closely related to the hearsay limb. This creates further complications in analysing *Emery*. By following the judge's instructions the jury would have been taking the approach to hearsay uses of expert evidence required by *Turner* and *Bradshaw*.[187] The jurors would have looked for direct evidence (such as Emery's testimony about Hedman's violence towards her) to support the expert diagnosis and, if they believed the direct evidence, they would have had grounds for accepting that diagnosis. Unfortunately, this does not provide a neat solution. From the case report, it is not exactly clear what the diagnosis had been based on. Certainly Emery's assertions were a large component, but direct observation also played a part: it was noted that a monotonous tone of speech was a BWS symptom—presumably one that Emery exhibited. The experts may also have administered tests such as 'locus of control' assessment to diagnose BWS symptoms. These indicia of BWS do not create hearsay problems, just as a doctor's diagnosis of bruises and broken bones would not have done. The problem, then, is that the experts' conclusions contain hearsay and non-hearsay components, just as they contain conclusions about both factual and personal credibility. It can be objected that it unfairly saps Emery's expert evidence of its full force if the jury cannot use it as evidence of Hedman's abuse and, deductively, of Emery's overall credibility.

If the experts' diagnoses in *Emery* were largely based on Emery's assertions, then perhaps the trial judge's approach was an appropriate, pragmatic one. But another approach would have been equally suitable. The judge could have instructed the jury that the diagnosis of BWS symptoms supported Emery's account, but that it should be aware that the diagnosis was also based on Emery's assertions and that she had an incentive to lie to the experts. This would alert the jury to the principal hearsay danger, but avoid forcing upon it an artificial, and rather illogical, analysis of the evidence.

It seems, then, that the courts' criticisms of the expert testimony in *Emery* were misfocused. Criticism was informed by the credibility taboo, not by the specific dangers of relying on expert evidence that is based largely on hearsay. Beyond this, there were far more important issues that were not addressed. In *Emery*, the Court of Appeal accepted the admissibility of BWS evidence because BWS is 'complex and not known [about] by the public at large'.[188] BWS evidence may pass the jury competence limb of the *Turner* rule, but that does not establish its relevance or validity. In ignoring these issues, the court ignored the most glaring problem of all. The experts apparently testified that BWS is characterized by a woman's 'inability to resist or stand up to her abuser . . . [it] makes her unable to leave, unable to seek help'.[189] Evidence of this categorical nature suggests an attribution error of the grossest sort, the error being to deny the woman free will by attributing all to situational factors. That, it hardly need be said, is wildly implausible.

There are other uses of BWS evidence that deserve consideration. It is often remarked that BWS evidence can play a valuable role in the courtroom by dispelling myths about battered women.[190] This function of the evidence was drawn on in *Lavallee* to bolster its admissibility. An obvious question about Lavallee's behaviour, Wilson J suggested, was 'if the violence was so intolerable, why did the appellant not leave the abuser long ago? This question . . . plays on the popular myth . . . that a woman who says she was battered yet stayed with her batterer was either not as badly beaten as she claimed or else she liked it.'[191] The expert evidence, therefore, was aimed at 'an area where the purported common knowledge of the jury may be very much mistaken, an area where jurors' logic, drawn from their own experience, may lead to a wholly incorrect conclusion, an area where expert knowledge would enable the jurors to disregard their prior conclusions as being common myths rather than common knowledge'.[192]

An expert testifying on BWS might refer to the cycle theory or to learned helplessness as a means of dispelling jury myths. But even if BWS research establishes that battering relationships typically include a cycle of violence, the hypothesis that the loving contrition phase of the cycle explains why some women remain in a battering relationship remains no more than a hypothesis; it has little support.[193] Learned helplessness is a more promising concept in this regard: if a defendant can be diagnosed as suffering from learned helplessness, that would help explain why she had not left a violent relationship. However, because there would be no need to demonstrate a link between the battering and the helplessness, there would be little need to introduce the concept of BWS. Alternatively, the expert may hypothesize that the violence described by D would have triggered learned helplessness and an inability to leave. Used in this manner, BWS would carry a lot of weight, and, on present research, it is unlikely that learned helplessness can be validly inferred from knowledge of exposure to violence.

Instead, an expert might rely on testimony of a more general sort. If the myth about which there is concern is that women simply will not remain in relationships where they are subjected to severe violence, all an expert need do is testify that there is ample evidence that women do remain in such relationships. Whether the reasons for this are psychological, financial or cultural matters little: all the jury need know is that not leaving is consistent

---

[190] See, e.g., Marilyn MacCrimmon, 'The Social Construction of Reality and the Rules of Evidence' (1991) 25 *U. Brit. Colum. L. Rev.* 36.

[191] *Supra* n. 47, 121.

[192] Ibid. 113, quoting *State* v. *Kelly* 478 A. 2d 364, 378 (1984).

[193] See, generally, Michael J. Strube, 'The Decision to Leave an Abusive Relationship: Empirical Evidence and Theoretical Issues' (1988) 104 *Psychological Bulletin* 236.

with the defendant's story of severe violence.[194] That is doubly fortunate, because it circumvents the need to rely on doubtful concepts such as learned helplessness, and because it may even remove the need for expert testimony. It may be that a judge is as well placed as an expert to inform the jury that failure to leave does not undermine the defendant's case. The respective merits of judge and jury instruction are explored in the following section.

Three further points need to be made about the merits of expert evidence— or its judicial equivalent—as a myth dispeller in cases involving battered women. First, the evidence would properly be characterized as group character evidence. The use of group character evidence in battered woman cases may be less problematic than it is in cases such as *Marquard,* because it can be given in a more general form (pointing out to the jury that some of their assumptions may be wrong). Secondly, I noted in the discussion of *Robinson* that it is sometimes argued that evidence supporting a witness's credibility should only be permitted when her credibility has been attacked. I am sceptical of that argument in cases like *Robinson* where credibility is the key issue. But even where credibility is not quite so central, the analogy with section 1(f) of the Criminal Evidence Act 1898 does not seem apt. If there is a danger of the trial being side-tracked by a discussion of what are essentially collateral issues, then that appears to be an argument in support of judicial instruction rather than expert testimony, which is not so easily controlled. This connects to a third point, which is that the danger of collateral side-tracks must be weighed against the probative value of the evidence. Evidence dispelling myths about battered women would have the equivalent of good probative value if there is good reason to believe that the myths are untrue and that jurors are likely to believe them.[195] The 'she would have left . . .' myth is undoubtedly untrue, but there is little evidence that jurors subscribe to it.[196] There may simply be no need to dispel myths in cases involving battered women.

---

[194] Earlier, I was critical of experts who give evidence in terms of 'consistent with', and in the previous section I suggested that experts giving group character evidence do so in Bayesian form. Lest the present proposal appear contradictory, I should explain. The fear that the 'she would have left' myth will distort the fact-finding process appears to be based on the assumption that jurors will employ categorical rather than probabilistic reasoning. In other words, they will think that remaining in the relationship is flatly inconsistent with suffering violence and conclude that the claims of violence are false, or at least grossly exaggerated. To block the categorical inference, all that is needed is the information that the two events could co-occur; probabilistic information is not necessary. In turn, this suggests that rigorous research is not needed as a foundation for the evidence. So long as some women remain in violent relationships, the evidence has a secure foundation.

[195] The rough Bayesian analysis, suggested in Saul M. Kassin, Phoebe C. Ellsworth, and Vicki L. Smith, 'The "General Acceptance" of Psychological Research on Eyewitness Testimony: A Survey of the Experts' (1989) 44 *Am. Psychol.* 1089, 1097, is a useful means of analysing the utility of expert evidence on such topics. One needs to consider both the validity of the evidence, and the probability that it will add something to the jury's knowledge.

[196] See Downs, *supra* n. 168, 169–73.

10. Expert Evidence on Eyewitness Identification

Writing in 1972, the Criminal Law Revision Committee stated that it regarded mistaken eyewitness identifications 'as by far the greatest cause of actual or possible wrong convictions. Several cases have occurred in recent years', it noted, 'when a person has been charged or convicted on what has later been shown beyond doubt to have been mistaken identification.'[197] Eyewitness identification, and the factors that affect its accuracy, are now the most researched of 'psycho-legal' topics; there are around 2,000 relevant books and articles.[198] Yet if a defendant who had been placed at the scene of the crime by an eyewitness were to call an expert to testify about the possibility of false identification, the expert testimony would almost certainly be excluded under the jury competence limb of the *Turner* rule.[199] At least, that would be the result in an English court; courts in the United States have been somewhat more receptive to this sort of evidence.

Since the Criminal Law Revision Committee wrote the words just quoted, much has been done to guard against the danger of mistaken convictions based on eyewitness evidence. Identification procedures used by the police have been improved.[200] And the courts themselves have taken steps to warn juries about the dangers of convicting on eyewitness evidence. In response to Lord Devlin's report on eyewitness misidentification,[201] the Court of Appeal laid down guidelines on the treatment of eyewitness evidence. The *Turnbull* guidelines[202] take the form of advice that judges should give to juries in cases that depend wholly or substantially on eyewitness evidence. The jury should be warned of the special need for caution before convicting and its attention drawn to the possibility that even a confident

---

[197] Criminal Law Revision Committee, *Eleventh Report: Evidence (General)*, Cmnd 4991 (London: HMSO, 1972), para. 196.

[198] See A. Daniel Yarmey, 'Probative v. Prejudicial Value of Eyewitness Memory Research' (1997) 5 *Expert Evidence* 89, 89. See also Michael J. Saks, 'The Law does not Live by Eyewitness-Testimony Alone' (1986) 10 *Law & Hum. Behav.* 279.

[199] The closest example may be *R. v. Browning* [1995] Crim. LR 227, where the Court of Appeal ruled that expert evidence on memory decay was caught by the *Turner* rule.

[200] See Police and Criminal Evidence Act 1984, Code of Practice D; Ian McKenzie, 'Psychology and Legal Practice: Fairness and Accuracy in Identification Parades' [1995] *Crim. LR* 200.

[201] P. Devlin, *Report to the Secretary of State for the Home Department of the Departmental Committee on Evidence of Identification in Criminal Cases*, HC 338 (London: HMSO, 1976).

[202] *R. v. Turnbull* [1977] 1 QB 224. The Court of Appeal's guidelines depart slightly from Devlin's recommendations: see Colin Tapper, *Cross and Tapper on Evidence*, 8th edn (London: Butterworths, 1995), 789–90; Patrick Devlin, 'Foreword' in John W. Shepherd, Hadyn D. Ellis, and Graham M. Davies (eds), *Identification Evidence: A Psychological Evaluation* (Aberdeen: Aberdeen University Press, 1982). For some relevant factors which are not mentioned in the guidelines, see Mark R. Kebbell and Graham F. Wagstaff, *Face Value? Evaluating the Accuracy of Eyewitness Information*, Police Research Series Paper 102 (London: Home Office Policing and Reducing Crime Unit, 1999), v–vi.

witness is mistaken. The judge should point out the factors affecting the reliability of the identification in the instant case, such as the length of observation, the distance from which the suspect was seen, and the time elapsed between observation and identification. If the quality of the identification evidence is considered to be poor, the case should be withdrawn from the jury unless there is corroborating evidence.

The *Turnbull* guidelines constitute an important attempt to alert juries to the frailties of eyewitness testimony. In relation to the discussion in the previous section, note that the guidelines are an example of group character evidence being presented to the jury through judicial instructions, rather than through expert testimony.[203] There is obviously a strong argument that the guidelines circumvent the need for expert evidence on eyewitness identification. Before addressing this claim, it is important to consider what more general objections there might be to the presentation of expert evidence on eyewitness performance. The United States jurisprudence provides a useful starting point for exploring the issues.

It is not uncommon for psychologists to be asked to testify on the facts affecting eyewitness accuracy in United States criminal courts. Frequent topics for testimony are the effect of post-event information on memory; the effect of stress on eyewitness accuracy; the relationship between eyewitness confidence and accuracy; the relative accuracy of within-race and cross-race identifications; unconscious transference of information that may affect memory; the rate at which memory decays; and the effect of 'weapon focus' on eyewitness accuracy.[204] Courts have traditionally been sceptical of this type of expert evidence, but the present trend seems to be to reject a blanket exclusionary rule, and to 'admit expert testimony on eyewitness identification under certain circumstances which should be examined on a case-by-case basis'.[205] Nevertheless, good reasons for admitting such evidence are rarely found to exist, and the vast majority of federal courts continue to exclude it when proffered. The decisions show a large degree of consensus on the reasons for exclusion: because psychologists usually testify about general trends among eyewitnesses as a group, the evidence is not sufficiently individualized; judicial instructions and cross-examination are adequate safeguards against mistaken identification; the issues on which the expert proposes to testify are matters of common sense; and the probative

---

[203] Note, as well, that a *Turnbull* instruction amounts to the jury being given advice about making credibility determinations; the existence of the guidelines, therefore, provides one more reason to be sceptical of claims that there exists a general taboo on evidence concerning credibility.

[204] The list is based on the survey reported in Kassin *et al.*, *supra* n. 195. The authors report the percentage of experts in their survey who had testified on the factors listed at least once; the results therefore present only a rough guide to the topics addressed most frequently.

[205] *United States* v. *Smith* 156 F. 3d 1046, 1053 (1998). See also *United States* v. *Harris* 995 F. 2d 532, 534 (1993).

value of the evidence is outweighed by the danger of prejudice.[206] Less often, doubts are voiced about the scientific soundness of the research on which the testimony is based.[207] There is a further factor that courts seem to take into account when considering admissibility. This is not a traditional evidentiary concern but a pragmatic one: if the case against the defendant relies largely on the testimony of a single eyewitness, the evidence is more likely to be admitted; if there are multiple eyewitnesses or there is corroborating evidence, exclusion is more probable.[208] Under a conventional Bayesian analysis, this practice might be criticized. The likelihood ratio for the eyewitness evidence depends only on the factors relating directly to the eyewitness, such as the conditions affecting encoding and recall of the event witnessed. The existence or otherwise of other evidence incriminating the defendant affects the prior probability of guilt, not the strength of the identification evidence. Nevertheless, the pragmatic concern is defensible. The weaker the other evidence against the defendant, the more probable it is that an eyewitness who identifies him is mistaken.[209] From the court's point of view, therefore, a miscarriage of justice is more likely to be prevented by admitting expert evidence in weak cases than in strong ones.

As I have said, there is a large amount of research on eyewitness identification. Most of the studies are carefully conducted and—in so far as that label is useful—deserve to be called scientific.[210] But it is not always easy to reconcile the results of different studies, and the lack of common measure for the factors examined makes inter-experiment comparison difficult.[211] There are also problems in establishing the forensic relevance of the research.[212] Nearly all eyewitness research has been conducted through laboratory experiments and it is not obvious how the results transfer to the

---

[206] See *United States* v. *Thevis* 665 F. 2d 616 (1982); *United States* v. *Ginn* 87 F. 3d 367 (1996); *United States* v. *Smith* 122 F. 3d 1355 (1997).

[207] See, e.g., *United States* v. *Watson* 587 F. 2d 365 (1978). Two cases that considered the issue under the *Daubert* standard have concluded that the proposed testimony falls foul of the criteria in that case. However, in both cases the defendant adduced little evidence to support admissibility and the courts allowed that a better argued proffer might well pass muster under *Daubert*. See *United States* v. *Rincon* 28 F. 3d 921 (1994); *United States* v. *Brien* 59 F. 3d 274 (1995). Cf. *United States* v. *Smithers* 212 F. 3d 306 (2000), where the analysis implies that such evidence would pass *Daubert*.

[208] See *Smithers*, ibid.; *Smith, supra* n. 205, 1053–4; *United States* v. *Smith* 736 F. 2d 1103, 1107–8 (1984).

[209] See Richard O. Lempert, 'Social Science in Court: On "Eyewitness Experts" and Other Issues' (1986) 10 *Law & Hum. Behav.* 167, 170–1.

[210] See David L. Faigman, 'The Evidentiary Status of Social Science Under *Daubert*: Is it "Scientific," "Technical," or "Other" Knowledge?' (1995) 1 *Psychol., Pub. Policy, & Law* 960, 966–7, 975.

[211] See, for example, the discussion of the effects of stress on encoding in Ebbe B. Ebbesen and Vladimir J. Konečni, 'Eyewitness Memory Research: Probative v. Prejudicial Value' (1997) 5 *Expert Evidence* 2, 8–12.

[212] For an example of a specific, rather counter-intuitive, problem—that involved in applying knowledge of cross-race effects to line-up identifications—see Howard E. Egeth, 'What Do We *Not* Know About Eyewitness Identification?' (1993) 48 *Am. Psychol.* 577, 579.

situations examined by courts.[213] An advantage of laboratory studies is that they allow psychologists to control relevant variables and therefore to be more confident about the factors that produce variations in the accuracy of identifications by subjects. However, 'this control may paradoxically make it less likely that the results are applicable to specific cases in the "real world" ', because 'internal and external validity are often inversely related'.[214] As critics of those eyewitness experts who testify in court observe, real cases involve a complex range of factors and very little is known about how the variables found to affect laboratory subjects interact.[215]

Psychologists who testify as expert witnesses appear to be aware of some of the limitations of the research. They do not tell juries that a particular identification is likely to be mistaken (though, on occasion, quite specific testimony can be given, and one should not overlook the important contribution this might make to criminal trials[216]). Instead, they testify in general terms about the factors thought to have a negative impact on eyewitness accuracy. The research, therefore, is not asked to bear all that much weight —certainly not as much as BWS evidence sometimes is. Nevertheless, critics of expert testimony on eyewitness identification argue that its generality may make it practically useless. For example, Elliot suggests that the following testimony might legitimately be given on the 'weapon focus' effect:

Psychological research shows that the presence of a weapon can lead to reduced identification accuracy. Some experiments show that the reduction can be moderately large, such as a difference of 20% accuracy, while other experiments show that there is no difference. The effect of a weapon also differs as a function of the individual. On average, the difference is about 10%. Unfortunately, the research does not yet tell us the circumstances under which weapon presence should produce a moderate or a small effect or which people are more susceptible to a weapon focus effect, so we don't know how weapon presence would have affected this witness's memory in this circumstance.[217]

---

[213] See John C. Yuille, 'We Must Study Forensic Eyewitnesses to Know About Them' (1993) 48 *Am. Psychol.* 572.

[214] Peter B. Ainsworth, *Psychology, Law and Eyewitness Testimony* (Chichester: John Wiley, 1998), 167.

[215] See Ebbesen and Konečni, *supra* n. 211.

[216] For example, Davies describes an experiment he conducted in which subjects who were given a description of the offender were able to pick the suspect from a photograph of the line-up on a substantially better than chance basis. This suggested that the line-up did not provide good evidence of identity. Graham M. Davies, 'Mistaken Identification: Where Law Meets Psychology Head On' (1996) 35 *Howard J. Crim. J.* 232, 238–9. See also Willem A. Wagenaar, 'The Proper Seat: A Bayesian Discussion of the Position of the Expert Witness' (1988) 12 *Law & Hum. Behav.* 499 (describing an experiment exploring the ability of a witness to identify the sex of the driver in a fast-moving car).

[217] Rogers Elliot, 'Expert Testimony About Eyewitness Identification: A Critique' (1993) 17 *Law & Hum. Behav.* 423, 428 (quoting a personal communication from Brian Cutler). Elliot notes that Cutler, who has given expert testimony on eyewitness identifications on a number of occasions, would not himself testify on weapon focus. Cf. Saul M. Kassin, Phoebe C. Ellsworth, and Vicki L. Smith, '*Déjà Vu* All Over Again: Elliot's Critique of Eyewitness Experts' (1994) 18 *Law & Hum. Behav.* 203.

The kinds of problems just discussed should certainly make psychologists pause for thought before they testify in court. All the same, so long as the expert is aware of the limitations of the research, it is not obvious that these are knock-down objections. It is in the nature of the research in this area that only general and rather weak conclusions will be available, but these may still provide useful information. Even the testimony quoted by Elliot, which is probably an extreme example, might have legitimate uses. If, as seems likely, jurors use explanation-based decision-making to decide cases,[218] then the testimony on weapon effect might provide an explanation as to why an otherwise credible witness has mistakenly identified the defendant. From another perspective, although the testimony would not allow the jury to accord a precise value to the witness's testimony, it would alert it to the risk of relying on it to achieve a conviction. That there is a risk associated with the weapon effect is something one might even argue the jury is entitled to know.

Apart from the problem of the generality of expert testimony on eyewitness identification, courts have expressed concerns about redundancy and prejudice. Taking the redundancy point, note that, although all lay people have considerable experience of making eyewitness identifications, they have much less experience of making identifications in crime-like contexts, and less again of judging the accuracy of identifications made by other people.[219] In any case, the redundancy claim has been explored empirically. Reviewing the evidence, Cutler and Penrod conclude that lay people are unaware of some, though not all, of the factors relevant to the evaluation of eyewitness testimony.[220] These authors also conclude that even though jurors may, when prompted, demonstrate awareness of the relevance of some factors (such as retention interval and the effect of disguise) on eyewitness accuracy, this does not mean that they will integrate those factors into their decision-making. By drawing particular attention to the significance of certain factors, expert testimony appears to prompt integration. If this result is generalizable beyond eyewitness cases, it suggests that one should be cautious in concluding that expert evidence on any issue is redundant simply because it overlaps with an area of common knowledge.

This brings me, finally, to prejudice. Why might expert evidence on eyewitness identification be considered prejudicial? There are familiar concerns about delay and confusion. A more subtle point is sometimes made, though. In an influential critique of eyewitness expertise, McCloskey and Egeth

---

[218] See Nancy Pennington and Reid Hastie, 'The Story Model for Juror Decision Making' in Reid Hastie (ed.), *Inside the Juror: The Psychology of Juror Decision Making* (Cambridge: Cambridge University Press, 1993).

[219] See Joseph Sanders, 'Expert Witnesses in Eyewitness Facial Identification Cases' (1986) 17 *Texas Tech L. Rev.* 1409, 1440.

[220] Brian L. Cutler and Steven D. Penrod, *Mistaken Identification: The Eyewitness, Psychology and the Law* (Cambridge: Cambridge University Press, 1995), 171–209.

argue that, although there are reasons to be cautious about eyewitness reports, it would be wrong to draw the conclusion that jurors should therefore be more sceptical of eyewitness testimony:

> It must be borne in mind that the degree of skepticism jurors exhibit toward eyewitnesses will affect not only the likelihood that an innocent defendant will be convicted but also the likelihood that a guilty defendant will be convicted. Thus an increase in juror skepticism toward eyewitness testimony would decrease convictions of the guilty as well as convictions of the innocent, and a degree of skepticism that eliminated wrongful conviction on the basis of eyewitness testimony would also eliminate any role of eyewitnesses in the conviction of the guilty.[221]

In other words, it cannot be established that jurors are prone to over-believe eyewitness testimony. There are two responses to this argument. One, which the authors acknowledge, is that if expert testimony enables fact-finders better to discriminate between trustworthy and non-trustworthy eyewitnesses, then convictions of the innocent might be decreased without a corresponding decrease in convictions of the guilty. McCloskey and Egeth, however, doubt that expert testimony could achieve this; they argue that its likely effect is to increase scepticism. A second response is that it is not obvious that we cannot reach a conclusion that fact-finders over-believe eyewitnesses. If we knew that, on average, 20 per cent of eyewitness identifications presented to jurors were false identifications, but that fact-finders decided cases on the basis that the figure was 5 per cent, then we would have good reasons for wishing to increase juror scepticism. Of course, we do not have anything like precise figures for either of these rates. Even if we did, the fact that estimates of eyewitness reliability are context-dependent means that such general figures would not map easily onto individual cases. Nevertheless, information about the likely value of either figure would give us some grounds for claiming that attempts to increase scepticism were appropriate.

Cutler and Penrod argue for the admissibility of expert evidence on eyewitness identifications on the basis of the first counter-argument; that is, they suggest that expert evidence can increase discrimination rather than scepticism.[222] This claim is based on a series of empirical studies they conducted in which mock jurors were asked to judge the accuracy of witnesses to a real event. The authors also contrasted the use of expert evidence with judicial instructions. They found that one commonly used instruction had little effect on juror judgements, while a revised (clearer) instruction on the factors affecting eyewitness testimony increased scepticism rather than discrimination.[223] These results are intriguing, although, like all laboratory

---

[221] Michael McCloskey and Howard E. Egeth, 'Eyewitness Identification: What Can a Psychologist Tell a Jury?' in Lawrence S. Wrightsman, Cynthia E. Willis, and Saul M. Kassin (eds), *On the Witness Stand: Controversies in the Courtroom* (Newbury Park, CA: Sage, 1987) (essay orig. 1983), 198.

[222] *Supra* n. 220, 225–42.   [223] Ibid. 255–64.

research, they should be treated with caution.[224] In particular, the conclusion that judicial instructions are inefficacious cannot necessarily be applied to English trials. The Cutler and Penrod experiments relied on pattern instructions commonly used in United States courts rather than a *Turnbull* style warning. One important way in which the *Turnbull* approach differs is that it requires the judge to identify the factors affecting the quality of the identification in the instant case, and to draw them to the jury's attention. In the United States, judges are generally not permitted to comment to the jury on the facts of a case.[225]

I have chosen expert testimony on eyewitness identification evidence as an illustrative example for a number of reasons. One is that it raises questions about the effectiveness of judicial instructions compared to that of expert testimony. Another is that it prompts thought about the relationship between expert evidence—especially group character evidence—and criminal trials. Unlike traditional forms of expert evidence, evidence on eyewitness identification is evidence about the probative value of the evidence of another witness in the trial. Its aim is to make the jury a better judge of fact when it evaluates eyewitness identifications, and it can only do this in fairly general terms. An expert can tell the jury that most studies have shown that, for example, stress, or the presence of a weapon, has a moderate negative effect on eyewitness performance. An expert might also testify that the majority of research shows that the best way of evaluating eyewitness evidence is by concentrating on 'witnessing identification conditions' rather than on factors relating to the witness, such as confidence and memory for peripheral detail.[226] Ideally, I suppose, we would want all jurors to be well informed about psychologists' findings on eyewitness performance. Then we could be confident that we were giving defendants the fairest trials possible, given the state of our knowledge. Does that mean, though, that we should spend time in trials alerting jurors to these issues? This may be a context where the rather vague notion of 'helpfulness' is appropriate. The question is

---

[224] Other studies have not found a discrimination effect: see R. C. L. Lindsay, 'Expectations of Eyewitness Performance: Jurors' Verdicts Do Not Follow From Their Beliefs' in David Frank Ross, J. Don Read, and Michael P. Toglia (eds), *Adult Eyewitness Testimony: Current Trends and Developments* (Cambridge: Cambridge University Press, 1994).

[225] See David Wolchover, 'Should Judges Sum up on the Facts?' [1989] *Crim. LR* 781. One study has examined the effect of detailed judicial instructions and case-commentary on mock jurors, and discovered a scepticism effect. However, the use of psychological research in the instructions probably made them closer to expert evidence than to an English judge's *Turnbull*-style summary. See Richard D. Katzev and Scott S. Wishart, 'The Impact of Judicial Commentary Concerning Eyewitness Identifications on Jury Decision Making' (1985) 76 *J. Crim. L. & Criminol.* 733.

[226] See Cutler and Penrod, *supra* n. 220, esp. 79–112; Douglas J. Narby, Brian L. Cutler, and Steven D. Penrod, 'The Effects of Witness, Target, and Situational Factors on Eyewitness Identifications' in Siegfried Ludwig Sporer, Roy S. Malpass, and Guenter Koehnken (eds), *Psychological Issues in Eyewitness Identification* (Mahwah, NJ: Lawrence Erlbaum, 1996).

whether the jury could make practical use of the information given to it, and whether the information would aid accurate decision-making. Absent research on more realistic trial conditions than those used by Cutler and Penrod, I am not confident that the answer is 'yes'. Real trials often involve complex masses of information, and it is not obvious that investing heavily in the jury's ability to assess one part of that information would be effective, nor that it would have a significant payoff in terms of verdict accuracy.

Nevertheless, even in England, where eyewitness identification evidence is governed by *Turnbull*, there is a better case for expert evidence on eyewitness identifications than most would realize. Under *Turnbull*, cases that depend wholly or largely on eyewitness identifications may still be left to the jury. It is in such cases that there is most reason to believe that eyewitnesses are mistaken. The jury will be warned by the judge about the danger of relying on the eyewitness evidence; but this may not be an appropriate approach if the risks are great and the jury is not well informed of their nature. Moreover, this strategy may not be particularly effective because the jury may reason that the judge would not let it decide the case if the risks really were great. A lot finally depends on how reliable eyewitness identifications are and whether they really are far more unreliable than the jury is likely to think. Cutler and Penrod's review of mock crime studies suggests that the likelihood ratio for eyewitness evidence may be as low as 1.2, although the experiments on which this figure is based involved short exposure times and unexceptional behaviour on the part of the targets—which limits the generalizability of the figure to real crimes.[227] Considering line-ups, Wagenaar *et al.* indicate that evidence of identification from a well-performed identity parade may have a likelihood ratio of 15; procedural biases, however, would lower this figure.[228] But this estimate is based on limited research. Far more pessimistic is Levi's conclusion—based on a thorough review of line-up research and a comparison with real crimes —that evidence that the defendant was chosen in a well-conducted line-up has a likelihood ratio of just 3.[229] It is not so easy to say how much juror likelihood ratio estimates differ from these figures. Common sense alone suggests that, if Levi's figure is anything like accurate, there is a substantial over-belief problem; studies of mock jury decision-making support fears of over-belief.[230] It may be, then, that even if expert evidence only increases scepticism, increased scepticism is entirely appropriate.[231] At the very least,

---

[227] See Cutler and Penrod, *supra* n. 220, esp. 13.

[228] *Supra* n. 160, 121.

[229] Avraham M. Levi, 'Are Defendants Guilty if They Were Chosen in a Lineup?' (1998) 22 *Law & Hum. Behav.* 389, 400.

[230] See Cutler and Penrod, *supra* n. 220, 225–42; Lindsay, *supra* n. 224.

[231] See Michael R. Leippe, 'The Case for Expert Testimony About Eyewitness Memory' (1995) 1 *Psychol., Pub. Policy, & L.* 908, 947.

this suggests that, if the *Turnbull* strategy of leaving some fairly weak cases to the jury continues, there is a good case for using experts to alert juries to psychologists' findings on eyewitness performance. I shall end this section by describing one case where expert evidence might have been appropriate.

In *R. v. Williams*[232] the defendant challenged the decision of the trial judge not to withdraw the case from the jury. The case against Williams was based almost entirely[233] on eyewitness identification evidence: he had been identified by a police officer. The officer had seen the criminal's face for two seconds from about fifteen feet away. Dismissing the appeal, the Court of Appeal referred to the observations in *R. v. Ramsden*[234] that '[h]onest police officers were likely to be more reliable than the general public, being trained and less likely to have their observations and recollections affected by the excitement of the situation.'[235] That police officers make better witnesses than lay people sounds to be common sense, and may well be believed by jurors.[236] The available psychological research, however, indicates that this assumption is mistaken.[237] If judges let cases such as *Williams* go to the jury, it seems to me that expert testimony should be allowed. Of course, the point that police officers are not necessarily better witnesses than lay people could be conveyed to the jury by the judge; but *Williams* implies that not all judges are aware of this finding. Although the practice of conveying information about eyewitness testimony to the jury through the judge has advantages over using an expert—particularly in terms of economy and control over the evidence—expert testimony has its advantages too. Experts are simply far more knowledgeable about the various factors than judges, and it is probably not feasible to educate judges about all of the factors that might be relevant. Additionally, defence lawyers have incentives to seek out expert evidence, incentives that judges lack. So, in a case like *Williams*, there are actually economic advantages in using an expert to convey the information to the court.[238] One of the problems with *Turner* is that it may discourage defence lawyers from seeking relevant psychological evidence in *Williams* type cases; that means that the courts, too, are deprived of important information.

[232] *The Times*, 7 October 1994.
[233] The other evidence was that Williams had been found near the scene of the crime.
[234] [1991] Crim. LR 295. Cf. *Reid v The Queen* [1990] AC 363; *R. v. Tyler* (1992) 96 Cr. App. R. 332.
[235] Quoted in *Williams*, LEXIS transcript.
[236] See Michael R. Leippe, 'The Appraisal of Eyewitness Testimony' in Ross *et al.*, *supra* n. 224, 390–1.
[237] See Ainsworth, *supra* n. 214, 43–5; Narby *et al.*, *supra* n. 226, 30; A. Daniel Yarmey, 'Police as Witnesses' (1998) 6 *Expert Evidence* 237.
[238] Though once the expert had alerted the judge to the relevant psychological findings, it would be open to the judge to present the evidence to the jury himself.

11. CONCLUSION

There have been many themes in this chapter and it is not easy to tie them into a neat conclusion. I shall, therefore, merely highlight what I take to be some of the more important ones. Although the *Turner* case law has come in for a fair amount of criticism, the results of most ôf the cases are perfectly sensible. Evaluated functionally, the *Turner* rule does a pretty good job of keeping bad expert evidence out of the courts. One significant point, I think, is that the rule often responds to reliability concerns (as in *Turner*, *Chard*, and the credibility cases), even when it is not obvious that that is what is going on.[239] Another is that evidence is rarely excluded because it is redundant—the expert evidence offered to the courts rarely is—instead, there usually exist other reasons for exclusion, even though they are not referred to explicitly.

It would, however, be misleading to issue the *Turner* rule with a clean bill of health. The rule does not encourage careful analysis of expert evidence, and that can lead to bad decisions. In particular, in the BWS cases dubious evidence has been admitted for questionable purposes. Additionally, it is possible that the blunt application of the credibility and jury competence limbs of the rule leads to the exclusion of evidence that could help the courts in their principal function: that of reaching accurate decisions. Although I have my doubts about expertise on eyewitness identifications and the personal credibility of witnesses, one should be wary of being too dismissive of what experts have to offer the courts on these subjects.

I do not pretend to offer any definitive reformulation of the *Turner* rule here. In fact, beyond something as vague as 'admit all helpful expert evidence', or 'admit expert evidence if its probative value outweighs its prejudicial effects', I rather doubt whether an explicit reformulation would be wise. Much depends on the context of each case and on the details of the expert evidence offered; that is one reason why I have taken particular examples—the facts of *Turner*, BWS evidence, eyewitness expertise—and examined them in detail. It seems to me that an ability carefully to analyse expert evidence and its link to the facts of a case is far more useful than any general rule. Linked to this, there is one general point that is worth returning to: that courts concerned about the impact of expert evidence offered by psychologists and psychiatrists should consider limiting the form in which it is presented. The Bayesian format helps to keep the expert within the bounds of her expertise, brings home to the jury the limited impact of

---

[239] It is not uncommon for a careful analysis of rules of evidence to show that those rules have hidden functions. For the suggestion that the similar fact rule often operates as a corroboration rule, see Mike Redmayne, 'Drugs, Money and Relevance: *R. v. Yalman* and *R. v. Guney*' (1999) 3 *Int. J. Ev. & Pr.* 128.

the expert evidence, and, by encouraging rigorous thinking, discourages bogus expertise.

Finally, I should draw attention to the connections between this chapter and the previous ones. Taken as a whole, the thrust of my argument is that, as the amount of expert evidence available to the criminal courts increases, we should rely less on traditional objections to it (the *Turner* concerns) and more on scrutinizing its reliability and the form in which it might be given. This, I admit, would mean that judges would have to become *au fait* with some of the rather technical issues I have discussed in this book, issues such as the problems affecting social science research and the probabilistic interpretation of evidence. I can only assert that I think such efforts would be worthwhile in terms of what I take to be the over-arching aim of criminal trials: making accurate decisions. It might be suggested, however, that this aim would be better served by procedural changes that would alter the way in which expert evidence is presented to the courts. It is to such arguments that I turn in the final chapter.

7

Adversarial Experts

Of all the concerns that are expressed about expert evidence, the complaint that the adversarial system has a deleterious effect on expert testimony is the most common. It is also the oldest.[1] Over the years it has led to numerous reform proposals, one of the most radical being to replace adversary-appointed experts with neutral experts.[2] In this chapter, I assess these criticisms and reforms that might allay them.

1. CRITICISMS OF ADVERSARY EXPERTISE

What is wrong with adversary expertise? The points made by two commentators cover most of the ground. According to Gross, the principal danger is bias.[3] The parties are able to choose the experts who best suit their case, and are then able to further bias their experts during the process of preparing for trial. Expert evidence is presented orally, and the mechanisms of direct and cross-examination can further distort it. Spencer echoes many of these criticisms.[4] He also draws attention to the exaggeration of expert disagreement in court, the reluctance of good experts to get involved, the lack of quality control, and the danger of 'expert shopping'—the process of seeking opinions from one expert after another, until a favourable one is found. Some of these difficulties may be compounded by the use of lay fact-finders. Juries make the problem of expert disagreement look particularly acute. And if jurors judge how much weight to give to expert evidence by reading the expert's credibility cues—rather than by scrutinizing the content of the expert's testimony—the expert's performance on cross-examination

---

[1] See Emory Washburn, 'Testimony of Experts' (1866) 1 *Am. L. Rev.* 45; William L. Foster, 'Expert Testimony: Prevalent Complaints and Proposed Remedies' (1897–8) 11 *Harv. L. Rev.* 169; Learned Hand, 'Historical and Practical Considerations Regarding Expert Testimony' (1901–2) 15 *Harv. L. Rev.* 40. For a review of early criticisms of expert witnesses in England, see Tal Golan, 'The History of Scientific Expert Testimony in the English Courtroom' (1999) 12 *Science in Context* 7.

[2] Perhaps the proposal that judges or juries be replaced or advised by expert assessors is more radical still. See, e.g., Edward V. Di Lello, 'Fighting Fire with Firefighters: A Proposal for Expert Judges at the Trial Level' (1993) 93 *Columbia L. Rev.* 473. This proposal has received little serious advocacy in reform proposals for the English criminal process. I do not discuss it here.

[3] Samuel R. Gross, 'Expert Evidence' [1991] *Wisconsin L. Rev.* 1113.

[4] J. R. Spencer, 'Court Experts and Expert Witnesses: Have we a Lesson to Learn from the French?' [1992] *Current Legal Problems* 213.

takes on particular significance. Rather than dealing with each of these criticisms in turn, I shall develop responses to them in a piecemeal fashion. In this section, I make some rather general preliminary points, before turning to a more detailed examination of whether various reforms that have been suggested offer satisfactory solutions.

To start with, it should be noted that some of these problems may be exaggerated—at least in the context of the English criminal justice system. There is a large American literature criticizing adversarial experts. One point that receives particular—and, I think, justified—censure is the practice of witness coaching, which allows parties to spend considerable time instructing witnesses on what to say, and how best to make particular points.[5] The coaching of non-expert witnesses in criminal cases is contrary to the rules of the English bar.[6] Although contact between the parties and their experts prior to trial is permitted, and even encouraged,[7] my impression is that such sessions do not involve the sort of fine-tuning of testimony that is the object of criticism in the United States. It is simply not part of English legal culture.[8] Expert shopping does occur, but the evidence suggests that it is rare in the criminal justice system. In Roberts and Willmore's study, the only example involved a defendant in a drink-driving case who was not dependent on legal aid.[9] Most defendants cannot afford to shop for experts, and the legal aid authorities are unlikely to allow them the funds to do so.

What of the problems of cross-examination, and the possibility that it deters some scientists from involvement with the legal system?[10] There are stories of experts being mercilessly destroyed by cross-examination—perhaps undeservedly—but they may be more lore than actuality.[11] After a year of observation in a Crown Court, Rock concluded that experts were

---

[5] See Gross, *supra* n. 3, 1136–53.

[6] See *Code of Conduct of the Bar of England and Wales,* paras 6.1–6.3.4. The rules imply that coaching of witnesses in any case is a breach of conduct (see para. 6.2.4). This is more explicit in criminal cases: '[a]s a general principle . . . with the exception of the lay client, character and expert witnesses, it is wholly inappropriate for a barrister in such a case to interview any potential witness. Interviewing includes discussing with any such witness the substance of his evidence or the evidence of other such witnesses' (para. 6.3.1).

[7] See, e.g., Trevor Rothwell, 'Presentation of Expert Evidence' in Peter White (ed.), *Crime Scene to Court: The Essentials of Forensic Science* (London: Royal Society of Chemistry, 1998), 346.

[8] For one possible counter-example, see Paul Roberts and Chris Willmore, *The Role of Forensic Science Evidence in Criminal Proceedings,* Royal Commission on Criminal Justice Research Study No. 11 (London: HMSO, 1993), 98.

[9] Ibid. 79.

[10] For a vivid example, see 'Getting Away with Murder', *Daily Telegraph,* 7 May 1997, which discusses the decision of the forensic entomologist, Zakaria Erzinçlioglu, to stop working in the courts until the system of expert evidence is reformed. See further Z. Erzinçlioglu, 'Reform of Forensic Science Provision: Some Basic Questions' (2000) 40 *Science & Justice* 147.

[11] Jones came across no examples of ruthless cross-examination in her study, and she quotes one barrister: '[t]hese days it is regarded as *infra dig.* to grill an expert witness.' Carol A. G. Jones, *Expert Witnesses: Science, Medicine and the Practice of Law* (Oxford: Clarendon Press, 1994), 149.

actually treated more respectfully than other witnesses.[12] The real problems of direct and cross-examination of experts are rather more mundane—though that is not to say that they should be taken lightly. They are the problems of getting all of one's points across, and of not being able to draw attention to the limitations of one's evidence.[13] But even if adversarial bullying of experts is rare, is not the fact that experts do not like giving evidence enough to count against it?[14] There are two difficulties here. While it is certainly true that some experts dislike testifying—often claiming that it is contrary to scientific practice—others appreciate that the process can be valuable. According to Wakeford, who acted as an expert during the Sellafield leukaemia trial:

I have seen several expert witnesses suffer greatly during cross-examination because they ventured into territory beyond their expertise, spoke with insufficient knowledge on particular studies or attempted to persist in a line of reasoning which could not be sustained. Unlike the seminar, during cross-examination the awkward questions will not go away. The structured questioning of a well-briefed barrister can be a searching and rigorous examination of scientific evidence and inference, and is an extremely effective way for the judge to come to appreciate what the evidence can and cannot support.... [W]here major differences of opinion exist, cross-examination appears to be the most effective means of determining the position that is best supported by the evidence.[15]

A second difficulty with the criticism of cross-examination is that it applies across the board. Many non-expert witnesses dislike it,[16] and witnesses other than experts find they have to put up with it, and have to put practice and effort into presenting their evidence well.[17] These problems are likely to persist so long as witnesses have to give oral evidence.[18] There is also a larger

[12] Paul Rock, 'Witnesses and Space in a Crown Court' (1991) 31 *Brit. J. Criminol.* 266, 268–9. This is not too surprising, as intimidatory tactics may well backfire by leading the jury to conclude that the person using them is desperate. A recent study of rape trials shows that barristers are aware of this sort of danger: see Jennifer Temkin, 'Prosecuting and Defending Rape: Perspectives From the Bar' (2000) 27 *J. Law & Soc.* 219, 229–30.

[13] See Roberts and Willmore, *supra* n. 8, 124–6. It could almost be said that this shows that the problem is that experts are cross-examined *too* leniently.

[14] See Peter Reder, Clare Lucey, and Elizabeth Fellow-Smith, 'Surviving Cross-Examination in Court' (1993) 4 *J. Forensic Psychiatry* 489.

[15] Richard Wakeford, 'Epidemiology and Litigation—the Sellafield Childhood Leukaemia Cases' (1998) 161 *J.R. Stat. Soc. (Series A)* 313, 321–3.

[16] See J. D. Jackson, 'Law's Truth, Lay Truth and Lawyer's Truth: The Representation of Evidence in Adversary Trials' (1992) 3 *Law & Critique* 29, 38–49. See also David Brereton, 'How Different are Rape Trials? A Comparison of the Cross-Examination of Complainants in Rape and Assault Trials' (1997) 37 *Brit. J. Criminol.* 242.

[17] See Janet E. Stockdale and Peter J. Gresham, *The Presentation of Police Evidence in Court*, Police Research Series Paper No. 15 (London: Home Office, 1995).

[18] Indeed, in inquisitorial systems experts also find the process of giving evidence daunting. See Loïc Chauveau, *Les traces du crime. Enquête sur la police scientifique* (Paris: Calmann-Lévy, 1993), 160. Even if expert evidence were always presented in written form, experts would doubtless still vary in their ability to write convincing reports. Again, research on the French system shows that judges deliberately choose those experts who write reports that are easily digestible. See Danièle Bourcier and Monique de Bonis, *Les paradoxes de l'expertise. Savoir ou juger?* (Le Plessis-Robinson: Institut Synthélabo pour le progrès de la connaissance, 1999), 17.

point here. Criticisms of adversarial expertise are often better seen as criticisms of the adversarial system in general. That is not to say that those criticisms are not valid—that witnesses other than experts complain may lend weight to criticisms of adversarial practices. But shifting the focus to the structure of the whole system serves as a reminder that rather more is at issue here than the proper treatment of expert evidence. There are long-standing debates about the virtues of adversarial systems as opposed to inquisitorial ones. Some commentators are attracted to the inquisitorial system because they view it as a superior method of fact-finding.[19] There is no good evidence for that claim, and there are reasons to doubt the armchair theorizing on which it is often based.[20] But even if it were true, the standard response is that adversarial systems may do a better job of promoting values other than verdict accuracy,[21] or that they deliver verdicts that blend normative and factual issues in such a way as to make comparisons with inquisitorial systems unhelpful.[22] A few of the observations in this chapter will bear on the relative merits and demerits of adversarial and inquisitorial systems, but I shall not explore the issue in depth. It may therefore be helpful to give some idea of the assumption that guides my approach. I take the view that, if one were designing a criminal justice system from scratch, there would not be an awful lot of reason for preferring an adversarial system to an inquisitorial one. Each has its good and bad points.[23] The systems, moreover, are relatively flexible, and much fine-tuning can be done to each without destroying its essentially adversarial or inquisitorial nature.

A major strand of the critique of adversarial expertise charges the adversarial process with producing biased expertise. This is partly due to what might be termed the 'bell curve' effect. We might imagine a range of different possible viewpoints on a technical question of interest to the criminal justice system—say, one relating to the reliability of a particular identification technique. If we polled a large number of experts on the question, we would doubtless find some variation in their views, but we would not expect to find the views randomly distributed along the range of opinions. We would expect the majority of opinions to be clustered around a particular point on the range, perhaps somewhat in the shape of a bell curve. Now anyone examining the reliability of the technique would be interested to know the point where the majority of views clustered. But in an adversarial system, where the parties choose their experts, we would not expect the

[19] See, e.g., Peter Brett, 'The Implications of Science for the Law' (1972) 18 *McGill LJ* 170, 191.
[20] See Richard A. Posner, 'An Economic Approach to the Law of Evidence' (1999) 51 *Stanford L. Rev.* 1477, 1487–97.
[21] See John Jackson and Sean Doran, *Judge Without Jury: Diplock Trials in the Adversary System* (Oxford: Clarendon Press, 1995), 77–8.
[22] See Mirjan Damaška, 'Presentation of Evidence and Factfinding Precision' (1975) 123 *U. Pa. L. Rev.* 1083, 1103–6.
[23] For a similar view, see David Luban, *Lawyers and Justice: An Ethical Study* (Princeton: Princeton University Press, 1988), ch. 5.

choice to be made from the central part of the bell curve. Each party would look for an opinion lending as much support as possible to its case, and this might lead to opinions being chosen from the tails, rather than the centre, of the bell curve.[24] This seems to me to be one of the most cogent criticisms of adversary expertise. There is a question, though, about how far it applies in the criminal justice system. In the United States, the bell curve argument works particularly well in toxic tort litigation, where experts are known to have particular views on the litigated issue, and can be chosen for those views.[25] But the majority of forensic science evidence does not involve analogous questions. Usually it is a question of an expert being instructed to examine trace evidence, or to review the findings of another expert, and there is no way for the parties to tell what opinion the expert will come to. There are exceptions: some experts are known for their views on DNA evidence, or on stylometry. Perhaps the views of mental health experts have a certain degree of predictability. But the bell curve argument does not apply to all experts.

The problem of expert bias is much wider than the bell curve problem. In Chapter 2, I touched on the difficulty of defining bias in scientific practice. This problem is again relevant. 'Partisanship', Edmond suggests, may be 'an unavoidable feature of knowledge production and expert opinion.'[26] If bias affects all scientific opinion, is there any point in worrying about the biases produced by adversary expertise? The appropriate response to this, as before, is to look at the concept of bias more carefully. Edmond's argument is informed by work in the sociology of science that makes much of the role social and political interests play in the shaping of scientific knowledge.[27] Even if one accepts that scientists' beliefs are always biased by these interests, it is still possible that the legal system further biases their beliefs, and that this extra bias is a bad thing. So bias should be taken seriously. The principal concern of critics of adversary expertise is that experts may be affected by 'party allegiance' bias. The most damning charge is that experts will deliberately mould their views to fit their employer's case (an example of motivational bias). There is evidence that this occurs. In a survey of psychologists who had worked as expert witnesses, Gudjonsson found that 27 per cent had been asked to alter a report; moreover, 56 per cent of these had complied. Some of the ensuing alterations were minor or clarificatory, but some seem to have involved making a report more favourable to the

---

[24] See, e.g., Joseph Sanders, 'Scientifically Complex Cases, Trial by Jury, and the Erosion of Adversarial Processes' (1998) 48 *DePaul L. Rev.* 355, 374–5.

[25] See Joseph Sanders, *Bendectin on Trial: A Study of Mass Tort Litigation* (Ann Arbor: University of Michigan Press, 1998), ch. 4.

[26] Gary Edmond, 'Judicial Representations of Scientific Evidence' (2000) 63 *Modern L. Rev.* 216, 244.

[27] See, e.g., Steven Shapin, 'History of Science and its Sociological Reconstructions' (1982) 20 *History of Science* 157.

instructing party.[28] These results are disturbing, but it is necessary to ask: just what is wrong with tailoring one's evidence to an employer's case? Sometimes there may be a range of possible opinions. The expert may prefer one of them, but feel able to switch to another if asked. Unless we regard the expert as being asked to give *her* preferred opinion, rather than *a* reasonable opinion, it is not obvious that there is anything wrong with emphasizing the opinion favoured by the employer. Of course, things are not so straightforward—it may be that the expert should have a duty to emphasize the range of reasonable opinions that might be taken. This is an ethical question, and the courts have only recently begun to address this sort of issue.[29] It would hardly be surprising, then, if experts were unclear what their role should be. But even if ethical codes were introduced that made it clear that experts should not make any concessions to a party's wishes, and experts followed the codes rigorously, critics of adversarial expertise would still have a point. As I observed in Chapter 2, biases can be subtle and unconscious. Experts report that they find it extremely difficult to avoid becoming biased towards the side that they are working for.[30] Once an expert starts to view one side of a case, or one theory, favourably, the group of cognitive biases that lead people to overestimate the support for a favoured hypothesis is likely to take effect.

It seems, then, that adversary expertise will produce biased experts. There are two reasons, though, for thinking that this is not as significant a problem as it might appear to be. First, when it comes to biases at the cognitive level, it is unlikely that any procedural arrangement can eliminate them entirely. A system of neutral experts might just replace party allegiance bias with 'own theory' bias.[31] This might well, though, be a milder, more acceptable form of bias.[32] A second argument against bias-based criticisms of adversary expertise involves claiming that bias can be a good thing. An expert who wants her employer to prevail will be motivationally biased. This may make her work harder, and uncover evidence that she would otherwise not have done. Motivational bias is also likely to engage cognitive biases,

[28] Gisli H. Gudjonsson, 'Psychological Evidence in Court' (1996) 5 *The Psychologist* 213. The sample comprised psychologists who had worked in both civil and criminal cases.

[29] See, e.g., *National Justice Compania Navier S.A.* v. *Prudential Assurance Co. Ltd.* ('The Ikarian Reefer') [1993] 2 Lloyd's LR 68, 81–2.

[30] See Bernard L. Diamond, 'The Fallacy of the Impartial Expert' (1959) 3 *Archives of Criminal Psychodynamics* 221; William Schofield, 'Psychology, Law and the Expert Witness' (1956) 11 *Am. Psychol.* 1, 2. For empirical evidence that bears on the issue, see Neil Vidmar and Nancy MacDonald Laird, 'Adversary Social Roles: Their Effects on Witnesses' Communication of Evidence and the Assessments of Adjudicators' (1983) 44 *J. Personality & Soc. Psychol.* 888.

[31] See Diamond, *supra* n. 30. For the view of one forensic scientist that such bias is inevitable, see Russell E. Stockdale, 'Running with the Hounds' (1991) 141 *New LJ* 772.

[32] It may, however, end up being a more baleful form of bias if it is less evident to a fact-finder. There is evidence that jurors are aware that adversary-appointed experts will be biased: see, e.g., Daniel W. Shuman, Elizabeth Whitaker, and Anthony Champagne, 'An Empirical Examination of the Use of Expert Witnesses in the Courts—Part II: A Three City Study' (1994) 34 *Jurimetrics J.* 193.

for example, the biases of salience and availability.[33] These, again, will make her more likely to uncover evidence and to think of theories supporting her employer's case. Now this might not be much comfort: cognitive biases are often seen in a negative light.[34] The expert may well overestimate the weight of evidence supporting her employer's case and ignore evidence that undermines it. Even so, these apparently pernicious biases may turn out to have a positive effect. Kitcher has suggested that science is less likely to advance if all the scientists in a particular field agree which theory is most promising, and all decide to pursue it, than if research effort is distributed between different theories.[35] There are several ways of getting a distribution of research effort: the incentives provided by money and status can play a role, as can differences in cognitive abilities, skills, and information.[36] Another way is through bias: if, for example, scientists give more weight to the theories they are most familiar with, they are less likely all to work on the same one.[37] The lesson is that what appears irrational at the level of individual cognition— here, bias—may turn out to be rational from the community's point of view.[38]

This argument for the rationality of bias can be applied directly to some examples involving expert evidence. In what became known as the 'DNA wars', proponents of various points of view were doubtless biased towards their own perspectives in various ways. Furthermore, the adversary system probably interacted with the scientific community to increase bias.[39] But this in turn led to intense scrutiny of DNA evidence, and developments in research that might not have occurred otherwise. One notable example is that the Forensic Science Service adopted a method of calculating DNA match probabilities that had been proposed by statisticians associated with the defence side of the DNA dispute.[40] 'Although there were times when the controversy became acrimonious and testifying was unusually stressful', Evett and Weir conclude, 'most would now agree that this extended debate has

[33] See Ziva Kunda, 'The Case for Motivated Reasoning' (1990) 108 *Psychological Bulletin* 480.

[34] See, generally, Thomas Gilovich, *How We Know What Isn't So: The Fallibility of Human Reason in Everyday Life* (New York: Free Press, 1991).

[35] Philip Kitcher, 'The Division of Cognitive Labour' (1990) 87 *J. Phil.* 5.

[36] Kitcher, ibid., stresses the former incentives. Giere has argued that the latter differences play a role in scientific disagreement: see Ronald N. Giere, *Explaining Science: A Cognitive Approach* (Chicago: University of Chicago Press, 1988), ch. 8.

[37] See Miriam Solomon, 'Scientific Rationality and Human Reasoning' (1992) 59 *Phil. Sci.* 439. See also Philip Kitcher, 'Patterns of Scientific Controversies' in Peter Machamer, Marcello Pera, and Arisitides Baltas (eds), *Scientific Controversies: Philosophical and Historical Perspectives* (New York: Oxford University Press, 2000).

[38] See further Miriam Solomon, 'Social Empiricism' (1994) 28 *Noûs* 325.

[39] See Mike Redmayne, 'Expert Evidence and Scientific Disagreement' (1997) 30 *UC Davis L. Rev.* 1027, esp. 1071–3.

[40] The method is outlined in D. J. Balding and R. A. Nichols, 'DNA Profile Match Calculations: How to Allow for Population Stratification, Relatedness, Database Selection and Single Bands' (1994) 64 *Forensic Sci. International* 125. See also Ian W. Evett, Lindsey A. Foreman, Graham Jackson, and James A. Lambert, 'DNA Profiling: A Discussion of Issues Relating to the Reporting of Very Small Match Probabilities' [2000] *Crim. LR* 341, 346.

been good for the science.'[41] They add that '[w]e can now say that we under-stand far more about the statistics of DNA profiles than about any other forensic technique'.[42] It is difficult to imagine the intense—and productive—period of research on DNA statistics that took place during the 1990s occurring in an inquisitorial system.

The DNA example is atypical. It was a relatively high level dispute, involving the reliability of a forensic science technique. Disagreement in forensic science usually occurs on a smaller scale. Scientists will agree about a technique, but differ in their interpretation of the results it produces in a particular case. Once the motivational argument, rehearsed above, is spent, it is harder to argue for the utility of bias in this more usual case. But cog-nitive bias may still be useful if it prevents premature closure of disagree-ment. If the two experts assessed the evidence in identical ways, they would quickly agree on its best interpretation. But they would not necessarily be right. By forestalling agreement, bias may be an effective way of getting a range of interpretations to the fact-finder and, in the long run, ensure that more true theories get considered in court.

In this section I have tried to suggest that the adversarial development and presentation of expert evidence may not be as bad as it is sometimes made out to be. Some of the criticisms of adversarial expertise may be exaggerated, and some of its supposed demerits can actually perform useful functions. Plainly, these arguments do not establish the superiority of adversarial expertise: they merely emphasize the need for caution in criti-cizing it. The next section develops these issues in a less abstract manner by examining a frequently proposed reform—the institution of a system of court experts. Even if adversarial expertise is not deeply flawed, it may be that a system using court experts is superior.

2. COURT-APPOINTED EXPERT WITNESSES

How might a system of court-appointed experts work, and what advantages might it bring? In order to steer the analysis of these questions away from the more theoretical considerations of the preceding section, I shall anchor the discussion in the workings of a jurisdiction that uses court-appointed experts. I choose the French criminal justice system for the simple reason that I have some familiarity with it. This choice also allows the discussion

---

[41] Ian W. Evett and Bruce S. Weir, *Interpreting DNA Evidence: Statistical Genetics for Forensic Scientists* (Sunderland, MA: Sinauer, 1998), xiv.

[42] Ibid. Similarly, Lempert writes that 'in this instance the importation of legal adversari-ness into the scientific world has spurred both valuable research and practical improvements in the way DNA evidence is analysed and presented'. Richard Lempert, 'Comment: Theory and Practice in DNA Fingerprinting' (1994) 9 *Statistical Science* 255, 258.

to track some of the points made by Spencer in his promotion of the French system of expertise.[43]

The French criminal justice system is often described as being inquisitorial in character. The word 'inquisitorial' is extremely vague, and most French commentators prefer to describe their system of criminal procedure as a mixture of inquisitorial and adversarial influences, rather than as a purely inquisitorial one.[44] Nevertheless, French criminal justice possesses key characteristics that common law commentators would characterize as inquisitorial. The parties play a smaller role in locating and developing evidence than in common law systems. Police investigations in more serious cases are subject to judicial control. There is greater emphasis on the pre-trial process, less on the trial. As a consequence, the trial involves less oral evidence and the parties play a smaller role in it—in particular, witnesses are questioned by the judge. All of these factors have a bearing on the way expert evidence is commissioned and challenged in the French criminal process.

Despite the differences just outlined, the majority of criminal investigations in France are likely to proceed much as they do in England, with the police playing the central role.[45] The *code de procédure pénale* (CPP) specifically gives police officers the power to commission expert evidence.[46] Significant differences emerge between English and French practices, though,

[43] *Supra* n. 4. For another sympathetic view of court experts, see Peter Alldridge, 'Forensic Science and Expert Evidence' (1994) 21 *J. Law & Soc.* 136, 142–4. In a discussion paper, the New Zealand Law Commission recommended moving to a system of court experts: see Law Commission, *Evidence Law: Expert Evidence and Opinion Evidence*, Preliminary Paper 18 (Wellington: Law Commission, 1991), 36–46. This proposal was later abandoned: see Law Commission, *Evidence: Reform of the Law*, Report 55, Vol. 1 (Wellington: Law Commission, 1999), 26–7.

[44] See Serge Guinchard and Jacques Buisson, *Procédure pénale* (Paris: Litec, 2000), ch. 2. This choice of classification is largely motivated by the desire to distinguish the modern criminal process from its counterpart of the seventeenth and eighteenth centuries. From a different perspective, Nijboer concludes that France, along with Spain, the Netherlands, and Belgium, retains the most inquisitorial of civil law procedural systems: J. F. Nijboer, 'Common Law Tradition in Evidence Scholarship Observed from a Continental Perspective' (1993) 41 *Am. J. Comp. L.* 299, 311.

[45] See Leonard H. Leigh and Lucia Zedner, *A Report on the Administration of Justice in the Pre-Trial Phase in France and Germany*, Royal Commission on Criminal Justice Research Study No. 1 (London: HMSO, 1992), 14. The authors add that the defence may be less favoured during the investigatory stage in France than in England. Since their study was published, certain reforms have improved the position of the defence slightly. See Helen Trouille, 'A Look at French Criminal Procedure' [1994] *Crim. LR* 735. Defence rights are being further strengthened: see Christine Lazerges, 'Le projet de loi renforçant la protection de la présomption d'innocence et les droits des victimes' (1999) *Rev. de science crim. et de droit comp.* 166.

[46] CPP arts 60, 77–1. These articles cover situations where a crime is *flagrant* (basically, has just been committed or discovered), or where an *enquête préliminaire* (preliminary enquiry) is instituted. In the latter scenario, the referral must be authorized by a prosecutor. These provisions give the police considerable scope for commissioning expert evidence. Nevertheless, it appears to be accepted that some types of expert evidence, such as psychiatric evaluations, will always be commissioned by a *juge d'instruction*. See Jean Pradel, 'L'Expertise psychiatrique' in Marie-Anne Frison-Roche and Denis Mazeaud (eds), *L'Expertise* (Paris: Dalloz, 1995), 13.

when it comes to the French system of judicial supervision of police investigations. There are two organs of judicial supervision in the French system: prosecutors (*le ministère public*)[47] and *juges d'instruction*.[48] As a rule, supervision only plays a significant part in the investigation of the more serious cases.[49] It does little harm to concentrate on serious cases, however, because it is in these that expert evidence is most likely to be used. Prosecutors are involved in all cases, but their supervision of the police investigation will usually be minimal: it is a matter of 'oversight and answerability' rather than control.[50] In the most serious cases—classified as *crimes*—investigations must be supervised by a *juge d'instruction*.[51] In an intermediate category—*délits*—the prosecutor makes a discretionary decision whether to appoint a *juge d'instruction*.[52] The *juge d'instruction*'s task is to conduct an investigation into the case, in order to discover the truth.[53] However, the *juge* will quite often delegate investigative powers to the police.[54] In the context of expert evidence, the significance of the involvement of a *juge d'instruction* is this: the *juge* has the power to commission an *expertise judiciaire*.[55] While the *CPP* simply talks in terms of *expertise*, I use the

---

[47] Also known as the *parquet*. Although prosecutors are part of the French judiciary, most will have taken up the job immediately on leaving the *école nationale de la magistrature*, so will not have served on the bench. On the training and status of French judges, see Richard S. Frase, 'Comparative Criminal Justice as a Guide to American Law Reform: How Do the French Do It, How Can We Find Out, and Why Should We Care?' (1990) 78 *Calif L. Rev.* 539, 559–67.

[48] The usual English translation is 'examining magistrate'. The courts also play a supervisory role in criminal investigations, the parties having various possibilities of appeal to the *chambre d'accusation*, a court that deals with pre-trial issues.

[49] See John Bell, 'The French Pre-Trial System' in Clive Walker and Keir Starmer (eds), *Miscarriages of Justice: A Review of Justice in Error* (London: Blackstone Press, 1999).

[50] Nigel Osner, Anne Quinn, and Giles Crown, *Criminal Justice Systems in Other Jurisdictions* (London: HMSO, 1993), 85.

[51] *CPP* art. 79.

[52] *CPP* art. 79. In 1988, out of 613,056 investigations, 40,370 (6.5 per cent) involved a *juge d'instruction*. The majority of these (34,494) were *délits*. See Guinchard and Buisson, *supra* n. 44, 23. However, only a minority of *délits* (around 8 per cent) are referred to the *juge d'instruction* (the decision usually depends on such matters as the complexity of the investigation and whether a suspect has been identified). Ibid. 509–10, 530. The fact that the best known feature of the French criminal process—the *juge d'instruction*—is only involved in a small proportion of investigations has led some commentators to see judicial supervision as a relatively insignificant aspect of the French system. Nevertheless, when one bears in mind that in England most cases generate guilty pleas, and that only 2 per cent of cases are deemed serious enough to be dealt with in the Crown Court, 6.5 per cent starts to seem a significant figure. On the pros and cons of judicial supervision, see Stewart Field, 'Judicial Supervision and the Pre-Trial Process' (1994) 21 *J. Law & Soc.* 119.

[53] *CPP* art. 81.

[54] By issuing a *commission rogatoire*: *CPP* arts 151–5. This power is widely used: see Commission justice pénale et droits de l'homme, *La mise en état des affaires pénales. Rapports* (Paris: Documentation Française, 1991), 57.

[55] *CPP* art. 156. The *juge d'instruction* need appoint only one expert, but has the power to appoint more than one in complex cases. If so, the experts should draw up a joint report, indicating areas of disagreement: art. 166. Exceptionally, in fraud cases, the appointment of experts is *contradictoire*, with one being appointed by the *juge d'instruction* and one by the suspect. See Jean Pradel, *Droit pénal comparé* (Paris: Dalloz, 1995), 470.

term '*expertise judiciaire*' to mark the distinction between expert evidence commissioned by the police and that commissioned by the *juge d'instruction*. Having said that, it is not clear just how significant the distinction is. In theory, the *juge d'instruction*'s choice of expert is restricted: the *expertise judiciaire* should normally be commissioned from a list of official experts.[56] The lists are compiled by the courts and are reviewed each year.[57] However, in practice, the majority of experts commissioned by the police will also be on the list.[58] A number of sources suggest that an *expertise judiciaire* carries more weight in court than other expert evidence,[59] but this may be wishful thinking, as there is no obvious mechanism for achieving differential weighting.[60]

Spencer suggests that the French system of expert lists provides an effective means of quality control.[61] But there is plenty of room for doubt on this score. First of all, the police will often be the ones requesting expert evidence, and they have a free choice of expert. Secondly, even though the *CPP* suggests that the *juge d'instruction* should choose from the list, the *juge* may, exceptionally, choose another expert.[62] In fact, this discretion seems to be used quite frequently, to the extent that commentators complain that one of the problems of the system is the *juge d'instruction*'s free choice of experts.[63] A third question about the French lists relates to the quality of the experts on them. The judiciary is not in a particularly good position to choose the best experts, and there is evidence that in some areas quality is not good. In the field of handwriting expertise, for example, the lists have been criticized for including graphologists rather than experts in handwriting identification.[64] The psychiatric experts on the lists—many of whom do little non-forensic work—are said to be out of touch with mainstream

[56] *CPP* art. 157.

[57] See Guinchard and Buisson, *supra* n. 44, 169. See further Bardet-Giraudon, 'The Place of the Expert in the French Legal System' in J. R. Spencer, G. Nicholson, R. Flin, and R. Bull (eds), *Children's Evidence in Legal Proceedings: An International Perspective* (Cambridge: University of Cambridge Faculty of Law, 1989), 68–70.

[58] See Guinchard and Buisson, *supra* n. 44, 168.

[59] See, e.g., Roger Merle and André Vitu, *Traité de droit criminel (tome II). Procédure pénale*, 3rd edn (Paris: Cujas, 1979), 227; Osner *et al.*, *supra* n. 50, 87.

[60] One possibility is that in the *cour d'assises* lay jurors sit with professional judges, who will obviously guide their deliberations. In cases where there is conflicting expert evidence, this may lead to an *expertise judiciaire* being given more weight. But such cases are rare and, when it is not a question of comparing one expert's opinion to another, it seems unlikely that the weight accorded to an expert's opinion will differ depending on whether it was commissioned by a *juge d'instruction* or not.

[61] *Supra* n. 4, 228–30.

[62] *CPP* art. 157. Reasons should be given when an expert is chosen from outside the list.

[63] See Jean-Philippe Dolt, 'L'Appréciation des preuves par les jurés pour la formation de leur conviction intime: mythe ou réalité?' (1995) *Rev. de droit pénal et de criminologie* 203, 210–14; Chauveau, *supra* n. 18, 157.

[64] See House of Lords Select Committee on Science and Technology, *Forensic Science: Evidence Received up to 31st July 1992*, HL 24–I, 1992–3 (London: HMSO, 1992), 136. Graphology —a French obsession—involves drawing conclusions about a person's character from her handwriting.

opinion.[65] These criticisms evidently do not mean that expert lists are a bad idea. It may be that the French system could be improved so that it worked as an effective form of quality control.[66] But it is wrong to presume that the French lists are a failsafe means of regulating the quality of expertise.

In theory, one of the attractive aspects of inquisitorial systems is that suspects are able to keep abreast of the investigation and to suggest alternative lines of enquiry to the judge who supervises it.[67] Given the importance of the pre-trial stage in France, these opportunities are crucial to the integrity of the process. Suspects are relatively well served by the provisions of the *CPP* that govern *expertises judiciaires*. The suspect is able to ask the *juge d'instruction* to commission an *expertise judiciaire*, and may suggest that the expert examine particular questions.[68] He is given a copy of any expert report, and may ask the *juge d'instruction* to commission a *contre-expertise* that will critically assess the first expert's report.[69] At trial, the expert can be questioned—though questions must be relayed through the judge—and the defence can call its own expert. This happens rarely, however, as there is no legal aid available to defendants for this purpose.[70] If there is a dispute over expert evidence at trial, the court can commission further *expertises judiciaires* to sort out the issues.[71]

The French system does, then, provide a number of mechanisms through which defendants can challenge expert evidence. At the same time, as Spencer notes, the emphasis is on consensus rather than confrontation.[72] There is an opportunity to consider conflicting opinions before the trial, and the *juge*

---

[65] See Jean-Pierre Olié, William de Carvalho, and Christian Spadone, 'Expertise mentale dans le déroulement du processus pénal: le point de vue du psychiatre-expert' in Frison-Roche and Mazeaud, *supra* n. 46, 21. The authors also criticize the way the lists are compiled, claiming that it is arbitrary and secretive.

[66] I suspect, however, that there are systemic factors that militate against this. If, as seems to be the case, challenges to expert evidence are rare in the French system, there may be a certain amount of complacency about the quality of experts on the list. Additionally, the role of judges in the French system may mean that they are reluctant to relinquish power over the accreditation of experts. The judge, as representative of the state, tends to be seen as the guardian of the rights and liberties of the suspect. Taking away from them their control of expert lists might rub against this vision of the judge's role. On this aspect of the French system, see Jean-Pierre Versini-Campinchi, 'Sauvez le juge d'instruction', *Libération*, 6 July 1999; J.-L. Sauron, 'Les vertus de l'inquisitoire, ou l'Etat au service des droits' (1990) 55 *Pouvoirs* 53.

[67] See M. McConville, 'Prosecuting Criminal Cases in England and Wales: Reflections of an Inquisitorial Adversary' (1984) 6 *Liverpool L. Rev.* 15, 30–1; Michael Mansfield and Tony Wardle, *Presumed Guilty: The British Legal System Exposed* (London: Mandarin, 1993), 187.

[68] *CPP* arts 156, 165.

[69] *CPP* arts 279, 167. Victims also have a right to challenge expert evidence (art. 167–1), and there are rights of appeal against decisions of the *juge d'instruction* not to commission an *expertise judiciaire* or a *contre-expertise* (186–1). Where a *juge d'instruction* has not been appointed, the suspect will not have these rights, and would have to rely on persuading the court to order further expert evidence. This may considerably disadvantage defendants.

[70] Osner *et al.*, *supra* n. 50, 87. Commentators also suggest that a party-appointed expert's standing *vis-à-vis* the *expert judiciaire* will deter defendants from calling their own experts at trial. See Spencer, *supra* n. 4, 232.

[71] *CPP* art. 169. See also art. 310.   [72] *Supra* n. 4, 232–3.

d'instruction can direct experts to meet to discuss their differences. This is doubtless valuable, as it may prevent opinions becoming unduly polarized through adversarial bias. The system cannot, of course, eliminate all bias: I suggested earlier that even experts who owe no allegiance to either party may be affected by 'own theory bias'. Other forms of bias also appear to operate in the French system. In the field of forensic psychiatry, *juges d'instruction* are said to be able to choose those experts who will simply confirm their own views; it has even been suggested that random selection of experts is needed to overcome this problem.[73] It is also claimed that the process of commissioning expert evidence can contaminate the expert with the *juge*'s view of the issues.[74] According to Chauveau, the very fact that an expert has been requested to provide a *contre-expertise* can cause her to take an over-critical approach to the original expert report.[75] He also notes that biases of a more motivational sort sometimes operate, because there are rivalries between different laboratories, especially between those in the public and private sectors.[76] Despite these problems, the elimination of adversarial bias is welcome, provided that—and this was questioned earlier—this bias does not play a useful role in expert investigations.

While a system that promotes consensus rather than confrontation has its advantages, there are reasons to think that the French system goes too far in deterring challenges to expert evidence.[77] Margot, who generally approves of the *CPP*'s provisions on expert evidence, claims that expert evidence is of worse quality in inquisitorial systems because it is infrequently challenged by the defence.[78] The French system might work better if defence lawyers did question expert evidence more vigorously; but it is difficult to change one element of the system in this way: the inquisitorial set-up seems to promote a culture in which the defence does not play a very active role.[79] In a more theoretical vein, Damaška argues that party-dominated fact-finding

[73] See Olié *et al.*, *supra* n. 65, 22; Bourcier and de Bonis, *supra* n. 18, 67–8.
[74] See Bourcier and de Bonis, *supra* n. 18, 60–76.
[75] *Supra* n. 18, 163.   [76] Ibid. 64, 192.
[77] For a critical account, see Jean-Pierre Marguénaud, 'Le droit à "l'expertise équitable"' (2000) *Recueil Dalloz-Sirey (chron.)* 111, 112–13. Marguénaud suggests that the lack of adversarial element in the appointment of experts in the criminal process would fall foul of the European Convention on Human Rights. He bases this argument on *Mantovanelli* v. *France* (1997) 24 EHRR 370, in which the court ruled that the lack of adversarial element in the commissioning of expert evidence in one civil case was a breach of art. 6–1 of the Convention because it was insufficiently adversarial. Given the facts of that case, though, it seems that the rights given to the defence under *CPP* arts 156, 165, and 167 might satisfy the requirements of the Convention. A better criticism, floated by Marguénaud at 114–15, is that the defence is disadvantaged by not having access to its own expert, who could advise it about the strengths and weaknesses of the expert's report and suggest lines of criticism. For further criticism of the French system, in particular of the fact that it is insufficiently adversarial, see Olié *et al.*, *supra* n. 65, 22–3; Henri Leclerc, 'L'Expertise psychiatrique et la défense' in Frison-Roche and Mazeaud, *supra* n. 46; Marie-Anne Frison-Roche, 'La procédure de l'expertise' in ibid. 93–4.
[78] Pierre Margot, 'The Role of the Forensic Scientist in an Inquisitorial System of Justice' (1998) 38 *Science & Justice* 71, 73.
[79] See Guinchard and Buisson, *supra* n. 44, 175–7, 186–8.

procedures instil epistemological scepticism,[80] a mindset more likely to lead to challenges to evidence. Challenges to expert evidence do, of course, create problems. If opposing expert views are presented at trial, it will be difficult for the fact-finder to choose between them. Even so, the adversarial clash of expert opinion has some advantages. 'Regularly subjected to duelling experts', Damaška suggests, 'adjudicators need not surrender to the authority of science as blindly as those confronted with a single opinion of their chosen expert.'[81] Dissension encourages critical scrutiny. It is no surprise, then, that one of the concerns voiced about expert evidence in the French criminal process is that judges too readily accept the conclusions of experts and that there is little critical examination of their reports.[82]

What this brief review of the use of court experts in the French criminal process suggests is that, while the system has certain merits, it also has a number of defects. Now it is possible that I have simply chosen the wrong system to review. There may be other criminal justice systems that have more satisfactory systems of court experts. But this is doubtful: the more theoretical reflections pursued in the preceding section suggest that adversarial bias can serve useful functions. Systems that attempt to eliminate it are likely to pay a price, even as they profit. Writings on other inquisitorial systems only confirm this view. Commentators tend to think that their systems work quite well, but they also worry that expert evidence is not challenged frequently enough and that it is not scrutinized closely at trial.[83]

Perhaps, though, it is a mistake to look abroad in the first place. Something like a system of court-appointed experts is being used in the English

---

[80] Mirjan R. Damaška, *The Faces of Justice and State Authority: A Comparative Approach to the Legal Process* (New Haven: Yale University Press, 1986), 75. See also 123, 160–4.

[81] Mirjan R. Damaška, *Evidence Law Adrift* (New Haven: Yale University Press, 1997), 152.

[82] See Dolt, *supra* n. 63, 217, 220; Chauveau, *supra* n. 18, 157; Laurence Bellon and Christian Guery, 'Juges et psy: la confusion des langues' (1999) *Rev. de science crim. et de droit pénal comp.* 783, 784–5.

[83] The most comprehensive English language treatment of expert evidence in a civil law jurisdiction is P. T. C. van Kampen, *Expert Evidence Compared: Rules and Practices in the Dutch and American Criminal Justice System* (Antwerp: Intersentia Rechtswetenschappen, 1998). See esp. 65–136. Van Kampen welcomes reform proposals that will make the Dutch system of expertise slightly more adversarial in nature, e.g. by giving the defence more opportunity to obtain expert evidence, a reform she expects to result in the presentation of more conflicting expert evidence at trial (at 131). She also suggests that experts should give oral evidence more often in Dutch trials (at 320). For other treatments of the Dutch system, criticizing the fact that courts are not sufficiently critical of experts, see H. F. M. Crombag, 'Expert Witnesses as Vicarious Anchors' in J. F. Nijboer, C. R. Callen, and N. Kwak (eds), *Forensic Expertise and the Law of Evidence* (Amsterdam: Royal Netherlands Academy of Arts and Sciences, 1993), 86; J. F. Nijboer, 'The Law of Evidence in Dutch Criminal Cases in a Nutshell: The Role of the Expert' in ibid. 68. On the Dutch system, see also Johannes F. Nijboer, 'Forensic Expertise in Dutch Criminal Procedure' (1992) 14 *Cardozo L. Rev.* 165. For criticism of the fact that experts in the German criminal process have too much power, and that defendants have insufficient opportunity to challenge their evidence, see K. Volk, 'Forensic Expertise and the Law of Evidence in Germany (Criminal Cases)' in ibid. 44–6. For descriptions of systems for commissioning and challenging expert evidence in a number of other civil law jurisdictions, see Osner *et al.*, *supra* n. 50.

civil process. Rule 35.7 of the Civil Procedure Rules allows a court to direct that expert evidence on an issue be given by a single expert only. The parties may agree who is to be the 'single joint expert', but if they cannot, the court can choose from a list prepared by the parties, or make its choice in some other manner.[84] This product of the Woolf reforms has only been in force for a year, but the scant evidence suggests that it is working quite well, and that litigants do not object to the appointment of a single joint expert.[85] Why not adopt this system in the criminal process? It would permit the parties to instruct their own experts to carry out an enquiry and to develop theories with the benefit of adversarial bias. It would allow cross-examination of the expert.[86] And it might present the fact-finder with a simpler and perhaps less biased picture of the technical questions in issue. The system, admittedly, is quite attractive. But it has its problems: unless the parties can agree, the choice of expert may prove crucial. Judges are probably not in a very good position to make it.[87] There are also disanalogies between the problem in civil and criminal trials that indicate that this solution is not needed in the criminal courts. Woolf's final report stresses that the appointment of a single joint expert will not be appropriate in all cases, especially not in those where legitimate disagreement is possible.[88] The scheme therefore seems designed to deal with the 'excessive' and 'inappropriate' use of experts, which Woolf identified as a problem,[89] rather than with differences of opinion between experts. The excessive use of expert evidence may have been the result of a tactical arms race that ultimately benefited no one, and judicial intervention may now have enabled a mutually

---

[84] See further the practice direction supplementing the rules, *Practice Direction—Experts and Assessors*, para. 5; and *Draft Code of Guidance for Experts Under the Civil Procedure Rules 1999 (CPR)* (London: Lord Chancellor's Department, 1999), paras 26–7. See also *Daniels v. Walker, The Times*, 17 May 2000.

[85] See Gavin Lightman *et al.* (eds), *The Civil Justice Reforms One Year On: Freshfields Assess Their Progress* (London: Butterworths, 2000), 123–43; Suzanne Burn, 'Woolf Reforms One Year On' *Legal Action*, April 2000, 24, 26–7.

[86] There is considerable confusion about whether or not it is possible to cross-examine court-appointed experts. Howard suggests that proposals for court-appointed experts envisage no cross-examination of the expert (M. N. Howard, 'The Neutral Expert: A Plausible Threat to Justice' [1991] *Crim. LR* 98, 104; id., 'Expert Witnesses' (Correspondence) [1991] *Crim. LR* 395, 396), while the Royal Commission on Criminal Justice contradicts itself on this point: see Royal Commission on Criminal Justice, *Report*, Cm 2263 (London: HMSO, 1993), ch. 9, paras 17 and 74. There is nothing that, in principle, rules out cross-examination of court experts, and Woolf suggests that it will be permitted under the new Civil Procedure Rules: Lord Woolf MR, *Access to Justice: Final Report to the Lord Chancellor on the Civil Justice System in England and Wales* (London: HMSO, 1996), ch. 13, para. 17.

[87] Gross, *supra* n. 3, 1191–3, suggests that this is why, in the United States, powers to appoint court experts are used infrequently. The new Civil Procedure Rules may overcome this problem because they allow the parties to agree a list from which a choice will be made, a solution suggested by Gross at 1227–9.

[88] *Supra* n. 86, ch. 13, para. 19.

[89] Harry Woolf, *Access to Justice: Interim Report to the Lord Chancellor on the Civil Justice System in England and Wales* (London: Lord Chancellor's Department, 1995), ch. 23, para. 17.

advantageous *détente*. But no one has diagnosed a similar problem in criminal cases, where defendants rarely enjoy the resources that would allow them regularly to employ expert evidence for tactical advantage.[90] In the absence of a problem to which it would be a good solution, the introduction of an equivalent to Civil Procedure Rule 35.7 seems excessive, especially as it could involve defendants being deprived of their right to present witnesses—a right guaranteed them under the European Convention on Human Rights.[91]

3. Restraining Adversarialism

So far, my arguments about tempering the adversarial nature of expert evidence in the criminal process have been fairly non-committal.[92] The contention has not been that the idea of using court experts is fundamentally flawed; just that, on balance, given the defects of such systems, this sort of reform is not very attractive.[93] While suggesting that some criticisms of adversarial expertise may be exaggerated, I do not allege that the present system is flawless. In this section some reforms that might improve it are put forward.

While the Royal Commission on Criminal Justice rejected a system of court experts, it did propose a number of less radical reforms to the system of presenting expert evidence at trial.[94] A primary concern was to introduce pre-trial procedures that would enable as much conflict between experts as possible to be resolved in the pre-trial phase. The Commission proposed that

[90] Roberts and Willmore found that some defence lawyers in their sample adopted a strategy of 'conflict confusion'. This was found to be relatively rare, and experts would sometimes resist. See *supra* n. 8, 103–5.

[91] Art. 6 para. 3(d).

[92] I suspect that the conclusion that there is not much to choose between adversarial and inquisitorial systems is rather inevitable. It is simply extraordinarily difficult to compare two legal systems in such a way as to conclude that one performs better than the other, and I am suspicious of those who do come to such conclusions. This is not a point about incommensurability—though there is something to that argument (see, e.g., Damaška, *supra* n. 81; Ellen E. Sward, 'Values, Ideology, and the Evolution of the Adversary System' (1989) 64 *Indiana LJ* 301). Even if the criteria on which one is comparing two systems are clear, it just seems to be very difficult to make global comparisons. It is not as if one has the two systems—like two apples the size of which is to be compared—in either hand and can just glance from one to another. With legal systems, data that would allow a 'bottom line' comparison (e.g. the number of miscarriages of justice in each) are unavailable, and it is difficult to gain a vantage point that will enable sufficient aspects of each one to be kept in view in such a way as to allow a serious comparison.

[93] I have not made much here of the difficulties that might be experienced in fitting a system of court experts into the adversarial system. Commentators vary on whether these are significant: cf. Christopher Oddie (Chair), *Science and the Administration of Justice* (London: JUSTICE, 1991), 35–6 and J. R. S. Spencer, 'French and English Criminal Procedure' in B. S. Markesinis (ed.), *The Gradual Convergence: Foreign Ideas, Foreign Influences, and English Law on the Eve of the Twenty-First Century* (Oxford: Clarendon Press, 1994), 42–3.

[94] Similar proposals were also put forward by a committee set up by JUSTICE and the Council for Science and Society (see Oddie, *supra* n. 93, 37–41); as well as by the House of Lords Select Committee on Science and Technology, in *Forensic Science: Report*, HL 24 1992–3 (London: HMSO, 1993), 44–8.

the defence disclose its grounds—if any—for disputing the prosecution's expert evidence before trial.[95] The intention here is to prevent the prosecution expert being caught off-guard by allowing her to consider responses to criticisms before the trial. The expert would be able to organize a pre-trial conference if necessary. Although a system of defence disclosure has been introduced since the Commission reported, this recommendation would probably go further than present requirements.[96] Some commentators object to defence disclosure requirements on the ground that they dilute the prosecution's burden of proof, but this line of reasoning is rarely well articulated.[97] Nevertheless, the Commission's proposal would tend to draw the sting out of cross-examination. The question is whether the sting should be drawn out. Those who are generally suspicious of the cross-examination of experts will be quick to answer 'yes', but things are not that simple. Might an expert's failure to predict criticisms of her work indicate that she is not particularly competent? The answer, surely, is that sometimes it will, and sometimes it will not. Another reason for being unenthusiastic about this proposal is that it may be quite legitimate for defence counsel to cross-examine an expert with no particular criticism of her evidence in mind—especially if the

[95] *Supra* n. 86, 157–8. When the Commission reported, a degree of defence disclosure was already required: the Crown Court (Advance Notice of Expert Evidence) Rules 1987 (SI 1987 No. 716) require a party to supply other parties with a written statement of any finding or opinion that will be relied upon. However, the Commission also had evidence that this requirement is quite frequently ignored by defendants: see Michael Zander and Paul Henderson, *Crown Court Study*, Royal Commission on Criminal Justice Research Study No. 19 (London: HMSO, 1993), 90–1.

[96] Criminal Procedure and Investigations Act 1996, s. 5. The exact scope of the disclosure requirement implemented by the Act remains unclear, and an empirical study of the new regime finds considerable variation in its interpretation by defence lawyers: Crown Prosecution Service Inspectorate, *The Inspectorate's Report on the Thematic Review of the Disclosure of Unused Material* (London: Crown Prosecution Service, 2000), 36–9. See also David Corker, 'The CPIA Disclosure Regime; PII and Third Party Disclosure, The Defence Perspective' (2000) 40 *Med. Sci. Law* 116, 119–20.

[97] For a clear expression of this view, see Zander's dissenting comments in Royal Commission on Criminal Justice, *supra* n. 86, 221; see also Steven Greer, 'The right to Silence, Defence Disclosure, and Confession Evidence' (1994) 21 *J. Law & Soc.* 103, 107. The problem with this view is that, however much evidence the defence must disclose, the prosecution (subject to well-known exceptions) still bears the legal burden of proving the defendant's guilt beyond reasonable doubt. It is true that defence disclosure may make it easier for the prosecution to discharge this burden, but then so does giving the police wider arrest powers or a larger budget. A different argument is that suspects should not have to cooperate in their prosecution (see Ben Fitzpatrick, 'Disclosure: Principles, Processes and Politics' in Walker and Starmer, *supra* n. 49, 167; see also Robert Nozick, *Anarchy, State, and Utopia* (Oxford: Blackwell, 1974), 102). But quite a lot of cooperation is already enforced by the system, such as attending interviews, giving samples, etc. A suspect can, of course, engage in these processes in a spirit of non-cooperation, but the police do have powers, in some cases, to arrest for questioning and to take samples by force. It is not too difficult to imagine the police being given similar powers in respect of disclosure—disclosure can be enforced, as the law now allows, by drawing adverse inferences from non-cooperation. In which case one could say—just as with interviews and samples—that the defendant need not cooperate in disclosure. In this manner, disclosure requirements can be reconciled—at least as much as other requirements can—with a right not to cooperate.

defence have not employed their own expert to specify criticisms. Cross-examination might be used to explore the limitations of the prosecution expert's evidence; in the process it might reveal more substantial lines of attack. There may sometimes be reasons to frown upon this tactic: a well-known defence strategy is to destabilize expert evidence by exploiting the expert's—professionally responsible—reluctance to express her evidence in terms of certainty.[98] But the potential for abuse does not justify a rule forbidding cross-examination on topics that have not been specified in advance. Perhaps a disclosure rule could be crafted that would overcome these problems; on balance, however, this does not look to be a particularly fruitful reform. Moreover, there are other reforms that might deal with many of the problems that this one is designed to combat.

Most obviously, there is the Commission's proposal that, in cases where the defence is calling its own expert, the opposing experts should meet before trial in order to discuss the issues and to draw up an agreed report. If substantial disagreements were revealed, there would be a pre-trial hearing.[99] The chief merit of the French system of expert evidence is that it provides opportunities for consensus to be established before trial. The proposal for pre-trial meetings looks promising because it institutes something similar. There is little point in presenting opposing viewpoints at trial if the experts would be able to reach agreement when the restrictions imposed by the legal system are absent. Obviously, disagreement will not always vanish when experts meet. But if a pre-trial meeting enables the experts to agree on the scope of and reasons for disagreement, it will at least make the fact-finder's task easier. Walker and Stockdale broadly welcome this proposal, but they add: 'this exercise should be limited to factual assertions rather than interpretations and inferences, the advance disclosure of which on the part of the defence seems to shift both the conduct of the case to scientists as well as the burden of proof'.[100] This is obscure,[101] but it may reflect one concern that defence lawyers seem to have about this sort of conference. They worry that they will not be able to prevent details of the defence case being revealed to the prosecution during such meetings. The Royal Commission may have recognized this problem but, as Roberts notes,[102] it appears to dodge it by recommending that the scientists meet 'on their own or in the presence of counsel or solicitors'.[103] The disadvantage of having lawyers attend the meeting in order to police disclosure is that this may detract from the full and frank discussion between scientists that the sessions are intended to promote. The issue is less charged now that the defence is required to

---

[98] See Oddie, *supra* n. 93, 24–5.   [99] *Supra* n. 86, 158.

[100] Clive Walker and Russell Stockdale, 'Forensic Evidence' in Walker and Stockdale, *supra* n. 49, 140.

[101] Does the burden of proof shift to the scientists? Or from prosecution to defence? If the latter, why?

[102] Paul Roberts, 'Forensic Science Evidence After Runciman' [1994] *Crim. LR* 780, 787.

[103] *Supra* n. 86, 158.

disclose some of the details of its case in advance of Crown Court trial.[104] But the defence scientist might still be privy to information that the defence need not, and would not want to, disclose. The problem is rather wider than the present context might suggest: Roberts and Willmore found that informal pre-trial contact between prosecution and defence experts was common and that it frequently involved disclosures that defence lawyers would rather have prevented.[105] Consequently, the best solution might be a code of practice for expert witnesses drawing the issue to their attention; prosecution experts might be forbidden from disclosing details of the defence case to the police or prosecutors.

A minority of the Commission would have strengthened the pre-trial meeting proposal by applying it to experts who are instructed by the defence, but whom the defence does not intend to call at trial.[106] The reason for this is that the defence often consults experts, makes use of their expertise, but does not have them testify. This might become more common if the disclosure and pre-trial meeting recommendations were implemented. Still, the proposal is odd: pre-trial meetings are supposed to dilute expert disagreement at trial. But if no defence expert is called, there will be no expert disagreement. There might be an equivalent to expert disagreement, that is, cross-examination by counsel who has been briefed by an expert. But the enhanced disclosure recommendation would catch this. Earlier, caution was expressed about the enhanced disclosure requirement, partly because, when the defence is not briefed by an expert, it has every right to conduct speculative cross-examination. The possibility of advisory experts blunts that argument, and makes the minority's recommendation look rather more useful, but, rather than discussing its pros and cons directly, I shall explore a slightly different suggestion. One aspect of adversarial bias, noted earlier, is the bell curve problem. Even though it does not happen very often, the possibility of expert shopping makes the bell curve problem more acute: the defendant might shop his way to the tail of the bell curve. A solution would be to make the defence reveal both that the expert it is calling is the nth of n experts consulted and what the n-1 experts said.[107] An analogy reveals the objection to this: why not require the defence to reveal any adverse evidence it has uncovered: the witnesses it tracked down who said D did it, or the contradictory statements of D's alibi witness? But why not impose this obligation? Once the question

---

See n. 96, *supra*.   [105] *Supra* n. 8, 107–19.   [106] *Supra* n. 86, 158.

This might be implemented in the following manner: require the defence to disclose to the expert it intends to call, as well as to the prosecution, any other reports it has commissioned. The expert called could then be cross-examined on the existence and contents of those other reports. Enforcement could be difficult: the defence might simply try to hide the fact that it has consulted other experts. But there would be ways of checking up on those relying on legal aid. Otherwise, the prosecution would sometimes discover by chance that the defence had instructed other experts: expert communities are not very large, word sometimes gets around, and occasionally the prosecution tries to instruct an expert who has already been instructed by the defence.

is asked, the objections are not quite as compelling as one might have thought.[108] It might be argued that it is simply not the defence's job to produce evidence for the prosecution; however, this simply prompts the question why it should be the prosecution's job to produce evidence for the defence. It is evident that we would want to end up saying that there is a lack of symmetry between what we expect the defence to do and what we expect the prosecution to do. But it is not so evident that the asymmetries that we might build into those job descriptions would justify the defence not revealing the inculpatory evidence that it has discovered. One way of justifying this particular asymmetry is to argue that the defence disclosure requirement would have a chilling effect on defence investigations: exculpatory evidence would not be discovered for fear of uncovering inculpatory evidence. Not everyone finds this argument convincing;[109] in any case, my proposal indulges it. The defence can consult all the experts it wants and keep this hidden from the prosecution, so long as it does not call an expert to give evidence at trial. A little chilling would still occur: having got one adverse opinion, commissioning a second in the hope that it will prove supportive would no longer be such an attractive option; the more the adverse opinions pile up, the less attractive it will be. But this seems a small price, one worth paying in order to present the fact-finder with a more accurate picture at trial.[110]

The Commission made one significant recommendation on the use of expert evidence at the trial stage: 'that trial judges, where the evidence is disputed, ask expert witnesses before they leave the witness box whether there is anything else that they wish to say'.[111] Experts would also be able to indicate, through their solicitors, that they wish to clarify their evidence. This seems good sense: experts often claim that the lack of control the question and answer format gives them over their evidence can mean that significant issues are not explored.[112] According to the Government's response to the Commission's report, the first proposal has been brought to the attention of the Judicial Studies Board.[113] The second is questioned on the ground that it 'gives a second chance to a witness who has performed badly under cross-examination'.[114] This presumes that expert witnesses should be treated like ordinary witnesses. That is not really justified: for one thing, credibility is

---

[108] See H. Richard Uviller, *The Tilted Playing Field: Is Criminal Justice Unfair?* (New Haven: Yale University Press, 1999), 244–9.

[109] See ibid. 247–9.

[110] The Commission's minority proposal, however, is open to the 'chilling effect' argument, because it is aimed at situations in which the defence is not planning to call any expert evidence.

[111] *Supra* n. 86, 160.   [112] See Roberts and Willmore, *supra* n. 8, 124–7.

[113] *Royal Commission on Criminal Justice: Final Government Response* (London: Home Office, 1996), 60.

[114] Ibid. These two recommendations are also criticized by Walker and Stockdale, *supra* n. 100, 139, who suggest that they reflect 'the mistaken belief that science, unlike other testimony [sic], cannot be an interpretation rather than an undiluted reflection of reality'. It is not clear how these recommendations do reflect such a view.

rarely in issue for experts. In any case, the Commission's proposal seems designed not to allow the expert to recover from cross-examination, so much as to allow clarification and additional points to be made.

The Royal Commission's proposals, then, largely offer welcome reforms to the present system. If implemented, they would go some way towards meeting the criticisms levelled at adversarial expertise, while retaining its strong points.[115] The Commission's proposals do not exhaust the agenda of possible reforms; I shall briefly mention four others. The first two take ideas from the French system. One of these was discussed in Chapter 2: a registration programme for expert witnesses, more comprehensive than the French lists. Work is already under way to implement this scheme.[116] A second positive point about the French system is that defendants have the opportunity to influence the work undertaken by experts at an early stage of the investigation. They may suggest issues to be explored, and request that certain tests be carried out. There seems no reason not to set up a formal procedure allowing defendants in England and Wales a similar opportunity. The opportunity might rarely be used—employing one's own expert would usually appear more attractive. But it might prove useful in situations where early input into an investigation is important: where, for example, a crime-scene cannot be preserved for long, or where samples will be destroyed during testing.

A third reform has been touched on very briefly already. It was suggested that a code of practice might clarify experts' responsibilities *vis-à-vis* disclosure of elements of the defence case. This is just one aspect of a wider problem: that the precise role and responsibilities of expert witnesses are unclear. This is likely to be a source of tension if experts and lawyers disagree as to precisely what their role should be. The lack of clear standards may also leave experts open to manipulation by lawyers. There already exist codes of practice set up by some bodies: the Forensic Science Service and the British Academy of Experts, for instance. The civil courts have recently gone some way towards clarifying the role of experts.[117] But it is doubtless time for something more detailed and comprehensive, acceptable to lawyers as well as to experts.[118]

Finally, Alldridge has suggested that some disputes about expert evidence might be resolved by a body outside the legal system.[119] Writing in the early

---

[115] It is a shame, then, that they have not really been implemented. The Government's response to the recommendations is rather evasive, drawing attention to other reforms, such as the general disclosure requirements, that do not implement exactly what the Commission proposed. See *supra* n. 113, 59–60.

[116] See E. A. V. Ebsworth, 'The Council for the Registration of Forensic Practitioners' (2000) 40 *Science & Justice* 134.

[117] See n. 29, *supra*.

[118] See further Christine Willmore, 'Codes of Practice: Communicating Between Science and Law' in Michael Freeman and Helen Reece (eds), *Science in Court* (Dartmouth: Ashgate, 1998).

[119] Peter Alldridge, 'Recognising Novel Scientific Techniques: DNA as a Test Case' [1992] *Crim. LR* 687.

1990s, he used the example of DNA evidence. Another area where the courts might receive useful advice is stylometry.[120] The proposal is attractive because, where a technique is controversial, an adversarial trial is hardly the best place to make decisions about its validity. There are precedents. In the United States, DNA evidence was twice referred to the National Research Council of the National Academy of Sciences.[121] It is difficult to imagine a permanent body playing this role, for there might not be sufficient work, and different questions would call for different areas of expertise. But on occasion it might prove useful to set up an *ad hoc* body. One should be aware of the problems, though. Controversy breeds controversy, and the conclusions of expert panels are not immune from criticism. The courts may misunderstand the conclusions. Science progresses, and a panel's conclusions may be outdated a few years after their pronouncement, yet still be treated as gospel by the courts. But if the courts take a very critical look at reports of expert bodies, the stabilizing effect they were intended to have may be endangered. All of these problems plagued the reports of the panels on DNA evidence.[122]

4. Conclusion

I cannot pretend to end this chapter with very strong conclusions about the best way of commissioning and presenting expert evidence. I have stressed that different procedures have their pros and cons, and can only reiterate that here. There may, though, be a moral to draw from this ambivalence. Among the topics I have discussed is cross-examination. Wigmore once praised cross-examination as 'the greatest legal engine ever invented for the discovery of the truth'.[123] But there is now a considerable literature that is critical of cross-examination, pointing to its ability to intimidate, confuse, and obfuscate. There is much truth in these criticisms, but they do not necessarily give the lie to Wigmore. As he observed, '[n]ot even the abuses, the misunderstandings, and the puerilities which are so often found associated with cross-examination have availed to nullify its value.'[124] Cross-examination can be

---

[120] See Bernard Robertson, G. A. Vignaux, and Isobel Egerton, 'Stylometric Evidence' [1994] *Crim. LR* 645.

[121] See National Research Council, Committee on DNA Technology in Forensic Science, *DNA Technology in Forensic Science* (Washington DC: National Academy Press, 1992); National Research Council, Committee on DNA Forensic Science: An Update, *The Evaluation of Forensic DNA Evidence* (Washington DC: National Academy Press, 1996).

[122] See Redmayne, *supra* n. 39, 1057–62; David H. Kaye, 'The Forensic Debut of the National Research Council's DNA Report: Population Structure, Ceiling Frequencies and the Need for Numbers' (1994) 34 *Jurimetrics J.* 369.

[123] John Henry Wigmore, *Evidence in Trials at Common Law*, rev. James H. Chadbourn (Boston: Little, Brown, 1974), § 1367.

[124] Ibid.

both the greatest legal engine for the discovery of truth and a pernicious means of generating confusion. It has its good and bad points. Bias and the adversarial system do too.

I am wary of sounding complacent here. There are certainly reforms that may improve the way the adversarial system handles expert evidence, and I have tried to suggest some. It may not always be possible, though, to fine-tune legal procedures so that we erase their defects while retaining their merits. Experts appear to differ in their views of the process of giving evidence. Some hate it, while others seem to enjoy it. It may be that these differences are best put down to human nature. If so, then procedural fine-tuning will be thwarted so long as we apply the same rules to people who differ in their likes and dislikes. This serves as a reminder that one can be complacent in a different way: by presuming that it is possible to construct procedures that function perfectly. Any system for utilizing expert knowledge in the courts aims to take the—sometimes divergent—conclusions of experts and present them to lay people in a way that is not only comprehensible, but that also provides some means of judging the validity of those conclusions. If the analysis in this book has shown anything, it is that that is an extraordinarily difficult thing to do. It would be quite remarkable if any procedure could always achieve it.

Index